Singing the English

Late nineteenth-century France was a nation undergoing an identity crisis: the uncertain infancy of the Third Republic and shifting alliances in the wake of the Franco-Prussian War forced France to interrogate the fundamental values and characteristics at the heart of its own national identity. Music was central to this national self-scrutiny. It comes as little surprise to us that Oriental fears, desires, and anxieties should be a fundamental part of this, but what has been overlooked to date is that Britain, too, provided a thinking space in the French musical world; it was often – surprisingly and paradoxically – represented through many of the same racialist terms and musical tropes as the Orient. However, at the same time, its shared history with France and the explosions of colonial rivalry between the two nations introduced an ever-present tension into this musical relationship. This book sheds light on this forgotten musical sphere through a rich variety of contemporary sources. It visits the café-concert and its tradition of 'Englishing up' with fake hair, mocking accents, and unflattering dances; it explores the reactions, both musical and physical, to British evangelical bands as they arrived in the streets of France and the colonies; it considers the French reception of, and fascination with, folk music from Ireland and Scotland; and it confronts the culture shock felt by French visitors to Britain as they witnessed British music-making for the first time. Throughout, it examines the ways in which this music allowed French society to grapple with the uncertainty of late nineteenth-century life, providing ordinary French citizens with a means of understanding and interrogating both the Franco-British relationship and French identity itself.

Hannah L. Scott is a Research Fellow at Newcastle University, with a particular interest in the world of performance in nineteenth-century France, especially popular songs, dance culture, and street spectacles. Her first monograph, *Broken glass, broken world: glass in French culture in the aftermath of 1870*, was published by Legenda in 2016.

Music in Nineteenth-Century Britain
Series Editor:
Bennett Zon, Durham University, UK

So much of our 'common' knowledge of music in nineteenth-century Britain is bound up with received ideas. This series disputes their validity through research critically reassessing our perceptions of the period. Volumes in the series cover wide-ranging areas such as composers and composition; conductors, management and entrepreneurship; performers and performing; music criticism and the press; concert venues and promoters; church music and music theology; repertoire, genre, analysis and theory; instruments and technology; music education and pedagogy; publishing, printing and book selling; reception, historiography and biography; women and music; masculinity and music; gender and sexuality; domestic music-making; empire, orientalism and exoticism; and music in literature, poetry, theatre and dance.

Music in the Girl's Own Paper: An Annotated Catalogue, 1880–1910
Judith Barger

Figures of the Imagination
Roger Hansford

Arthur Sullivan
Benedict Taylor

Richard D'Oyly Carte
Paul Seeley

Music and World-Building in the Colonial City: Newcastle, NSW, and its Townships, 1860–1880
Helen English

French Music in Britain 1830–1914
Paul J Rodmell

Singing the English: Britain in the French Musical Lowbrow, 1870–1904
Hannah L. Scott

For more information about this series, please visit: www.routledge.com/music/series/MNCB

Singing the English
Britain in the French Musical
Lowbrow, 1870–1904

Hannah L. Scott

LONDON AND NEW YORK

First published 2022
by Routledge
4 Park Square, Milton Park, Abingdon, Oxon OX14 4RN

and by Routledge
605 Third Avenue, New York, NY 10158

Routledge is an imprint of the Taylor & Francis Group, an informa business

© 2022 Hannah L. Scott

The right of Hannah L. Scott to be identified as author of this work has been
asserted in accordance with sections 77 and 78 of the Copyright, Designs and
Patents Act 1988.

All rights reserved. No part of this book may be reprinted or reproduced or utilised
in any form or by any electronic, mechanical, or other means, now known or
hereafter invented, including photocopying and recording, or in any information
storage or retrieval system, without permission in writing from the publishers.

Trademark notice: Product or corporate names may be trademarks or registered trademarks,
and are used only for identification and explanation without intent to infringe.

British Library Cataloguing-in-Publication Data
A catalogue record for this book is available from the British Library

Library of Congress Cataloging-in-Publication Data
A catalog record has been requested for this book

ISBN: 978-0-367-41612-6 (hbk)
ISBN: 978-1-032-23522-6 (pbk)
ISBN: 978-0-367-81543-1 (ebk)

DOI: 10.4324/9780367815431

Typeset in Times New Roman
by Newgen Publishing UK

For My Parents

Contents

	List of figures	viii
	Acknowledgements	ix
	Introduction	1
1	Singing the English: at the café-concert	28
2	Singing for salvation: music and British evangelism in France	80
3	Singing the Celts: British folk music and French identity	132
4	Singing in London: dubious music in French travel writing	181
	Epilogue	220
	Appendix	230
	Index	242

Figures

1.1	Sheet music cover from 'Le Chic anglais' (1894)	39
1.2	Sheet music cover from 'Miss Gig' (1885)	40
1.3	Sheet music cover from 'Mylord Gig-Gig' (1879)	41
1.4	Sheet music cover from 'Oh! le Angleterre' (1878)	42
2.1	Sheet music cover from 'L'Armée du Chahut' (1887)	110
2.2	Sheet music cover from 'Viv' l'armée du Chahut-u-u-u-ut' (1893)	111
3.1	The first page of W.R. Binfield's *Bluette*, with variations on the theme of 'Scots wha hae wi' Wallace bled'	153
3.2	One of several plates with images of bagpipe players from Marie-Anne de Bovet's *L'Écosse: Souvenirs et impressions de voyage* (1898)	159

Acknowledgements

This book owes its existence to the generous support of the British Academy and the University of Nottingham, who granted me the time and freedom to dedicate three years as a postdoctoral fellow to exploring the music and culture of the French fin de siècle. I am continually indebted to Susan Harrow who, though long-liberated from the responsibility of superintending my studies, has been a constant and generous source of support and advice. My thanks also go out to the companionship and comradery of Rebecca Sugden and Daniel Finch-Race, and to Katherine Shingler, Olivia Walsh, and Ewa Szypula for their encouragement and rallying cups of coffee.

The production of this book went smoothly thanks to great support from the team at Routledge and invaluable suggestions from their anonymous readers. An earlier version of sections from the final chapter of this book appeared in *Forum for Modern Language Studies* (October 2019), and I am grateful to Oxford University Press and the editors of the journal for their feedback and for their permission to adapt and use the material again here. Thanks also to the Being Human Humanities Festival, without whom I would not have dared to take some rather uncertain steps onto the stage to perform parts of this repertoire with my undergraduate students at the British Academy in 2018.

And finally, the greatest thanks of all are due, first, to my endlessly supportive husband Simon, who has listened so patiently to my effusions and frustrations, has supported me unfailingly through the trials of early-career academia, and who has never once complained at my dubious renditions of Fragson on the tuneless old piano in our dining room; and to my wonderful daughter Heather, who waited patiently to let me finish the manuscript for this book before being born.

Introduction

'Aucun art ne joue un rôle aussi important dans la vie moderne, aucun ne passionne autant le public et les masses que la musique.'

'No art plays such a substantial role in modern life, no art so fascinates the public and the masses as music.'

François-Auguste Gevaert (1876, p. 357)

Angleterre: a land without music?

Late nineteenth-century France was a nation undergoing an identity crisis: the uncertain infancy of the Third Republic and shifting alliances in the wake of the Franco-Prussian War forced France to interrogate the fundamental values and characteristics at the heart of its own national identity. Music was central to this self-scrutiny. In the era of *Carmen*, *Samson et Dalila*, and *Lakmé*, it comes as little surprise to us that desires, fears, and anxieties about the exotic and the Orient should be a fundamental part of such an interrogation, but what has been largely overlooked to date is that Britain, too, provided a musical thinking space in the French mind – one that primarily inhabited the 'lowbrow' musical sphere and one that was often, surprisingly and paradoxically, represented using many of the same racialist terms and musical tropes as the Orient. However, Britain's shared history with France and the explosions of rivalry between the two nations for colonial dominance introduced an ever-present tension into this musical relationship during the Third Republic. This book explores the ever-shifting soundscape of this relationship, visiting the café-concert and its tradition of 'Englishing up' with fake hair, mocking accents, and unflattering dances; exploring the reactions, both musical and physical, to British evangelical church bands as they arrived in the streets of France and its colonies; questioning the French fascination with traditional music from the Celtic margins of Britain; and confronting the culture shock felt by French visitors to Britain as they witnessed British music-making in situ for the first time.

DOI: 10.4324/9780367815431-1

2   *Introduction*

The focus on music in a study of the British place in French culture may strike the reader initially with some surprise. It was, after all, a commonplace to express, as did the influential music theorist François-Joseph Fétis, that 'l'opinion souvent manifestée par les écrivains du continent place les Anglais au degré le plus bas de l'échelle des facultés musicales' ['the opinion often held by continental writers places the English on the lowest rung of the ladder of musical talent'] (1833, p. 130). As far as art music was concerned, the French in the nineteenth century demonstrated minimal respect for, or awareness of, British composers of any calibre. Most contemporaneous publications on the composing stars past and present contain no one from Britain: for example, in two collections entitled *Musiciens d'aujourd'hui* (*Musicians of Today*, 1892 and 1908) and another, longer book on the best musicians of all time, *Musiciens d'hier et d'aujourd'hui* (*Musicians of Yesterday and Today*, 1910), we find a repertoire of Frenchmen (Hector Berlioz, Ambroise Thomas, Charles Gounod, Edouard Lalo, Camille Saint-Saëns, Georges Bizet, Ernest Reyer, Jules Massenet, Claude Debussy, Vincent d'Indy, Emmanuel Chabrier, Camille Erlanger, Gustave Charpentier, François-Adrien Boieldieu, Étienne Méhul, Charles Lamoureux), Italians (Verdi, Rossini, Puccini), Germans (Wagner, Brahms, Schumann, Gluck, Mozart, Beethoven, Richard Strauss), one Belgian (César Franck), and a Slovenian (Hugo Wolf). Edward Elgar and Frederick Delius are conspicuously absent from all such texts: Handel alone – generally treated as English rather than German despite his birthplace – is occasionally mentioned as a composer of quality, but then this level of skill is used to elevate him to the status of a universal artist rather than one belonging to England. This was played out at the 1889 World Fair when the performance of his *Messiah* was the most popular concert of the entire musical programme and hundreds had to be turned away at the door; but, rather than this opus being billed as an English work in line with publicity for similar compositions by other international musicians, it was performed in French translation and the reviewer Fourcaud for the *Gaulois* felt the need to reassure his readers that 'le génie du maître n'a rien d'anglais' ['the master's genius has nothing English about it'] (1889, p. 2). As for any other British-composed art music that made its way to Paris, if it was mentioned at all, it was in terms of its atypicality: in his musical news column for the music journal *Le Ménéstrel*, Gustave Bertrand records the premier of *Javotte* (a French adaptation of an English opéra entitled *Cinderella*) at the Théâtre Lyrique de l'Athénée on Friday 22 December 1871 – he does so not because it was especially good, since his review is rather lukewarm, but largely because 'c'est un des bien rares opéras qui sont venus d'Angleterre en France' ['it is one the very rare operas to have come from England to France'] (1871, p. 28).

The precise reason for Britain's judged lack of compositional talent was open to debate. Fétis, whose influence endured throughout the century, had explained that part of the reason for the dearth of British music in France was the English language, and part was that British composers lacked the skill to compose anything more than fashionable, lightweight songs. He writes

Introduction   3

that 'la langue anglaise est si peu favorable à la musique, et si peu connue des étrangers, que jamais on ne publie la partition d'un opéra anglais. Quelques airs, devenus populaires, sont seuls achetés par les marchands de musique qui, moyennant une somme peu considérable, profitent de la vogue qu'ils obtiennent' ['the English language is markedly unfavourable to music, and it is so little known by foreigners that nobody ever publishes the scores to English operas. Only a handful of airs in vogue are sold by music merchants who, for a meagre sum, profit from their temporary popularity'] (1833, p. 163). Later he suggests – with a different logic – that the cause is in fact from within contemporary English *society* rather than being attributable to language or aptitude. He indicates that it is at least in part due to the stupidity of the English aristocracy, who impede quality musicians from emerging: 'si cette aristocratie était moins sotte, si tout ce qui honore l'intelligence humaine n'était lettres closes pour elle, on verrait bientôt les artistes anglais se distinguer dans la musique, comme ils le font en quelques parties de la peinture' ['if the aristocracy were less stupid, if everything that honours human intelligence was not a closed book to them, we would soon see English artists distinguishing themselves in music as they have done in some areas of painting'] (1833, p. 169). On still another occasion, in a later text written at the end of the Second Empire, Fétis turns to emphasize evolutionary, racial discourses to explain the musical capacities of different peoples, asserting that 'l'histoire de la musique est inséparable de l'appréciation des facultés spéciales des races qui l'ont cultivée' ['the history of music is inseparable from an understanding of the features particular to the races who have cultivated it'] (1869, I, p. i). Fétis's own apparent indecision as to the true causes of musical talent – judged through the lens of French aesthetic values – is representative of the confusion in French writing on British music and musicality more generally. This ambiguity, as we shall see, leaves considerable scope to use the subject as a platform on which to address quite other agendas.

However, beyond the disregard for British art-music composers, wider music-making culture in Britain is by no means a topic on which the French are silent in the nineteenth century. The eyes of French music journalists were rivetted upon the musical performance landscape in London for three to four months every year for the duration of the Season. To take a sample case from one of the leading musical papers, *Le Ménéstrel*, the special correspondent H. Moreno took up residence in London from the very start of the season on 10 March 1872 to satisfy demand among French readers for every detail: in his 'Saison de Londres' column, he minutely sets out the movements of musicians to and fro across the Channel, the release of concert bills for the Season, and the crème of the musical events. The amateur music-lover was given everything they needed to converse in French salons and cafés about the performances taking place at the Drury Lane theatre, the Covent Garden Opera house, Palace Crystal [sic], the Albert Hall, the Floral Theatre, and more, as well as enjoying special reports to slake their thirst for minute details such as exact tickets prices, the projected immensity of each West End

4 Introduction

theatre's income, and the dazzling aristocratic audiences at the Rothschilds' private concerts ('Nouvelles diverses: étranger,' 26 May 1872, pp. 214–5). As the Season rose to its climax, Moreno commented that the English addiction to music was 'à n'y pas croire' ['unbelievable'], with a great wave of demand for song and music that burst beyond the walls of West End theatres and flooded across the entire city, 'dans tous les quartiers de Londres, sur tous les théâtres, dans toutes les salles de concerts et en mille autres lieux transformés en *salons à musique* pour satisfaire l'insatiable appétit des innombrables dilettanti anglais' ['in every district of London, in every theatre, in every concert hall and in a thousand other spaces converted into *musical rooms* to satisfy the insatiable appetite of all those English dilettanti'] (30 June 1872, p. 253). In fact, the demand for music and theatre in London was sufficiently substantial all year long that the Lyceum, the Charing Cross Theatre, and the Opéra Comique on the Strand were able to host and sustain the theatrical companies of the Parisian Vaudeville, Théâtre-Dejazet, and Comédie Française respectively when they fled the Franco-Prussian War in 1870–71 (Pougin, 1871, p. 36). Indeed, any time that a journal such as the *Ménéstrel* remarks upon the arrival of a new opera or orchestral composition in Paris, to mention that it had already been sung or performed in Covent Garden (and/or New York) is a recurrent publicity trope. A surprising state of affairs, one might think, for a land 'on the lowest rung of the ladder of musical talent.'

Yet beyond the journalistic records of specific musical events, sociological texts and travel narratives which attempt to capture the British character in more general terms repeatedly deprecate the place of music in British culture. Music writer Gustave Bertrand remarked in his 1872 work on *Nationalités musicales*, 'on ne se connaît et l'on ne s'affirme jamais plus franchement qu'en se comparant aux autres' ['we come to know ourselves and to affirm who we are most clearly when comparing ourselves to other people'] – thus, to be a musical nation France must affirm its musicality by placing a non-musical nation in counterpoint, and Britain, especially England, forms this counterpoint for nineteenth-century France (1872, p. 6). A prominent stereotype enforced by, among others, the novelist and architect Félix Narjoux, is that 'l'Anglaise est rarement bonne musicienne' ['the English woman is rarely a good musician'] because of her fanaticism for physical and sporting activities (1886, p. 13). On the rare occasion that a young woman might have talent, it is not nurtured because she has a deep-seated need for passionate self-expression, but in order to charm – or hoodwink – a man into marrying her (1886, p. 215). Such condemnations recall Edmond de Goncourt's unflattering portrayal of the gorilla-wristed cousin of Lord Annandale in *La Faustin* who, 'sans repos, sans relâche, avec un entêtement de femelle britannique, [...] jouait du piano seize heures par jour, ne possédant pas la plus petite aptitude musicale et la moindre "oreille"' ['without resting, without ceasing, with the stubbornness of a British female, played the piano for sixteen hours a day despite not possessing the smallest aptitude or the slightest ear for music'] (1882, p. 302). His contemporary Fernand de Jupilles proclaims that London ladies 'sabot[ent] du matin au soir et du soir au matin sur leurs discordants pianos ou leurs orgues mélancoliques' ['fudge notes from dawn until dusk and dusk until dawn on their discordant pianos or melancholic organs'] (1885, p. 269). That Jupilles could actually have gained access to all those drawing rooms in order to state this fact with such assurance is open to doubt, but what we see here is women and their (lack of) musical qualities behind used at least in part as a persuasive metonym for British culture and character more widely, which these writers seek to lambast as woeful, inferior – indeed, as almost savage.[1]

The imperative to assign musical talent and the ability to appreciate music to one or another nation is rooted in contemporaneous theorizations of the absence of 'quality' (i.e. Western, orchestral) music in primitive races. Pamela Potter has observed that for many scholars 'interest in music as a manifestation of racial differences grew [...] as European explorers visited Africa and Asia and recorded their observations' (2007, p. 50). Scientific and sociological thought was increasingly influenced by Charles Darwin, Herbert Spencer, Hippolyte Taine, and their contemporaries, and though there is not space here for an in-depth survey of the numerous race theories dominating nineteenth-century thought – and others have done this in far more incisive detail than would be possible in this introduction[2] – it is a prominent feature of these theories that musicality was one of the key indicators of evolutionary advancement for any one ethnic group. Notably, Charles Darwin studied musical behaviours in species from insects, to gibbons, to human races including Hottentots and Negroes, and hypothesized that singing had developed from mating calls and thus could be considered natural to all humans; the process of natural selection would therefore logically dictate that the best singer would get the most mates – implying that the more complex the music, the more highly evolved the group of individuals who make that music. Consequently, music and musical complexity became seen as signifiers of evolutionary sophistication (1882, pp. 566–74). Pursuing this line of logic, Hippolyte Taine recommended that in order to analyse any art work, especially music, one must first examine the ethnic origins of the composer, since racial character and the influence of milieu are fundamental to any creative enterprise (1865, I, pp. 116–20). In all such cases, music is taken to be not merely a general sign of a loosely-defined national spirit, but as fundamental evidence of the inherent, subconscious impulses of what we would now call genetics. Music, in the light of such racialist discourses, was a key to unlocking the scientific secrets of a nation's place in the struggle for life and for finding out where it stood in the hierarchy of civilization and evolution.

There were two main poles to the debate on racial traits regarding music: some, who argued that humanity developed from monogeneic origins, used music to underwrite the primacy of evolutionary adaptation to geographical and cultural milieus over unchanging racial impulses. The Orientalist and artist Félix Clément, for example, argued against the idea that races have intrinsic levels of musical ability but rather that musical talent reflects cultural customs related to climate and habitat (in his *Histoire de la musique depuis les*

6 *Introduction*

temps anciens jusqu'à nos jours [*History of Music from the Ancient World to the Modern Day*], 1885, p. 6). In contrast, many polygeneists believed that certain races are inherently sophisticated musically speaking, while others are bereft of such talent, in line with their perceived intellectual capacities more widely. Indeed, the lasting influence of music scholar François-Joseph Fétis had done much to engrain the belief in the direct correlation between racial origin and musicality in contemporary thought; Fétis had asserted that 'il était réservé à la race blanche de créer l'art véritable de la musique, mission que n'ont pu remplir les races noires et jaunes' ['it is the province of the white race to create the true art of music, a mission that the black and yellow races have been unable to fulfil'] (1833, p. 119). However, in practice this link between race and musical capacity was used to create much finer distinctions than the general hierarchy of three racial groups (delineated by black, yellow, and white skin colour) would initially imply. The 'Anglo-Saxon' nations of England, America, and Australia were also seen as musically bereft by French writers despite their white skin. France, on the other hand, was cast as 'le royaume de la chanson, car le Français naît chansonnier' ['France is the kingdom of song, for the Frenchman is born a songsmith'] by the patriotic composer and music theorist Jean-Baptiste Weckerlin (1886, p. 3). Julien Tiersot takes a position focused primarily on the European and not-European – which it will later transpire means essentially Germany, Italy, and France in contrast to everybody else – and he opens his discussion of world music with a declaration that 'l'Europe ayant toujours été le foyer principal de la civilisation humaine, il est tout simple que la musique qu'on y pratique ait acquis une supériorité à laquelle n'ont pu atteindre les peuples des autres parties du monde' ['Europe has always been the principal home of human civilization, and so it is logical that the music played there has acquired a degree of superiority that people in other parts of the world have been unable to achieve'] (1905, p. 1). For all their divergences of opinion about the precise reasons for the musical differences manifested by different populations, all of these writers concur that music is an indicator of value by which hierarchies of ethnic superiority and inferiority may be established. It is hardly surprising, given that many of the intellectuals setting the parameters on which this hierarchy rested were from France, and often Paris, that they generally considered the French as the superior race when it comes to music – and, extrapolating from this, the superior race in general.

Complex, Western art music is seen, then, as the marker par excellence of civilization; thus, to emphasize its absence from Britain, France's major rival on the global stage, provides a compelling 'scientific' indication of France's superiority over its powerful neighbour. This becomes entwined with the idea that a binary opposition existed between northern, Germanic (barbarian) races and southern, Latinate (civilized) races – a concept that became common currency in France in the wake of the Franco-Prussian War. When it comes to music, it is not their recent enemy Germany but Britain that is often of greatest interest to French writers engaged in this debate. In part this may simply be because it would be an audacious writer who dared

Introduction 7

to declare the homeland of Bach and Beethoven bereft of music. However, this interest also derives from Britain's mixed heritage of Celtic, Germanic, Scandinavian, Roman, and Norman invaders. Many writers went to considerable pains to prove that the Germanic Saxon blood in Britain – especially England – had dominated the Celtic, Roman, and French. This was essential because it marked out the superior evolutionary trajectory of the French nation, which had had a similar history of invasion but which considered its Celtic and Latinate qualities to have remained dominant through the process of natural selection (as will be explored further in the course of the present book). Thus, if musical prowess was the key trait of civilization, and if the barbaric bloodlines had won through in Britain, then logic dictated that the British population could not have any serious capacity for musical talent.

With these ideas of evolution, race, and national character in mind, popular-music circles in France discuss, sing about, and dance about the British and Britishness with astounding frequency – including in terms of café-concert songs, protest songs, cabaret skits, music hall, street music, and folk music, as shall be examined in the course of this book. Yet despite the remarkable, wide-reaching, and ever-present interest in British ideas and the idea of Britishness in popular music, this significant part of French musical culture has seldom been explored by historians beyond a general acknowledgement of the influence of music hall, and it has in large part been forgotten in all its rich detail. Indeed, the influence of English popular music on parallel genres in France was remarkably pervasive – in particular the tradition of music hall, whose venues were emulated and acts were adapted to the great acclaim of Parisian audiences. While this was nothing new in the world of circus and pantomime, where thoroughgoing Franco-British exchanges date back at least to the 1820s (noted in Gordon, 2001, p. 114), French song historian Louis-Jean Calvet has noted the mass influence of music hall, the imitation of music-hall style shows, and that the adoption of the theatre-style seating facing the stage that was typical in London became increasingly prevalent around the 1880s in Paris (1981, p. 69). Additionally, Angèle David-Guillou observes that the political rapprochement of the Entente Cordiale was only confirmed at a cultural level thanks in large part to the music hall in the first decades of the twentieth century (2010, p. 62). *Singing the English* seeks to build upon these revelatory glimpses into the cross-Channel world of popular music, to deepen our understanding of the role of popular music in thinking about Britishness and, by contrast, about Frenchness at this turning point in Franco-British relations, and to return popular music to its rightful place in our shared cultural memory.

A case for the 'lowbrow'

High-culture music, in its various guises, is often said to be extra-expressive in its aesthetic complexity, reaching recesses of the mind and fulfilling a communicative function that no other mode of expression can attain; these qualities

8   *Introduction*

have attracted detailed analyses by psychologists, linguisticians, and music theorists alike.[3] A substantial part of its value has frequently been held to reside in this extra-expressiveness and complexity, focusing on music's ability to say something that we cannot define but can ascertain obliquely through our subconscious, our feelings, or other intangible realms of reception and response. It is this quality that so often attracts the epithet of 'the universal language' for art music, elevated beyond the hum-drum realities of daily life as lived by any one group or culture at any one fleeting moment in history. Whilst I have no intention of either dismissing the undoubted power of art music, nor of critiquing its aesthetic interest, it should, however, be acknowledged that the elevation of art music to this 'higher' plane in comparison to a purportedly more shallow, more mundane popular sphere is itself a cultural construct and one that springs in many ways from the late eighteenth and nineteenth centuries. Simon Frith remarks succinctly that 'we can only hear music as having value, whether aesthetic or any other sort of value, when we know what to listen to and how to listen for it. Our reception of music, our expectations from it, are not inherent in the music itself' (1990, pp. 96–7). Lawrence Levine, in his study of high- and lowbrow music in post-Revolutionary America, underlines the importance of recognizing the active intentionality and class tensions which initiated the separation of the artistic and popular spheres in music. He explains that the 'process of sacralization endowed the music it focused upon with unique aesthetic and spiritual properties that rendered it inviolate, exclusive, and eternal. This was not the mere ephemera of the world of entertainment, but something lasting, something permanent.' An important element of this process was the deprecation of popular music, to enshrine an insurmountable divide between the divinity of symphonic music and the banality of more popular genres (2009, pp. 132, 136). A parallel situation can be found in France, drawing upon the shift that had taken place through the Romantic era to privilege the emotional extra-expressiveness of art music: James H. Johnson traces in detail in his *Listening in Paris* the transition from detached half-listening to displays of ecstatic captivation from Gluck onwards, demonstrating persuasively the central influences affected by issues of class, philosophy, and shifts in the political landscape on the perception of art music as something divine, pure, and enthralling (see Johnson, 1995).

Critics have often been damning of the dearth of intellectual, aesthetic, or social worth in popular music and among its listeners. Perhaps quintessential in this regard is Theodor Adorno, whose *Introduction to the Sociology of Music*, though published in the second half of the twentieth century, reflects many attitudes to the musical lowbrow that had already been central to thought in Third Republican society (as will be discussed further in Chapter 1). He defines popular music as 'the decoration of empty time' (1976, p. 47) for 'a "lonely crowd" of the atomized, [...] the immature, [...] those who cannot express their emotions and experiences' (pp. 26–7). He asserts that entertainment music, the epitome of cultural decay (p. 22),

Introduction 9

no longer does anything but confirm, repeat, and reinforce the psychological debasement ultimately wrought in people by the way society is set up. The masses are swamped with that music, and in it they unwittingly enjoy the depth of their debasement.

(p. 225)

Its listeners are merely passive drones to consumerism comparable with drug addicts (p. 15). This elitist attitude to popular music voids it of all meaningful content, either aesthetic or cultural, except as a negative symptom of the capitalist class system and oppression – indeed, still today, we have all felt the pressure not to really enjoy pop music, or if we do, to dismiss it as a guilty pleasure. Yet such a reductive position overlooks, among other positive attributes, popular music's place in working- and lower-middle class subcultures and protest movements, youth culture (Rutherford, 1986, p. 133), each generation's understanding of time, and the mediation of the dynamics of gender, sexuality, race, and class identities (Pasler, 2009, p. 4). Jane Goodall has shown that popular performance culture's relationship with the world of scientific ideas was mischievous yet often insightful, active in its reflections on dominant discourses and able to establish new forms of ironic distance from the views and the messages disseminated by the opinion-making classes (2002, p. 6).

In musical terms, too, popular music may have inherent value – a prospect that Adorno stumbles against uncomfortably when he tries to explain away the enduring appeal of some popular songs. He does acknowledge that 'evergreens' – 'hits that seem to defy aging and to outlast all fashions' – have a certain quality that is 'very hard to describe but honoured by listeners,' yet he assures us that they 'can scarcely be counted as art' (1976, p. 35). From the twentieth century alone one might think, for example, of songs such as Judy Garland's rendition of 'Over the Rainbow' (Harold Arlen and Yip Harburg, 1939), Bing Crosby's 'White Christmas' (Irving Berlin, 1942), Bill Haley and His Comets 'Rock around the Clock' (Max C. Freedman and James E. Myers, 1954), or Frank Sinatra's 'My Way' (Claude François, Jacques Revaux, and Paul Anka, 1967/68), which all still get air time on the radio, find their way into wedding and funeral playlists, or are popular choices for television TV talent show audition pieces despite being over half a century old. Were these to be composed of nothing but 'an unmercifully rigid pattern' of melody and lyrics (1976, p. 25), were they to succeed only in as much as they produce 'standardized reactions and […] its adherents' fierce aversion to anything different' (p. 29), then the sentimental crooning of Crosby or the big-band flair of Sinatra could hardly retain an appeal to the post-electronic, digital generation who would have no possibility of reacting to these songs in the same way as their original intended audiences – and there has, after all, been plenty of other pop music produced in the intervening years to push these songs from the contemporary consciousness. Yet my working-class grandmother (born more than sixty years before me in 1923) and I long enjoyed similar popular songs from her youth without sharing the sociological factors across our large

10   *Introduction*

generational, cultural, and educational gap that Adorno sees as the only possible substance of any value in pop music. Neither her romanticism nor her bittersweet memories of wartime nor her views on gender roles nor her religious faith informed my reaction to this music, but we met in enthusiastic agreement from a musical point of view over the pleasure to be gained from the progression of harmonies, melodic lines, danceable rhythms, and so on.

This enforced aesthetic hierarchy separating the pure and the puerile, the eternal and the ephemeral, not only denigrates popular culture: it also belies that art music, far from soaring above the banality of daily life, has always been embedded in the transient ephemera and political conflagrations of its age. In the French Third Republic, we can see both art and popular music genres engaging with the wider political context. Some local governments cut bursaries to musical societies for political infractions, often as simple as the unsanctioned playing of the Marseillaise (such as that reported in the *Journal Officiel de la République*, 1879, p. 7754); the first celebration of 14 July as a national holiday in 1880 saw the revival and public performance of Revolutionary songs and operas;[4] more than 370 songs, both high- and lowbrow, were written about General Boulanger between 1886 and 1889 (Tombs, 1996, p. 448); and the promotion of popular *orphéons* and Mimi Pinson choirs by bourgeois sponsors reveals a belief that art music had the power to affect social and moral change among the popular classes. Jane Fulcher remarks in her detailed discussion of the music and politics of the Third Republic that prominent art musicians publicly adhered to the two camps of the Dreyfus Affair, signing either the 'Manifeste des intellectuelles' (including composer Charles Koechlin, music historian Henry Prunières, composer Alfred Bruneau, and scholar Lionel Dauriac) or the opposing petition from the Ligue de la Patrie française (including Vincent d'Indy, composer Augusta Holmès, director of the Opéra Comique Albert Carré, critic Henri Gauthier-Villars, composer Pierre de Bréville, and professor of music history at the Conservatoire Louis-Albert Bourgault-Ducoudray) (see Fulcher, 1999, pp. 15–18). As Fulcher argues persuasively, such ideological and political positioning of music and musicians affected the breadth and depth of the world of musical education, from primary schooling to the training of lead violinists. Republican idealists sought to provide models of beauty and of unified, cross-class Republican identity through both art music and folksong education in primary schools and through concerts for the working-class family. Meanwhile, Vincent d'Indy set up the Schola Cantorum to rival the musical ideology of the state-run Conservatoire, which

> challenged the Republic's educational hegemony and established a discourse that related its conception of national identity to a canon and style; the Republic responded with [...] its own set of meaning and values, as well as a canon in the context of both the programmes of the 1900 Exposition and academic music history.
>
> (Fulcher, 1999, p. 64)

Introduction   11

Indeed, as Jann Pasler demonstrates, art music practitioners and governmental bodies used music actively as a political apparatus, disseminating ideas to the masses, mediating class and cultural differences, and forging a shared idea of Frenchness (2009, p. 30).

Just as art music was more rooted in the everyday than many of the elites chose to recognize in their writings on music, so too popular music clearly had wider social importance than the offhand dismissals of its banality might imply. Due to the evidenced potential of music to galvanize the populace (discussed by Laura Mason in her 1996 study of music in the Revolutionary years), legislators and the ruling elites in all nineteenth-century political regimes policed public performances of music – in particular, performance by and for the working classes. For example, Josette Parrain has analysed censorship of public entertainments surrounding the Commune of 1871 (1971, p. 330), and Clélia Anfray has noted how group singing was forbidden by the censor in the theatrical adaptation of *L'Assommoir* during the scene from Gervaise's birthday party for fear of rousing lower-class members of the audience (2009, p. 229). The material performed at popular theatres and cafés-concerts was strictly censored until 1906, with an interdiction on any songs whose lyrics might threaten the political status quo or challenge loosely defined 'public morals'; fines, closures, and sometimes prison sentences were meted out as punishment for performing illicit songs or for performing songs in unauthorized places (see Lethbridge, 1991). Restrictions were also imposed upon the mode of performance: until 1867 there was a ban on the use of costumes, props, dance, acrobatics, and gesture during songs or entre-actes to circumvent the challenges posed by satire, parodic impressions, or subversive double-entendres and innuendo (noted by Héros, 1919, p. 12). The significance of popular as well as art music for Third Republican culture, then, went far beyond questions of a fleeting cultural phenomenon and light entertainment, and it is well worthy of serious scholarly attention both as music and as socio-political product.

Indeed, these tensions were already evident in the conflicted responses from the bourgeoisie to popular-music performance venues such as the café-concert during the latter half of the nineteenth century. On the one hand, the textual response was often vehemently condemnatory, belittling, and elitist, expressing fears that the café-concert had already become a symptom of the decay of art and predicting that before long it would also be the cause of the decay of society as a whole (as will be discussed in more detail in Chapter 1). On the other hand, the bourgeoisie also constituted a significant proportion of café-concert audiences, composers, and proprietors; whilst no exact data exists on audience attendance by class, numerous establishments in the wealthier quartiers of Paris were known for attracting large bourgeois audiences from among young middle-class university students, adult men looking for a release from bourgeois rectitude, and fashionable upper-class men and women from the *tout Paris*. The former song-writer and director Eugène Héros (born 1860) remarked in 1919 that the 'les hommes de

12 *Introduction*

ma génération ont tous, plus ou moins, dans leur prime jeunesse, chahuté aux Ambassadeurs' ['the men of my generation all, more or less, cancaned at the Ambassadeurs in the flower of their youth'] and that their fathers 'nous parlaient avec tant d'admiration [de l'Eldorado] et […] les anciens habitués ne s'en souviennent qu'avec une pointe d'émotion' ['spoke to us with so much admiration of the Eldorado, and the erstwhile regulars cannot remember it without a quiver of emotion']. Héros goes on to observe that even a fairly conventional slice of society could be tempted, a little later, to the family-friendly shows at the Eden-Concert from 1881 (1919, pp. 10, 12, 15). On closer examination, then, it becomes clear that, as Theodore Gracyk has remarked,

> what they [pop songs] *sound* like is more or less beside the point; for the disinterested, elite listener, the value of music has little or nothing to do with listening. Its value is the platform it offers for evaluating the tastes, and social standing, of other listeners.
>
> (2010, p. 29)

Singing the English, then, seeks to revalorize the musical 'lowbrow' and its centrality for exploring, negotiating, and mediating national identity and the importance of Britain in Third Republican society, politics, and culture. This book journeys through a wide range of fascinating archival sources that have been largely forgotten since the nineteenth century, including café-concert songs, political protest songs, reviews, newspaper articles, letters, travel narratives, memoirs, prefaces from drawing-room music books, song translations and commentaries, sociological texts on musical cultures, and early works of ethnomusicology. In doing so doing so it examines the different ways in which France's neighbour and rival across the Channel – too different to embrace as brother, yet too similar to dismiss as Other – affected French ideas of their own place in the world and of their identity as a newly-formed Republic.

The British in the French Third Republic

It is well known that the French looked across the Channel for inspiration (both positive and negative) in myriad areas of life and thought in the nineteenth century. Due to the broad nature of Franco-British relations, an all-encompassing history of their connections and conflicts is more than usually impractical and little scholarship has attempted such a monumental task. Exceptional in this respect is Isabelle and Robert Tombs's masterly *That Sweet Enemy* (2007), which gives an unusually wide vision and a detailed historical narrative of the Franco-British relationship from the sixteenth century to the present, placing major political events into context alongside journalistic cuttings and socio-cultural anecdotes. The present book pretends to no such universality of insight but, rather, it seeks to explore in depth one aspect in nineteenth-century France's understanding of Britain and the British – popular

Introduction   13

music – and to examine its place in the varied manifestations of Britain in French culture and thought. It will at times draw a variety of locations from around France into its scope, but Paris remains its principal focus due to the concentration of British visitors, residents, and influences in the nation's capital; due to the considerable scale of Paris's popular entertainments and cultural events; and due to the innovativeness and responsiveness of popular culture to wider political and socio-cultural events in this urban, rapidly modernizing environment. Both in France as a whole and in Paris in particular, lowbrow music plays a significant part in mediating the ambivalence of Franco-British relations, and folk musicians, popular songwriters, comic singers, art-music composers, early ethnomusicologists, and music journalists all grapple with the perplexing nature of Britishness and its implications for France through music.

Whilst it is not my intention to attempt a thorough cultural history of the Franco-British relationship from the French perspective in this introduction, it will be useful to take a brief glance here at key areas of British life and history that drew French attention during the Third Republic in order to set the wider scene for music. Britain – and the idea of Britain – had shared a history with France for so long that it had itself become a part of French culture. French writers on all manner of subjects repeatedly evoke the parallel histories of the two countries and their series of 'curieux rapprochements' ['curious parallels']: the Revolutions in 1640 and 1789; the executions of Charles I and Louis XVI; post-revolutionary civil wars; Cromwell and Napoleon; the Stuart and Orléans restoration monarchies; the Glorious Revolution of 1688 and *trois glorieuses* of 1830; the Stuarts in exile in France and the Bourbons in exile in Scotland, and so on – implying that England's experiments in revolution, republicanism, and parliamentary democracy might offer useful lessons on which France could build (such as the discussion of parallel histories in Colombel, 1853, pp. 263–4). On the other hand, Jules Garsou suggests that French culture had often seen England as a useful Other – he observes that 'les traditions nationales françaises sont, avant tout, anti-anglaises' ['French national traditions are, above all, anti-English'] (1900, p. 3). Of course, there is also the history of military conflict which earned England its infamous monikers as *la perfide albion* (perfidious Albion) and *l'ennemie séculaire* or *héréditaire* (the age-old or hereditary enemy). This is not negligible, certainly: although the precise dates are often debated, Linda Colley notes that France and Britain had been at war in the years 1689–97, 1702–13, 1743–48, 1756–63, 1778–83, 1793–1802, and 1803–1815, and even that the apparently peaceful interludes were characterized by spying, plotting, jostling for political dominance in the colonial sphere and by critical scrutiny of each other's societies, politics, and national characters (1998, p. 12). In addition to this timeline, there were also conflicts over the arrest of the missionary-agitator Pritchard in Tahiti in 1843, Britain's decision to remain neutral during the Franco-Prussian War in 1870, its manoeuvring to control the Suez Canal in 1875 and the West African coast in 1895, its public support for Dreyfus in the

14 *Introduction*

late 1890s, the Fashoda Incident in 1898, and the 1899–1902 Boer War (see Tholoniat, 2010, pp. 20–23). Occasionally, around the signing of the Entente Cordiale and the 1908 Franco-British Exhibition in London, writers chose to focus on the history of *friendly* relations – for example, the Franco-British alliance in the Crimea, the 1860 free-trade agreement, and the British decision to send expeditionary forces to Mexico alongside French and Spanish troops (discussed by Millot, 2003, p. 149).

The historical vacillation between conflict and peace for Britain and France is foundational to the French understanding of its own history. The British feature in memories of recent historical events: for example, during the Année Terrible of 1870–71, although the British government declined to take sides, many British residents stayed in France in spite of the danger. Notable individuals such as Richard Wallace gave substantial aid to Paris, including donating a medical station, two hospitals, and an air balloon during the war, and the famous Wallace Fountains afterwards, and the Lord Mayor of London sent food supplies to help relieve Parisian residents after the siege fell (see Lapie, 1976, p. 269). Meanwhile, when Republican school curricula sought historical role models to inspire school boys to become patriotic soldiers and defenders of the homeland, nearly all of the examples entail French heroes resisting English rather than Germanic adversaries – for example, the French armies of the Hundred Years' War, the Seven Years War, and those who defended the values of 1789 in the Revolutionary Wars (discussed in detail in Guiffon, 2006, p. 256). Moreover, Britain can be found embedded in numerous facets of the official Republican education syllabi: not only are modern languages – particularly English and German – promoted for the first time after 1874, but Britain appears as a topic area in school subjects such as philosophy, history, and 'géographie générale.' The geography syllabus for final-year lycée pupils in both the Science and Lettres streams included sections on British racial character, institutions, wealth, farming, mining, industry, commerce, the colonial empire, and their maritime transport routes. Although other countries do also appear on the syllabus – notably, Germany, Russia, Austrio-Hungary, and Italy – none of them feature in so many parts of the curriculum, and for no other Western nation is a study of their racial make-up and character prescribed in the French school room (listed in *Plan d'études*, 1891, p. 69).

Additionally, areas of socio-cultural interest in this period were multifaceted and wide-ranging. French philosophers and psychologists were drawn to the writings of Mill, Spencer, Bain, Lewes, Bailey, Morell, and Murphy.[5] The English language was scrutinized by philologists thanks to its hybrid linguistic history,[6] and British literature was collated and translated for French readers and analysed by French scholars, such as Hippolyte Taine, the diplomat J. J. Jusserand, and, on official governmental commission under Jules Ferry, by the scholar H. d'Arbois de Jubainville.[7] Politicians and sociological thinkers debated the lessons to be learned from British social structures and ideologies,[8] and pedagogical theorists and policy makers continuously turned their eyes in the direction of the cricket pitches of Harrow, Rugby,

Introduction   15

and Eton and the ladies' lawn-tennis courts of Girton College.[9] Ireland and Scotland provided opportunities to consider issues of governmental centralization and regional marginalization, and British colonialism, patriotism, and derring-do supplied meat for both criticism and envy.[10] A steady stream of travel writers produced a steady stream of accounts on the horrors of London's East End (while overlooking the distastefulness of indulging in poverty tourism) and, occasionally, they wrote of expeditions to the northern industrial cities and the major beauty spots of Scotland and Ireland.[11] Throughout accounts of these diverse areas of British life, topic-specific commentary is interspersed with opinions – often stated as facts – which reveal a fascination with British cultural, sexual, and religious mores, and the inherent traits of British character.

Indeed, it is a notable peculiarity of the Franco-British relationship that there seems to be a continual appetite among readers for all such publications, despite their tendency to be distinctly repetitive and to recycle the same elegies or vituperations over and over again. Max O'Rell's rather sarcastic accounts of British mores and morality – aptly described by Jana Verhoeven as 'jovial bigotry'[12] – sold immense numbers of copies in France (and, indeed, in Britain, America, and worldwide): his first book *John Bull et son île* (*John Bull and his Island*, 1883), went into fifty-seven editions in France in two years, and 48,000 copies of his second book *Les Filles de John Bull* (*The Daughters of John Bull*) sold in the very first week in 1884 (Verhoeven, 2012, pp. 1, 193). The publishing house Plon had a whole catalogue of anti-English works on their holdings list – keen Anglophobes were evidently a large enough market to justify this systematic espousal of prejudice regardless of its lack of originality – and, often, verifiability.[13] In the competitive print market of magazine publishing, it must be assumed that articles on Britain were appealing enough not just to be passively consumed but to garner enough *active* interest that they helped to sell individual titles; for example, the *Vie parisienne* elected to prominently serialize the *Notes sur Londres* (*Notes on London*) by Brada [pseud. Henriette Consuelo Samson Puliga] in the 1890s, in spite of the fact that its structure and chapter headings strongly parallel those seen many times before (admittedly, the content on female emancipation differs considerably from its predecessors, but this is neither immediately obvious in the first few instalments of the series nor in the section headings for the browsing eye). In short, there is hardly a sphere of existence in which France's cross-Channel cousin does not galvanize the pens and opinions of French writers. Deep significance is read into even such minutiae as an English company deciding to develop their own brand of tuning fork, a move which one journalist confidently declares to be motivated 'rien que pour faire échec au diapason français' ['simply to provoke the failure of the French tuning fork'] – the Covent Garden theatre's subsequent decision to order tuning forks from France in spite of this is hailed as a massive snub for British jingoism ('Nouvelles diverses: étranger,' 10 March 1872, p. 118). The smallest details and events garner keen interest and are approached as reflections of national rivalries, politics, and character.

16 *Introduction*

At the same time, it became an increasingly feasible endeavour for even home-loving Third Republicans to visit London and, as infrastructure improved, to explore the further reaches of Britain. A journey from Paris to London that had taken somewhere in the region of fifty-four hours in 1803 could take as little as seven hours and forty minutes in 1899, and although a first-class ticket on the fastest route cost a considerable 71Fr10, the cheapest route from Dunkerque to London via the Thames was an accessible 8Fr75 (see Léribault, 1994, p. 13; Joanne, 1898–99, pp. 3, 14). It was now not only the Baron Henri de Rothschild who could traverse the Channel and publish his travel notes (1889), but the entire Société bourguignonne de géographie et d'histoire could take a group nostalgia trip to Battle and Hastings in 1893 (see Bon d'Avout, 1895, p. ix), and fiction readers could find it perfectly believable that Huysmans's working-class seamstress Jeanne might have travelled for work to England in around 1880 (1881, p. 265). After all, although the French at the time had a reputation for being disinclined to move abroad, there were nonetheless 26,000 French citizens living in the United Kingdom by 1891 (*Statistiques générales de la France*, 1894, p. 64).

Still, the British were more familiar to the French as visitors to France than vice-versa, and by the Third Republic their physical presence across the Channel was no novelty. There had long been both a resident and a transient body of British people in the country, particularly from the wealthy echelons of society. After the Revolution, impoverished French nobles such as Alfred de Vigny and Lamartine had married into English money, London-style clubs had been founded in Paris, such as the Cercle Français in 1824 and Jockey Club in 1834, and there were already approximately 13,800 British people in the capital by 1815 (see Léribault, 1994, pp. 27, 30, 26). By the latter half of the century, this presence had more than tripled and it no longer retained its aristocratic exclusivity. Census documents show an ever-rising British population in France (recorded as 'Anglais'), rising from 26,003 in 1872, to 30,007 in 1878, 37,006 in 1881, and 39,687 in 1894, with particularly high concentrations in the Seine, Pas-de-Calais, Alpes-Maritimes, Seine-Inférieure, Nord, Basses-Pyrénées, and Oise départements. In Paris, English-speaking residents were sufficiently widespread to demand not one but six anglophone churches by 1889.[14] Indeed, only a couple of the more remote départements ever register no British residents at all (Cantal and Haut-Rhin in 1878; Creuse in 1881; Basses-Alpes and Cantal in 1891). Strikingly, British women in France outnumber British men in successive censuses throughout the 1870s and 1880s, and they are the only foreign nation for which this is the case. As most British women would, most likely, have resided in France as wives, or as employed governesses, teachers, and nursemaids, this means that the British were not merely anonymous faces on the street but members of the family or household, part of the private sphere, and part of a French child's upbringing (see *Statistiques de la France*, 1878; 1883; 1894). As for tourism, the flow of British visitors was so substantial that the census of 1891, which normally only reports upon the fixed population, makes special mention of the

Introduction 17

'très-considérable' rate of 'Anglais de passage en France' ['very considerable' rate of 'English people passing through France'] (1876, p. 35). One newspaper account specifically records that there were 500,000 English (read: British) visitors in France at the 1889 World Fair, although it does not deem it of interest to give an equivalent statistic for any other nationality (*Exposition universelle internationale*, 1889, n.p.). This ebb and flow of visitors was so significant that, by 1908, British tourism was worth approximately 500 million Francs per annum (noted in *Exposition Franco-Britannique, ca.* 1908, p. 249). So, although there was a higher population of resident immigrants from Belgium, Italy, Germany, Switzerland, and Spain, it is not surprising that the British seem to have been considered as the second nationality in France.[15]

The British presence also had a prominent place on the daily horizons of French citizens, theatregoers, and readers. The British formed part of the artistic landscape: artists from across the Channel exhibited at the Salons, the World Fairs, and in Bing's gallery (Puvis de Chavannes discovered Aubrey Beardsley's work there in 1892), and Shakespeare was adapted and readapted for the French stage (including, at the new Parisian Opéra, with Saint-Saëns's *Henri VIII* in 1883 and Charles Gounod's *Roméo et Juliette* in 1888). Parisian cabarets were so habitually frequented by the British that they are memorialized in Toulouse-Lautrec's *L'Anglais au Moulin rouge* (1892), in Richard Ranft's *L'Anglais aux Folies-Bergère* (1899), and in Otero's poster 'Tout Paris à la revue des Folies-Bergère' (1905) where the distinctive heavy eyes of Edward VII fill the right-hand side of the frame. British fiction, too, formed a substantial part of the literary market: collections such as the *Bibliothèque universelle des romans* encouraged textual traffic across the Channel; translations of English writing were serialized in the *Journal des Débats* and *Lectures pour tous*; and reviews and publications could be enjoyed by the literati readers of Henry Davay's 'Lettres anglais' in the *Mercure de France* and of Valéry Larbaud's 'Études anglais' in *La Phalange*.

Still more present are British characters in French literature, who range from minor cameo parts – such as the lady's maid Miss Forest in Hector Malot's *Une bonne affaire* (*A Good Deal*) – to fundamental, central protagonists. It is beyond the realms of the present book to explore all of these, but a sample will give a sense of their ubiquity. Guy de Maupassant has the buffoonish English businessman who strays into the brothel of *À la feuille de rose, maison turque* (*At the Rose Leaf, Turkish Brothel* – 1875), his fictionalized Swinburne invites the narrator to dine in 'L'Anglais d'Étretat' ('The Englishman of Etretat,' 1882), and the love-lorn eponymous 'Miss Harriet' throws herself into a Bénouville well (1883). Auguste de Villiers de l'Isle-Adam creates the chronically melancholic Lord Ewald in *L'Ève future* (*Future Eve*, 1886), Edmond de Goncourt the phlegmatic Lord Annandale in *La Faustin* (1882), and Joris-Karl Huysmans populates Gallieni's Messenger, a basement tavern, and the station bar with bespectacled parsons and long-toothed Englishwomen in *À rebours* (*Against the Grain*, 1884). Alphonse Daudet chooses a psychologically distressed Welsh woman as a symbol for

18 *Introduction*

destructive evangelical Protestantism in *L'Évangéliste* (*The Evangelist*, 1883), and equivocal members of the Salvation Army march through the pages of J.-H. Rosny aîné's *Nell Horn de l'Armée du Salut* (*Nell Horn of the Salvation Army*, 1886) and Henry Maystre *L'Adversaire* (*The Adversary*, 1886). Mirbeau's *Le Jardin des supplices* (*The Torture Garden*, 1899) is animated by the sadistic English femme fatale Clara, and perhaps the least sadistic character of Rachilde's corpus is her Englishwoman Ellen in *L'Homme roux* (*The Red-haired Man*, 1889). With a distinctly decadent persuasion, Jean Lorrain's pages are filled with cruel, perverse Englishmen; most famous is Lord Ethal, who tortures the Irish Sir Thomas Welcôme in *Monsieur de Phocas* (1901), but they also murder, ruin lives, and drink throughout *Le Vice errant* (*Wandering Vice*, 1901) and *Les Crimes des riches* (*The Crimes of the Rich*, 1905). For more popular tastes, Victor Cherbuliez's title character *Miss Rovel* and her mother are two impetuous, daring Englishwomen (1875), whilst Hector Malot creates a courageous yet angelic Miss Clifton as a counterpoint to the fickle Frenchwoman Suzanne in his two-part war novel *Souvenirs d'un blessé* (*Memoires of an Injured Soldier*, 1872), as well as two opposing English families of perfect affection (on the one hand) and criminal neglect (on the other) in his best-selling *Sans famille* (*Nobody's Boy*, 1878). In novels of travel and adventure, Pierre Loti's recurrent narrator is an English naval officer named Harry Grant – and were all the British characters to be removed from Jules Verne's novels his corpus would be desperately depopulated.[16] British figures, then, are part of daily life for French literature readers in the late nineteenth century: not just aristocratic heroes, and not just Romantic ones, but in all genres and no matter what the class status of the characters.

Many of the areas of interest noted above predated, and often also post-dated, the Third Republic, but the specific time period of 1870–1904 is particularly worthy of our attention. On the one hand, old rivalries lingered on in new guises. As French engagement with colonization grew, Britain remained a focus of tense interest militarily; though it had been some time since Britain posed any threat to France in the European interior, the imperial drive of the Victorians, their skilled navy, and their highly-organized colonial administration posed a constant threat to France's own ambitions in this regard. Alfred Weil observed pointedly that, for most of this period, 'ce sont des noms anglais et non pas des noms allemands qui pullulent sur les cartes géographiques du globe, et qu'on trouve attachés aux grandes entreprises destinées à envelopper et à transformer le monde' ['it is English and not German names that proliferate on world maps, and that one finds associated with grand projects destined to envelop and transform the world'] (1872, p. 133). Garsou is more explicit, remarking that 'de tous les peuples qui, successivement, ont été ennemis de la France, les Anglais lui ont inspiré la haine la plus vive. De nos jours même, la germanophobie semble dépassée par l'anglophobie' ['of all the people who have successively been the enemies of France, the English have inspired the most violent hatred. Even today, Anglophobia seems to surpass Germanophobia'] (1900, p. 3). Thus, as France vacillated between historical

Introduction 19

enmity and a desire to forge new alliances in the wake of the Franco-Prussian defeat, representations of Britain are particularly varied. They depend upon the individual composer, writer, or performer's politics and ideology, upon the politics of their intended audience, and upon the exact moment that a representation was created. As these aspects shifted, sometimes from one month to the next, song and text became embroiled in a morass of contradictory 'facts,' opinions, and stereotypes that add ever-more complexity and perplexity to every effort to understand their neighbour and, by extension, to understand themselves.

At the same time, crucially, other new rivalries and enmities began to loom large in the French mind during this period which had an impact upon the general perception of Britain. For some, in the wake of the Franco-Prussian War the heavy financial penalty for peace and the loss of Alsace-Lorraine meant that Germany had replaced England as its enemy number one. It is to Sedan that the philosopher Alfred Fouillée referred when trying to encourage improvements in education in 1891 – 'au Sedan militaire n'ajoutons pas nous-mêmes un Sedan intellectuel' ['let us not add an intellectual Sedan to the military one'] (1891, p. 239). At the turn of the twentieth century, clear signs of Germany's colonial ambitions reopened the scars of 1870 anew, and both France and Britain turned to the Entente Cordiale as a sign of at least an official intention that the two powers would henceforth be collaborators, allies, and friends. As the British choirs at the 1908 Franco-British Exhibition in London sang out the Marseillaise (Guyot et al., 1918, II, p. 74), it was indicated that mutual suspicion and fear were now misplaced and that the French should focus their attention across the Rhine rather than across the Channel – foreshadowing things to come in 1914. Concurrently, to the east, the 'yellow peril' threatened as Japan's successes in the Russo-Japanese War destabilized the perceived hierarchy of strength and superiority between Orient and Occident; and to the west, the rising influence of America started to mediate the understanding and the place of Britain in the French cultural psyche.

With this transitional period of 1870–1904 in mind, then, Chapter 1 explores comic songs from Parisian popular theatres in which French performers pretended to be English, putting on absurd accents and costumes and performing outrageous dances to mock their cross-Channel neighbour and rival. During the Third Republic, the golden age of the café-concert, the comic character of the Englishman was a firm favourite of French audiences. This chapter delves into the vibrant and persistent play on the idea of Englishness through a repertoire of over eighty comic songs (catalogued in the Appendix). These songs have never before been the subject of academic study, yet the sheer quantity of pieces and the regularity with which they debuted on the stages of Paris throughout this period clearly demonstrate that their appeal went beyond a simple desire for novelty or frivolity. These English songs not only make jokes and present stereotypes about the English, but their French performers also habitually *embody* the English persona – 'Englishing up' as they would

20   *Introduction*

shortly afterwards 'black up,' with exaggerated and unflattering hair, freckles, costumes, accessories, dance steps, physical comportment, and comedy accents. Indeed, this parallel with blackface minstrelsy is particularly apt when taking into account the lexicon of race that accompanies these acts, both in the songs themselves and under the pens of their reviewers, emphasizing English primitivism, asserting the influence of Anglo-Saxon racial imperatives, and mocking the English accent through explicit comparison to a *patois nègre*. By analysing this forgotten song tradition, it becomes possible to examine reasons for its appeal and its longevity, and to consider the implications of these acts for the audience and for the performer alike – both mediating and problematizing concepts of national identity at the turn of the century.

The second chapter turns to the noisy invasion of Parisian streets by Salvation Army bands, seen as the *sine qua non* of British culture and religion. Physical, written, and musical reactions to these marching bands became a locus for wider concerns about race and religion in France from Catherine Booth's arrival in 1881 and throughout the organization's rapid growth, to the point that it became the second-largest religious group in the capital city (after Catholicism) within just ten years. With this success came considerable persecution, forgotten today in the shadow of the violent anti-Semitism of the Dreyfus Affair. Salvationists were murdered, grievously injured, sexually harassed, and routinely abused in the streets – and it is remarkable to find that newspapers, on reporting these events, foreground not theological or political concerns but the *acoustic* horrors of the brass instruments, percussion, group singing, and its Halleluiah Lasses. Chapter 2 explores the insistence on music and song in the polemic surrounding the Salvation Army, examining the fears and anxieties that coalesce around their music. Their sonic presence was often explicitly scrutinized in terms of contemporaneous theories of brainwashing and hypnotism, leading to a remarkable range of accusations being levelled against their military-style bands: their music is accused of inciting class conflict, political subterfuge, colonial uprisings, and of committing such serious sonic aggression that the murder and injury of Salvationists is treated with clemency and as an understandable response. And, like most aspects of Englishness, comic song made the Salvation Army another target for its wit, with musical merriment at the organization's expense appearing in opéra-comique, dance hall, pantomime ballet, opéra-bouffe, carnival parades, and the café-concert, to the point that Salvationist music becomes an important signifier of wider religious, class, and generational tensions in nineteenth-century France.

Chapter 3 examines the French reception of, and fascination with, folk music from the mist-laden Celtic margins of Britain, and it analyses ways in which the French used the folksongs of Scotland, Ireland, and, on occasion, Wales, as a way of renegotiating ideas about their own racial and cultural identity. In a considerable majority of texts in nineteenth-century France, the terms 'English' and 'British' are used with cavalier interchangeability; however, when it comes to traditional music, the distinction between England and

Introduction 21

its Celtic neighbours is carefully upheld. As the Third Republic sought to find a common origins story behind which the French nation could unite – one that was tainted neither by religious or political appurtenance nor by implications of Germanness in the wake of the Franco-Prussian War – a popular choice was to focus on the Celtic origins of the Gauls, an origin distant enough to be plausible but neither finally refutable nor verifiable for any one individual or region. With this Celtic dawn in mind, many French musicians and folk scholars turned their attention to the Celtic margins of Britain as a primitive cousin and a living relic of the French past – and importantly one with fewer complex political implications than Brittany. This chapter tours Britain alongside French travel writers as they respond to both the haunting pipes and the raucous singing of drunken peasants in situ, and it explores the texts of composers, writers, journalists, and early ethnomusicologists as they are torn between, on the one hand, the powerful appeal of exotic reductionism and, on the other hand, as they try to draw 'scientific' conclusions regarding the racial impulses behind such music, in the context of the nineteenth-century racial theories. It goes on to explore translations and arrangements of the songs of Robert Burns, Walter Scott, and Thomas Moore (seen as representative of Scottish and Irish folk traditions) for French amateur musicians by French song collectors and publishers, and ways in which they are adopted and appropriated, stripped of their original contexts and content as they enter French culture – but, at the same time, ways in which they also pose subtle challenges for concepts of French national and racial unity and for the use of music to make conclusions about ethnic hierarchies in the first place.

Looking in the other direction across the Channel, Chapter 4 interrogates the place of music in the work of French writers travelling to Britain and the ways in which music at once challenges their pre-conceptions and is adopted as a means of coping with their alien surroundings. French travel writers in the fin de siècle remark repeatedly on their astonishing, lowbrow musical encounters in London – in the salons, music halls, tawdry bars, spit-and-saw-dust theatres, and strip joints of the nation's capital. As the brass bands blare out, as amateurs play mechanically on dull-sounding pianos, as black-faced minstrels twang their banjos, as sexually-exploited young girls sing bawdy songs, and as the strains of jig after jig assail their ears and eyes, French writers present their readers with an intriguing and ambivalent textual form. This chapter explores the musical culture shock experienced by a number of French writers from this period – rich and poor, male and female, anglophile and anglophobe – and it traces their acoustic, physical, textual, and emotional reactions to these startling encounters. Often, these texts insistently reach beyond the anecdotal nature of their author's experience to extrapolate overarching sociological conclusions about the national characteristics of the English and about their character relative to France. Not unsurprisingly, such extrapolation is riven with inconsistencies and contradictions as the authors try to reconcile these strange musical experiences with the familiar stereotypes and the ethnographic assessments that had solidified over the generations in

22   *Introduction*

France. The music they hear in Britain – and especially in London – resists easy conceptualization and it challenges many of the tropes that had for so long underwritten French ideas of the English Other.

As a whole, this study of French musical representations and engagements with the British from the Franco-Prussian War to the Entente Cordiale offers an insight into the little-studied role of 'lowbrow' musical culture in the critical years of the fin de siècle and illuminates a gap in our cultural memory and understanding of nationalistic feeling in nineteenth-century popular culture. It explores ways in which French writers and musicians from across the sociopolitical spectrum used music to conceptualize Britain within ethnographic discourse, for diverse and often competing ends, and seeks to open lines of enquiry into musical relations and representations that are often dismissed as trivial.

Notes

1 Jana Verhoeven discusses the use of feminine gender and sexuality as flexible metaphors for judging Britain and as means of finding shared values among Max O'Rell's diverse international audience at this time (2012).

2 One of the most thorough studies summarizing the key racialist 'science' and ideologies of the nineteenth century is Tzvetan Todorov's *On Human Diversity* (1994), which analyses in keen detail the principle theories from the Enlightenment to mid-twentieth century. A small sample of other useful references include: Alice Conklin's discussion of these theories in the context of efforts to reconcile racialist and Republican ideology in the Third Republic's 'civilizing mission' (*A Mission to Civilize*, 1997); William B. Cohen's analysis of thinking about race and slavery from the sixteenth to nineteenth centuries (*The French Encounter with Africans*, 1980); and the collected essays on France's 'human zoos' which give useful detail on the intersection between colonial and scientific racism in contemporaneous popular culture (Nicholas Bancel, Pascal Blanchard, et al., *Zoos humains: de la Vénus hottentote aux Reality Shows*, 2002).

3 Such issues have been approached from a wide range of different angles: for example, Tia DeNora (2000) discusses how individuals construct a sense of identity and socialization using music; Byron Almén and Edward Pearsall (2006) explore different theoretical perspectives that may be brought to bear upon meaning in music; John Shepherd and Peter Wicke (1997) contemplate the ascription of value to music and ways in which the structures of the mind relate to the structures of music; and the mental affect of performance has been examined in adults by Christopher Small (1998) and in children by Patricia Shehan Campbell (1998).

4 Jann Pasler engages in a detailed discussion of the role of music in forming the political subject under the Third Republic in *Composing the Citizen* (2009).

5 The publisher Alcan, in their Bibliothèque scientifique internationale collection in 1888, included twenty-two British philosophers among their sixty-four international authors, and the Philosophie contemporaine anglaise series included forty-five works, whereas the corresponding German and Italian collections contained only twenty-four and twelve works respectively.

Introduction 23

6 Including G. de la Quesnerie, *Éléments germaniques, vocabulaire anglais* (1895), and the notorious, eccentric *Les Mots anglais* by Mallarmé (1877).

7 Hippolyte Taine, *Histoire de la littérature anglaise* (1866–78); J. J. Jusserand, *Histoire littéraire du peuple anglais* (1894); Arbois de Jubainville, *Rapport sur une mission littéraire* (1883).

8 Charles Valframbert, *Régime Municipal et Institutions locales* (1873); M. le docteur Vaudremer, *Une visite express aux hôpitaux de Londres* (1904); and on women's rights, Clarisse Coignet, *De l'affranchissement politique des femmes en Angleterre* (1874).

9 For example, commentaries on English education throughout this period in Jules Simon, *La Réforme de l'enseignement secondaire* (1874); from founder of the modern Olympics, Pierre de Coubertin, *L'Éducation anglaise en France* (1889); Alfred Fouillée, *L'Enseignement au point-de-vue national* (1891); Arthur Dessoye, *L'Enseignement secondaire de la République* (1902); and on women's education in B. Buisson, *De l'enseignement supérieur des femmes en Angleterre* (1883).

10 This is a particularly fruitful field in the Third Republic: for instance, on the state of the imperial venture, Victor Bérard, *L'Angleterre et l'impérialisme* (1900); on the imperialistic mindset, G. Poton, *L'Impérialisme en Angleterre* (1905); on the (effectively) colonial repression of Scottish highlanders, Charles Guernier, *Les Crofters écossais* (1897); and on the embattled state of affairs in Ireland, Gustave de Beaumont, *L'Irlande sociale, politique et religieuse* (1881).

11 Including simple tourist guidebooks, such as the Paul Joanne, *Guide Joanne* series published by Hachette; romanticized visions of Scotland and Ireland (notably by the novelist Marie-Anne de Bovet, *L'Écosse* (1898) and *Trois Mois en Irlande* (1908); and utterly damning portraits of England, of which some of the most strongly worded are Fernand de Jupilles, *Moderne Babylone* (1886) and Hector France, *Les Va-nu-pieds de Londres* (1883).

12 See the title of her study on O'Rell, *Jovial Bigotry* (2012).

13 Including Félix Narjoux, *En Angleterre* (1886); H. Saint-Thomas, *Le Rêve de Paddy et le Cauchemar de John Bull* (1886); E. Plauchent, *L'Égypte et l'occupation anglaise* (1889); E. de Mandat-Grancey, *Chez John Bull* (1895); Alfred Bourguet, *La France et l'Angleterre en Égypte* (1897); and Jean de la Poulaine, *La Colosse aux pieds d'argile* (1899).

14 Listed in an 1889 World Fair guide: the Église épiscopale, rue d'Aguesseau; the Église anglais, 7 cité du Retiro and 7 rue des Bassins; the Église du Christ, 49 Boulevard Bineau; the Église wesleyenne, 4 rue Roquépine; and the Église écossaise, 160 rue de Rivoli (*Exposition universelle internationale*, 1889, p. 370).

15 In 1891, there were 465,860 Belgians, 286,042 Italians, 83,333 Germans, 83,117 Swiss, and 77,736 Spanish residents in France, in comparison to only 39,687 British. This false perception of the magnitude of the British presence may have been in part because 38 per cent of that 39,687 lived in the Paris area and were thus more striking for the writers, composers, and journalists living in the capital.

16 For example, in Verne's Third Republic novels alone, the British play a substantial role in *Le Tour du monde en quatre-vingt jours* (1872), the *Aventures de trois Russes et de trois Anglais* set in Southern Africa (1872), the Scottish Lord Glenarvan and Tom Ayrton in *L'Île mystérieuse* (1874), and the British colonialists and inventors in *La Maison de vapeur* set in India (1880).

24   *Introduction*

Works cited

Adorno, T. W., 1976. *Introduction to the Sociology of Music*. Translated from German by E. B. Ashton. New York: Seabury Press.

Almén, B. and Pearsall, E. R., 2006. *Approaches to Meaning in Music*. Bloomington and Indianapolis: Indiana University Press.

Anfray, C., 2009. 'La Scène surveillée: les adaptations théâtrales des *Rougon-Macquart* face à la censure.' *Les Cahiers naturalistes*, 55 (83), pp. 223–44.

Avout, B. d', 1895. 'Notes de voyage en Angleterre et en Écosse, 1893.' In: *Mémoires de la Société bourguignonne de géographie et d'histoire*. Dijon: Darantière.

Bancel, N., P. Blanchard, et al., 2002. *Zoos humains: de la Vénus hottentote aux Reality Shows*. Paris: La Découverte.

Beaumont, G. de, 1881. *L'Irlande sociale, politique et religieuse*. Paris: Calmann-Lévy.

Bérard, V., 1900. *L'Angleterre et l'impérialisme*. Paris: s.n.

Bertrand, G., 1871. 'Semaine théâtrale,' *Le Ménéstrel*. 24 Dec, p. 28.

Bertrand, G., 1872. *Les Nationalités musicales*. Paris: Didier.

Bovet, M-A. de, 1898. *L'Écosse, souvenirs et impressions de voyage*. Paris: s.n.

Bovet, M-A. de, 1908. *Trois Mois en Irlande*. Paris: s.n.

Brada [pseud. Henriette Consuelo Samson Puliga], 1895. *Notes sur Londres*. Paris: Calmann-Lévy.

Bruneau, A., 1900. *Musiques d'hier et de demain*. Paris: Charpentier.

Buisson, B., 1883. *De l'enseignement supérieur des femmes en Angleterre*. Paris: Chamerol.

Calvet, L.-J., 1981. *Chanson et société*. Paris: Payot.

Campbell, P. S., 1998. *Songs in their Heads: Music and its Meaning in Children's Lives*. Oxford and New York: Oxford University Press.

'Chambre des députés: séances du 29 juillet,' 1879. *Journal Officiel de la République*. 30 July, pp. 7740–72.

Clément, F., 1885. *Histoire de la musique depuis les temps anciens jusqu'à nos jours*. Paris: Hachette.

Cohen, W. B., 1980. *The French Encounter with Africans: White Response to Blacks, 1530–1880*. Bloomington, IN: Indiana University Press.

Coignet, C., 1874. *De l'affranchissement politique des femmes en Angleterre*. Paris: Revue politique et littéraire.

Colley, L., 1998. *Britons: Forging the Nation, 1707–1770*. Oxford: Voltaire Foundation.

Colombel, A. de, 1853. *L'Angleterre et l'Écosse à vol d'oiseau: Souvenirs d'un touriste*. Paris: Ledoyen.

Conklin, A., 1997. *A Mission to Civilize: the Republican Idea of Empire in France and West Africa, 1895–1930*. Stanford, CA: Stanford University Press.

Coubertin, P. de, 1889. *L'Éducation anglaise en France*. Paris: Hachette.

Darwin, C., 1882. *The Descent of Man, and Selection in Relation to Sex*. 2nd edn. London: John Murray.

David-Guillou, A., 2010. 'L'Entente cordiale au music-hall: nouvel statut de l'artiste de musique populaire et échanges artistiques entre la France et l'Angleterre.' In: François Poirier, ed. *Cordiale Angleterre: regards trans-Manche à la Belle-Époque*. Paris: Orphys. pp. 42–62.

DeNora, T., 2000. *Music in Everyday Life*. Cambridge: Cambridge University Press.

Dessoye, A., 1902. *L'Enseignement secondaire de la République*. Paris: Alcide Picard.

Introduction 25

Exposition Franco-Britannique, Londres 1908: Les Colonies françaises, ca. 1908. Paris: Comité national des expositions coloniales.

Exposition universelle internationale: Guide définitif, technique et pittoresque, 1889. Paris: Librairie de la nouvelle revue.

Fétis, F.-J., 1833. 'Essai sur la musique en Angleterre.' *Revue des Deux Mondes*, 3, pp. 129–70.

Fétis, F.-J., 1869. *Histoire générale de la musique*, 6 vols. Paris: Firmin-Didot.

Fouillée, A., 1891. *L'Enseignement au point-de-vue national*. Paris: Hachette.

Fourcaud, 1889. 'Musique,' *Le Gaulois*. 9 June, p. 2.

France, H., 1883. *Les Va-nu-pieds de Londres*. Paris: Charpentier.

Frith, S., 1990. 'What is good music?' *Alternative Musicologies*, 10 (2), pp. 92–102.

Fulcher, J. F., 1999. *French Cultural Politics and Music: From the Dreyfus Affair to the First World War*. Oxford and New York: Oxford University Press.

Garsou, J., 1900. *L'Anglophobie chez Barthélemy et Méry*. Paris: Fischbacher.

Gevaert, F.-A., 1876. 'De l'enseignement public de l'art musical à l'époque moderne,' *Le Ménéstrel*. 8 Oct, pp. 356–9.

Goncourt, E. de, 1882. *La Faustin*. Paris: Charpentier.

Goodall, J. R., 2002. *Performance and Evolution in the Age of Darwin: Out of the Natural Order*. London and New York: Routledge.

Gordon, R. B., 2001. *Why the French Love Jerry Lewis: from Cabaret to Early Cinema*. Stanford, CA: Stanford University Press.

Gracyk, T., 2010. *Listening to Popular Music: Or, How I learned to stop worrying and love Led Zepplin*. Ann Arbor: University of Michigan Press.

Guernier, C., 1897. *Les Crofters écossais*. Paris: Arthur Rousseau.

Guiffon, J., 2006. 'L'Anglophobie dans les premiers manuels d'histoire de l'enseignement primaire sous la Troisième République.' In: S. Aprile and F. Bensimon, eds. *La France et l'Angleterre au XIXe siècle: échanges, représentations, comparaisons*. Paris: Creaphis. pp. 255–67.

Guyot, Y., Sandoz, G.-R., Bourgeois, P., and Claretie, L., 1913. *Exposition Franco-britannique de Londres, 1908*, 3 vols. Paris: Comité français des expositions à l'étranger.

Héros, E., 1919. 'Les Cafés-Chantants: Les Cafés-Concerts: Les Music-halls.' *La Rampe*. 13 April, pp. 8–37.

Huysmans, J.-K., 1881. *En ménage*. Paris: Charpentier.

Joanne, P., 1898-99. *Guides-Joanne: Londres et ses environs*. Paris: Hachette.

Johnson, J. H., 1995. *Listening in Paris: a Cultural History*. Berkeley, CA: University of California Press.

Jubainville, A. de, 1883. *Rapport sur une mission littéraire dans les îles britanniques*. Paris: Imprimerie nationale.

Jullien, A., 1892. *Musiciens d'aujourd'hui*. Paris: Librairie de l'art.

Jullien, A., 1910. *Musiciens d'hier et d'aujourd'hui*. Paris: s.n.

Jupilles, F. de, 1885. *Jacques Bonhomme chez John Bull*. Paris: Calmann-Lévy.

Jupilles, F. de, 1886. *Moderne Babylone: Londres et les Anglais*. Paris: St. Quentin.

Jusserand, J. J., 1894. *Histoire littéraire du peuple anglais des origines à la Renaissance*, 2 vols. Paris: Firmin-Didot.

Lapie, P.-O., 1976. *Les Anglais à Paris: de la Renaissance à l'Entente cordiale*. Paris: Fayard.

Leribault, C., 1994. *Les Anglais à Paris au 19e siècle*. Paris: Paris-Musées.

26 Introduction

Lethbridge, R., 1991. 'Reading the Songs of *L'Assommoir*,' *French Studies*, 45 (4), pp. 435–44.

Levine, L., 2009. *Highbrow/lowbrow: the Emergence of Cultural Hierarchy in America*. Cambridge, MA: Harvard University Press.

Mallarmé, S., 1877. *Les Mots anglais*. Paris: Truchy.

Mason, L., 1996. *Singing the French Revolution: Popular Culture and Politics 1787–1799*. Ithaca, NY: Cornell University Press.

Millot, H., 2003. 'Discours de Jacques Bonhomme à John Bull ou le retour du refoulé (article « Angleterre » du *Grand dictionnaire universel du XIXe siècle*).' In: A. Court and P. Charreton, eds. *Regards populaire sur l'Anglo-Saxon: Drôles de types*. Saint-Étienne: Publications de l'Université de Saint-Étienne. pp. 149–63.

Moreno, H., 1872. 'Saison de Londres,' *Le Ménéstrel*. 10 March–30 June.

Narjoux, F., 1886. *En Angleterre: Angleterre, Écosse (Les Orcades, Les Hébrides), Irlande: Le Pays, Les Habitants, La Vie intérieure*. Paris: E. Plon, Nourrit et Cie.

'Nouvelles diverses: étranger,' 10 March 1872. *Le Ménéstrel*. p. 118.

'Nouvelles diverses: étranger,' 26 May 1872. *Le Ménéstrel*, pp. 214–15.

Parrain, J., 1971. 'Censure, théâtre et Commune.' In: C. Talès, ed. *La Commune de 1871*. Paris: Éditions ouvrières. pp. 327–42.

Pasler, J., 2009. *Composing the Citizen: Music as Public Utility in Third Republic France*. Berkeley, CA: University of California Press.

Plan d'études et programmes de l'enseignement secondaire moderne dans les lycées et collèges (Arrêté du 15 juin 1891), 1891. Paris: Delalain frères.

Poton, G., 1905. *L'Impérialisme en Angleterre*. Paris: Librairie militaire R. Chapelot.

Potter, P. M., 2007. 'The Concept of Race in German Musical Discourse.' In: J. Brown, ed. *Western Music and Race*. Cambridge: Cambridge University Press. pp. 49–62.

Pougin, A., 1871. 'Tablettes artistiques,' *Le Ménéstrel*. 31 Dec, p. 36.

Quesnerie, G. de la, 1895. *Eléments germaniques, vocabulaire anglais*. Paris: Laisney.

Rolland, R., 1908. *Musiciens d'aujourd'hui*. Paris: Hachette.

Rothschild, Baron H. de, 1889. *Notes sur l'Angleterre*. Lille: s.n.

Rutherford, L., 1986. 'Harmless Nonsense: the Comic Sketch and the Development of Music-Hall Entertainment.' In: J. S. Bratton, ed. *Music Hall: Performance and Style*. Milton Keynes and Philadelphia: Open University Press. pp. 131–57.

Shepherd, J. and Wicke, P., 1997. *Music and Cultural Theory*. Cambridge: Polity Press.

Simon, J., 1874. *La Réforme de l'enseignement secondaire*. Paris: Hachette.

Small, C., 1998. *Musicking: the Meanings of Performance and Listening*. Hanover, NH and London: Wesleyen University Press.

Statistiques de la France – résultats généraux du dénombrement de 1876, 1878. Paris: Imprimerie nationale.

Statistiques du dénombrement de 1881: France et Algérie, 1883. Paris: Imprimerie nationale.

Statistiques générales de la France – Résultats statistiques du dénombrement de 1891, 1894. Paris: Imprimerie nationale.

Taine, H., 1866–78. *Histoire de la littérature anglaise*, 5 vols. Paris: Hachette.

Taine, H., 1865. *Philosophie de l'art*, 5 vols. Reprint 1881. Paris: Hachette.

Tholoniat, R., 2010. 'La Caricature anglophobe de Fachoda à l'Entente cordiale.' In: F. Poirier, ed. *Cordiale Angleterre: regards trans-Manche à la Belle-Époque*. Paris: Ophrys. pp. 19–32.

Tiersot, J., 1905. *Notes d'ethnologie musicale*. Paris: Fischbacher.

Todorov, T., 1994. *On Human Diversity: Nationalism, Racism, and Exoticism in French Thought*. Cambridge, MA: Harvard University Press.

Tombs, R., 1996. *France 1814–1914*. London and New York: Longman.

Tombs, R., 2007. *That Sweet Enemy: the French and the British from the Sun King to the Present*. London: Pimlico.

Valframbert, C., 1873. *Régime Municipal et Institutions locales de l'Angleterre, de l'Écosse et de l'Irlande*. Paris: Marescq ainé.

Vaudremer, M. le docteur, 1904. *Une visite express aux hôpitaux de Londres*. Paris: Jean Gainche.

Verhoeven, J., 2012. *Jovial Bigotry: Max O'Rell and the Debate over Manners and Morals in Nineteenth-Century France, Britain, and the United States*. Newcastle-upon-Tyne: Cambridge Scholars' Press.

Weckerlin, J.-B., 1886. *La Chanson populaire*. Paris: Firmin-Didot.

Weil, A. 1872. *Du Programme de l'enseignement secondaire précédé d'une lettre de M. Édouard Laboulaye*. Paris: Charpentier.

1 Singing the English
At the café-concert

'Pourquoi ne peut-on mettre des Anglais au théâtre sans les forcer à danser la gigue?'

'Why can't we have English characters on stage without forcing them to dance a jig?'

Frou-Frou, 'Les Premières' (1872)

In the 1840s, the composer Adrien de la Fage explained that song was an absolute essential of life for the ordinary Frenchman; his sensitivity to music meant that it was not a mere frivolous pleasure, but 'c'est sa consolation, c'est son bien, c'est son droit; il jouit de la chanson comme de l'air qu'il respire, comme du soleil qui l'éclaire et le rechauffe' ['it is his consolation, it is his riches, it is his right; he delights in song like the air that he breathes, like the sun that lights his way and warms his skin'] (1844, p. 62). In the Third Republic, a newly burgeoning space for song arose for the ordinary Frenchman at the café-concert, and it immediately had a magnetic appeal. Earlier in the century, the granting of licences to new cafés-concerts had been severely limited and, even when permission was given, performers had been forbidden from wearing costumes, dancing, gesturing, doing impressions, or using clowning or pantomime – in short, they could essentially just stand and sing (Héros, 1919, Chapter 2). When these restrictions were lifted in 1864 and 1867 respectively, they gave way to an immediate explosion of café-concert culture – and by 1870, more than one hundred such venues could be admired lining Paris's streets and boulevards, providing access to musical entertainment for the ordinary, urban-dwelling Frenchman.

However, as a popular, urban mode of song and entertainment, the artistic and social elites were instinctively suspicious of its content for political, cultural, social, and aesthetic reasons, particularly in the wake of the Paris Commune. The influential musicologist and composer Jean-Baptiste Weckerlin was emphatic in rejecting café-concert music absolutely from his definition of admirable, worthy French song culture. He subdivides French song into three valid categories: art song, city song (the by-then-traditional

DOI: 10.4324/9780367815431-2

Singing the English 29

noël de cour and vaudevilles), and folk song, but scorns and renounces the '*turlutaines* de cafés-concerts, que le peuple braille sur les boulevards' ['café-concert *ditties* that the populace bawls out in the boulevards'] (1886, p. xxix). Its pernicious influence, he feared, would go so far as to suffocate the more valuable but delicate blooms of folk song and traditional city song, since, even in the regions, the 'bonnes vieilles chansons de nos aïeux [...] ont été remplacés par les ineptes rhapsodies, les immorales bêtises des *cafés-concerts*' ['the good old songs of our ancestors have been replaced by the inept rhapsodies, the immoral idiocies of the cafés-concerts'] (1886, p. 21).

Yet despite Weckerlin's categorical rejection of café-concert culture as both aesthetically bereft and of interest only to the undiscerning populace, the appeal of its songs seems to have been no less pervasive and far-reaching to the Frenchman's delight in songs 'like the air that he breathes.' Initially, these venues were frequented by a mostly popular audience (Attali, 2009, p. 76), becoming the standard entertainment of the urban working classes and the petite bourgeoisie, in part for reasons of cultural preference, and in particular because entrance was free on the condition that attendees did not linger long without replenishing their beer glasses (Moore Whiting, 1999, p. 1). However, it was not long before the genre's appeal spread rapidly up the class ladder. First, its shows drew upper-class and bourgeois men into its audiences, and, by the 1890s, high-society women, too, could take pleasure in the evening's entertainment without committing a grave infraction against social decorum. Gabriel Tarde commented in 1901, 'voici un auditoire de café-concert; des Parisiens et des Parisiennes de goût raffiné s'y rassemblent. Pris séparément, ils sont dégustateurs de fine musique, de littérature pimentée mais savoureuse. Réunis, ils ne font leurs délices que de stupides chansons' ['here is a café-concert audience; Parisian men and women of fine taste gathered together. Taken separately, they enjoy sophisticated music and spicy but flavoursome literature. Taken together, they only get their pleasure from idiotic songs'] (1901, p. 186). So, although the *aesthetic* of the café-concert and the atmosphere it encouraged might be said to be more 'popular,' audiences were characterized increasingly by social mixity. Indeed, by the turn of the century, many venues largely edged the working classes and petits employés out with entrance fees and an increasing focus on luxuriance (discussed in Rearick, 1985, pp. 95–96).

Jann Pasler remarks upon the democratization of demand for music in the Third Republic, while French thinkers, composers, writers, musicians, educators, and policymakers alike sought the key to an elusive concept of national identity, and while the idea of finding, fostering, or forging a shared, cross-class French musical spirit and genius repeatedly came to the fore (2009, esp. Chapter 8). Many members of the cultural and social elites were invested in widening access to art music for more popular audiences, be it through affordable public concerts (such as those organized by Pasdeloup – see Bernard, 1971) or through the provision of music-making societies such as wind bands and orphéon choirs (see Baker, 2017) and, for women, with Charpentier's

30 *Singing the English*

Mimi Pinson choirs (see Poole, 1997). Art music outreach and dissemination programmes were actively explored and nourished by the elites as a means of calming and unifying the populace, of educating and improving, and of nurturing national sentiment whether for politically strategic or genuinely philanthropic purposes – and all this was typically couched in language contrasting these ventures with the banality, even the dangerousness, of popular café-concert music. Yet in reality, as Pasler observes, this widening of audiences went in both directions, and those who proscribed the cafés-concerts for the lower classes were no less tempted through their doors; the 'democratization of demand' not only meant that 'the lower classes got into establishments previously reserved for the bourgeoisie, albeit in the upper seats, but also that the appeal of "democratized theatre" or "theatres of the poor" – the *cafés-concerts* – was spreading to all social classes' (2009, p. 477).

Whatever the snobbery surrounding these guilty pleasures, the immense popularity of the café-concert during this period meant that it provided a crucial setting in which the preoccupations of the day could be acted out – both literally and in psychological terms. It offered a mediatory space where tensions could be dissolved into humour, alarm replaced with determination, and fear transformed into resolution and a sense of community. Steven Moore Whiting has observed that the repertoire of the Parisian cafés-concerts was interwoven tightly with the shifting landscape of politics and society, and it embraced the events of the contemporary world from the Franco-Prussian War and Algerian conflicts, to cultural novelties such as the introduction of the telephone, trams, or automobiles (1999, p. 20). Song content, as a result, presented audiences with a rich panoply of content, genre, and performance style, varying both over time and over the spectrum of performers, venues, and favourite character types. There was the troupier [soldier], gambilleur [prancer], pochard(e) [drunkard], pierreuse [low-class prostitute], gommeux/euse [dandy], épileptique [saucy singers pretending to have various hysterical and neurological disorders], paysan(nne) [peasant], and many, many more – but in all their various manifestations, as the novelist and civil servant André Chadourne observed in 1889, 'autant que le journal et le livre, et beaucoup plus que la chaire, la tribune, le barreau, il est, pour ainsi dire, le miroir résonant de nos croyances, de nos mœurs, de nos fantaisies, de nos goûts, de nos passions' ['just as much as newspapers and books, and much more than the pulpit, political platform, or judicial bar, the café-concert is, so to speak, the resonating mirror of our beliefs, our customs, our fantasies, our tastes, our passions'] (1889, p. 3).

Such dynamism and sensitivity to socio-cultural and political change could not but reflect contemporaneous dealings with Britain, given the ever-changing, important, and affective nature of the cross-Channel relationship. England (and it is usually England rather than Scotland, Ireland, or Wales in this case) was the subject of an entire genre of café-concert song; yet, to the best of my knowledge, no scholarship to date has explored the representations of England and the English in this vastly influential musical

Singing the English 31

culture. Unlike so many subjects for song such as the World Fairs or the latest technological gadgetry, songs about the English were no mere transient novelty, nor a periodic topic that came and went with fleeting moments of conflict or rivalry; rather, they were an embedded, fundamental part of café-concert culture throughout the fin-de-siècle era. Moore Whiting mentions in passing a *genre anglais* favoured by the performers Harry Fragson and Max Dearly in the 1890s (1999, p. 15), but archival research conducted for the present book reveals that the genre of comic English songs was considerably more substantial and long-lived. It seems to have appeared on the popular-music scene in France around the 1830s, with a marked spike around and in the immediate wake of the 1855 World Fair, and then it flourished at the café-concert during the Third Republic with at least eighty-nine songs and musical skits about the English that I have (so far) been able to discover from between 1870 and the signing of the Entente cordiale in 1904. Such a wealth of musical material significantly outnumbers comparable bodies of popular song about the Far East, Spain, or Algeria in this period – all cultures that we are accustomed to thinking of as central obsessions of Third Republican culture – and there is no equivalent corpus of café-concert songs for any other nationality. It is an astonishing quantity of songs to cluster around one repeated theme, appearing on the stages of at least twenty-three different Parisian cafés-concerts, music halls, and, occasionally, cabarets (see details in Appendix), giving a sense of the pervasiveness and the longevity of this comic song tradition.

That so many of these songs were subsequently published in music magazines (such as the popular and affordable *Chanson illustrée*) and as sheet music in both *grand* and *petit format* for the repeated enjoyment of singers and pianists at home and at smaller theatres suggests that publishers also had a comfortable expectation of their continued appeal; and, considering the prohibitive price of pianos for those on a working-class income, it can be assumed that there was a substantial petit-bourgeois and bourgeois market for this music, too. For a publisher to break even on their investment, the playwright and songwriter Eugène Héros noted that about a thousand print copies would need to be purchased in the 1890s (1894, p. 1) – of course, he concedes, not every song published would have crossed that threshold but many far exceeded it and were an editorial goldmine. A number of the comic English songs were among these demonstrable successes and remained popular for many years, in spite of the continuous production of new songs on the same topic. For example, in 1895 the editor Le Bailly advertised a collection of 'Chansonnettes anglaises' ('English comic songs' – 3 Fr *petit format* / 10 Fr *grand format* with piano), all but two of which pre-date 1867 – Le Bailly clearly understood the continued market for (and lucrative potential of) reviving these songs for the next generation of comic English-song lovers. The *Figaro* even reported in 1896 that Fragson, Briollet, and Mortreuil's 'L'Anglais parisien' (1895 – featuring a French singer pretending to be an Englishman who comes to Paris to learn French but unwittingly

32 *Singing the English*

learns Montmartre argot), figured among the best-received entertainments at the Marquis and Marquise de Barbentane's house party at the Château de Saint-Jean-la-Priche; such songs, it appears, held substantial appeal even to the cream of high society (Ferrari, 1896, p. 2).

Of course, the comic English character existed in genres beyond the café-concert too, and I do not imply that popular song invented a unique character type here: on the contrary, buffoonish English characters were present in a broad swathe of stage entertainments, both the musical and the unmusical. Hugh Macdonald has noted the proliferation of foolish English men and women in successful comic operas, notably during the Restoration period by Scribe, Aubert, and Halévy.[1] Comic plays and farces, too, often enlivened their scenes with English characters.[2] However, the unique context of the café-concert performance demands that its English characters become a concentrated, hyperbolic version of this already-exaggerated, comic Anglo-Saxon. Whereas shows at the comic opera, theatre, and circus provided a narrative framework in which to fit the fictional English individual, situating him among a network of other characters and in an extended comic scenario, the café-concert Englishman would only appear on stage for a few short minutes, in a largely self-contained skit, with an often only partially-attentive audience amid the noise of waitresses, conversations, grinding chairs, footsteps, and glassware. As a result, he had to be all the more instantly recognizable, and to be funny in and of himself without recourse to wider farcical plotlines.

This chapter, then, explores the vibrant and persistent play on ideas of Englishness in this forgotten song tradition. The pleasure audiences seem to have taken in these songs for so many years is complex and multi-faceted in spite of the simplicity of the music itself, and this chapter examines the appeal of these songs and the messages that they promulgated. First, it sets out an overview of the musical corpus and the key features of the café-concert English stereotype, its costumes, and its contrast to the English characters of French literature and of political song. It then turns to focus on accent and language, the comedy that these elicit, and the often-awkward positioning of these jokes given the wider context of language learning in France after the Franco-Prussian War. Language, furthermore, is used to 'Other' the English – using, perhaps somewhat surprisingly, the tropes and representational strategies more familiar to us from the representation of colonial, exoticized, non-European Others. The English body, too, is depicted as a site of radical Otherness as the French performers 'English up' in their tweeds and sideburns and contort their elegant frames into the angular peculiarities of the jig. Throughout, this chapter seeks to understand where the crux of the comedy lies for French fin-de-siècle audiences, why it makes them laugh, and what wider implications this laughter may have had; while, of course, the café-concert's treatment of the English is wildly exaggerated, this chapter explores its capacity to mediate and problematize wider concepts of French national identity at the turn of the century.

The English 'type'

Before entering into the finer details of this analysis, it is worth pausing briefly to summarize the salient features of this substantial corpus of songs. A number of notable repeating themes can be identified, and it is these repeated themes that were at the heart of the audience's recognition, understanding, and enjoyment of the comic English act. The general premise is that the French performer enters the stage and announces themselves to be an Englishman or woman: the first lines of twenty-seven out of the eighty-nine songs I have traced open explicitly with a grammatically-dubious statement such as 'J'arrive de la Hangleterr' ('Mylord Gig-gig,' 1879), 'Je hâvais quitté l'Angleterre' ('Milady Plumpudding,' 1887), 'Je vins à Péris en France' ('L'Anglais poivrot,' 1897). They go on to explain that they are travelling or have recently travelled to France, generally to Paris – there are, to my knowledge, only two examples of a French character giving their impressions of the English after having themselves travelled to England ('Miss, Oh! Yes!' 1895; 'L'Anglais gêlé, ou John c'est épatant,' 1898). Almost all of these characters' language is scattered liberally with errors in French grammar and vocabulary, and is still more equivocal in terms of accent, with indications of the desired mispronunciation provided in the lyrics – commonly, 'moâ' for 'moi,' 'mosseu' for 'monsieur,' 'pôvais' for 'pouvais,' and so on. This is elaborated with a smattering of English vocabulary, though this rarely extends beyond 'very good,' 'very well,' 'shocking,' 'goddam,' 'yes / no,' and 'alright'; indeed, a subset of these songs explicitly thematize the French language skills of English visitors to Paris, including several about those who travel to France specifically to learn the language (these will be discussed in more detail below). Around the turn of the century, it became increasingly popular to sing *about* the English rather than for the performer to pretend to *be* English – I have found twenty-three such songs, nearly all of which post-date 1898 – though in terms of themes, jokes, stereotypes, and English lexicon they very much draw from the familiar catalogue established by their predecessors.

In almost all cases, the English character in question is wealthy, genteel, and from London. The stage is graced by the well-to-do Englishman in every possible mood; as the list of these songs in the Appendix indicates, over a quarter are simply entitled 'L'Anglais + adjective,' with the drunk and the sober, the joyous and the sad, the infuriated and the guffawing, the formal, the annoyed ... Yet this repetitiveness did nothing to diminish the popularity of this genre as the years went on. I have found only four songs obviously representing English people from other social classes, and although these are not explicit about whether the character is a nouveau riche industrialist or an ordinary petty bourgeois, their ungenteel social status is made clear in a number of possible ways. First, by explicitly mentioning their provenance from the supposedly cultureless industrial cities of Manchester and Liverpool ('L'Anglais embarrassé,' 1887; 'L'Anglais triste,' 1892; 'L'Apéritif d'un Anglais 1894). Secondly, by their financial savviness or stinginess; for example, the 'Anglais

34 *Singing the English*

embarrassé' asks a number of questions to get directions, menu suggestions, and so on from people he meets in Paris but understands none of their rapidly-spoken responses – except the one in which a French girl asks him for an expensive gold necklace, which despite her charms he flatly refuses to buy for her, unlike the typical behaviour of the Mylord. Thirdly, by their rude refusal to even try to speak French; in the case of 'L'Apéritif d'un Anglais,' the English character neatly rhymes 'Liverpool' with 'speak bloody English, fool.' Or fourth, by a hard-luck story, such as the teacher in 'Ratatapoum purée' (1893) who comes to Paris to look for work but goes from one disaster to another with exclamations of 'bladdy goddem' in what appears to be a pseudo-cockney accent. Women, too, are in the minority for these comic English songs (even though male performers were not particularly dominant at the café-concert in general), with only nineteen songs in which the performers take on a female English persona or sing primarily about English women – and several of these are drag acts performed by men, such as 'Miss Kokett' (1877), which was played at the Excelsior Concert in 1896 by the 'homme-femme' M. Modanel in faded pink frock and five-day beard.

Male or female, genteel or not, all these English characters recount that they have come to France in search of some kind of enriching life-experience – cultural, linguistic, and/or sexual – which their own more northerly, more prudish shores could not afford them. This focus on experiential travel often elicits a series of contrasts between England and France, with favoured sets of opposites arising around sense of humour, corporeal mannerisms in dance, attitude to sports, elegance, seduction, class structures, and ideas of politesse. The 'Anglais à Paris' (1881), for example, compares English and French dancehalls (and their women), 'Le Joyeux Anglais' (1889) juxtaposes alcohol consumption and food habits, and the 'Revanche de John Bull' (1894) self-referentially compares the means by which each nation caricatures the other in comedy, complete with an introduction to the tune of 'God Save the Queen' and coda based on the well-known hornpipe 'Jack's the lad' to fully maximize the French audience's appreciation of national difference. Even in those songs where national difference is not the explicit topic of the lyrics, the English characters are frequently portrayed as so utterly different to the French that this game of us-and-them remains the dominant force of the act. For example, in the 'Anglais formaliste' (1888), English social etiquette is so rigid (and ridiculous) in contrast to the French that the English gent refrains from informing a fellow diner at a chic Parisian restaurant that his trousers are on fire until they have been formally introduced. Very often, national difference is displayed through bodily difference, and by far the most frequent manifestation of this is in 'national' dance (as shall be analysed in more detail later in this chapter). The generic motif in such songs of jaunty, dotted-rhythms of the English jig and the hyper-energetic jigging body are repeatedly contrasted to the straight-rhythmed measures of either the waltz or the quadrille and their more aesthetically-appealing steps – a juxtaposition subsequently used to extrapolate fundamental distinctions between the French

Singing the English   35

and English in terms of race, body, culture, psyche, and politics. As Richard Hibbitt has observed in his study of literary exchanges, in both France and the United Kingdom, 'we find evidence not just of stereotypical views of so-called national characteristics, but also a widespread belief in fixed differences between each culture as if it were a question of different species' (2012, p. 35).

The insistence on caricatural, clichéd personality types has much in common with the aesthetic processes at the heart of Realism and melo-drama. As Christopher Prendergast has explained, the mimetic function of Realist types was rooted, not in a verifiable reality outside the textual world, but in concepts of plausibility based on readerly expectations, fostered in large part by the reader's past literary and theatrical experiences (1986, Introduction). Indeed, English characters were everywhere to be found in novels throughout the nineteenth century and they tended to cohere around a few key manifestations of Englishness; for example, the phlegmatic but honourable type, such as Verne's Phileas Fogg (*Voyage autour du monde en 80 jours* [*Around the World in 80 Days*], 1872). There is the melancholic and despairing type, such as Maupassant's eponymous and suicidal Miss Harriet (1883), Villiers de l'Isle-Adam's suicidal Lord Ewald (*L'Ève future* [*The Future Eve*], 1886), or Robert de Bonnière's eponymous and depressive Lord Hyland (1895). In Swinburnian vein, there is the cold and cruel type, such as Jean Lorrain's sadistic Lord Ethal (*Monsieur de Phocas*, 1901), the lower-class Whitechapel gang of murderers in his 'Masques de Londres' from *Le Vice errant* (*Wandering Vice*, 1901), or Mirbeau's torture-loving Clara in *Le Jardin des supplices* (*The Torture Garden*, 1899). And there are the heart-of-gold, sentimental Dickensian types, such as those in the hugely popular Hector Malot novels *Sans famille* (*Nobody's Boy*, 1878) and *Miss Clifton: souvenirs d'un blessé* (*Miss Clifton: memories of an injured soldier*, 1872). These 'types' are reinforced by contemporary sociological discourses on Englishness, not least by Hippolyte Taine, whose *Notes sur l'Angleterre* (*Notes on England*, 1872) repeatedly insist that English national traits emerge from the depths of their racial temperament, always subtended by the essence of 'l'homme du Nord, [...] violent et plus militant [pour lequel] le plaisir est chose brutale et bestiale' ['the man of the North, violent and more militant, for whom pleasure is a brutal and bestial thing'] (1872, p. 16).

Character types at the café-concert are produced and function in a similar way: they are instantly recognizable as 'English' through constant reiter-ation and through intertextual and intermusical references between songs that, over time, solidify into audience expectations – and eventually audience requirements. The audience may suspect that, *really*, they would be unlikely to find the streets of London filled with such caricatures if they were to tra-verse the Channel – but the overbearing familiarity of the character types also results in a base-level belief that there might indeed be some fundamental truth in them; they are driven by an enjoyment, as Ruth Amossy notes of stereotypes generally, 'à laquelle nous prenons d'autant plus plaisir que nous en avons déjà assimilé les règles' ['in which we take all the more pleasure

36 *Singing the English*

because we have already learned its rules'] (1991, p. 15). However, though the mechanism is similar between the café-concert and literary Realism, it is striking to note that the 'English' character types in comic songs often diverge in fundamental ways from the stereotypes consecrated by literary mimesis. The melancholic Englishman who remained a stalwart companion for the literature reader had featured in some earlier songs from cafés chantants and vaudevilles during the Romantic period, but he had faded from the stage almost entirely by the end of the 1860s. For example, audiences had enjoyed the suffering of the aristocratic gentleman of 'Les Jolies Petites Songes d'un Anglais' ['The Lovely Little Dreams of an Englishman,' *ca.* 1836], who sighed in delight at his dreams of death by violent misadventure to a lullaby-like melody which pastiches the most sentimental offerings of Romanticism. In 'L'Anglais en traversée' ['The Englishman Crossing,' 1850], Milord could be witnessed longing for his homeland as he set sail for France – partly out of patriotism, partly due to a desire for terra firma in the midst of harrowing bursts of seasickness and an accompaniment which lurches just as violently up and down the scale as the boat does upon the waves. 'L'Anglais mélancolique' ['The Melancholic Englishman,' 1855] had confessed his feelings of profound spleen when confronted by such sad sensations as the sight of pretty girls, the song of nightingales, or the warmth of the sun. Yet this absurd melancholic had drifted away by the late-1850s – a fact we might perhaps ascribe to real-life contact between ordinary Parisians (the café-concert target audience) and non-aristocratic English visitors during the 1855 World Fair. After 1870, melancholic characters such as these appear as primary characteristics in only four songs – even though this character type remains prominent well into the twentieth century in both the operatic and literary spheres.

Notable too, from the other end of the spectrum, is the absence of cruelty among English café-concert characters – even though we could well imagine a pantomime-villain-style aristocratic character working well here. The 'Anglais malcontent' (1888) is certainly grumpy and inclined to put his fists up at the first apparent affront to himself or his wife (the scatalogically-named Lady Centris [= la dysenterie]): he threatens to box with a man who smokes in the train carriage; with a waiter when the beef sauce has a hair in it; and with a passing youth who says his wife looks like a hippopotamus – but for all that he is depicted as gruff rather than villainous. The 'Anglais chez nous' (1891) might be 'pas chouett's pour les Français' ['not nice to the French'] in not honouring the Opéra with adequately smart evening dress and in nonchalantly treating Paris like a tourist resort, but there is no suggestion that their rudeness might thinly veil a perverse taste for inflicting psychological or physical torture. The English character at the café-concert might be unnecessarily proud of his peculiar culture, and he or she may be hypocritical by professing straight-laced moralism in England whilst indulging in sexual looseness in France, but there is no suggestion that they are fundamentally malevolent.

This is all the more striking because profound and inherent cruelty are precisely the characteristics ascribed to the English in explicitly *political* songs

Singing the English   37

from the same era, often pitched at similar audiences and performed in identical venues. Unlike comic English songs, these political songs are not a constant cultural companion of the fin-de-siècle generations but emerge in flurries during the intermittent spikes of political tension – particularly during the fraught atmosphere of the Fashoda crisis and the Boer War. For example, the successful song writer Lucien Boyer not only wrote comic Englishman ditties for café-concert comic stars Mayol and Fragson, but also created 'La Balle "Dum-Dum"' (1889) to the tune of the 'Frou-frou' waltz, about England's use of the expanding bullet during the First Boer War (performed by Louise France to the socially-mixed audiences at the Grand Guignol and by Jules Mévisto to the artistic crowd at the Quat'z-Arts). In this, he remarks with dark sarcasm that:

> L'Anglais vraiment humanitaire,
> Vient d'trouver un nouvel engin
> Pour civiliser tout' la terre:
> C'est un bijou d'plomb et d'nickel
> Qui s'ouvre comme un parapluie;
> Ça découpe comme une scie,
> Ça fouill'la chair comme un scalpel.

> [The truly humanitarian Englishman,
> Has just found a new contraption
> To civilize the whole world:
> It's a gem of lead and nickel
> That opens like an umbrella;
> It cuts like a saw,
> It probes flesh like a scalpel.]

Similarly, the café-concert and music-hall composer Léo Lelièvre's 'La Marche des Boers' from the Second Boer War (1900, performed by the famous singer Dona at the Eldorado – one of the most successful venues of the fin de siècle), excoriates an England defined by greed, imperious oppressiveness, and a callous disregard for human life and valour (compared to France as a lover of liberty and the spiritual brother of the Boers):

> Employant le même sans-gêne,
> Que nous vîmes à Fachoda,
> Dans la République Africaine
> L'Angleterre envoie ses soldats,
> Voulant écraser ce qui vibre
> Dans le cœur des hommes ardents.

> [With the same brazenness,
> That we saw at Fashoda,
> To the African Republic

38 *Singing the English*

> England is sending its soldiers,
> Hoping to crush the life
> From the hearts of ardent men.]

Yet this inhumanity – here depicted as a habitual trait of English national character – is conspicuously absent from the bulk of those comic café-concert English characters who form an ever-present figure in contemporary performance culture.

What, then, might be at the root of these discrepancies between literature and the café-concert, and between political and comic song? One might initially be tempted to put this discrepancy down to a question of social class: that the audiences reading literary texts and going to the opera, and those enjoying an evening of 'light' music at the café-concert were not the same, and thus that they had their own familiar images of what 'the English' were like, according to their likely exposure to the English in politics, tourism, and so on. However, the increasing 'democratization of demand,' to reprise Pasler's term, meant that the educated classes enjoying literary writing and art music were also frequently attendees at the café-concert, and the lower classes were increasingly familiar with opera and opéra-comique. Café-concert venues with a substantial popular audience (such as the Pépinière and Gaité-Rochechouart) and the most chic venues (such as the Café des Ambassadeurs) frequently drew from the same repertoire, including for comic English songs, and for much of this period venues in popular districts such as Montmartre and the 10th arrondissement drew a mixed-class clientele. The disparity – even sometimes mutual incompatibility – between the sets of stereotypes elaborated on operatic stages and in novels vis-à-vis those at the café-concert would, then, have been obvious to many of the audience members.

The use of costume, I contend, offers some explanation for this striking divergence. Costume held a place of central importance in the comic English performance; there is little detailed record of this in performance reviews – reflecting, indeed, just how little it called for a commentary for the familiar contemporaneous audiences – but the images on the covers of sheet music allow us a glimpse into the visual spectacle. The English wardrobe could best be stylistically defined as frumpy; it reliably consisted of a tweed jacket and absurd stick-on ginger or blonde mutton chops, and then combined these with an assortment of button-down gloves, a hat (generally a tweed deer-stalker or tweed bowler), tweed trousers or white riding knee-britches with stockings, shiny black boots, an ill-fitted waistcoat, and a number of cumbersome accessories for good measure such as a monocle, umbrella, walking cane, cross-body travel bag, or binoculars (see Figures 1.1–1.4). Women's costumes varied somewhat more, depending on whether the butt of the humour is that Englishwomen are appallingly unattractive (like the unalluring and markedly un-self-aware 'Miss Kokett,' 1877, played in drag) or that they are secretly nymphets (like the 'Anglaises Misses,' 1885, who assure us they are very modest and that, when dancing, they never kick their legs up ... above nose

Singing the English 39

Figure 1.1 Sheet music cover from 'Le Chic anglais' (1894).
Source: Bibliothèque nationale de France.

level). However, in both cases tweed or tartan fabrics and a flagrant disregard for elegant style dominate, and the costumes for these two kinds of women differ principally in terms of the length of the skirts and whether they were to be worn by male or female performers.

In the heyday of the comic English genre around the turn of the century, such a costume was of course divorced from contemporary sartorial reality in England, yet it was no less accepted as a clear visual signifier of Englishness by French audiences – not unlike the habitual but historically-misguided insistence today that a stripy tee-shirt, beret, and string of onions constitute dressing as 'French.' Much like that beret-clad onion seller, these visual stereotypes of the English are in fact rooted in a real, small-scale historical

40 *Singing the English*

Figure 1.2 Sheet music cover from 'Miss Gig' (1885).
Source: Bibliothèque nationale de France.

moment of encounter, but were then expanded for use as a universal and lasting visual signifier. The writer Hector France remarks with some frustration in 1900 that 'voici donc bientôt cinquante ans que le long et grotesque favori a disparu des visages anglais, mais il est probable que dans cinquante ans, nos artistes et nos fumistes boulevardiers en orneront encore nos voisins d'Outre-Manche, pour donner à la badauderie parisienne un *parfait specimen* du type britannique' ['it's now nearly fifty years since those long, grotesque sideburns have disappeared from English faces, but in another fifty years our artists and boulevard shams will still be plastering them on our cross-Channel neighbours to give idle Parisians a *parfait specimen* of Britishness'] (1900, pp. 23–25). He locates this tweedy, muttonchop-bearing Englishman as a

Singing the English 41

Figure 1.3 Sheet music cover from 'Mylord Gig-Gig' (1879).
Source: Bibliothèque nationale de France.

product of the 1850s, when floods of the English middle classes descended upon Paris for the 1855 World Fair, often for the first time. By the time the World Fair of 1889 came to pass, the initial shock of encounter, greater familiarity over the intervening decades, the normalization of photography, images, and pictures in many newspapers (especially in the penny press), and the homogenization of fashion through mass production and expanding trade networks meant that such immediate visual differences and visual surprises had largely disappeared. This is reflected in Gontron Jollivet's 'Mme de Charvy' segment in the *Figaro-Exhibition* guide from 1889, which recounts how Mme de Charvy and her friend tried to guess the nationality of different visitors based on outward appearance with distinctly limited success:

42 *Singing the English*

Figure 1.4 Sheet music cover from 'Oh! le Angleterre' (1878).
Source: Bibliothèque nationale de France.

> Ceux-ci, qui passent raides et muets consultant à chaque instant leur guide? – Des Anglais sans doute. […] Je t'avouerai que nos devinettes […] n'ont pas été toujours absolument exactes. Tel que nous prenions pour un citoyen de Manchester ou de Berlin s'est trouvé parler, en passant près de nous, le plus pur auvergnat. […] Elles nous prouvaient simplement qu'avec l'uniformité colportée dans le monde entier, précisément par ces mêmes chemins de fer qui nous dégorgent tant d'étrangers, c'est le diable de mettre les pays des gens sur leur visage.
>
> (Jollivet, 1889, pp. 123–34)

Singing the English 43

[These ones, walking along rigid, silent, with their noses constantly in their guidebooks? – English, no doubt about it. [...] I confess that our guessing game wasn't always absolutely successful. Someone we took for a citizen of Manchester or Berlin could be heard, on passing near to us, speaking in the purest Auvergnat accent. [...] It simply proved to us that, with the uniformity spreading across the world due precisely to the same railways that are currently spilling out foreigners into Paris, it's a devil of a job to work out people's origins from their appearance.]

Nonetheless, the insistence at the café-concert on the existence of a quintessentially English appearance proves tenacious and it repeatedly presents and re-presents a visual image of an Englishman who, by the Third Republic, scarcely existed anymore across the Channel.

What can be observed here is a striking process of detemporalization which stops the clock in the 1850s – a retrograde tendency all the more surprising given the café-concert's general inclination for reacting to the immediate novelties of contemporary life. This atypical detemporalization suggests that not only a physical importance but also a psychological one was attached in the French cultural psyche to these garments and the stereotypes that they bring to life. Back in the 1850s, as the rather puritanical social mores of the early Victorian regime prospered and as the growing British Empire fostered loyalty to the crown rather than revolutionary ferment, there was indeed a cultural chasm far wider than the few miles of sea between France and England. Converging as this did with the first major encounter between substantial segments of the French population and English people (other than on the battlefield), and converging too with the burgeoning popularization of early ethnology from Buffon, Darwin, Taine, and their contemporaries, cultural divergence at this time was read as a fundamental expression of difference in racial and national character. By lingering doggedly, then, on a visual image based on an Englishman of the early Victorian period, the café-concert song ignores all the subsequent cultural changes that reduced that gulf between French and English character, such as diminishing prudery, the relaxation of Sunday observance, the increased aesthetic appreciation marked by Pre-Raphaelitism, improving workers' rights, and the gradual weakening of traditional class hierarchies in England, and the increasing hunger for colonial expansion in France.

The English voice

Homi Bhabha says of the stereotype that it is 'a form of knowledge and identification that vacillates between what is always "in place," already known, and something that must be anxiously repeated' (1994, p. 66). Anxiety of repetition is apparent in these costume choices and it extends, too, into the content

44 *Singing the English*

of the songs. Another striking difference between the literary and the comic café-concert English character – perhaps the most striking – is that the latter has a limited mastery of French. When the literary Englishman (or woman) first graces the page, as Corinne Perrin observes, 'le personnage adopte instantanément le français pur et le "beau langage" de ses interlocuteurs (on invoque, comme justification, le don des Anglais pour les langues étrangères...)' ['the character immediately adopts the purest French and the elegant register of those he is talking to (this is justified by invoking the English gift for foreign languages...')] (2003, p. 19). The same cannot be said for the café-concert English character; in contrast to their literary counterparts, the enthusiasm of their efforts to speak French is woefully out of proportion to their success. A characteristic example can be found in 'L'Anglais en voyage' (1882), where the entire basis for humour in the chorus is the misguided woman's comic accent and its distortion of the familiar sounds of French – emphasized by the placement of the most heinous errors as both rhyme words and on held notes at the end of each musical phrase. The female traveller explains to a chic French man who is, of course, trying to seduce her in the street, that:

Aôh, very well, vô êtes beaucoup bon (prononcer: beune)
Mais il me manquait le prononciation (prononnciécheune)
Exquiousez môa je étais de London (Lonndeune)
Je comprenais pas je demandais pardon (pardeune)!

[Oh, very well, you are very good
But my pronunciation needed work
Excuse me I am from London
I didn't understand and asked him to excuse me!]

This song is by no means unique; on the contrary, punning on mispronunciation, misremembered idioms, and category slips gives rise to a whole genre of café-concert humour. Sometimes the Englishman is aware of his errors and the audience is invited to guffaw at the spectacle of him mentally or literally thumbing through the dictionary to recall the correct phrase. In 'Je pôvais pas' (1885), an English gentleman is in the midst of his first experience of French cuisine at a bistro and has just struggled valiantly with a very tough French beefsteak.[3] He exclaims: 'à la première mâchement j'avais cassé ma ... comment vous dites? Ma râteau? No! Ma râtelier de dents dans mon baouche!' ['at the first bite I broke my... ..how do you say it? My rake? No! My false teeth in my mouth!']. Despite the jibe at French cookery, the audience is invited to laugh at both the Englishman's imperfect dentistry and his imperfect French. On other occasions, the Englishman is belligerently sure of himself and takes exception at French people who misunderstand him or who, when he misunderstands them, seem to make the most outlandish and bizarre suggestions. For example, the 'Anglais au dictionnaire' (1875) claims with tremendous confidence that 'je comprenais n'importe quoa, / avec mon

Singing the English   45

fêmeux dictionnaire / je pôvais jêmais tromper moâ' ['I understood absolutely anything, / With my fantastic dictionary / I couldn't make a mistake'];
yet on going to the theatre, he is infuriated when the ticket girl offers him
a 'baignoire' [in a theatre, this refers to the boxed seating just above and
around the stalls – but also, literally, means a bath] since, after consulting
the dictionary, he thinks she is offering him a chance to have a soak in the
tub instead of seeing the show. Having refused this, she offers him a place
in the 'poulailler' [the gods – but also, literally, a hen house]; this time, the
infallible dictionary informs him this is a chicken coop and, as he is par-
tial to chicken, he accepts gleefully. But on arrival – what disappointment –
the audience members who were already seated must have eaten every single
chicken before he entered. Completely unenlightened and unabashed by this
experience, he later steals a horse and rides it into the Bal Mabille after seeing
the term 'cavalier' on the ticket price list [literally, horse rider, but also the
term for a male dance partner]; and subsequently he thinks the girl he has
taken to a private 'cabinet particulier' for an intimate dinner has gone to buy
cake when she dismisses both him and his terrible French with a curt exclamation of 'du flan!' ['waffle!'].

Novelty and surprise are often held to be central concepts to comedy, yet
they are distinctly absent from this genre and provide scant explanation for
the continued pleasure found in these songs by generation after generation of
audiences. Already in 1864, a journalist for the *Figaro* complained about the
mystifying popularity of the comedy English accent in comic opera:

> Je n'ai jamais compris le côté plaisant de ces grossières caricatures, et cela
> ne m'amuse pas du tout d'entendre un dialogue lardé de *come, shocking,
> very well* et autres lambeaux de conversation britannique. Mlle Clarisse
> Miroy parle cette langue mi-partie et sautille en marchant comme un
> oiseau qui se brûlerait les pattes. Est-ce bien comique? Je ne trouve pas. Il
> est vrai que le public ne paraît pas être du même avis que moi.
>
> (Villemessant, 1864, p. 2)]

> [I have never understood what's so comical about these coarse caricatures,
> and it doesn't amuse me at all to hear a dialogue strewn with *come,
> shocking, very well*, and other scraps of British conversation. Mlle Clarisse
> Miroy half speaks this language and hops about as she walks like a bird
> burning its feet. Is it funny? I don't think so. But it's true that the audience
> don't seem to feel the same way.]

By 1904, so ever-present were songs littered with English words by singers
such as Max Dearly, Harry Fragson, and Fordyce (all French performers
under English pseudonyms) that one reviewer of the Olympia's 'The Magic
Kettle' revue show quipped that the Parisian audience was surely well on their
way to fluency in English thanks to the continual presence of English jargon
on stage (M[onsieur] du B[alcon], 1904, p. 4).

46 *Singing the English*

The humour in this mockery of English linguistic capabilities takes multiple forms and taps into a number of tensions that were troubling the waters of contemporaneous French society. Summarizing the history of laughter in theatrical tradition, Eric Weitz notes that classic humour theories can be grouped into three main subsets: 'the Incongruity Theory proposes generally that laughter is caused by the perception of a clash between incompatible ideas or images; the Superiority Theory claims that laughter is brought about by a spontaneous validation of higher status with regard to some joking target; and the Relief Theory suggests that laughter derives from psychic or social tension suddenly defused, demobilized, or otherwise released' (2016, p. 12). The comic English speaker of French draws upon all these comic methodologies and is thus entertaining on several levels. First, at the most obvious level, he or she is comic in the peculiarly incongruous way in which they speak French, jarring the ear with the same errors and the same verbal ticks over and over. Secondly, the buffoonish English character offers the audience a strong feeling of superiority – no matter how much a French audience member might struggle to cope with life, economic disadvantage, and social stigmatization within French society, the English were always more awkward, more lacking in social ease and charm, and less desirable in spite of their often aristocratic status. Indeed, in Ludovic Dugas's contemporaneous work on the psychology of laughter, he evokes the English specifically as a perfect target for superiority laughter among the French: Dugas observes that 'quand des hommes appartiennent à des milieux trop différents pour sympathiser entre eux, ils se trouvent ridicules: un paysan est ridicule pour un citadin, un militaire pour un civil, un Anglais pour un Français' ['when people belong to milieus too different to allow sympathy between them, they find each other ridiculous: a peasant is ridiculous to a city dweller, a military man to a civilian, an Englishman to a Frenchman'] (1902, p. 41).

However, the pleasure in laughing at the English character from a position of superiority is not entirely unproblematic, and this is particularly evident in Delormel and Perpignan's 'Miss! Oh yes!' (1895) where the singer presents us with a tension between the relative importance of foreign language skills and social skills. In this song, we have the rare case of a Frenchman who has just ventured to England for six months to learn English, but in all that time 'Oh yes!' is all that he has learned to say. Why so little? Because his superior charm and savoir-faire have ensured that he says yes to all the right people at all the right times and lands on his feet regardless of his extremely limited vocabulary, rendering linguistic skill unnecessary. In this way, he gets good stock options from a fat rich banker, he earns a packet from wealthy businessmen, and finally he advises his French listeners that 'pour se faire un peu d'braise / je crois bien que la langue anglaise, / entre nous, c'est d' l'extra' ['to make a bit of dough / I firmly believe that the English language, / just between us, is superfluous']. The musical style underwrites this message of suave Gallic confidence; the verses where he describes his interactions with the English are predominantly staccato and in 2/4 time, creating a somewhat stilted, clunky feeling, whereas the choruses shift to a smooth waltz precisely as we discover how smooth a Frenchman can be. This is witty, certainly – but it is also all highly improbable.

In the wake of the Franco-Prussian War, and the severe blow this dealt to French self-assurance, the learning of languages was the source of frequent and often embattled debates and anxieties. G.-A. Heinrich was one among many to see language skills as an important practical endeavour to save the nation from the humiliation of future military defeat in Europe or in the colonial sphere, and he laments that

> Dans ce grand travail de reconstitution de notre pauvre patrie écrasée, il faut nécessairement faire disparaître toutes les causes de notre infériorité. Les étrangers connaissent bien notre pays parce qu'ils parlent notre langue; nous ignorons ce qui se passe au-delà de nos frontières parce que nous savons peu ou mal les langues étrangères.
>
> (1871, p. 5)

> [In the great effort to rebuild our poor, crushed homeland, it is necessary to remove all sources of our inferiority. Foreigners know our country well because they speak our language; we know nothing of what happens beyond our borders because we speak foreign languages little or badly.]

The pedagogue and linguist Alfred Weil goes further, arguing in his programme for secondary education that

> Celui qui parvient à connaître une langue jusqu'à dans ses plus intimes détails, à en sonder tous les secrets, à en apprécier tout le génie, a une idée plus exacte du peuple qui la parle [...]. Tandis que toutes les autres nations [...] s'immisçaient à notre vie, analysaient nos mœurs, s'adaptaient nos idées, nos tendances, notre manière de penser, pénétraient, en un mot, au cœur de la patrie par l'étude de notre idiome, [...] nous nous sommes laissés entraîner à croire qu'il était inutile de plier notre esprit à l'étude des langues étrangères, nous condamnant volontairement ainsi à une ignorance presque absolue du caractère, de l'esprit, des mœurs de nos voisins.
>
> (1872, p. 26)

> [A person who gets to know a language in its most intimate details, to penetrate all its secrets, to appreciate its genius, has a more exact idea of the people who speak it. [...] Whilst all other nations involved themselves in our life, analysed our cultural habits, adapted themselves to our ideas, our tendencies, our way of thinking, and penetrated, in a word, right to the heart of our nation by way of learning our language, we have let ourselves think that there is no need to turn our minds to language learning – voluntarily condemning ourselves to an almost entire ignorance of the characters, mentalities, and cultural mores of our neighbours.]

48 *Singing the English*

With this in mind, the enjoyment of superiority over the café-concert English character's awkward efforts to speak French is not as simple as it might initially appear, but in fact manifests an uneasy, only partially-concealed need for a coping strategy and for reassurance; in this we see much of Bhabha's 'anxiety of repetition,' with the audience being driven back to the same jokes again and again for comfort – and certainly, Third Republican France was not a society brimming with unalloyed self-confidence.

Although France's most recent major military defeat in the fin de siècle may have been at the hands of Germany, it is notable that the English language and nation form the most frequent reference point here. Indeed, there are very few mocking, comic songs with German characters, accents, or linguistic jokes during this period – to my knowledge, only fourteen – most of which espouse an angrily dark humour and are concentrated between 1870–72. Whereas the English accent can be mimicked relatively unproblematically, when it comes to the German accent there is a considerable obstacle to successful humour. Up to this point, German characters had featured at the café-concert as mostly romantic figures rather than comic ones, and thus a humorous German accent had not featured heavily or become familiar to Parisian audiences. When comic German songs are attempted after 1871, in order for the audience to recognize the accent as Germanic, performers are obliged to fall back upon the accent traits typically ascribed in the past to comic Alsatians, such as in Offenbach's *Lischen et Fritzchen* (where we find ch used for j, c for g, p for b, and so on). By being obliged to conflate Germany and Alsace through their accents, these songs are tainted by a linguistic echo of the military absorption of Alsace into the new German state that was rather too close to home and not necessarily a natural wellspring for laughter.

The English and the English language, on the other hand, entailed no such painful remembrance. As attention turned away from conflict on the European mainland to colonialism, dominance in military and political spheres abroad was seen as still within France's grasp, even though military victory against Germany on European soil may not have been. Consequently, it is the language skills of the English, as France's major colonial rivals, that tended to attract particular attention in this period. It is in the context of the relative linguistic competency of this powerful rival that weak efforts to learn languages in France were primarily a cause of concern. For example, one examiner for the Certificat d'aptitude à l'enseignement de la langue anglaise in 1899 remarked, with a tone of wearied frustration after failing 132 out of 143 candidates, that: 'le Jury est d'avis que des Anglais doivent comprendre l'anglais que les professeurs parlent et enseignent en France' ['the Jury is of the opinion that the English should be able to understand the English that is spoken and taught by teachers in France'] ('Concours des certificats d'aptitude,' 1899–1900, n.p.). In contrast to this, as Justin Améro explains, the English may not be entirely fluent but they are substantially more advanced in their knowledge: 'les Anglais sont aux *difficultés* de notre syntaxe, tandis

Singing the English 49

que nous n'en sommes encore qu'aux *mots* de leur vocabulaire' ['the English have got to the finer details of our syntax, whereas we are only on the words of their vocabulary'] (1879, p. 8).

For all the buffoonery and blundering of the Englishman in 'Je pôvais pas,' in the first refrain he can nonetheless quip that:

> Pour vous plaiser jé serais aise,
> De chanter un' chanson française,
> J'aimerais mieux dire en anglais
> Mais vous ne comprendriez d'jémais!

> [To please you, I would be glad
> To sing a French song,
> I'd rather speak in English
> But you'd never understand it!]

Twelve years later, the same point is still being made in 'L'Anglais et le Bourgeois' (1897) – though here, the skill deficit is referred to with implied rolled eyes and the insouciant tone of a teenager ignoring sound parental advice. Repetition of the same old broken record has clearly done nothing to improve learning standards or motivation over time. In the monologue section of this skit, the bourgeois Frenchman explains to an Englishman who has stopped him in the street that

> je suis force de vous avouer que je ne speak pas English et je vais vous expliquer pourquoi? C'est tout simplement à cause du mauvais système d'éducation qu'on a adopté en France. Je trouve absolument ridicule qu'étant au collège, on m'ait fait piocher la langue latine et la langue grecque que j'ignore du reste, au lieu de m'enseigner les langues vivantes, ce qui me procurerait le plaisir de pouvoir causer avec vous.

> [I have to admit that I don't *speak English* and shall I tell you why? It's quite simply because of the bad education system that has been adopted in France. I find it entirely ridiculous that at secondary school, they forced me to slave away at Latin and Greek – which I don't understand in any case – instead of teaching me living languages, which would give me the pleasure of talking with you.]

The conversation then continues in the broken French familiar from this comic song tradition more generally, and revolves around the same outrageously bad pronunciation on the part of the Englishman. Clearly, it is the Englishman's limitations that are meant to be the ultimate butt of the joke – but nonetheless the French audience are confronted here with their own still greater lack of linguistic agency. Though not as directly disconcerting as songs about Germany, songs revolving around the English and language skills, then, do not offer unalloyed, unproblematic pleasure.

50 *Singing the English*

Another means of denigrating and laughing at the English character for his dubious linguistic mastery goes beyond the purely practical and pedagogical, and links the world of popular song to the widely-disseminated ideas and theories of civilization and evolution. On complaining of the difficulties of learning English, the novelist and journalist Camille Debans exclaims: 'un fameux patois du reste que l'anglais. C'est la langue nègre mise hors de la portée des autres humaines' ['what's more, English is a renowned patois. It's black pidgin, placed beyond the grasp of other humans'] (1884, pp. 286–7). English, far from being treated here as a linguistic product of a developed European civilization, is instead placed on a par with the 'patois' of sub-Saharan colonies – seen at this time as barbaric and backward. This tallies with the emphasis on the rough, unsophisticated nature of the English language and population by writers and scholars such as the essayist and critic Émile Montégut, who repeatedly discusses them in ethnographical terms of barbarism, savagery, blood, race, and violence.[4] From colonial discourses, we are familiar with the idea that black was seen as the opposite of white, Eastern as the opposite of Western, African as the opposite of European – but Englishness, too, is posited here as the polar opposite of Frenchness in terms not only of taste or temperament but of language, ethnicity, and civilization. Montégut asserts that the English (Anglo-Saxon, Germanic) and the French (Celtic, Latinate) spirits represent 'les deux pôles d'un même aimant dont le nom est civilisation' ['the two opposite poles of a magnet which bears the name of civilisation'] (1883, p. 53).

From our post-colonial perspective, England and France as major colonial powers have typically been studied together; they were rivals, yes, but tend to be placed at one end of the spectrum as colonizers wielding power vis-à-vis colonized nations. In the post-colonial era, and with this dichotomy of colonizer and colonized in mind, the term 'race' is used almost synonymously with skin colour; Michael Pickering explains that

> in contemporary discourse, 'race' refers to people who are non-white, and denotes cultural 'difference.' 'Race' is used as a way of designating certain categories within our culture, and it does this from an invisible, undesignated position. This is the position of whiteness.
>
> (2004, p. 91)

Yet in nineteenth-century representations of the English by the French, England is by no means depicted as inhabiting the same end of the ethnic spectrum as France despite their similar whiteness. Indeed, the idea of Englishness is couched in terms which go further than distinguishing between the English and French as northern and southern Europeans; risible English attempts to speak French are performed and received as a kind of pidgin that reformulates French grammar and phonetics, and they are recounted in vocabulary which uses tropes remarkably similar to those at the heart of blackface minstrelsy. The lines between the users and targets of racialist discourse were not as

Singing the English 51

clear cut in the nineteenth century as they are now; England was as likely to be explicitly discussed and described using the derogatory terminology and ideology of racialist 'science' as were supposedly 'exotic' lands, despite the similarity in skin colour.

In making this observation I do not intend to deny or diminish the racism inherent in colonialism and colonial discourses, or the inhumanity of acts of literal and structural violence perpetuated by colonial powers. Rather, what I wish to highlight here is that the same racialist lexicon, reductive rhetoric, and performative strategies are being used here to *represent* the English; the English character is being represented in texts and on the stage, first and foremost, *as a racial Other*, and this is an essential element in France's conceptualization of England during the fin-de-siècle period. French performers 'English up' using the same theatrical methodologies and performance tropes as they might to 'black up': in order to take on an English stage persona – as for a blackface persona – French performers put on a hyperbolic costume that exaggerates certain body parts in an absurd and derogatory fashion; they dance in an ungainly and energetic way, emphasizing the lower body to indicate base and uncivilized impulses; they are stubborn; they are obsessed with consuming food and drink to suggest the dominance of animal tendencies over cerebral ones; they use gesture, facial expression, and words or lyrics to imply that they are of limited intelligence and unsophisticated habits but they nonetheless take themselves very seriously; and, above all, they express themselves in a kind of pidgin French. Pickering explains that the first step of racial stereotyping is taken when a behavioural category becomes racially marked, when it assumes particular (inferior) characteristics because of its origins and its distance from a presumed position of superiority (2004, p. 91). Far from England being treated as the polar opposite of the 'exotic,' far from it being a country, as Perrin contends, 'où il ne reste guère de place pour l'étrangeté et l'exotisme' ['where there is hardly any remaining space for strangeness or exoticism'] (2003, p. 12), a close examination of these songs demonstrates that England is, in fact, represented using many of the same racially-marked representational strategies as the non-white, exotic Other in popular music.

Of course, the radical imbalance of political and economic power that fundamentally defined the relationship between France and its colonies did *not* characterize the Franco-English relationship; the English were not politically and militarily subordinated by the French colonizer; they were not at risk of cultural erasure through colonial education policies; and the English were able to assume a voice, to represent themselves, and to answer back using the same cultural and economic apparatuses as the French – indeed, English music-hall songs mocking the French are by no means in short supply.[5] Fundamentally, comic French café-concert acts are powerless to cause the English individual the deep psychological trauma commented upon by Frantz Fanon in his book *Peau noire, Masques blancs* [*Black Skin, White Masks*] (1952, Chapter 1).

The fact that, in spite of all of this, the *machinery* of representation remains remarkably similar for the English racial Other and for the non-white Other

52   *Singing the English*

is all the more intriguing. It suggests a degree of wish fulfilment taking place in these café-concert comic acts. Just as perspicacious analyses have revealed the cracks and tensions in nineteenth-century representations and stereotypes of the exotic Other,[6] so this linguistic and humorous hierarchy between France and England is as revealing of French anxieties as it is of confident jingoistic bluster or scientific conviction. For all the differences suggested on the stage between the English speaker of French and the French native speaker, it was no less an inevitable reality that France and England shared a significant common ancestry in terms of both language and ethnicity. The English language was composed of, 'sous le costume anglo-saxon, les vieux mots de notre langue' ['under an Anglo-Saxon disguise, the ancient words of our own language'] (Bréal, 1900, p. 79), and, as the diplomat Jusserand remarks, 'les mêmes races se sont mélangées, à peu près aux mêmes époques, mais dans des proportions et des conditions sociales différentes' ['the same races mixed together, at more or less the same historical moment, but in different proportions and social contexts']. Jusserand seeks to reassure his readers that France and England 'sont trop différentes pour qu'ils risquent de perdre, à se copier, leur caractère national, et ils se ressemblent trop pour que les emprunts faits demeurent stériles' ['are too different to risk losing their national character if they copy each other, and they are too alike to make any such borrowing a sterile one'] (1894, I, p. 1). Yet the fact that he feels the need to stipulate this to ease the concerns of his audience indicates that a fear of the dilution of Frenchness by Englishness lingered unsettlingly in the subconscious of contemporary society.

The drive, then, to assert the existence of insurmountable national and ethnic differences in these representational choices appears to *envisage* through repeated performance the satisfaction of an ideal hierarchy of mocker and mocked. The linguistic jokes in these songs, focusing as they do around key English traits of ethnicity, sexuality, and religion, encourage, as Michael Billig argues, not innocent forms of stereotyping but a 'suspension of empathy' (2001, p. 268), broadening the divide and the sense of difference between the French and the English. Language is used to insist upon a hierarchy of civilizations, placing England below France in essence, even if this was not matched in contemporary realities of military, economic, or colonial practice. This is reflected in songs which make the French Anglomaniac as well as the Englishman the target of their mockery. In 'Gigue-obsession' (1900), a Parisian girl is having a fling with an English gentleman (who speaks, on this occasion, exemplary French). In her glee at her – lucrative – relationship, she babbles out a string of nonsensical, more or less accurate English words:

> Yes! Very well!
> My dear! Old England!
> High life Tailor! Water closet!
> West minster! Et Manchester!
> Gentleman! Et sportswoman!

Singing the English 53

Beefsteack, roomsteack! [i.e. rump steak]
All right! God save the queen!

Far from this giving her the chic appearance she thinks it does, it leaves an impression akin to that more famously made by Proust's Odette a few years later in 1913 – that is, that she is using English to overcompensate for her lack of culture and education. It is girls like her and similar victims of anglomania that the 'Anglais parisien' (1895) meets on his trip to France, where he travels in the hope of imbibing all that French culture has to offer. However, everywhere he goes in Paris he is confronted with English vocabulary and English fashions, not least at the very same music halls in which such songs as this were sung:

Le soir je me rendis au Français
Où l'on jouait Hamlet de *Shakspeure*
Comm' cette pièc' là je la connais
Au *Music-Hall* je me fais conduire.
Mais là j'entendis chanter *All right!*
J'vois danser les sœurs Barrisson
J'écout' le duo d'miss Helyett
Lingaling et l'chanteur Fragson.

[In the evening I went to the Comédie Française theatre
Where they were showing Hamlet by Shakespeare.
Since I know that play already
I got a cab to the music hall.
But there I heard them singing *All right!*
I saw the Barrisson Sisters dance,
I heard the Miss Helyett duet,
Ling-a-ling and the singer Harry Fragson]

At the end of the song, he returns home and assures his parents that 'il n'y a rien d'tel que Paris / pour faire un Anglais accompli' ['there's nothing like Paris / to make a really polished Englishman']. Though at first glance this is merely a comic look at the shared cross-Channel cultural reference points of the fin de siècle, it is also quite a worrying prospect; Parisian culture, here, is eroded to the point of becoming a veritable conduit and finishing school for *English* national identity. In the context of the theories of evolutionary dominance and natural selection which are so often aired in relation to the English, this augurs that Frenchness could be on the verge of losing the struggle for existence – unless a drastic effort be made to protect it.

The French anglomaniac is all the more to be disdained than the Englishman because they should know better, because they make an *active* choice to behave that way, and because they are not simply hapless victims born into an inferior culture, race, and nation. Thus, in these songs, we see an

54 *Singing the English*

additional use of laughter to discipline and to demonstrate the boundaries of cultural acceptability within French culture. In 'Le Chic anglais' (1900, rereleased as 'Pourvu' que j'ai l'chic anglais' in 1901), a Parisian – to judge from the use of slang, a member of the popular classes – copies everything English, desirable or otherwise, in spite of biting reprimands metred out by his friends and family. He wears English clothes even though they are uncomfortable (verse 1), he gets drunk until he makes 'dirty jokes in his pants' (verse 2), he lets his wife play 'fout-ball' with an English lord (verse 3 – there is a vulgar pun here on *le football* and *foutre*, meaning 'fuck'), he narrowly avoids getting lynched by a crowd on the Champ de Mars but still insists on wearing an English suit (verse 4 – bear in mind this song is released at the height of French popular support for the Boers), he brags about making the conquest of a flat-chested and ugly English girl (verse 5), he lets himself get punched on the nose by a Boer rather than admit that he is in fact French (verse 6), and finally he ends by dancing an absurd jig (verse 7).

Some songs are still more emphatic and direct; 'Les Mots anglais' (1897) does not just teach by example but gets straight to the point with a clearly anti-anglomania statement. The opening verse states with evident distaste that:

> Y en a qui s' serv'nt de mots englisches,
> Comm' si la langu' de notr' pays
> Pour eux n'était pas assez riche,
> Moi, j' trouv' que c'est des abrutis.

> [There are those who use English words,
> As if our own country's language
> Wasn't rich enough for them,
> Personally, I think they're morons]

At the end of each verse, the singer shouts 'C' qu'ils feraient pas mieux d'parler français?' ['wouldn't they do better to speak in French?'], and by the sixth repetition we can well imagine the audience joining in with this catchphrase, shouting down those ridiculous anglomaniacs with one unified voice. Here, the message is clear and the community-building power of music is reinforced by the use of the third-person plural to distance 'those people,' those 'abrutis,' from both the singer and the audience and to cure any audience members of their anglicizing folly through the stinging shame of mockery.

Reflected here is a fear with which we are still familiar today, as the Académie repeatedly pits itself against anglicisms just as linguists such as Justin Améro (among others) were already doing in 1877. Améro is not against people learning English – on the contrary, he firmly supports language learning and linguistic competency. Rather, he opposes the pointless, inelegant, and often down-right inaccurate assimilation of English words into French purely for the purposes of empty-headed modishness: he warns against 'ce débordement de l'anglais dans le français dont nous sommes, qui

Singing the English 55

les auteurs, qui les témoins, ce débordement, loin d'augmenter la richesse de notre langue, n'y est qu'un élément de désordre et de confusion' ['this flood of English into French, of which we are either the perpetrators or the witnesses – this flood, far from increasing the richness of our language, is nothing but a source of disorder and confusion']. Like the English character's pidgin French, dragged down as it is by the influence of the inferior accent, syntax, and elegance of the Englishman's own more 'primitive' language, the French *themselves* risk turning French into just such a barbarous tongue. Améro begs 'n'est-il pas temps de s'arrêter, si nous ne voulons pas que le français tombe au rang, – je ne dirai pas d'un *patois*, ni d'un jargon, mais – d'un argot?' ['isn't it time to stop, if we don't want French to descend to the status of – I won't say a patois, or a jargon – but a slang?'] (1879, pp. 7, 20). The café-concert anglomane, then, serves as a warning: laugh at him, but remember to ensure that in laughing you do not become him.

The English body

It is not language alone that marks out the Otherness of the English in popular entertainments but also the 'English' body, and never more so than when it is being contorted joltingly into the ungainly, grotesque, angular, unseductive shapes of the jig. Indeed, dance is often understood at this time in terms similar to language and is elided by some with the latter as two sides of the same coin. A reviewer for *L'Europe artiste*, for example, commented after a production of Offenbach's comic opera *La Fille du tambour major* that 'le petit cocher anglais est charmant dans sa gigue, le rythme haletant, pressé, comme s'il était dansé et prononcé avec l'accent britannique' ['the little English cab driver is charming during his jig, with its breath-taking, hurried rhythm, as though it were danced and pronounced with a British accent'] (X.D., 1880, p. 2). By the same token, the racializing tropes used to represent the English language and accent are also present in discourse surrounding the jig. Unlike the polka or waltz, which had shed most of their original Bohemian or Germanic cultural associations on being appropriated by the Parisian social scene in the first half of the century, the jig continued to be understood as inherently English – indeed, this perception dominated in spite of the fact that there was a long 'gigue' tradition in French folk-dance culture. Whereas today we are more accustomed to associating the jig with Irish and Scottish folk culture, this was not the case in nineteenth-century France; though jigs are included in plays based in Irish and Scottish settings as well as English ones – for example, in the Irish wedding scene from the French adaptation of Dion-Boucicault's *Jean la Poste* (1876) or in Hervé's *Le Trône d'Écosse* (*The Throne of Scotland*, 1871) – this is due to a perception that the constituent nations of the United Kingdom shared a common dance culture, rather than in recognition or celebration of a separate Celtic identity.

As early as 1872, the jig was already a familiar staple of comic English acts on the stages of the café-concert, comic opera, and comic theatre – to the

56 *Singing the English*

point that the reviewer 'Frou-Frou' already questioned 'pourquoi ne peut-on mettre des Anglais au théâtre sans les forcer à danser la gigue?' ['why can't we have English characters on stage without forcing them to dance the jig?'] (1872, p. 3). Nonetheless, throughout this period numerous dramas and theatrical comedies continued to find pretexts to incorporate jig scenes, just as they frequently incorporated balletic interludes.[7] A quarter of a century later, a review of the Olympia's *La Demoiselle de magasin, opérette anglaise* (*The Shopgirl, English Operetta*, 1896) again remarked upon the burning desire for there to be an English jig after every single couplet (Ryvez, 1896, p. 5). Yet for all its lack of newness, the café-concert audience still seemed avid for its hyper-energetic leaps and jaunty rhythms and it could even make or break the success of a show or a dancer; in 1887, the *Gaulois* reviewer Frimousse asserted with confidence that the comic singer Duhamel's chaotic jig would stand out as one of the high points of his career – and that, on sadly omitting to offer the audience the same pleasurable spectacle in *La Petite Fronde* the following year, the performer deprived himself 'd'un sûr élément de succès' ['of a sure-fire element of success'] (Frimousse, 7 Oct. 1887, p. 3; 17 Nov. 1888, p. 3).

Indeed, at the café-concert, this dance was not only an entertaining interlude in a theatrical plotline but formed a substantial and essential crux of the comic English genre. Of the eighty-nine songs listed in the Appendix, only five mention jigs in the titles (5.7%), but 42.5% open with a jig (either immediately or as part of the introductory music); 26% end with a jig after the final verse; 33.3% have jig music between every verse; 12.6% mention the jig in the lyrics as a means of explicitly contrasting the French and the English; and 10.3% juxtapose the jig rhythm with dance genres generally associated with Parisian culture to make a point about English character or eccentricity (usually the waltz, occasionally the polka, sometimes even the cancan). For example, in 'Mylord Gig-Gig: excentricité anglaise' (1879), the gentleman visits France specifically to show the French the jig, a dance he says they simply cannot master, and he actively contrasts it in verse 2 with the polka and in verse 3 with the waltz. In 'Ell's danse pas le d'gigue' (1893), a frumpy English lady of a certain age uses the jig and the cancan as the ultimate manifestation of the differences in the bodies, ideals of beauty, and cultures of the two nations. Note that the 'jig' referred to in these songs is not a jig from a technical point of view. It is identified here inaccurately, but in accordance with the style that was referred to insistently in nineteenth-century France as the jig; it is in 2/4 time with a rapid dotted rhythm (usually alternating between dotted semi-quavers and demi-semi-quavers), rather than in compound time with groups of three quavers as is more traditional. However, this form is identified consistently as a jig in nineteenth-century France, and habitually bears a shared set of bold, brassy stylistic features, including forte or fortissimo dynamics, a liberal use of stress marks, and often the rapid tempo marking *gigue* or *mouvement de gigue*. A typical example can be found at the opening of 'Ell's danse pas le d'gigue':

Extract 1.1 'Ell's danse pas le d'gigue' ['They don't dance the jig'], by Chassaigne and Aupto (1893).

Adapted from source: Bibliothèque nationale de France.

The constant inclusion of jigs of this kind in café-concert English acts nourishes a feedback loop between Englishness and jigging in the French cultural imagination. This did not go so far as to attempt to convey any particular folkish naivety in the choice of instruments (piano or small orchestra) or the arrangement: though the music is rather facile and the texture thin, there is little evidence of any further thoroughgoing effort to communicate a specifically English traditional musicality beyond the aural evocation of the generic 'jig' form. Harmonically speaking, this music often differs little from dances and songs seen as typically Parisian or French such as the chahut or quadrille, certainly not to the extent of developing a unique musical 'style anglais.' The main factors which catch the ear are a tendency to use the discordant augmented second, a familiar cliché from much generically exotic music, and the still-more discordant augmented fourth, with both of these most often appearing as part of frequent chromatic passages. These were by no means unique to comic English songs, though they do appear here with considerably regularity and contribute towards a sense of foreignness (for the former) and a lack of elegance (for the latter). It is in the ever-present insistence on these dotted 'jig' rhythms, however, that the main difference can be heard, and this becomes an aural tag which the audience would immediately associate with Englishness. Indeed, unlike dance crazes such as the redowa, danse du kangaroo, or boston, which each peaked and began to disappear from French

58 *Singing the English*

stages within a decade or two or its first appearance, the jig remains a primary feature of English skits throughout the 1870–1904 period, and even still remains so at the eve of the First World War (such as in Batifort and Cabrol's 1910 hit, 'La Gigue! Aôh yes!').

In the text and print culture surrounding these acts, the national specificity of the jig is everywhere emphasized. Collections of 'typical' music from around the world for amateur musicians subtitle pieces called 'La Gigue' as the 'danse nationale anglaise' ['the English national dance'] (for example in Rabuteau and Vilbac, *ca.* 1890). Major newspapers reinforce this link in their theatre reviews, with throw-away witticisms that the English include jigs in all their shows because 'la danse est "nationale" et qu'elle est nécessaire comme le plum-pudding' ['the dance is "national" and is as necessary as plum pudding'] (Duquesnel, 1899, p. 3), or with lengthier explanations such as this advice to Yvette Guilbert upon her tour of English music halls:

> toute chanson qui se respecte finit, en Angleterre, par une danse, qui est la gigue, la danse nationale et obligatoire. [...] Si Yvette Guilbert [...] veut poursuivre sa veine chez nos voisins, il lui faudra bien en arriver là. *Gigue is money.* Yvette dansant la gigue! On traversera la Manche pour aller voir ça.
> (Tout Paris, 1896, p. 1)

> [every self-respecting song ends, in England, with a dance; the jig, the national and obligatory dance. If Yvette Guilbert wants to build on her popularity with our neighbours, she'll surely end up doing it too. *Jig is money.* Yvette dancing the jig! That would be worth crossing the Channel for.]

This is not to say that the popular audiences at the English music hall did *not* in reality delight in the jig – on the contrary, it was a central part of popular stage entertainments, street performances, Derby-day entertainments, and more. However, the class-specific nature of the entertainment is effaced on the French stage, where it is, as often as not, an aristocratic character who is made to dance the jig with gay abandon – 'Mylord Gig-gig' (1879), for example, is both a nobleman of the blood and a nobleman of the dancefloor. Where it had become commonplace in the age of Wagner for art music to ally *leitmotifs* with characters in a narrative, the English character's leitmotif was, indubitably, the dotted rhythm of the jig.[8]

Also like a leitmotif, this intertwining of English character and English jig brings with it a freight of signification. The interrelation between the jig and English national character is not just an entertainment convention but becomes deeply racinated in contemporaneous French ideas about England on a more profound level. That native dance and song were key signifiers of national character was a widely-held belief expressed in travel literature, academic study, and journalism in this period. The journalist Jules Clarétie, for example, in an article on the cake-walk in 1903, explains that:

Singing the English 59

Quand j'ai voyagé, avant d'étudier les cœurs intimes ou les institutions politiques d'un peuple, j'ai voulu, dès le premier jour, connaître ses danses et ses chansons. Ne croyez pas à un paradoxe. [...] Avant d'entendre les orateurs du Parlement anglais j'ai tenu à voir les gigues du peuple. Le *horn-pipe* que dansaient avec rage les marins de Nelson au matin de Trafalgar m'a révélé sur le tempérament britannique autant de traits inconnus que le pourrait faire une harangue de M. Chamberlain. *Dis-moi ce que tu danses et chantes et je te dirai qui tu es.*

(1903, p. 1 – emphasis added)

[When I have travelled, before studying private lives or political institutions, I have wanted from the very first day to find out about dances and songs. Don't think I'm being paradoxical. Before hearing speakers at the English parliament, I set store in seeing the jigs of the populace. The *hornpipe* that Nelson's sailors danced with such passion on the morning of Trafalgar revealed to me more hidden traits of the British temperament than any harangue by Mr. Chamberlain could. *Tell me what you dance and sing, and I'll tell you who you are.*]

Dance is understood here as a bodily manifestation of traits integral to the blood and the mind of the nation – dance is seen as a physical testimony which grants access to a hidden but fundamental nature. Indeed, the more scholarly voice of Fernand Delzangles, folklorist and dramatist, summarizing a half-century that had seen rapid developments in ideas on the body and mind from Darwin, Taine, Charcot, and Delsarte, asserted that dance is the product of 'le développement des facultés intellectuelles, [elle a] évolué suivant le caractère et le tempérament des peuples, s'est perfectionnée, embellie, harmoniée, eurythmie suivant le degré de leur civilisation, le raffinement des mœurs' ['the development of the intellectual faculties; [dance has] evolved according to the character and temperament of each people, has perfected itself, become beautiful and harmonious, with eurhythmics in accordance with the degree of civilization and the refinement of their cultural mores'] (1914, pp. 1–2). If this be the case, the ungainly jig does not reflect well upon the 'degree of civilization' of the English; they are highly energetic but more physical than cerebral or artistic, and they manifest themselves as bizarre and eccentric as much as they do jovial and spirited. Indeed, at the café-concert the jig is not presented as a misguided aesthetic choice, but an insurmountable bodily imperative. 'Miss Gig' (1885), for example, simply cannot control herself despite her strongest efforts; when she enters a ballroom or takes to the Opéra stage as a ballet dancer – and even at her husband's funeral – her legs start jigging of their own accord. The place of the jig within the rhetorical field of contemporaneous ethnographic vocabulary, then, suggests that these apparently frivolous and funny interludes are in fact echoing and playing with substantially more meaningful ideas and concepts familiar to nineteenth-century audiences.

60 *Singing the English*

The Englishness of the café-concert jig tallies with contemporaneous thought more generally on the body as a site of meaning and as a useful device for establishing stable social categories. Catherine Hindson has observed that at this time, 'current thinking, indeed cutting-edge research, about criminality, degeneration, sexuality, and psychology were explored, explained, and defined through visual systems of physical code' (2007, p. 35). While Hindson is primarily discussing issues of gender, class, and sexuality, the same can be said of the perception of national identity, including – and perhaps especially – English identity. The English body is thought by the French to be all the more revealing of the impulses of its national blood because, according to numerous contemporary theorists such as Émile Montégut, Cartesian dualism does not apply in their case. He contends that 'l'homme de chair et de sang n'a pas été brusquement séparé de l'homme intellectuel et moral; la civilisation ne s'est pas superposée à la barbarie pour l'écraser et l'étouffer, mais elle est sortie de cette barbarie même dans laquelle elle a ses racines et sa semence' ['the flesh and blood man has not been rent from the intellectual and moral man; civilization was not imposed upon barbarism to crush and suffocate it, but rather it emerged directly from that very barbarism and they share the same roots and seeds'] (1883, p. 96). Furthermore he asserts, for the English and the Germans, 'l'idée de nationalité n'est pas distincte de l'idée de race' ['the idea of nationality is not separate from the idea of race'] (1883, p. 93) – thus any national dance evinces not only national but, more fundamentally, *racial* character; it is the product of imperatives that run far deeper than any apparent, transient manifestations of modernization, political reform, or cultural progress.

This feeds into the assertion that the English are the sole global race to have completed their evolutionary trajectory. Montégut and, like him, the influential Gustave le Bon, maintain that 'la plupart des races historiques de l'Europe sont encore en voie de formation [...]. Seul l'Anglais actuel représente une race presque entièrement fixée' ['most of the historic European races are still evolving. The English today are alone in representing a race that is almost entirely fixed'] (Le Bon, 1894, pp. 50–1; Montégut, 1883, pp. 52–3). The precise reasons for reaching this conclusion are not made entirely clear by either but its implications for the jig are significant. If dance reveals the race; if, for the English, nationhood and race are one and the same; and if that still-barbarous English race has reached a henceforth unchanging state, then the jig as a national dance should offer an open book on English nature.

Gordon remarks of the *gommeuses épileptiques* and the cake-walk dancers that the 'mechanical gestures, disjoined and convulsive movement (apparently) issuing directly from the nervous system and the instincts (what nineteenth-century psychiatry and physiology called the "lower faculties")' were seen as evidence that lower-class women and the Afro-American racial Other were less-evolved peoples, 'since, for centuries, in the development of species only the lower forms of mental activity had existed, with the higher forms being recent additions' (2000, p. 221). The same association

Singing the English 61

between the jig and 'lower forms' of instinct also prevails, both in terms of racial Otherness and mental deficiency. One might well expect the white, northern-European jig to be portrayed in an entirely different manner to these racially-Othered performances, but in fact the jig often shares a stage with and is described in similar ways to dances that we are more accustomed to thinking of as nineteenth-century exotic acts. For example, in this description of an event at the 1900 World Fair, there is nothing to suggest that the reader would find it peculiar to see the jig listed here among other exoticized dances and nations: 'après le fandango des Andalouses, nous aurons la cachucha des Castillanes, la séguidille des gitanes, le boléro des Madrilènes, la gigue des Anglaises, le boutichek des Cosaques, sans compter la bamboula des rois nègres' ['after the Andalusian fandango, we will have the Castilian cachucha, the gypsy seguidilla, the Madrileño bolero, the English jig, the Cossack boutichek, not to mention the bamboula of the black kings'] (Gaston Deschamps, 1900, p. 1). Moreover, the jig is firmly engrained with associations of lower, degenerate mental activity in contemporaneous culture. On more than one occasion, people tried to feign madness by dancing the jig, trusting that this external bodily comportment would be read as a sign of mental insanity. For example, during the Commune a M. Chambareaud avoided execution by Communard firing squad when 'il dansa une gigue héroïque, simulant la folie avec une perfection qui aurait trompé un expert' ['he danced a heroic jig, feigning madness so perfectly that it would have fooled an expert'] (Paul Roche, 1898, p. 1) – earning him incarceration in the Bicêtre asylum instead of a death sentence. Similarly, a man arrested for a heist at the Magasins de la Bénédictine in 1895 'se mit à chanter, à danser la gigue, à déclamer des vers de Lord Byron' ['began to sing, to dance the jig, and to recite poetry by Lord Byron'] to simulate madness and avoid serious punishment (Albert Bataille, 1895, p. 5).

Madness, the jig, and their combined implication that the English national character is dominated by 'lower forms' of mental activity is a much-loved feature of dozens of café-concert comic English songs. In 'L'Anglais triste' (1892), for example, a part-sung, part-spoken skit, the Englishman is first introduced to us as he bursts onto the stage in the full throes of a vigorous jig, which he suddenly interrupts, coming to an abrupt halt and cutting off the orchestra with a cry of 'Nao! Nao! Je voulais pas danser le gigue, je étais triste, beaucoup fort triste' ['no! no! I don't want to dance the jig, I'm sad, really very sad']. He goes on to recount that he had married a pretty girl from a good family, and they had had a son – a wonderful, adorable, good-tempered little boy – but the baby had such a tremendous thirst for milk that they had hired a French wet-nurse to cater to his needs (playing on the stereotype of French women having more ample chests than their English counterparts). However, this French nursemaid gave him so much milk and then bounced him around so vigorously after feeding that all the milk in his stomach churned into butter and the little boy died. Maddened by grief, the thin vestiges of English self-control fall away, and the Englishman's intellect has no power to stop his body

62   *Singing the English*

from returning to its default impulse – jigging. Even as he articulates the last words of his story, expressing his painful sense of grief, he starts jigging again and is carried by his legs from the stage.

Of course, it should be taken into account that the bodies on stage performing these English characters are, for the most part, not English but *French* bodies, and the songs and jokes are *French* compositions – they are not, in fact, the outpourings of national character from the inner impulses of the English body that they claim to be and, more surprisingly, that they were often treated as being by reviewers and commentators. Consequently, the apparently insuperable boundaries and distinctions dividing the French and English body are broken here. The dances are based upon, even sometimes learned directly from, English theatrical dancers, but the spectacle witnessed by the café-concert audience is in reality seldom the behaviour of an English body. Paul Bourget, in his remarks on farce, stipulated that the French always ensured that 'ces débordements de vie animale sont soigneusement mis en dehors' ['these outbursts of animality are careful excluded'] (1889, II, p. 36) – but in much of this extensive comic genre the French comic singer and dancer must precisely take on those 'outbursts of animality' that were seen as so antithetical to the French mind and body alike. Although, of course, this is all a construct, a performance, and largely just a bit of fun, the context of racializing discourse does raise troublesome questions as to the oft-asserted disparity in the fundamental nature of French and English bodies. The jig being so very English means that for the French dancer to perform it, they must embody, for the space of five minutes at least, an English body. Far from the folklorist and historian Fernand Delzangles's declaration that dance is 'le divertissement qui permet le mieux aux Français de déployer leurs plus aimables et brillantes qualités: la gaieté, l'entrain, la fierté, la crânerie gauloises, la politesse, l'amabilité, l'élégance, la grâce, l'esprit, la galanterie et la coquetterie françaises' ['the entertainment that best allows the French to demonstrate their most pleasant and brilliant qualities: gaiety, liveliness, pride, gallic swagger, politeness, courtesy, elegance, grace, spirit, gallantry, and French coquetry'] (1914, p. 203), instead the French bodies dancing here demonstrate that they are, in fact, perfectly able to dance without manifesting most or any of those positive qualities.

According to contemporaneous ideas about the relationship between body and mind, this embodiment of Englishness is not without psychological importance. Fears of degeneration were rooted in the idea that the French mind and national character could be toppled from their position at the peak of civilization – as the Romans had been – and that care had to be taken to protect the national blood and character from the diluting effects of outside influence. O'Rell notes that children of French birth who lived and were schooled in England began to assimilate traits seen as inherently English; he writes that numerous French parents resident in London had intimated to him 'd'un air triste: "Ces écoles anglaises *corrompent* mes fils et je ne sais comment je pourrai les conserver à la France"' ['with a sad air: "these English schools

Singing the English 63

are *corrupting* my sons and I don't know how to keep them for France"']
(1894, p. 298). The widely-admired Delsarte system of bodily expression
held that outer movements express the inner mind (if one thinks beautiful
thoughts, one will express beauty with the body) but it also implies that this
can operate in the inverse direction too (that beautiful postures can develop a
beautiful state of mind – summarized in Delzangles, 1914, pp. 1–3). Indeed,
this tallies with more recent studies in cognitive science which have found that
the formation of a sense identity depends on the activity of the body as well as
the brain.[9] Logically, then, if the seasoned performer of English acts perfects
a certain 'Englishness' of body, this could also have an 'anglicizing' effect on
the mind – questioning the degree to which national bodily characteristics,
and by extension national identity, are in fact inherent and inalienable.

In this context, it is significant that reviewers depict the jig and the explicitly-
racialized Other of the cake-walk provoking similar, involuntary responses in
the bodies of their French audiences. When both dances shared a bill at the
Moulin-Rouge in June 1903, for example, the audience members 'avaient été à
ce point mis en joie [...] que d'aucuns sortaient en dansant involontairement la
gigue, cependant que d'autres esquissaient de folâtres pas de cake-walk' ['were
so delighted [...] that some left involuntarily dancing the jig, while others did
some crazy moves from the cake walk'] (Raoul Ralph, 1903, p. 2). The same
performers – particularly female performers – who are associated with the
sexual and corporeal equivocation of the cake-walk and the epileptic genre
(in which female singers adopt gestures associated with hysteria, epilepsy,
and neurological conditions) are also prominent performers of the English
jig, such as Émilie Bécat (immortalized by Degas as a *gommeuse épileptique*
at the Ambassadeurs in 1877–8 and 1885, and appearing as an English jig
dancer in 'Bébé-revue' at the Fantaisies Oller in 1878), Polaire (the focus of
Rae Beth Gordon's discussion for the former two genres [2000, 2003, 2004]
and appearing as a jig dancer in the song 'Schoking!' in 1894), and Eugénie
Fougère (appearing on the cover of *Paris qui chante* on 18 October 1903
dancing to 'Oh! Ce cake-walk!' and singing and dancing as the jigging 'Miss
Rodin' in 1895).

Of course, this is not to suggest that these French performers or audiences
literally become English or become somehow temporarily possessed by some
kind of Englishness, but rather that it casts doubt upon any extrapolations
that one might make about national character based on musical, linguistic,
or corporeal behaviours. If the French performer can convincingly take on
bodily behaviours that are said to spring directly from the source of English
blood without ever traversing the intellect, this evinces that national identity,
much like gender identity, is in fact fluid and performative. In the same way
that Judith Butler, building on Monique Wittig, argues that discursive acts
bring the gendered body into being, so these songs, lyrics, and dances bring
the learned, cultural quality of national character into being on the French
stage (see Butler, 1990, esp. Chapter 1). Indeed, it is through a performative
speech act at the start of many songs – 'moi je suis de Angleterre' – that the

64 *Singing the English*

French body 'becomes' English, or at least, becomes English enough to convey stereotypes about the English to the audience that will become perceived as essentially based in truth.

National laughter

In addition to dance, music, and language, laughter itself is seen as a signifier of national character in this period. In many ways, there is nothing surprising here. Individuals are, after all, raised in a particular culture with exposure to certain kinds of comedy which often call upon their knowledge of their homeland's particular way of life, its peculiarities and foibles, its systems of education and governance, its traditional religious and moral conventions, and so on. It is in that community that they learn when laughter is inappropriate, appropriate, even essential; Henri Bergson indicates that 'le rire doit répondre à certaines exigences de la vie en commun. Le rire doit avoir une signification sociale' ['laughter must respond to certain requirements raised by life in society. Laughter must have a social significance'] (1900, p. 80). However, in the nineteenth century this understanding goes further, with a national sense of humour being seen not only as a response to the lived needs of a society at any one time, but also as emerging from deeper imperatives that were a question of nature not of nurture. As Charles Rearick has observed in his work on belle-époque entertainments, 'in an era of intense anti-German feeling and persistent anti-English prejudice, promoters of a belle-époque spirit contended that the French were by nature and inheritance Gauls blessed with an unsurpassed capacity to enjoy this world's delights. [...] To laugh was now considered not so much a characteristic of humanity as an endangered and essentially *French* trait' (1985, p. 36). Certainly, the audience at the café-concert do give themselves over to unbridled mirth. However, that this laughter is an inherently French trait – one that can be used to create a sense of unified national identity – is challenged in a number of key ways when put into practice. These will each be treated in turn in the final part of this chapter; first, with the sense of humour failures provoked by the English character among certain segments of the French audience; and secondly, by bourgeois snobbery directed towards the café-concert in general that rejects it as a lowbrow, lower-class deviation from 'national' cultural values.

The propensity for laughter and mirth is thematized with particular aptness in 'L'Anglais rieur' (1887, subtitled 'éclat de rire' ['a burst of laughter']) – the Laughing Policeman song for the fin-de-siècle generation. The visit to Paris that this English character recounts is a staple of the English genre: he goes to Paris for pleasure, meets a prostitute, goes to the Folies-Bergère, dances, and generally has a whale of a time. However, in this song, between each of the lines narrating his experiences, the character guffaws with hyperbolic merriment.

Extract 1.2 'L'Anglais rieur: éclat de rire' ['The Laughing Englishman: burst of laughter'], by Ouvrard and Pizoir (1887).

Adapted from source: Bibliothèque nationale de France.

    This song dramatizes in exaggerated fashion what happens when the Englishman in Paris is unleashed from Victorian rigidity; the Laughing Englishman does not just relax his solemn everyday demeanour, but positively explodes out of it with infectious exuberance. In the descending musical scale as he laughs, in this extract we can almost *hear* him bending at the waist with intense mirth. However, in shedding the weight of social expectations, he does not cease to be inherently English; it is not the *gaieté* of the French that he assumes, but rather a robust, rather violent kind of laughter that was often associated with Englishness. The celebrated café-concert star Yvette Guilbert, for example, in associating different kinds of laughter with different colours,

66 *Singing the English*

writes that there is a bright red ('vermillon') laughter that does not and never has existed as part of the French tradition of witty *esprit*; it is more hilarity than jollity, having been first imported to France from Italy in the seventeenth century, and now being best articulated in the English concept of the clown (1928, pp. 133–4). Its absence from French tradition, for Guilbert and many of her contemporaries, reflects that 'l'esprit comique est même quelquefois un don national. Le sens du comique est plus développé chez les latins que chez les Anglo-Saxons, c'est [...] *la capacité comique d'une race*' ['sense of humour is even sometimes a national gift. Sense of humour is more developed in Latinate people than in the Anglo-Saxons, it's the *comic capacity of a race*'] (1928, p. 120 – italics in original text).

This is problematized, however, by 'Le Joyeux Anglais' (1889) – a song first popularized at the café-concert and then adapted, cleaned-up, and republished in a music collection for boarding schools, and which therefore reached a particularly wide-ranging audience. In this song, the Englishman has a similar tendency to the 'Anglais rieur' to laugh heartily between each line in the chorus as he tells us what a merry old soul he is (for the twenty-first century audience, this is strongly reminiscent of the Sherman Brothers' 'I love to laugh' song from Disney's 1964 film *Mary Poppins*). However, unlike the 'Anglais rieur,' here the distinctive Englishness of his humour is challenged by his explanation that despite his place of birth, 'pour le caractère / jé le souis oun vrai Français' ['in terms of character / I'm a true Frenchman']. Unlike the splenetic tendencies of his compatriots ('chagrins comme oun chapeau de nouit' ['miserable as a night cap']), he is naturally inclined to a specifically French kind of jollity – he likes a witty turn of phrase, a clever play on words, he is filled with *joie de vivre*, he has 'le gaîté,' and of course, he has a predilection for French comic songs. In the final verse, he takes this a step further by conducting a little scientific experiment. On one occasion when he was feeling glum, he went home and drank a glass of Bordeaux and immediately felt better. On another, when his beloved pet dog died, he took a quick trip away from the fogs of England to the sun of France and he was suddenly filled with happiness. In this song, then, we have an alternative thesis on the roots of national character and humour. Whilst theorists such as Hippolyte Taine do refer to climate and diet as factors in the development of racial traits, the implication tends to be that long-term exposure is required before these are influential and are able to become engrained characteristics; yet here, all that stands between the English and French citizen being identical in their *esprit* is the application of a beverage or the purchase of a holiday.

A further means by which clearly demarcated ideas about national character are disrupted can be found in the representation of English priggishness and moral hypocrisy. Hyper-sensitivity to social norms is a recurrent topic of humour in these acts, though one that contains more ambivalence than might be expected. A firm belief held by many at this time saw the English – and particularly the large swathes of middle-class

Singing the English 67

'John Bulls' – as synonymous with moral hypocrisy, that infamous English *cant* (false piousness) which was considered the complex product of a puritanical Germanic temperament, an engrained sense of self-interest, and a littleness of spirit that was unconcerned with genuine honour. Taine states categorically in his *Histoire de la littérature anglaise* that 'le premier fruit de la société anglaise est l'hypocrisie. Il y mûrit au double souffle de la religion et de la morale' ['the principal product of English society is hypocrisy. It matures under the double influence of religion and morality'] (1921, V, p. 45). Max O'Rell explained wryly to his readers that 'les Anglaises sont beaucoup plus facilement choquées par le mot que par la chose' ['English women are much more easily shocked by the word than by the thing itself'] (1884, p. 69). Meanwhile, the significantly more explicit Anglophobic writer Fernand de Jupilles enumerates lengthy chapters of supposedly documentary information on English life, but does so largely via an immensely hyperbolic narrative of concealed debauchery and sexual misdemeanour: for example, he subverts English pride in their education system through a long description of bare-bottomed spankings in girls' boarding schools (apparently intimated to him by un-named mothers – an unlikely confession for a mother to make to a male acquaintance, we might assume, in the Victorian era); he dismisses admiration for English nursemaids by asserting that they sexually initiate their young charges whilst they are still infants and then fail to watch over them at night because they are busy being 'serviced' by bobbies on the beat (1886, pp. 39, 50–1); and he repudiates the cosy ideal of the English hearth and home by asserting that 'le moment n'est peut-être pas très éloigné où [...] la bigamie, si commune déjà en Albion, sera autorisée par la loi' ['it is not perhaps long before bigamy, which is already so common in Albion, will be legalized'] (1886, p. 221).

Though without nearly the same level of vitriol, the stereotype of English moral hypocrisy can also be found at the café-concert, with songs mocking the general propensity of the English to contravene in private the puritanical moral code that they claim to revere, whilst still loudly condemning anybody who contravenes it in public – and most especially the French. The strict expectation of moral rectitude, like the outfits and the facial hair, was genuinely characteristic of a portion of British society in the mid-century, which clamped down upon Sunday observance, elevated the centrality of marriage and the sanctity of children, and bowdlerized the naughtiness out of everything from fairy tales to Shakespeare. This peculiarity was mocked and criticized as much by the English as the French and forms the premise of a significant body of Punch cartoons. However, as the century progressed these strictures gradually loosened (see Bailey, 1998, pp. 29, 49); a transition in cultural mores which is seldom reflected at the café-concert. Songs being composed and performed in the fin de siècle still perpetuate the idea that the English exclaim 'shocking!' with every other breath, either out of excessive prudish sensitivity or out of a hypocritical desire to appear more morally upright than they really are. For example, in Eugène Lemercier and

68 *Singing the English*

Henri Waïss's 'Miss Plumpudding' (1894), the English *miss* opens with the unequivocal statement that 'Je fais point du tout oun' mystère, / Qu'en Franc' tout il était schoking' ['I make no mystery about the fact / that everything in France was shocking']. She goes on to explain what those shocks to her morality are, as she travels her way independently around Paris. First, she observes that blond men in England leave her cold, but when she sees French men with dark hair and beards,

> Ils troublaient le piodor de moi.
> Aimante, charmante, mon cœur d'amante,
> Sans tâche, s'attache au potache.

> [They unsettled my prudishness.
> Loving, charming, my lover's heart,
> Which is still unblemished, is drawn to these young students.]

She may well manage to be moral and pure in England – understandable, this implies, given the untempting specimens of masculinity available to her there – but when faced with a dark-haired Frenchman she feels her moral rectitude being shaken. The fragility of her modesty is also audible in the music; throughout the verse section, the tune is a calm, lilting waltz, but with this confession that her virginal heart feels the flutterings of desire, the music suddenly accelerates and switches to a rowdy 2/4 rhythm and melody. With this shift, as though the words burst forth without her being able to control them, she confesses that 'Quand je vois oun' petit' jeune homme / Je voulais lui *sucer le pomme*' ['When I see a little young man / I wanted to snog him']. This eruption of inner desire shocks Miss Plumpudding to the point that, '*s'adressant à elle-même d'un ton de reproche*' ['*to herself in a reproachful tone*'], she reprimands herself: 'Aoh! Miss Plumpudding!'

Undeterred, however, Miss Plumpudding continues her Parisian expeditions in the subsequent three verses: in verse two, she confesses that she wants to get drunk at parties with French men; in verse three, that she likes stuffing herself full of good food, but especially with French foods which act as aphrodisiacs; and in verse four, she always enjoys a night out dancing, but prefers one in France when she can show men what she is made of on the dancefloor at the Bal Bullier – a popular dancehall and bar in the 5th arrondissement, particularly favoured by students and young people, where lively dance crazes including the cancan-chahut, polka, and cakewalk saw great success (see *Bal Bullier*, 1908). The shift in rhythm, tempo, and musical style, as above, for each of these confessions gives the impression that they are not willed but are a spontaneous and involuntary explosion of repressed, voracious sexual desires; the Englishwoman here is not a pure, moral woman like Dickens's Little Dorrit, but has simply learned to dissemble her lust from herself and from those around her – until the temptations of Paris and its smoulderingly handsome men prove too much.

Extract 1.3 'Schoking!', by Chaudoir, Damien, and Flic-Flac (1894).
Adapted from source: Bibliothèque nationale de France.

Another number from the same year, simply entitled 'Schoking!' [sic], takes up a similar theme. Here, the singer does not adopt an English persona, but rather presents herself as a Parisienne describing English visitors. The chorus declares 'Schocking, schocking / Voilà le cri d'Anglaise / Aoh yes, aoh yes! / Si vous avez de la braise' ['Shocking, shocking / That's the Englishwoman's battle cry / Aoh yes, aoh yes! / If you're feeling hot under the collar'].

These lyrics are set to an extremely catchy tune that begs the audience to join in and to lend voice to this stereotype. However, the evidence that the song provides to justify this claim of moral hypocrisy is somewhat curious. The main criticism in each verse seems to be that Englishwomen are plain featured and lack feminine curves – 'raid's comme un paratonnerre' (v1), 'leurs jambes sont

70 *Singing the English*

des échasses,' 'leurs pieds des bateaux,' 'leurs dents des trompes de chasses' (v2) ['rigid as a lightning rod,' 'their legs are stilts,' 'their feet are like ships,' 'their teeth are hunting horns']. Initially, it seems logically unsound to present physical appearance as evidence of hypocritical prudery – the English woman's plain looks from the perspective of French beauty standards, even if true, are hardly her fault or the product of her morality. However, a link is made through the implication that ugly women must be all the more deviant. The chorus tells us euphemistically that 'malgré leurs airs d'innocence / ell's sav'nt plumer un pigeon' ['despite their air of innocence / they know how to pluck a pigeon'], indicating that, given their unalluring physique, it is all the more unlikely that they are innocents led astray by men who desire them for their beauty, but rather that they are instead active and perverse in order to seduce men who would not otherwise give them a second look. Indeed, in verse three we are offered the eye-popping image of sporty but unappealing English women flashing their arseholes at the men on the path below them whilst hiking up steep mountain trails. Even the French audience, here, are invited to be shocked.

It is an interesting paradox of the 'shocking' stereotype in songs such as these that, in critiquing English morality by shocking the moral sensitivity of the French audience, the French audience are in effect incited to exhibit a supposedly 'English' trait, claimed by these songs to be anathema to Frenchness. More precisely, they exhibit an *inverted* version of an English trait; where the English claim to be all innocence and probity but are in fact savvy and sin merrily in private and/or when in France, the songs suggest that the French national character is all savoir-faire and laissez-vivre, but in fact French bourgeois culture requires even stricter interdictions on female desire, freedom of movement, and knowledge than their English counterparts. When discussing *middle-class female* sexual desires and behaviours, it is the French who cry 'shocking!' at the English: indeed, O'Rell exemplifies this by commenting that 'la jeune fille anglaise est plus au courant de la vie que la jeune fille française; elle peut être aussi pure, mais elle est moins innocente, moins intacte' ['the young English girl knows more about how life works than the young French girl; she might be as pure, but she is less innocent and less intact'] (1884, p. 33). Thus, this French cry of 'shocking' raises two possible interpretations. Either, first, that the English are not as exceptionally hypocritical as the stereotypes would have them be, and therefore that they are more like the French than was generally admitted on either side of the Channel; or secondly, and perhaps more disconcertingly, that French culture contains within it more prudery and moral hypocrisy than stereotypes allow, and that it is more like English culture than they generally confess.

This leads us on to one final, important aspect of ambivalence – that the café-concert was looked down upon or outright rejected by many prominent voices from the bourgeoisie as a lowbrow subculture only able to afford pleasure to the least educated and vulgar at the margins of society. Whilst, on the one hand, this chapter has largely focused on the Parisian audiences in terms of their national identity and how it is reflected, confirmed, and

Singing the English 71

problematized vis-à-vis the English, on the other hand, the café-concert itself was still treated insistently by many vocal middle- and upper-class French critics as lowbrow trash, as aesthetically bereft, and as socially pernicious. Indeed, the scandalized voices crying 'shocking' at the English in the above examples espouse a certain bourgeois social and moral position. The author and journalist André Chadourne, despite his participation in the bohemian lifestyle of Montmartre, certainly wanted it to be understood publicly that he gave no quarter to the café-concert, lambasting 'le café-cancer avec sa lèpre hideuse et puante qui nous ronge, qui dévore notre société et qui risque, s'il n'est fortement combattu, d'en faire tomber les membres en putréfaction' ['the café-cancer, with its hideous and stinking leprosy, eats away at us, is devouring our society, and we risk losing limbs to putrefaction if it is not stringently combatted'] (1889, p. 371). He exhibits a French moral *cant* in parallel to the English one which, though perhaps less explicitly religious, still espouses many of the same traits; indeed, this *cant français* provided fuel for some 250 contemporaneous satirical periodicals, as Rearick has noted, whose 'stock-in trade was mockery of authority, marriage, bourgeois "respectability" and hypocrisy, pretension and power' (1985, p. 49). Likewise, in a 1878 speech by Albert Dupaigne, inspector of Paris's primary schools, advocating for the improvement of musical education, he vociferates that 'vous savez quelle est l'institution moderne qui fait partout aujourd'hui concurrence, non pas seulement aux théâtres, mais à la famille, à l'école du soir, aux orphéons, à toutes les réunions honnêtes, c'est le *café-concert*. (Applaudissements)' ['you all know the modern institution that competes today, not just with the theatre, but with family, evening school, *orphéon* music groups, with all honest social gatherings; it's the café-concert. (Applause)'] (1878, p. 288). In derogatory fashion, both Chadourne and Dupaigne dismiss the café-concert as empty, idiotic, and poisonous rubbish in which only the most culturally deprived and intellectually under-developed could possibly find pleasure.

Yet, as has already been remarked, the café-concert audience drew widely from all social classes; it was by no means only the less-educated masses who saw the appeal in these acts, and the gradual marginalization of popular audiences from many venues by the increasingly luxuriant music halls in the 1890s further belies this snobbery along class lines. Moreover, while there is a certain element of the carnivalesque in the popular audience and the means by which they express their pleasure – they espouse little of the studied non-chalance or polite appreciation of the bourgeoisie and upper classes – there is no reason to ascribe their enjoyment *purely* to the bodily, the grotesque, and the raucous, or to imagine that the musical, lyrical, and performed content of these acts bypassed their brains any more than ballet did for audiences at Opéra. The lower classes are just as likely as their social superiors to engage with these comic English songs in terms of their network of humour, competitiveness, disquiet, and nationalistic jingoism, as well as with their sauciness or silliness. The comic Englishman, then, sits across lines of class and aesthetic snobbery. The degradation of core bourgeois and patriarchal values by

72   *Singing the English*

the café-concert in general was of serious concern to many among the social elites – first because of their influence on an unruly lower class and their provision of a space for popular subculture, and secondly because it risked, as Gordon has noted, dragging the upper classes into the realm of the lower as they found themselves in thrall to these fun and catchy tunes (2001, p. 84). Yet for all this class division and disquiet, when it comes to the English character in particular, the café-concert provides a target of mockery that could be shared by people from across the social spectrum – and no doubt it is this cross-societal appeal that goes a long way to explaining its enduring popularity.

David Scott suggests of the humour in exotic and travel texts that,

> of course, there is a deliberate element of parody and humour in these writers' presentation of the other culture, one that is not necessarily intended to belittle it, but on the contrary to express a cultural gap that can only be filled by irony and humour.
>
> (2004, p. 212)

To some extent, these comic English acts appeal for precisely these reasons – the pleasures of parody, the explosive humour of slapstick, and the comforting delight found in old, familiar gags express the cultural gap of the Channel. However, the significance of the comic songs treated in this chapter runs deeper than this: in laughing at the English foreigner and treating them in terms of a *racial* Other, these songs teeter on the line between processes of racial Othering (dehumanizing the English person through the medium of comedy and consequently anaesthetizing the public to the idea of the violence of conflict), and an understandable need for reassurance and for the maintenance of peace and cohesiveness at home. They offer something most members of the French audience could get behind, something that provided a sense of national community and self – and it is perhaps preferable, from an ideological point of view, that if a target were needed to be Othered by French wit, ire, and insecurity, that it picks on the English as someone their own size, who had a reasonable chance of answering back.

However, unlike in exotic and travel writing, the cultural gap between England and France was by no means vast – singers, musicians, dancers, writers, artists, educators, politicians, policymakers, journalists, and an endless string of others exchanged ideas and practices across the Channel, influencing each other's cultures, even if one was Republican and the other remained a monarchy. Both the absurdity of seeing this gap in culture and character as insuperable, and the ubiquity of references to it in contemporary discourse, song, and humour, are neatly dramatized in Del, Fragson, Garnier, and Héros's song and monologue, 'Paris-London' (1897). In this skit, Fragson, dressed à l'Anglais, sings liltingly in an equivocal accent – as convention dictates – that he has come to Paris to amuse himself, and then he sets about enumerating all the striking differences between the two countries. He lists differences of such unsurmountable magnitude as the politeness of

Singing the English 73

the London police compared to the brusquerie of the Parisian gendarmes; the fog versus the sun; driving on the left versus the right; coachmen sitting on the back versus the front of their cabs; public execution by 'lengthening' (hanging) versus 'shortening' (guillotine); soldiers wearing a red jacket with blue trousers versus a blue jacket with red trousers; calling each other 'sir' (with the pun that it is pronounced *sœur* – sister) versus calling each other 'frère' (brother); vertical-opening sash windows versus horizontal-opening windows; whistling versus applauding performers to express delight; industrial workers having Saturday and Sunday off versus Monday; and having women with blonde hair, big feet, and little breasts versus brown hair, small feet, and big breasts. The singer concludes, in summary, that

> En France c'est tout le contraire
> De ce qu'on fait en Angleterre.
> À London, c'est je vous le dit
> Tout le contraire de Paris.

> [In France it's just the opposite
> Of what you do in England.
> In London, I'm telling you,
> It's the opposite of Paris.]

This lengthy accumulation would seem to imply monumental national differences, yet the triviality of the content undermines the widespread belief that the two nations contrast in any significant way that could justify the prevalent discourses of fundamental racial difference or mutual political incomprehension.

So, while the café-concert's treatment of the English may be anachronistic, exaggerated, often down-right fictional, what is does provide is a mirror image of French – and especially Parisian – Republican society and its underlying web of concerns, interests, ideas, and beliefs. Chadourne complains that, 'cette phrase: "tout en France finit par des chansons" est donc, à juste titre, passée en proverbe. Eh bien! Cette forme particulière de notre esprit gaulois ne nous a pas abandonnés, [...] [mais] le répertoire actuel des cafés-concerts ne s'alimente généralement que de platitude et de honte' ['that phrase "everything in France ends with a song" has, quite fairly, become proverbial. Well! That particular aspect of our gaulois spirit hasn't abandoned us, but the current repertoire of the café-concert is generally fed only by platitudes and shame'] (1889, pp. 213–14). However, his elitist tastes appear to blind him from the substance behind the repetitive jokes and ditties. Yvette Guilbert is nearer the mark when she comments, quoting François Coppée, that 'pour chanter les refrains modernes, il faut connaître son Paris' ['to sing modern songs, you have to know your Paris'] (1928, p. 54) – and this is an essential factor in understanding the extent of the relevance of the comic English genre. The comic English character, as this chapter has demonstrated, is a particularly

74 *Singing the English*

eloquent Other; it has a crucial role to play in both drawing attention to and palliating the anxieties that define this period in France.

Notes

1 Hugh Macdonald enumerates, among others, Lord Elmvood and Dr Sandfort in *Simple histoire* (1826); Lord and Lady Cokbourg in *Fra Diavolo* (1830); Mistress Carrington, Miss Indiana, Miss Pretty, and Edgard Mandlebert in *Camille* (1832); and Dr Neuborough in *L'Ambitieux* (1834) (1996, pp. 155–62).

2 Some typical examples of English characters in English-themed theatricals include: Albert Debeilly's *Miss Shocking!* (1883), a short sketch in which a French girl who is about to be introduced to her first suitor contemplates her English governess, who is plain and sad because a fiancé once abandoned her, and so the girl resolves to take her time in her choice of husbands and keep her standards set high; Meilhac and Halévy's *Fanny Lear* (1868), in which the wealthy Parisian gentleman Birnheim, in disgrace after falling in love with an English actress called Fanny Lear, is hiding away at his friend Fondeville's provincial estate – but Fanny has, it will transpire, made an advantageous marriage and is now the mysterious Madame de Noriolis, Frondeville's neighbour; Matrat and Fordyce's *English Tailor* (1897), in which the wily English tailor Leadpool outwits the foolish French provincial Lapoire into exorbitant tailoring bills, despite his limited sewing skills – whilst at the same time helping Lapoire to win the girl of his dreams; and the gentlemanly English aristocrat in an anonymous vaudeville *Le Prélude de l'Entente cordiale* (1906), who wishes to court a spirited young Parisienne, but the latter decides to play a trick on him by switching places with her maid servant – eventually, the truth outs, and the English gent accepts the test patiently and still asks for her hand in marriage in a cordiale entente.

3 It is an interesting culinary reversal that in the nineteenth century, the English were known for cooking their beef rare and the French for serving it woefully well done – in complete contrast with today when the opposite is presumed to be both typical and traditional.

4 In the first chapter alone, Montégut uses 'barbare' / 'barbarisme' / 'barbarie' thirty times, 'sauvage' seven times, 'sang' (bloodline) nine times, 'race' twenty-seven times, and 'violent' / 'violence' seven times (1883, pp. 3–53).

5 The English songs laughing at the French and Franco-British relations are too numerous to list here, but include titles such as Ella Kelly's *I will speak French* (1876), William Benson and F. Bowyer's *À la française* (1876), Arthur West's *The Paris Exhibition* (1889), R.A. Roberts's *That's How you Parley voo* (1895), and Tozer Ferris and W. Gill's *In Gay Paree* (1902).

6 Among many rich studies, see Jennifer Yee, *Exotic Subversions* (2008) and *Clichés de la femme exotique* (2000); and Lisa Lowe, *Critical Terrains* (1991).

7 See, for example, in 1881 alone, 'La Voleuse d'enfant' set in London and with a jig danced by four chorus girls at the start of scene five; 'La Fille de Lovelace,' in which one male and one female actor dance a jig together; and 'Le Secret de Miss Aurore' which drew audiences to the Théâtre Montmartre with the appeal of a jig in its second scene.

8 Jann Pasler elaborates on the normalization of this use of the leitmotif in art music after Wagner in her *Writing through Music* (2008, pp. 27–28).

Singing the English 75

9 Recent studies exploring the body's central role in shaping the mind include, for example: Wilson, 'Six Views of Embodied Cognition' (2002); Gallagher, *How the Body Shapes the Mind* (2005); and Raymond Gibbs Jr, *Embodiment and Cognitive Science* (2006).

Songs cited

'À la française.' W. Benson and F. Bowyer, 1876. London: Hopwood and Crew.

'L'Anglais à Paris! Chansonnette.' D.Fourcand, W.-D. S. Frieda and Suirain, n.d. [1881]. Paris: 7 rue d'Enghien.

'L'Anglais au dictionnaire. Scène comique.' D. Langat and H. C. de Ploosen, n.d. [1875]. Paris: H. C. de Ploosen.

'Les Anglais chez nous. Chansonnette.' É. Duhem and J. Jouy, n.d. [1891]. Paris: L. Bathlot-Joubert.

'L'Anglais embarrassé. Chansonnette comique.' P. Courtois, Delormel, and Garnier, n.d. [1887]. Paris: Répertoire Paulus.

'L'Anglais en traversée! Oppression de voyage.' P. Bourget and E. Lhuillier, n.d. [1850]. Paris: J. Meissonnier et fils.

'L'Anglais en voyage: Chansonnette.' L. Collin, Villemer, and Delormel, n.d. [1882]. Paris: L. Bathlot.

'L'Anglais et le bourgeois: scène comique à deux personnages.' Gerny and A. Queyriaux, n.d. [1897]. Paris: Veuve Émile Benoît.

'L'Anglais formaliste: chansonnette monologue.' Delormel and Garnier, n.d. [1888]. Paris: Répertoire moderne.

'L'Anglais gêlé, ou John, c'est épatant. Chansonnette comique.' H. Christiné and A. Grimaldi, n.d. [1898]. Paris: Albert Grimaldi.

'L'Anglais malcontent. Chansonnette comique.' É. Duhem, and L. Laroche, n.d. [1888]. Paris: Alfred Forest.

'L'Anglais mélancolique! Scène comique.' S. Mangeant, and E. de Richemont, n.d. [1855]. Paris: Au Ménéstrel.

'L'Anglais parisien! Chansonnette.' Mortreuil Briollet, and Fragson, n.d. [1895]. Paris: 7 rue d'Enghien.

'L'Anglais poivrot!' L. Cologne and J. Graves, n.d. [1897]. Paris: L. Gillot.

'L'Anglais rieur! Éclat de rire.' E. Ouvrard and Pizoir, n.d. [1887]. Paris: Duval.

'L'Anglais triste: chanson monologue.' Gerny and P. Léonvic, n.d. [1892]. Paris: Émile Benoît.

'Anglaises misses: chansonnette.' É. Duhem and C. Durozel, n.d. [1895]. Paris: C. Joubert.

'L'Apéritif d'un Anglais. Chanson comique.' Disle and A. Ducreux, n.d. [1894]. Paris: Renoult.

'La Balle "Dum-Dum," Chansonnette.' L. Boyer, 1899. Paris: G. Ondet.

'Le Chic anglais!' L. Bans, Jeunil Garnier, and J. Lasaiques, n.d. [1900]. Paris: Delormel-Garnier.

'Ell's danse pas le d'gigue.' E. Auplo and F. Chassaigne, 1893. Paris: R. Cathelineau et Cie.

'La Gigue, aoh! yes!' O. Batifort and J. Cabrol, n.d. [1910]. Saint-Mandé: Bergerat.

'Gigue-obsession!' E. Lemercier and E. Poncin, n.d. [1900]. Paris: E.-Meuriot.

'I will speak French.' E. Kelly, 1876. London: s.n.

76 *Singing the English*

'In Gay Paree.' T. Ferris, and W. Gill, 1902. London: Reynolds and Co.

'Je pôvais pas! Chansonnette anglaise avec gigue.' C. Hurbain, J. Paulet, and J. Strauss, n.d. [1885]. Paris: A. Corcier.

'Les jolies petites Songes d'un Anglais, ou Qué ne peut-on rêver toujours! Romance.' E. Lhuillier, n.d. [1836]. Paris: A. Petibon.

'Le joyeux Anglais! Scène comique avec parlé.' C. Letellier, n.d. [1889]. Paris: O. Bornemann.

'La Marche des Boërs, chanson-marche.' L. Lelièvre, 1900. Paris: H. Pascal.

'Milady Plumpudding! Chansonnette anglaise avec danses et parlé.' A. Jambom, Stainville, and Tac-Coen, n.d. [1887]. Paris: P. Clair.

'Miss Gig. Chansonnette avec danse.' Delormel, É. Duhem, and Villemer, n.d. [1885]. Paris: Le Bailly.

'Miss Kokett.' F. Berthel, and L. Bousquet, n.d. [1877]. Paris: Brandus.

'Miss, Oh! Yes! Chansonnette.' Delormel and F. Perpignan, n.d. [1895]. Paris: 7 rue d'Enghien.

'Miss Plumpudding! Chansonnette.' E. Lemercier, and H. Waïss, n.d. [1894]. Paris: G. Ondet.

'Les Mots anglais. Chansonnette.' Delormel Briollet and Gerny, n.d. [1897]. Paris: 7 rue d'Enghien.

'Mylord Gig-Gig! Excentricité anglaise.' L.Gabillaud, J. Rocca and Tac-Coen, n.d. [1879]. Paris: L. Bathlot.

'Paris-London! Chanson monologue.' Del Fragson, Garnier, and Héros, n.d. [1897]. Paris: F. Vargues.

'Ratatapoum purée! Type réaliste d'Anglais.' F. Dufor, and E. Paigne, n.d. [1893]. Paris: 16 passage de l'Industrie.

'La Revanche de John Bull! Scène comique.' C. Letellier, n.d. [1894]. Paris: O. Bornemann.

'Schoking! Chansonnette.' F. Chaudoir, V. Damien and Flic-Flac, n.d. [1894]. Paris: Édition Contemporaine.

'That's How you Parley-voo.' R. A. Roberts, 1895. London: Francis, Day, and Hunter.

'The Paris Exhibition.' A. West, 1889. London: Francis Bros. & Day.

Works cited

Améro, J., 1879. *L'Anglomanie dans le français et les Barbarismes anglais usités en France.* Paris: Abbeville.

Amossy, R., 1991. *Les Idées reçues: Sémiologie du stéréotype.* Paris: Éditions Nathan.

Attali, J., 2009. *Noise: the Political Economy of Music.* Translated from Italian by B. Massumi. Minneapolis: University of Minnesota Press.

Bailey, P., 1998. *Popular Culture and Performance in the Victorian City.* Cambridge: Cambridge University Press.

Baker, A., 2017. *Amateur Musical Societies and Sports Clubs in Provincial France, 1848–1914: Harmony and Hostility.* Basingstoke: Palgrave Macmillan.

Un Bal d'étudiants (Bullier), notice historique, accompagnée d'une photogravure, et suivie d'un appendice bibliographique par un ancien contrôleur du droit des pauvres, 1908. Paris: H. Champion.

Bataille, A., 1895. 'Gazette de tribunaux.' *Le Figaro,* 10 April, p. 5.

Bellenger, H., n.d. [1877]. *Londres pittoresque et la vie anglaise.* Paris: Georges Decaux.

Singing the English 77

Bergson, H., 1900. *Le Rire: essai sur la signification du comique.* Paris: Félix Alcan.

Bernard, É., 1971. 'Jules Pasdeloup et les Concerts populaires', *Revue de musicologie*, 57 (2). pp. 150–78.

Bhabha, H., 1994. 'The Other Question: Stereotypes, Discrimination and the Discourse of Colonialism.' In: H. Bhabha, ed. *The Location of Culture.* London: Routledge. pp. 66–84.

Billig, M., 2001. *Laughter and Ridicule: Towards a Social Critique of Humour.* London: Sage.

Bon, G. le, 1894. *Les Lois psychologique de l'évolution des peuples.* Paris: Félix Alcan.

Bourget, P., 1889. *Études et portraits*, 2 vols. Paris: Lemerre.

Bréal, M., 1900. *De l'enseignement des langues vivantes – conférences.* Paris: Hachette.

Butler, J., 1990. *Gender Trouble: Feminism and the Subversion of Identity.* London and New York: Routledge.

Chadourne, A., 1889. *Les Cafés-Concerts.* Paris: E. Dentu.

Clarétie, J., 1903. 'Le Cake-walk.' *Le Figaro*, 13 Feb., p. 1.

'Concours des certificats d'aptitude à l'enseignement de la langue anglaise,' 1899–1900. *Revue de l'enseignement des langues vivantes*, 16 (9). n.p.

Debans, C., 1884. *Les Malheurs de John Bull.* Paris: Marpon and Flammarion.

Debeilly, A., 1883. *Miss Shocking! Saynète en vers.* Paris: L. Michaud.

Delzangles, F., 1914. *La Danse: son utilité, sa rénovation.* Paris: Librairie Universitaire J. Gamber.

Deschamps, G., 1900. 'Les Jeunes filles et l'exposition.' *Le Figaro*, 3 April, p. 1.

Dugas, L., 1902. *Psychologie du rire.* Paris: Félix Alcan.

Dupaigne, A., 1878. 'Conférence sur le chant dans les écoles.' In: *Les Conférences pédagogiques faites aux instituteurs délégués à l'exposition universelles de 1878.* Paris: Ch. Delagrave.

Duquesnel, F., 1899. 'Les Premiers.' *Gaulois*, 21 Oct., p. 3.

Fage, A. de la, 1844. *Miscellanées musicales.* Paris: Comptoirs des imprimeurs unis.

Fanon, F., 1952. *Peau noire, masques blancs.* Paris: Seuil.

Ferrari [pseud.], 1896. 'Le Monde et la ville.' *Le Figaro*, 14 Oct., p. 2.

Fordyce and Matrat, 1897. *English Tailor: Fantaisie en 3 petits actes.* Paris: P.-V. Stock.

France, H., 1900. *Croquis d'Outre-Manche.* Paris: Charpentier.

Frimousse [pseud.], 7 October 1887 and 17 November 1888. 'La Soirée parisienne,' *Gaulois.* p. 3.

Frou-Frou [pseud.], 1872. 'Les Premières.' *Le Figaro*, 15 May, p. 3.

Gallagher, S., 2005. *How the Body Shapes the Mind.* Oxford: Clarendon Press.

Gordon, R. B., 2000. 'Epileptic Singers on the Parisian Stage.' In: R. Lloyd and B. Nelson, eds. *Women Seeking Expression: France, 1794–1914.* Monash: Monash Romance Studies.

Gordon, R. B., 2001. *Why the French Love Jerry Lewis from Cabaret to Early Cinema.* Stanford, CA: Stanford University Press.

Gordon, R. B., 2003. 'Natural Rhythm: La Parisienne Dances with Darwin: 1875-1910,' *Modernism/Modernity*, 10 (4). pp. 617–56.

Gordon, R. B., 2004. 'Fashion and the White Savage in the Parisian Music Hall,' *Fashion Theory*, 8 (3). pp. 267–99.

Guilbert, Y., 1928. *L'Art de chanter une chanson.* Paris: Bernard Grasset.

Halévy, L. and Meilhac, H., 1868. *Fanny Lear, comédie en 5 actes.* Paris: M. Lévy.

Heinrich, G.-A., 1871. *L'Enseignement des langues vivantes en France.* Paris: Charles Douniol.

78 *Singing the English*

Héros, E., 1894. 'Les Succès du Café-concert.' *Le Figaro*, 31 March, p. 1.

Héros, E., 1919. 'Les Cafés-Chantants: Les Cafés-Concerts: Les Music-Halls,' *La Rampe*, 140. pp. 8–37.

Hibbitt, R., 2012. 'Entente asymétrique? Franco-British literary exchanges in 1908.' In: A. Radford and V. Reid, eds. *Franco-British Cultural Exchanges, 1880–1940*. Basingstoke: Palgrave Macmillan. pp. 34–51.

Hindson, C., 2007. *Female Performance Practice on the Fin-de-Siècle Popular Stages of London and Paris: Experiment and Advertisement*. Manchester: Manchester University Press.

Jollivet, G., 1889. 'Les Adieux: Mme de Charvy à sa mère.' In: *Figaro-Exposition*. Paris: Goupil et Cie.

Jupilles, F. de, 1886. *Au pays des brouillards (Mœurs britanniques)*. Paris: Librairie illustrée.

Jusserand, J. J., 1894. *Histoire littéraire du peuple anglais des origines à la*

Lowe, L., 1991. Critical Terrains: French and British Orientalisms. Ithaca, NY: Cornell University Press.

Macdonald, H., 1996. 'The Outre-Manche in Nineteenth-Century French Opera,' *D'un opéra à l'autre: hommages à Jean Mongrédien*. Paris: Presses de l'Université de Paris-Sorbonne. pp. 155–62.

M[onsieur] du B[alcon], 1904. 'Spectacles et Concerts.' *Le Figaro*, 25 Sept., p. 4.

Montégut, É., 1883. *Essais sur la littérature anglaise*. Paris: Hachette.

Moore Whiting, S., 1999. *Satie the Bohemian: from Cabaret to Concert Hall*. Oxford: Oxford University Press.

O'Rell, M. [pseud. Léon Paul Blouet], 1884. *Les Filles de John Bull*. Paris: Calmann-Lévy.

O'Rell, M., 1894. *La Maison John Bull et Cie*. Paris: Calmann-Lévy.

Pasler, J., 2008. *Writing through Music Essays on Music, Culture, and Politics*. Oxford: Oxford University Press.

Pasler, J., 2009. *Composing the Citizen: Music as Public Utility in Third Republican France*. Berkeley, CA: University of California Press.

Perrin, C., 2003. 'Angleterre en papier: le cliché et le miroir.' In: A. Court and P. Charreton, eds. *Regards populaires sur l'Anglo-Saxon*. Saint-Étienne: Publications de l'Université de Saint-Étienne. pp. 9–29.

Pickering, M., 2004. 'Racial stereotypes.' In: G. Taylor and S. Spencer, eds. *Social Identities: Multidisciplinary approaches*. New York: Routledge. pp. 91–106.

Poole, M. E., 1997. 'Gustave Charpentier and the Conservatoire Populaire de Mimi Pinson,' *19th-Century Music*, 20 (3). pp. 231–52.

Le Prélude de l'entente cordiale, saynète, 1906. Tours: imprimerie de Deslis frères.

Prendergast, C., 1986. *The Order of Mimesis: Balzac, Stendhal, Nerval and Flaubert*. Cambridge: Cambridge University Press.

Rabuteau, A. and Vilbac, R. de, *ca.* 1890. *Airs populaires: Chants nationaux et motifs célèbres de tous les pays, arrangés pour piano et violon*, 8th edn. Paris: Henri Lemoine.

Ralph, R., 1903. 'Théâtres – Moulin Rouge: "La Belle de New York".' *Courrier français*, 7 June, p. 2.

Raymond, G., 2006. *Embodiment and Cognitive Science*. Cambridge: Cambridge University Press.

Rearick, C., 1985. *Pleasures of the Belle Epoque: Entertainment and Festivity in Turn-of-the-Century France*. New Haven and London: Yale University Press.

Roche, P., 1898. 'Cour de Cassation.' *Gaulois*, 3 April, p. 1.

Ryvez, 1896. 'Premières représentations.' *L'Art lyrique et le music-hall*, 13 Dec., p. 5.

Scott, D., 2004. *Semiologies of Travel: from Gautier to Baudrillard*. Cambridge: Cambridge University Press.

Taine, H., 1872. *Notes sur l'Angleterre*. Paris: Hachette.

Taine, H., 1921. *Histoire de la littérature anglaise*, 5 vols. Paris: Hachette.

Tarde, G., 1901. *L'Opinion et la foule*. Paris: Félix Alcan.

Tout Paris [pseud.], 1896. 'Bloc-notes parisien.' *Gaulois*, 28 Sept., p. 1.

Villemessant, H. de, 1864. 'Les Hasards de la plume.' *Le Figaro*, 17 Nov., pp. 1–2.

Wéckerlin, J.-B., 1886. *La Chanson populaire*. Paris: Firmin-Didot.

Weil, A., 1872. *Du Programme de l'enseignement secondaire précédé d'une lettre de M. Édouard Laboulaye*. Paris: Charpentier.

Weitz, E., 2016. *Theatre and Laughter*. Basingstoke: Palgrave Macmillan.

Wilson, M., 2002. 'Six Views of Embodied Cognition,' *Psychological Bulletin*, 9 (4). pp. 625–36.

X.D. [pseud.], 1880. 'Province: Cherbourg.' *L'Europe artiste*, 4 Jan., p. 2.

Yee, J., 2000. Clichés de la femme exotique: un regard sur la littérature coloniale française entre 1871 et 1914. Paris: L'Harmattan.

Yee, J., 2008. *Exotic Subversions in Nineteenth-Century French Fiction*. Oxford: MHRA Legenda.

2 Singing for salvation
Music and British evangelism in France

'Toutes ces Anglais's pudiques,
Qui march'nt en rangs dans la ru,
Baragouinant des cantiques
Compos'nt l'armée du salut'

'All those prudish English women
Who march through the streets in their ranks,
Jabbering their hymns,
Make up the Salvation Army'
      Nalray, Deransart, Siégel, and Lémon,
      'Viv' l'Armée du Chahut-u-u-u-ut' (1893)

At some point in every discussion of the English, from every conceivable standpoint, the French nineteenth-century observer will remark upon England's religiosity and ardent Protestantism as defining features of the nation. Six out of thirty-two chapters in Max O'Rell's [pseud. Léon Paul Blouet] *John Bull et son Île* (1884b) are dedicated specifically to religion and religious sects, and he quips in *Les Filles de John Bull* that whilst any new line of thinking in France 'fait école' ['forms a school of thought'], in England it inevitably 'fait église' ['forms a church'] (1884a, p. 227). For him, as for many of his contemporaries, English Protestantism and French Catholicism crystallize fundamental differences in how the two nations are hard-wired to think, act, and feel.

'Protestantism' and 'Catholicism,' it should be noted, are used as uncritical explanations for a much wider spectrum of negative and positive character traits. For Jean Lorrain, a notorious Anglophobe, Puritanical Protestantism and English character are synonymous as he lambasts English tourists for supressing *French joie de vivre*, invading the south coast with 'leur puritanisme [qui] a attristé le monde' with its 'humeur de brouillard' ['their Puritanism that has saddened the world' with its 'foggy mood'] (1900, p. 58). It is not clear precisely why a branch of Protestantism – a religious practice born with Martin Luther in Germany – should be the religious equivalent of English fog, except that these clichés had been repeated so often that this would not jar at all with the reader's sense of plausibility. Even musical taste and the

DOI: 10.4324/9780367815431-3

Singing for salvation 81

ways in which people listened to music in England were taken as definite manifestations of Protestantism, and in turn were seen as the sine qua non of Englishness. O'Rell comments upon John Bull's predilection for the oratorio form and depicts him, 'les yeux fermés, pour mieux entendre, tout comme au sermon. Il est heureux: il a l'air d'être venu au temple. L'oratorio est pour lui un avant-goût des délices qui l'attendent dans l'autre monde' ['eyes closed the better to hear, just like at a sermon. He is happy: he has the air of a man at church. For him, the oratorio is a foretaste of the delights that await him in the next world'] (1884b, p. 190). John Bull, O'Rell implies, does not have the temperament to appreciate music for its purely artistic qualities, but rather only in as much as it provides him with a spiritual experience.

Furthermore, just as 'Frenchness' and 'Catholicism' had become associated with corruption and decadence in Britain, so 'Englishness' and 'Protestantism' became an intertwined shorthand for moral hypocrisy for French writers in this period. The English are said to be content to make loud public claims to moral rectitude whilst sinning freely in private; whilst using religion to garner power, self-importance, money, or sexual influence; and all the while declaring themselves scandalized by the dens of iniquity in Paris – as the sarcastic epigraph to the present chapter implies. Fernand Jupilles scoffs that 'dans ce pays, la religion offre un vaste champ d'exploitation' ['in this country, religion offers a vast field to be exploited'] (1885, p. 69), and he makes murky accusations of widespread sexual misconduct. With this association in mind, it was of little wonder to many when William Stead published his scandalous revelations about child prostitution in England in the *Pall Mall Gazette* in 1885 – and writers such as Auguste de Villiers de L'Isle-Adam, Octave Mirbeau, and Jean Lorrain capitalized on this engrained association. In 'Le Sadisme anglais' ('English Sadism,' 1888), *Le Jardin des supplices* (*The Torture Garden*, 1899), *Monsieur de Phocas* (1901), *Le Vice errant* (*Wandering Vice*, 1900), the *Histoire de masques* (*The Story of the Masks*, 1900), and the *Crimes des riches* (*Crimes of the Rich*, 1906), they dramatize, as though they were inherently inextricable, the religious hypocrisy, immorality, and cruelty of Englishness. Indeed, the evangelical enthusiasm of late nineteenth-century England, Scotland, and Wales reinvigorates this stereotype, and it becomes a fundamental feature of novels about new religious groups such as the Salvation Army. For example, J.-H. Rosny aîné, in his novel *Nell Horn, de l'Armée du Salut* (*Nell Horn of the Salvation Army*, 1886), takes apparent pleasure in (over-) dramatizing Nell's disenchantment with the Salvation Army: Rosny imagines episodes in which Nell sees two unmarried church leaders kissing passionately after a prayer meeting on sexual purity; in which a church-going policeman tries to sexually assault Nell after she raises the alarm that her father is physically abusing her and her mother; and in which Christian nurses treat the dying poor with cruel inhumanity (1900, pp. 29, 45, 64–65).

However, the renowned novelist Brada challenges these engrained stereotypes. She questions whether English national character and national religion really are so easily defined and so inextricable. After all, Shakespeare's bawdy,

82   *Singing for salvation*

earthy humour seems irreconcilable with Anglo-Saxon stuffy, foggy, hard puritanism and Brada suggests that he, like Chaucer, William Langland, and other old English authors, is in fact representative of the way English culture originally was and that they indicate a vein that still runs deep in the national psyche. The Reformation and the imposition of puritanical Protestantism from Germanic Europe led to an acquisition of habits that *deformed* the 'génie anglaise,' 'forcé de dévier de sa véritable nature [...] libre, hardi, joyeux' ['forced to deviate from its true nature – free, bold, and joyous'] (1895, p. 46). Taine, too, though lacking nuance in many aspects of his analysis, also deems this shift in national habits to be unnatural, looking back at 'la *Merry England* de Shakespeare, la pleine sève primitive de l'arbre que le puritanisme est venu tordre, élaguer et rendre rigide autant que droit' ['the Merry England of Shakespeare, the flowing sap of the tree that Puritanism would twist, prune, and train to be as rigid as it is straight'] (1872, p. 47). Clearly, the issue of the characteristics habitually associated with Protestantism and Catholicism by the French are more fluid than these learned clichés allow. Further, if English religiosity is not in fact an inherent racial impulse of Englishness as so many have suggested, but rather a cultural trait that can change for better or worse when exposed to other influences, this also has worrying implications for the fledgling Third Republic – not least taking into account the growth in popularity of mass pilgrimage centres such as Lourdes and La Salette in the late nineteenth century.

This becomes particularly pertinent from the perspective of French Republicanism, in the context of the push for secularization in contemporaneous France. If to be English is to be Protestant, but to be French is no longer to be Catholic, then what precisely *is* the new French equivalent that the Republic should offer up to take Catholicism's place for the secular era? The anxiety caused by this uncertainty can be seen in the trepidation over the 'Protestant question' in Third-Republican political circles. This period is often presented as a struggle between those wishing to maintain Catholic influence over education, society, and politics, and those looking to free the system from all religious influence; however, as Gilbert Chaitin clearly demonstrates, Protestantism was also a key player here (2009, p. 29). As control of schools was wrested from Catholic religious orders under Jules Ferry, many of their replacements were not secularists but Protestants and those influenced by Protestant, Kantian philosophy, notably Ferdinand Buisson (director of primary education, 1895), Jules Steeg (inspector general of the Université), and Julie Charlotte Velton (first director of the ENS Sèvres to prepare teachers for the new girls' secondary schools). Further, many Catholic conservatives blamed Protestant powers at home and abroad for ruinous events threatening France, such as the success of Prussian (and later German) anti-Catholic kulturkampfen, the unification of Italy through the machinations of Palmerston, Gladstone, and Bismarck, and generally 'les menées de sociétés protestantes, anglaises et allemandes, bibliques, salutistes, méthodistes et autres' ['the machinations of Protestant societies, English and

Singing for salvation 83

German, Bibleists, Salvationists, Methodists, and others'] (see Tombs, 1996, p. 90).[1] Furthermore, Protestant evangelical groups such as the Salvation Army – who are taken by the French as the epitome of English religiosity in the late nineteenth century – pose troubling questions about social levelling across the spectrum of socio-cultural hierarchies at work in France. Although newspaper articles systematically portray the Salvation Army as blonde, English, middle-class ladies, by 1904 there were in fact thousands of members in America, Germany, the Netherlands, France, Italy, and Belgium, as well as China, Turkey, Greece, Hawaii, sub-Saharan Africa, and South Africa, comprising both the upper and lower classes, white and non-white populations, men and women.

In the final decades of the century, concerns over French identity, religion, and social cohesion, and cross-Channel concerns over rivalry and cultural interpenetration coalesce around the image, the idea, and, above all, the music and the sounds of the Salvation Army – given the sobriquet of 'culte mystico-tapageur' ['mystic-racket-making cult'] by one writer for the *Revue encyclopédique* ('L'Armée du Salut,' 1892, pp. 230–1). This is not to claim that music is the *only* concern for the French regarding English religion and the Salvation Army; rather, music stands in the foreground of a discussion that would be difficult to tackle cogently without this discursive inroad. It provides a means of grappling with complex and unsettling issues regarding France's international status, its national identity, and its ability to resist cultural and political invasion. This chapter explores this musical engagement with the Salvation Army from a number of different angles: the acoustic horror of hearing the Salvation Army bands in Britain; the nexus of anxieties experienced on meeting these same bands in the streets of France and France's colonies; the associations of the specific combination of religion and brass music; and musical ripostes to these sonic assaults, as the risible Salvationist became a figure of popular musical fun. Throughout these, French reactions to this religious group are inextricable from the Salvationists' aural impact, and this becomes a defining facet of France's musical engagement with Britain at the turn of the century.

Hearing the Salvation Army in Britain

It is with surprising unanimity that French writers on Britain remark about the noisy horrors of Salvation Army bands and other evangelical groups as they march and preach through British towns and cities. Time after time, it is a reflex gesture when introducing a depiction or discussion of British religion to criticize religious street music. Despite Marie-Anne de Bovet's habitual eagerness to approve of Scottish culture, when it comes to religious street music she depicts a musical milieu that hardly qualifies as musical at all, 'rien n'étant plus étranger à l'harmonie que ces litanies traînantes et nasillardes, vociférées sur des pont-neufs [...] avec des éclats de fausset acides comme un citron vert fusant au-dessus d'une bouillie confuse de basses sourdes et ternes' ['nothing

84   *Singing for salvation*

being more alien to harmony than these drawling, nasal litanies, hollered out upon public byways with bursts of acidic falsetto like a lime dripping over a muddled pulp of muffled, dull bass notes'] (1898, p. 120). Such multifaceted aesthetic critique – the tone, tempo, volume, pitch, and timbre are all summarily rejected here – taints the soundscape of nearly every Scottish town. De Bovet is saddened by the sonic interruption of her Shetland reverie in Lerwick when a Majoress 'à la voix toniturante' ['with a booming voice'] sings and cries out her sermon (1898, p. 237), and Louis Lafond's largely positive impression of Edinburgh is somewhat blighted by 'des groupes de jeunes gens qui chantent en chœur des hymnes pieux, du reste avec ce parfait mépris de toute règle musicale qui distingue le peuple britannique' ['groups of young people singing pious hymns in chorus, with the perfect disdain for all the rules of music that characterizes the British people'] (1887, p. 3). Similarly, in London, Hector France is aghast when William Booth's Hallelujah Band crosses his path; and, whilst France is aghast at almost everything English throughout his text, the top spot on his list of horrors is reserved for the Salvation Army's noise music, filling the streets 'avec le fracas d'un cirque forain. L'on s'arrêtait aux carrefours populaires, l'on chantait des hymnes, l'on prêchait et priait' ['with the din of a travelling circus. They stopped at busy crossroads, sang hymns, preached, and prayed'] (1900, p. 101). Even French commentators who were generally more measured in their remarks, for example the exiled Henri Bellenger, still show a marked distaste for the sounds of British evangelical groups, as 'la predication de la Bible alterne avec le chant des cantiques, qui d'habitude ne se recommandent ni par la facture des vers ni par la mélodie qu'on a plaqué dessus' ['Bible preaching alternates with singing hymns, which normally recommend themselves neither by the craftsmanship of the verses nor by the melody that has been stuck on top of them'] (1877, p. 167).

So striking are these aural experiences that some writers seek to transmit them to the reader through the medium of the text. Hector France, showing particular sensitivity to sound, evokes the sound of drummers to describe the Salvation Army: 'c'est par les rues et en chantant qu'ils font leur prosélytes. [...] Elle marche à la conquête des âmes, militairement: *Une, deux, une deux, ran plan plan*' ['it is by going singing through the streets that they make their converts. They march to conquer souls, militarily: *One, two, one, two, rum-pa-pa-pum*'] (1883, pp. 138–9). O'Rell, too, turns his attention to the Salvation Army's music, using a pithy contrast in song styles to cement the otherwise visual juxtaposition of the ragged poor and an evangelical crowd during a Teetotal Movement Meeting in London:

> C'est un spectacle bien anglais que de voir, d'un côté d'une rue – le côté nord du Strand – des groupes édifiants, onctueux, spécimens de la plus austère vertu; de l'autre, à quatre ou cinq mètres de distance, des groupes de malheureuses éhontées, sales, ivres, sans vergogne, spécimens de la plus grossière débauche: *à droite, les cantiques; à gauche, les chansons obscènes.*
> (1884a, p. 79 – italics in original text)

Singing for salvation   85

[It's a very British spectacle to see, on the one side of the road – the North side of the Strand – edifying, oily specimens of the most austere virtue; on the other, four or five metres away, groups of brazen, dirty, drunken, shameless specimens of the crudest debauchery: *to the right, hymns; to the left, dirty songs.*]

The average French reader probably cannot imagine with any precision what this street corner of London looks like or the particular clothing choices of English teetotallers, but they would be able to evoke the aural antithesis between hymns and dirty songs.

Paul Bourget goes into particularly extensive detail in his desire to convey the aural impression of a Salvation Army procession to the reader, so they can almost hear by proxy the music and the sounds that he hears. Into the quiet of a London Sunday,

Soudain une sonnerie de trompettes éclate, accompagnée de chants étranges. Une centaine de personnes paraissent, conduites par une femme qui marche à reculons. Les voix chantent: '*The lamb, the lamb, the bleeding lamb!* – L'Agneau, l'agneau, l'agneau qui saigne! ...' Les gens s'arrêtent et forment le cercle, autour d'un homme vêtu d'un uniforme presque militaire, et sur le collet duquel sont brodées en argent des S majuscules. Cet homme commence une sorte d'oraison jaculatoire; la tête se renverse, la bouche se tord, les yeux se révulsent. Il appelle 'le Seigneur! le Seigneur! ...' Une expression de désespoir ou d'extase se lit sur tous les visages. Une jeune fille, toute frêle et gracieuse, avec un chapeau fermé, pleure silencieusement. Elle parle à son tour. Puis les cuivres ronflent. Le cantique recommence et la troupe part ... C'est un bataillon de l'Armée du Salut qui vient de défiler devant moi. Il faut venir en Angleterre pour rencontrer de ces phénomènes de ferveur, qui attestent combien la sève religieuse est vivace encore dans le pays des puritains.

(1889, I, pp. 168–9)

[Suddenly a blast of trumpets bursts out, accompanied by strange singing. A hundred or so people appear, led by a woman walking backwards. The voices sing: '*The lamb, the lamb, the blood of the lamb!*' The people stop and form a circle around a man dressed in an almost military uniform, on the collar of which capital 'S's are embroidered in silver. This man begins a sort of yelled prayer; his head is thrown back, his mouth is twisted, his eyes are turned backwards in his head. He calls out 'the Lord! The Lord!...' An expression of despair or ecstasy can be seen upon every face. A young woman, delicate and graceful, with a closed bonnet, cries silently. She speaks in her turn. Then the brass instruments roar. The hymn begins again and the troop leave ... It's a battalion of the Salvation Army who have just processed in front of me. One has to come to England to see this phenomenon of fervour, showing just how much the religious sap still runs hardy in this puritan land.]

86   *Singing for salvation*

Note here the density of descriptors that privilege the mind's ear over the mind's eye and the constant return to music, which frames each ejaculatory outburst of preaching. Although we are given a rough mental visual image – vague figures in the processions, the military uniform of the man, his gestures, his congregation's expressions, and a young woman – the richness of the mental sound image is stronger still: we are given to hear trumpets, strange singing, chanted words, a shouted prayer, his precise cries to the Lord, the voice of the young woman, brass instruments, a hymn, and we are even told that we do *not* hear the silent tears of the young woman. Indeed, the fact that Bourget returns to a very similar passage eighty pages later leads the reader to wonder whether this musical procession has been circulating around London constantly in the intervening pages, retrospectively filling the book with a soundscape of the brassy notes of a religious marching band.[2]

Such repeated emphasis on the music and soundscape surrounding British evangelical groups indicates that this music is deemed significant in ways that go beyond its purely aesthetic qualities (or lack thereof) for French observers: it not only features in these travel texts as local colour, but the music seems to be experienced profoundly and personally, provoking a strength of response riven with horrified fascination, frustration, distress, even outrage. The causes and expression of this outrage are surprising for several reasons. First, because brass band music, played by amateur musicians, is treated here as musically as well as contextually exceptional but in fact it was far from unfamiliar to the French listener: Alan Baker sets out in detail the considerable prevalence of amateur musical societies across France from the 1860s onwards which frequently met in competitive *fanfare* or *harmonie* gatherings and performed in bandstands, parks, and squares (2007, Chapter 2, esp. p. 28); Pasler remarks that more than 80,000 Fr were dedicated to funding both amateur and military band performances at the 1878 World Fair (2009, p. 278); and far from being horrifying, these amateur bands were treated as offering the possibility of 'social solidarity, self-improvement, [...] escape from the banality of everyday life, [and] liberation from the prejudices commonly associated with the masses' (2009, p. 89).[3] Despite their aural similarity, none of this positivity or familiarity transfers over to influence French perceptions of religious community bands and music in Britain. Further, their outrage is all the more surprising because it does not seem to be caused by the fact that this music is being used in a religious context rather than a secular setting, as one might have expected; very few mainstream journalists remark upon the music as sacrilege, as a contravention of liturgical traditions or an insult to deeply held religious or ideological beliefs. Instead, the aural offensive of bass drums and trombones is seen as an oblique clue to deeper, murkier moral offences committed by France's perfidious neighbour.

Such a means of accusing the British of moral hypocrisy is a peculiar one. French Anglophobes could no doubt have found (or indeed fabricated) examples from the law courts or church councils about preachers being convicted for swindling, sexual abuse, or criminal intent – this would be clear

Singing for salvation 87

and unequivocal evidence of moral iniquity with which to condemn church and worshippers alike. However, instead the reader is invited to extrapolate heinous morality *obliquely*, by seeing it as a natural corollary of the heinous sounds of their music. Hector France, for example, places religious music as a signifier for moral hypocrisy in his nauseated description of English church-goers who 's'en va gravement, la Bible sous le bras, se sanctifier au prêche, à cette heure sacrée des hymnes en chœur et de l'hypocrisie en musique' ['go along gravely, Bible under arm, to get sanctified at a sermon at that holy hour of choral hymns and hypocrisy set to music'] (1883, p. 61). Elsewhere, he depicts the Salvation Army in London using music deliberately to drown out the noise of the suffering poor, about whom they merely claim to care so much: 'les sons d'un orgue portatif, unis aux voix des chanteurs d'hymnes, empêchaient les cris de la malheureuse d'être entendus' ['the sounds of a portative organ, together with the voices of the people singing hymns, blocked out the sound of the poor woman's cries'] (1886, p. 144). O'Rell makes the same connection between music and hypocrisy in still stronger terms, asserting that street preachers in Edinburgh are 'ou des hypocrites de la pire espèce ou des fanatiques de la plus belle eau. La monotonie de leurs chants, les lieux communs de leurs soi-disant sermons, la longueur de leurs figures de carême, les grimaces horribles qu'ils font en priant, tout cela est repoussant' ['either hypocrites of the worst sort or fanatics of the purest kind. The monotony of their songs, the commonplaces of their so-called sermons, the length of their miserable-as-sin faces, the horrible grimaces they make while praying, all of it is repulsive'] (1887, p. 126). After all, if the pure choral music of Catholic cathedrals reflects divinity through its musical exquisiteness, the brassy, circus-like music of 'ce Barnum évangélique' ['this evangelical Barnum'] (1887, p. 179), of this 'fracas de trombones [comme] une parade de cirque' ['din of trombones like a circus parade'] (Bovet, 1898, p. 143) surely crystallizes moral turpitude.

O'Rell's best-selling *Les Filles de John Bull* incorporates another more fantastical and lengthier iteration of this commonplace analogy between English bad character and Salvation Army music. In his clearly-fictional penultimate chapter – in a book that otherwise invites the reader to accept the veracity of its content on the basis that these are his first-hand experiences – he depicts a group of English women as they wait at the gates of Heaven for St Peter to allow them entry. This peculiar section of text, presented like a theatrical script, revolves around the arrival of a band of Salvationists at the pearly gates. Before the reader even knows who they are, their music bursts into the text: 'Un vacarme de trompettes, du tambours de basque, de cornets à piston, d'accordéons, une cacaphonie épouvantable venait de se faire entendre, et la foule inquiète des élus se précipitait vers la porte pour s'expliquer ces bruits étranges et si insolites dans le royaume de repos et de l'harmonie' ['a din of trumpets, tambourines, cornets, accordions, a terrible cacophony was heard, and the worried crowds of the chosen rushed to the gates to identify the source of these strange noises, so out of place in the kingdom of repose and

88   *Singing for salvation*

harmony']. The first identifiable human presence among this barrage of noise is 'une dame [...] brandissant son parapluie, gesticulant, vociférant, paraissant au comble de l'indignation' ['a lady brandishing her umbrella, gesticulating, vociferating, appearing to be in great high dudgeon'] – who, it transpires, is Mistress Bull, who also calls herself 'la Maréchale de l'Armée du Salut' ('Field Marshaless of the Salvation Army – 1884a, p. 290). In making the everyday English Mistress Bull fully synonymous with the Salvation Army, O'Rell merges the Salvation Army into all the priggish, self-interested stereotypes that had been daubed upon the brutish figure of John Bull and his wife since the eighteenth century. It rolls John Bull and the various accusations levelled at the Salvation Army into one powerful, resonant allegory that condemns the English for their religion, and the religion for its Englishness, and both for their dearth of refinement or aesthetic understanding. O'Rell takes advantage of the phonetic proximity between Mrs Bull and Mrs Booth to blend the former fictional character into the latter real one, allowing him to whitewash in one easy step all the genuinely useful social work carried out by Catherine Booth and many members of the organization. Instead, Mistress B. refuses to listen to St Peter, bragging instead of all the worthy roles she has fulfilled in her earthly life – all presented as degraded parodies of valorized masculine roles (leading the Army, running their newspaper, establishing colonial outposts around the world). When she introduces her – all-female – troupe, they identify themselves only by the instruments they play: Sallie is the drummer, Mary-Ann the cornet player, Betsy the singer, and Sukie the trombonist. St Peter chastises them for treating Heaven like a country fair or for taking a wrong turn on the way to Bedlam, and the ensuing argument is only finally quelled when the choir of seraphim pass by with 'une musique délicieuse [et] le son des harpes' ['a delicious music and the sound of harps'].

It is not merely that O'Rell describes these grossly caricatured Salvationists making noise with their musical instruments; rather, and moreover, the noise that they make is *all* that he tells us about them. The reader can tell that it is not their religious practice per se that O'Rell contests: first, because his St Peter is happy to admit Zooloos and Inca into Heaven if they have been good people, which was certainly not standard Catholic doctrine; and secondly because, after all, O'Rell is perfectly prepared to exploit the image of a farcical St Peter in a tin-pot Heaven to make his point. Rather, O'Rell uses the twin irritants of noise music and pushy women as anchoring points for his wider socio-cultural opinions about the English. Part of this is his condemnation of the increasing independence and social influence of women in England – O'Rell is certainly no feminist – and the Salvation Army with its female officers is simply the worst manifestation of this social ill.[4] However, this point could have been easily made without the insistence on music; he has after all, by this point, already made it several times in the preceding chapters of the *Filles de John Bull*. Rather, these references to noisy music are essential for the introduction of a key metaphor (and his reader may well suspect that all the apparently jovial sarcasm in this book had been building up this moment): that the

Singing for salvation 89

English are a nation of people who blow their own trumpets and beat their own drums. O'Rell has St Peter condemn 'celui qui a sonné la trompette, et qui s'en est allé dans les carrefours et les temples pour y brailler et y afficher sa vertu' ['the person who blows their trumpet and who goes to crossroads and temples to bellow and advertise their own virtue'] (1884a, p. 292). O'Rell writes the parable of the Salvation Army women and their noisy music: the French reader would do well both to refuse to join their ranks and to never reflect their example; French women would do well to maintain their elegant exclusion from masculine social roles; and everyone would do well to be circumspect in their dealings with the sect and the English nation as a whole.

This is, no doubt, a tidy analogization – noxious British evangelical music on the surface signifies noxious British moral habits below. However, when these travel narratives are read in conjunction with contemporaneous reports in the French press, the clear waters of this neat conceptualization are muddied. It was by no means unusual for a newspaper correspondent to send reports from Britain about antagonism or aggression by the wider British population in opposition to the Army's evangelical parades. For example, the reaction against the Salvation Army in Eastbourne in 1891 – indeed, the press reports on these protests are published in France in papers from across the breadth of the religious-ideological spectrum, underlining that there is much more than matters of faith at issue here. From May 1891, the Salvation Army took to the streets of this Victorian seaside resort town on Sundays with their brass bands, hymns, and public preaching. Complaints against this public nuisance, in spite of the gradual reduction of Sunday observance towards the end of the century, resulted in a ban on street music and the arrest of Salvation Army musicians during June of that year – not a ban on processions or preaching, it should be noted, but specifically an interdiction against the *music*. Naturally, the Salvationist bands continued their mission to save souls regardless of the ban, and consequently fines were levied and, in the case of non-payment, arrests were made. New musicians immediately emerged to take their places and the papers report that 'des scènes de désordre n'ont pas tardé à éclater' ['it was not long before scenes of disorder exploded'].[5] Indeed, so persistent was the English hostility against these musical nuisances that public protests against the Salvationists were still ongoing well into 1892. When one band progressed 'en processionnant à travers la ville, musique en tête,' rapidly 'une foule hostile de plusieurs milliers de personnes s'était portée sur le passage des salutistes. La police a dû interdire à la musique de jouer' ['processing through the town with their band before them' – 'a hostile crowd of several thousand people gathered in the path of the Salvationists. The police had to forbid the musicians from playing'] ('Dépêches télégraphiques: Angleterre,' 6 October 1891, p. 3). Even Church of England vicars (generally tarred by French commentators with the same brush of protestant hypocrisy) are acknowledged by O'Rell as joining the protest against the Salvationists for a combination of religious and musical reasons so tightly intertwined that they are inseparable: one vicar lambasts groups 'qui venaient brailler et gesticuler

90 *Singing for salvation*

jusque sous ses fenêtres et vociférer des chants blasphématoires, accompagnés de trombones, de cornets à piston, d'accordéons, de grosses caisses et de tambours' ['who came to bawl and gesticulate right under his windows, vociferating blasphemous songs accompanied by trombones, cornets, accordions, drums, and bass drums'] (1884a, p. 258). These accounts present the Salvation Army as a group strongly opposed by other sections of the British population; they are far from a simple hyperbolization of the wider feelings of the nation – and this indicates that the somewhat simple analogy foregrounded by French texts about British life requires deeper exploration.

Indeed, there is a further problematization of the neat parallelism between heinous music and heinous British moral character to be found lingering within these texts. We see this in the French visitors' persistent depictions of evangelical musicians and their audiences as uncanny. Rather than being roundly condemned and summarily dismissed, there remains something more subconsciously unsettling that gravitates around the performance of this music, and that lingers on after the moral condemnation has been administered. In Kirkwall, for example, writer and architect Félix Narjoux describes two female evangelists who sing a hymn or psalm whilst the crowd of passers-by listens in an eerie silence, and 'on ne les assaille ni de railleries, ni de quolibets' ['nobody assails them with mockery or jeers'] (1886, p. 169). These unmoving figures are unnervingly calm. On other occasions, it is the Salvationists who are uncanny: when Hector France comes across a crowd in a poor district of London bombarding Salvationist singers and musicians with stones and detritus, 'l'hymne joyeuse continua avec accompagnement des fifres et des tambours' ['the joyous hymn continued with its accompaniment of pipes and drums']; they show no awareness of and make no emotional response to their surroundings. They not only keep singing, but do so joyously, and in both sound and motion they present the French viewer with a definite impression of strangeness (1883, p. 144). They seem to reside in the uncanny valley, a locus where, as cyber-psychologist Angela Tinwell has noted, 'any deviations from the human norm in sound and motion will alert the viewer to a sense of strangeness in that character'; this is attributed to the absence of detectable empathy because 'being human is characterized by the ability to understand the cognitive and emotive processes of others' (2015, pp. 29, 100). Though human in form, the British reactions to evangelical street music and preaching are often antithetical to the reactions expected of them by the French observer. Within British culture and with a greater grasp of the context these reactions may make perfect sense – for example, taking local conventions of politeness or a belief in religious liberties into account in the first instance, or taking phlegmatism, bodily self-control, and deep religious convictions into account in the latter. Yet these reactions are so unlike those the French visitor expects that they provoke a feeling of lingering disquiet, auguring that more complex undercurrents are at work. British evangelical street music clearly leaves its mark on the French psyche, and this is underlined by taking into account that – although, strikingly, none of these

Singing for salvation 91

travel accounts mention the fact – from 1881 the Salvation Army was also present, brass bands and all, on the streets of France.

Religious brainwashing?

It is not the aim of this chapter to provide a detailed history of the Salvation Army in France, but it will be useful to set out some of the principal milestones of the organization's installation and growth on French soil before delving further into the acoustic antagonism that it provoked. Catherine Booth, daughter of the founder William Booth, began to establish the Salvation Army in France at the request of a small group of French Protestants and, with the help of Adélaide Cox and Florence Soper, she set up the first mission house in Paris in February 1881. Far from being a niche community as one might imagine in this nation already torn between traditional, nationalistic Catholicism, secularist Republicanism, and many shades in between, instead the Salvation Army became the subject of considerable attention: for some, the church appealed as a mode of worship, a centre of charitable works, and a source of strong community feeling in an alienating modern world; for others, it was an aesthetic travesty, a sign of English politico-cultural invasion, a religious heresy, or an unwanted additional complication in an already complex socio-religious environment.

Interestingly, in newspapers from across the ideological spectrum, the Salvation Army became the subject of persistent and sustained media attention throughout the last two decades of the nineteenth century; regardless of their wider standpoint on faith or politics, reports about the Salvation Army feature regularly in papers as diverse as *L'Aurore*, *Le Figaro*, *Le Gaulois*, *Le XIXe Siècle*, *Le Petit Parisien*, *Le Rappel*, *Le Radical*, *L'Univers*, and *La Croix*, as well as numerous regional newspapers, and they appear much more regularly than one might imagine for a newly-introduced religious community. From about 1883 onwards, the press regularly tracks the Salvation Army's movements around Europe; for example, when the organization was banned in Bern, when Catherine Booth was arrested in Switzerland in 1883, throughout the violence in towns such as Geneva, Bern, and Neuchâtel from 1883–7, and when the Booth-Clibborns were expelled from the country in 1892. They even follow the progression of the Salvation Army in far-flung reaches of the globe; editors believe that the French readership will be interested to know that Argentina, for example, banned the organization in 1891 on the grounds that it was an unofficial religion ('Dépêches télégraphiques,' 6 April 1891, n.p.).[6] Moreover, the Salvation Army features not only in articles detailing socio-political events, but it even features in the gossip columns of major French newspapers. They recount the engagement, wedding ceremony, and honeymoon of Catherine Booth and Arthur Clibborn (Dejuinne, 1886, n.p.; 'Faits divers,' 27 January 1887, n.p.; Gérôme, 1887, p. 131); they report that Catherine Booth launched a cigarette-free September campaign among members to raise funds in 1886 (Brichanteau, 1886, n.p.; Blum, 1886, n.p.);

92 *Singing for salvation*

and they even comment upon the re-styling of the regulation Salvationist uniform bonnet in September 1894 ('Échos et Nouvelles,' 1894, n.p.; O'Monroy, 1894, p. 563). In brief, the press shows a preoccupation with the Salvation Army that seems incongruous with their professed distaste for the organization, and this augments rather than diminishes the presence of the movement in the contemporary French psyche.

Concurrently, the Salvation Army was also winning over worshippers from among the French population, and while conversions did not pour in with the same elan as in Britain, the numbers no less steadily accumulated. While no French newspaper shows particular delight at this – the best that can be expected is neutrality or a wry smile – even if their endgame is to express concern the prevalence of their articles no less draws attention to the organization's upward trajectory. In April 1888, the *Petit Parisien* reported that 1887 was a successful year for the Salvation Army in France, having established footholds in sixteen new départements, created forty-six new 'posts,' and enrolled five hundred new male and female cadets and ninety-five missionaries. The organization's newspaper *En avant* had sold 720,000 copies – that is, the *Petit Parisien* specifies, an impressive 17,000 per week – as well as selling 112,000 pamphlets. Still more surprising, given the remarks already noted about the frightful impression made on French visitors to Britain by Salvationist music, 80,000 song books had been sold that year in France alone ('L'Armée du Salut,' 1888, n.p.). The *XIXe Siècle* remarked upon the establishment of major depots for charity and worship in Nîmes, Saint-Jean-du-Gard, Villeneuve, and twenty or so other towns in the Midi – particularly, but not exclusively, in areas with already notable Protestant communities ('La Presse au jour le jour,' 1887). By October 1889, the *Figaro* extended this list of successes, mentioning centres in Lyon, Marseille, Bordeaux, Dunkerque, and Valence, with a total of seventy-seven established posts and outposts, as well as, perhaps most unexpectedly, three successful centres in Paris on the Quai Valmy, in the old Folies theatre on the Rue de Belleville, and the hall on the Rue Auber, all of which, the journalist reports, 'surtout le dimanche, ne désemplissent pas' ['are never empty, especially on Sundays'] (Chincholle, 1889, p. 2).

By the end of 1892, the tally of Salvationists in Paris was over four thousand, giving it the status of the second-largest religious group in the capital city after the Catholic Church, and the national sales of *En avant* had risen still further to surpass the 800,000 threshold ('Les Religions à Paris, 1893, n.p.). Typically, French newspapers surround their reports on these statistics with sarcastic remarks or more or less belittling comments about the organization, its music, and its leadership – but this disdain was not enough to eclipse the fact that a growing number of French citizens were being drawn to this expanding movement. When considered in the context of the movement's progress on French soil, the travel writers' accounts of Salvation Army music in Britain appear in a new light and can no longer be contemplated in isolation as a purely foreign peculiarity. Depictions of the organization may

Singing for salvation 93

now be seen to have significantly deeper implications for both French writer and French reader. The journalist Augustin Léger may level an accusation of naivety at the Booth biographer who had remarked that 'avec leur facilité d'émotion, leur instinct de l'effet artistique, leur amour des parades militaires, leur passion pour la musique et leur humeur impressionnable, on aurait pu s'attendre à ce que les Français accueillissent bien une religion qui faisait appel à toutes ces qualités' ['with their emotional nature, their instinct for artistic effects, their love of military parades, their passion for music, and their impressionable spirit, one could have expected that the French would welcome a religion which appealed to all of these qualities'] (1901, p. 465) – but perhaps this was not so naïve after all, given that it is precisely those French susceptibilities to which the movement did successfully appeal in the 1880s on a scale significant enough to be both surprising and concerning to many.

To some extent, objections to the Salvation Army in France arise from a question of fairness; several newspapers from diverse ideological standpoints remonstrate that since Catholic processions are banned in the streets of Paris, it is unjust to extend this freedom to the Salvation Army – particularly taking into account the obtrusiveness of their noisy brass bands – and they call for consistency from the government (Jean de Paris, 1888, p. 2; Jean de Paris, 1891, p. 2; 'Bigoterie,' 1888, n.p.; 'Chronique,' 1892, n.p.). However, the dominant means of objecting to the Salvation Army and its music is in terms of the contemporaneous language of psychology.[7] Unlike when French writers observe the organization in England, there is no assumption in these texts that insidious moral hypocrisy is the root cause of the powerful attraction of its music and the gradually growing appeal of the Salvation Army *in France*; whilst such writers generally consider Salvationist music to be a clear signifier of moral hypocrisy in England, there is never the slightest suggestion that the same signification applies to music-making by French Salvationists. Instead, concepts of madness and psychological manipulation are implemented to explain the inroads being made by the Salvation Army on French shores – and concerns about the enervating, sinister influence of their music form the central axis of these critiques.

The lexicon of insanity runs like a refrain through newspaper articles on the movement's presence in France and is intertwined with references to Salvationist music. Here, it takes two forms. First, in texts both about the movement in England and in France, the language of madness is implemented to degrade the members of the religious movement by diagnosing them as maniacs. Marie-Anne de Bovet witnesses singers in Scotland who, 'pour activer le chant, [...] frappent dans leurs mains en cadence [...] et peu à peu cela provoque, chez eux au moins, une véritable danse de Saint-Guy' ['to stimulate the singing, clap their hands in time; and little by little, among themselves at least, this provokes a veritable St. Vitus's dance'] (1898, p. 238). Félicien Champsaur, a correspondent for the *Figaro* reporting from a Salvationist meeting on Guernsey, writes that he has witnessed a trombonist '[qui] se tord dans des convulsions épileptiques' and the journalist asks himself 'suis-je à

94 *Singing for salvation*

Charenton, avec les fous furieux dans la septième section? [...] Ce sont des figures hagardes, prunelles dilatées, lèvres tremblantes d'énervement, des extases, des cris' ['who contorts himself in epileptic convulsions' – 'am I at the Charenton asylum, with the raving lunatics of the seventh section? There are haggard faces, pupils dilated, lips trembling with agitation, they go into ecstasies, they scream'] (1885, p. 2). He projects any apparent religious fervour away from being interpreted as a spiritual leap of faith made by a rational mind, and instead imprisons it within a familiar medicalized discourse – religious fervour here is a madness manifested in insane music and the uncontrolled body. Even in a comic context, such as in the parodic journal *En arrière* produced by the students of Paris for their 1893 Mi-Carême cavalcade, there is an assumption that most Parisians would be familiar with the sight and sounds of Salvationist women in the streets, and that everyone could agree that they appear insane. The opening paragraph describes them as 'de vraies vierges vraiment folles, aussi pures de chair que détraquées d'esprit' ['real virgins who are really mad, as pure in the flesh as they are crazy in the mind'] (Général Boum-Boum, 1893, p. 1).

At first glance, these descriptions read as largely metaphorical, and the use of psychological vocabulary seems primarily to prescribe the writer's perceived boundaries of cultural appropriateness as much as to imply that sanity genuinely is at stake from a medical point of view.[8] However, more seriously – and this time uniquely in articles discussing the Salvation Army on the French side of the Channel – there appear to be growing suspicions that Salvationist music may *literally* manipulate or cause serious damage to the psychological stability of French listeners. The *Petit Parisien* warns, specifically, that their music may be injurious to people who, otherwise, would be left unmoved by printed propaganda or street preaching. Jean Frollo wrote in 1883, just as the numbers of adherents were increasing that,

> avec le temps, le système musical énervant usité dans les réunions de l'armée, avec la tentation [...] de chanter des airs interminables, il se peut très bien que des cas de folie du sacrifice, de monomanie religieuse, se déclarent assez fréquemment chez les jeunes filles de Paris et les amènent à quitter famille et patrie
>
> ['over time the system of enervating music used at the Army's meetings, with the temptation to sing interminable songs, may well cause frequent cases of self-sacrificial madness and of religious monomania in the young women of Paris, leading them to abandon their families and nation']
>
> (1883, n.p.)

Without its music, Frollo contends, the Salvation Army's potential for influence would be negligible, but these musical experiences are powerful

Singing for salvation   95

weapons capable of drawing women in against their volition and driving them to hysteria:

> Les yeux de ces fillettes, à la fin des chants, après avoir eu le système nerveux ébranlé pendant une heure par une grosse caisse, un piano, un triangle (joué par une dame!), un violon, un ophicléide, les yeux de tous ces innocents curieux, dis-je, étaient follement allumés, et je ne doute pas que [...] l'extase hystérique ne soit le résultat inhumain des exercices pieux de l'Armée du Salut.

> [The eyes of these girls at the end of the songs, after having had their nervous systems shaken up for an hour by a bass drum, a piano, a triangle (played by a lady!), a violin, an ophicleide – the eyes of all these curious innocents, I declare, were lit up crazily, and I have no doubt that hysterical ecstasy will be the inhumane result of the pious exercises of the Salvation Army.]

He concludes, leaving no room for doubt, that:

> Je regarde comme très-dangereux le spectacle bruyant et comique des Salutistes, par la continuité de l'action perturbante qu'il exerce sur le frêle organisme naissant des enfants et des jeunes filles qu'attire d'abord la curiosité, puis que ramène et retient le plaisir de chanter, de chanter sans cesse et toujours.
>
> (1883, n.p.)

> [I regard the noisy and comical spectacle of the Salvationists as highly dangerous, in its continued perturbation of the fragile developing organisms of children and young women, who are first attracted out of curiosity, then drawn back and captured by the pleasure of constantly and ceaselessly singing.]

Here, the English officers of the Salvation Army are not being diagnosed as insane in themselves, but, far more worryingly, as the entirely sane master manipulators of fragile French psyches.

There is no quarter given by Frollo for this being desirable to young women as a space of feminine freedom. He makes no allowance for the possibility it might offer independence and a sense of purpose beyond hearth and home, and that group music-making might provide a sense of community and self-expression (even when playing instruments not prescribed by bourgeois ideals of ladylike grace and accomplishment, such as the rather trivial triangle in the above passage). Instead, unequivocally, he depicts the Army officers as scheming wrongdoers who use music as a means of driving innocent young French girls to madness for their own malevolent purposes – the precise, no-doubt horrific details of which we are left to imagine for ourselves. In the

96 *Singing for salvation*

Intransigeant newspaper, too, though generally more neutral than the *XIXe Siècle* on the organization from a religious perspective, the reader is no less warned about the hysterical frenzy that may be whipped up by the Salvation Army's music, '[qui] exerce une influence pernicieuse sur les cerveaux mal équilibrés, qu'elle accomplit une œuvre mauvaise et trouble l'ordre public' ['exercises a pernicious influence on unbalanced minds, and its actions are harmful and disruptive to the public order'] (Dubois, 1890, p. 2). It is particularly interesting to note that the reception in the press is depicted with equal suspicion, even hostility, in areas of France with significant Protestant populations: the *Lyon-Revue* tellingly observes that 'les salutistes sont une branche du protestantisme [...] et n'ont pas de pires ennemis que leurs anciens coreligionnaires' ['the Salvation Army is a branch of Protestantism and has no worse enemy than their former co-believers'] (Félix Desvernay, 1886, p. 190).[9] Nonetheless, ten years later, a report in the *XIXe Siècle* on the religions of Paris suggests that this 'système musical énervant' had seen considerable success, as 'le premier [culte à Paris] par le chiffre de ses adhérents, par sa tapageuse réclame, est l'*Armée du Salut*, qui, quoi qu'on dise et quoi qu'on rie, à coups de cornet à piston, a obtenu même chez nous des résultats surprenants' ['the largest religious group in Paris by number of adherents, and by the noise of its publicity, is the Salvation Army, who, whatever people say and however much people laugh, has made surprising inroads even in France with each blast of its brass instruments'] ('Les Religions à Paris,' 1893, n.p.).

Psychologists and musicologists in recent years have dedicated considerable attention to understanding the manifold ways in which music can influence and control the mind. For example, Maja Djikic's psychology studies have demonstrated that music has a marked impact upon our short-term perception of our own identities (2011, pp. 237–40), and work by Jonathan Pieslak (2010, pp. 1–11) and Bruce Johnson (2002, pp. 27–39) has explored music's ability to provoke psychological breakdowns when it manifests as a social nuisance (the neighbour playing loud music at all hours of the night) or when it is used as an instrument of torture (as American soldiers were believed to do at Guantanamo Bay). James Kennaway remarks that musical ecstasy, whilst potentially exhilarating, 'can also be very disturbing, raising complex questions about the porous boundaries of the self and the ability of others to manipulate it' (2011, pp. 271–89). Indeed, it is not only recent scholarship that has taken an interest in the psychological influences of music: Charcot famously used tuning forks and gongs in his studies of hypnosis and hysteria at the Salpêtrière, and Mesmer used pianos, violins, harps, and the glass armonica in his work.

All of these analyses agree that it is not principally the mind of the performer but the mind of the listener – or worse, the unwilling hearer – that may be altered and manipulated by the power of musical sounds. This is not just when sound takes the pure form of Mesmer or Charcot's vibrating tuning forks or gongs; it is a quality that it was believed could be harnessed within

Singing for salvation 97

a musical composition. At the same time as the Salvation Army bands were marching in the streets of Paris, the physician and cultural critic Max Nordau warned that Wagner's music, for example,

> was certainly of a nature to fascinate the hysterical. Its powerful orchestral effects produced in them hypnotic states (at the Salpêtrière hospital in Paris the hypnotic state is often induced by suddenly striking a gong), and the formlessness of the unending melody was exactly suited to the dreamy vagaries of their own thought.
>
> (1895, pp. 210–11)

This is no mere metaphorical connection: music is seen as capable of *literally* driving the individual listener to hysterical madness and a loss of self. Perhaps, then, hypnosis, hysteria, or madness could provide a logical reason why citizens of the nation of artistic taste par excellence were drawn to what seemed, from every aesthetic perspective, to be abhorrent. The ethnomusicologist Bruno Nettl has observed the universality of the human propensity to move the body spontaneously to music (2000, pp. 463–72); can we divine the French bystanders trying hard not to let the march rhythms of the Army's brass bands control and regiment the pace of their steps as they walk alongside them down the boulevard, resisting the first signs of a loss of self? Little wonder that French commentators on the Salvation Army in Britain and France alike manifests signs of hostility and anxiety that go well beyond any objections to liturgical practices when confronted with the strange sonic and psychological experience of this evangelical music.

Behind these fears that English manipulators might brainwash innocent French victims into their seemingly cultic religious community, a deeper concern also lingers: that in fact, the seeds of this madness lurked in the French psyche itself all along, just waiting to be activated by their music. This comes to light in medical texts diagnosing different kinds of religion-related insanity. Jean-Marie Dupain's overview of these psychological conditions in his *Étude clinique sur le délire religieux* (1888) summarizes the nineteenth-century corpus of medical analyses on religious madness, and he details trigger factors, symptoms, and the progression of mental conditions in his series of case-studies. For one subject, a French husband and father, signs of increasingly ardent evangelism are treated as a symptom of mania; although he does join the Salvation Army as an *En avant* subscription seller, it is significant to note that the Salvationists did not *drive* him to madness – he was already in the full throes of insanity before becoming a member, and his Army membership is merely one of the later symptoms (1888, pp. 89–91). Similarly, a young female simpleton is already said to be in a state of imbecility before she starts attending Salvation Army meetings; these just aggravate and give a particularly puritanical manifestation to her folly (1888, p. 193). A male sufferer struck with what would probably be diagnosed today as bipolar disorder, takes periodically to singing endless religious songs in his cell with ecstatic expressions

98 *Singing for salvation*

of exaltation – and in this case, strikingly, there is no suggestion that he has had any contact at all with the Salvation Army (1888, pp. 134–5). It is clear, Dupain concludes, that religious delirium is never the root of the problem, but always a symptom of a deeper, pre-existing psychological problem.

This medical revelation brings with it problematic implications for those journalists remonstrating that the Salvation Army's sonic presence in the streets of France is a profound threat to the French psyche in itself. Such understanding of religious delirium by contemporaneous psychological experts means that the French psyche must *already* have been flawed, damaged by one of the various conditions Dupain lists as leading to religious madness, such as intoxication, masturbation, hysteria, epilepsy, genetic degeneration, depression, or heredity. It is not a contagion caught through the ear from the British – that could thus be purged, cured, or avoided – but a sign that the fin-de-siècle French psyche was itself already sick.

Concerns about the possible degeneration of the French race sit uncomfortably just below the surface here: the music of the Salvation Army is just one trigger for a ticking psychological time-bomb. This is felt all the more keenly because worries about the same conditions were being raised in other contexts at the same time, notably in debates on the state of France in the wake of the Franco-Prussian War. After all, France is not devoid of similar home-grown religious or spiritual movements filled with enervating music and that incite passionate, even hysterical behaviours with cultic qualities that disrupt socio-cultural norms. For example, Henry Fouquier notes in the *XIXe Siècle* that the Salvationists are hardly original, but that they are in fact merely copying the musical practices of the French Saint-Simoniens who, in 1832, 'eux aussi, chantaient des cantiques, revêtus de costumes bizarres, et attiraient la foule à leurs musiques' ['they too sang hymns, dressed in bizarre outfits, and drew a crowd to their music'] (1888, n.p.). This curiously-placed jingoistic cry of national precedence seems to claim that the willed manipulation of religious feeling through music is in fact a skill more French than English. The same conclusion arises again, though with less satisfaction, in descriptions of the worshipping practices of the pilgrims at Lourdes. In an article by Fouquier on the fanaticisms of the 1880s in France, he even compares the Salvation Army favourably to the paganistic, decadent, sickening, and saddening prestidigitation around the pilgrimage site (1883, n.p.). In Zola's description of the annual Lourdes pilgrimage – based on his real experience of the journey, though naturally embellished for literary purposes – the whole sojourn at the shrine is framed by fervent hymn singing on the train both en route and on the return to Paris, and it is this incessant, repetitious singing and loud hailing of Mary that is posited as bringing about the heightened, hysterical state needed to effectuate the 'miracles' (1894, Part I, Chapter 1; Part III, Chapter 3; Part V, Chapter 5).

Yet in spite of these medical discourses, when most journalists and commentators discuss the Salvation Army's presence in France they *continue* to insist that the Salvation Army is a contagion brought by the English to

Singing for salvation 99

France and that is likely to hypnotize the innocent French listener through the ear. However, an overview of these reports suggests that it is not primarily a *religious* brainwashing that was feared as a consequence of this hypnotism – rather, there are two key aspects that caused concern, each of which I will now treat in turn: first, a question of cultural invasion, and secondly, one of political influence.

Salvation Army – invading France?

It is telling that across the spectrum of newspapers and travel guides, whatever their wider political affiliations, all repeatedly insist on the inherent *Englishness* of the Salvation Army and its music. The singers, for the *XIXe Siècle* reporter Paul Ginisty, are all 'maigres misses encapuchonnées' ['skinny, capped young misses'] – not 'femmes' or 'filles' or 'demoiselles' or 'dames,' but always *misses* to insist upon the foreignness of the organization and evoke those stereotypes of skinny English plainness (1890, n.p.). When a *Petit Parisien* article dedicates its four leading, front-page columns in 1883 to describing this relatively new, invading force with its 'système musicale énervant' ['enervating musical system'], it refers repeatedly to 'cette secte anglaise' ['this English sect'] (Frollo, 1883, n.p.). The journalist Georges Daniel from *Le Matin*, in an unusually sympathetic article on the Salvation Army, no less opens with the overarching statement that the Salvationist to the French mind, regardless of his actual nationality, 'a une religion à part, dans laquelle la musique joue un grand rôle, et, de plus, il est toujours Anglais' ['a special religion, in which music plays a large part and which, moreover, is always English'] (1900, pp. 1–2). Furthermore, in the case of a grievous physical assault on two un-named Salvation Army members in the street in 1885, the three adolescent assailants, when asked why they attacked the men, gave 'C'est des Anglais' ['they were Englishmen'] as their whole explanation (Jean de Paris, 1886, p. 2). Even as late as 1902, by which point there were thousands of French adherents, the Salvation Army is depicted as a cornerstone of English national character in the music-hall revue *Miss! Miss!* at the Théâtre Marigny, in which a song-and-dance 'salutiste' act features alongside bridges over the Thames, lights in the fog, policemen, and clowns in a series of 'scènes typiques de la vie anglaise' ['typical scenes of English life'] (reviewed in 'Spectacles divers,' 1902, p. 5). Throughout this period, stereotypes persist that England is both the 'pays de la Bible par excellence' ['the country par excellence of the Bible'] (Finot, 1903, p. 2), and a land deprived of musical taste – thus it is hardly surprising that the stereotype of inherent Englishness persists around the Salvation Army. Even when newspaper reports mention Salvationists with such evidently French names as Armand Liotard and Eugène Barbier, the overall notion of the Englishness of the movement endures (these young men are reported as the victims of a stoning on the Rue d'Allemagne, in 'Paris: une brute,' 1887, n.p.). Rather than being dismissed as a relatively small religious movement, the strangeness of the Salvation Army leads writers to present it

100 *Singing for salvation*

as a metonym for everything that is wrong – and threatening – in their eyes about Englishness for the French. Indeed, the Salvation Army first appears in France at a moment when the race for colonial dominance was heightening, when many were eager for a means of asserting superiority over England directly and a means of asserting superiority over the Germanic races (in the wake of the Franco-Prussian defeat) more indirectly. Conveniently, the Salvation Army's lowbrow musical aesthetics, its unattractive uniforms, its Protestant religious convictions and earnestness, and its pseudo-military symbolism all provide scope to harness multiple areas of French anxiety around one, convenient bête noire.

In this context, the possibility that the Salvation Army might use its music to hypnotize and brainwash the French crowd becomes a question not merely of a religious brainwashing, but of an attack on French cultural and national identity. Gustave le Bon had, after all, asserted in his *Psychologie des foules* [*The Crowd: a Study of the Popular Mind*] that from the influences upon the individual in the *foule* 'résultent certains caractères psychologiques nouveaux qui se superposent aux caractères de race, et qui parfois en diffèrent profondément' ['certain new psychological characteristics result which superimpose themselves over racial character, and sometimes differ from it considerably'] (1895, p. i). Le Bon may claim that a 'foule latine' and 'foule anglo-saxonne' are strikingly different, but if the 'caractères psychologiques nouveaux' being acquired are ones of Englishness through the 'affirmation, répétition et contagion' of music, then this distinction between the Latin and Anglo-Saxon is dissolved (1895, pp. 27, 116). The movement's proselytization puts at risk the very Frenchness of its potential converts; if they adopt Salvationist modes of worship, evangelism, dress, and community, they inevitably become *misses* themselves and become, as Daniel's article stated, 'toujours Anglais.' They must replace their French musical, linguistic, and corporeal behaviours with antithetical English equivalents. For those in the ruling classes – who presume that they are themselves immune to such manipulation – this raises the spectre that the lower orders, women, and children might be led to lose their attachment to their own French cultural identity in favour of that of their rival. Those transient bouts of anglophilia that had periodically come into vogue since at least the eighteenth century might finally, through an underhand manipulation of the subconscious mind, make deeper and more permanent inroads into France through the influence of mesmeric, maddening music. As a consequence, journalists and travel writers appear to make concerted efforts to underline the foreignness of the Salvation Army and to paint them in as unappealing a light as possible at every opportunity.

Henri Bellenger is emphatic that the appeal of evangelical religion is necessarily incomprehensible for a French person. He does not simply state that he, personally, does not take to it, but instead extrapolates wildly that this antipathy is a characteristic of the French race as a whole; the French mind, he states categorically, is wired in such a way that it is constitutionally incapable

Singing for salvation   101

of understanding the appeal of their endless hymns (1877, p. 177). He asserts that there are aesthetic, spiritual, temperamental, and ethnic barriers rendering it inconceivable that a French individual could grasp the why and wherefore of Salvationist worship, let alone be won over by its infectious music. Similarly, Paul Ginisty insists on the absolute disconnect between English and French nature. Given that the combination of music and evangelical expression of faith is so antithetical to what he considers to be 'Frenchness,' Ginisty asserts – with daring disregard for statistical realities – that the organization 'n'a jamais réussi à Paris' and that it remains exclusively 'une puissance en Angleterre' ['has never succeeded in Paris' – 'a power in England'] (1890, n.p).

In such textual assertions of national identity and culture as these, references to the Salvation Army's music form an obsessive refrain. As Theodore Gracyk observes in his analysis of popular music more widely, the actual sound of the music ceases to be the crux of the issue. For these commentators, 'the value of music has little or nothing to do with listening. Its value is the platform it offers for evaluating the tastes and social standing of other listeners' (2010, p. 29). Anyone who enjoys this music or in whom it strikes a profound chord is evaluated as not having the essential characteristics of Frenchness; thus, theoretically, the instinctive response by an individual to the aural shock of a Salvation Army band should be a clear and simple litmus test for national identity. This implies that 'Englishness' is used as a rather sinister weapon beyond its normal role as France's foreign opposite alter ego. In an insidious reprise of the Revocation of the Edict of Nantes, the journalist André Balz states that 'la vertu rèche, huguenote, [...] est insupportable à notre caractère national, avant tout de bonne humeur et de franche gaité' ['dry, Huguenot virtue is intolerable to our national character, above all characterized by good humour and honest gaiety']. He asserts confidently and that the 'ligue néo-salutiste' ['neo-Salvationist league'] cannot possibly gain any ground in France (1893, n.p.). Ginisty asserts that it is only 'les mœurs protestants [qui] s'accommodent de ces prédications, des ces espèces de représentations [...] dont les sons d'un harmonium soulignent les cris de contrition' ['protestant customs that can tolerate this preaching, these kinds of show in which the strains of a harmonium underline the screams of contrition'] (1890, n.p.). Both journalists imply that, if it is impossible to be both French and to feel the draw of the Army's music at the same time, then France's long-standing Protestant communities cannot be seen as truly French either, much as the anti-Semitism surrounding the Dreyfus Affair would question the Frenchness of the Franco-Jewish community. It appears, then, that such writers as these attempt to use criticism of the Salvation Army's noxious music – on the surface an apparently harmless, aesthetic criticism – to spread wider suspicion about both the English and the Protestants within France. They imply that, no matter how much the members manifest French cultural identity in terms of dress, language, literature, customs, food, and even birthplace and citizenship, one day their Germanic character and/or blood will out.

102   *Singing for salvation*

Ironically, had these commentators removed music from their critiques and focused on liturgical aspects, their arguments that the average French person would not be drawn to the movement would have held somewhat more weight; though membership of the Salvation Army did steadily rise throughout the fin-de-siècle period, it never swept vast swathes of the population off their feet like the century's numerous revolutionary movements had done. Even among the French Protestant population, by no means everybody gave up their more reserved, long-held worshipping practices to join this new church. Yet the repeated emphasis on a positive response *to their music* being the indicator of non-Frenchness is distinctly problematic. The average Pierre and Marie Dupont might be comparatively unlikely to convert to a religious movement for reasons of faith or worshipping practices during the fin de siècle, but numerous forms of musical culture testify to the fact that the French were *not* constitutionally unfitted to throw their 'raison' to the wind and to respond passionately to affective, 'lowbrow' music: the crowds responded emotionally to French military band processions;[10] to persuasive political songs (as was seen in myriad songs emerging from the meteoric popularity of Boulanger);[11] to songs from cafés-concerts and bals musettes (inspiring celebrity worship of stars such as Aristide Bruant, Thérésa, Yvette Guilbert, and Dranem); and, indeed, to the fads for music-hall songs imported from England itself.

Some writers go still further and make direct accusations that the Salvation Army are waging an underhand political war on the stability of the French state. Rumours circulated in August 1885 that Catherine Booth intended to stand for election in France (for example, in 'Choses et gens,' 1885, p. 3), or that she had made a deal with Freycinet's government to have all French Salvationists vote for his party in the Ardèche to sway his majority in exchange for being left in peace to proselytize (Dejuinne, 1886, n.p.). Hector France claims that William Booth consciously employed music to manipulate the populace – 'il faut du bruit à la masse' ['the masses need noise'] – and that he did so with a regimented and psychologizing intentionality redolent of mass political movements (1900, p. 112). Whatever Booth's intentions, the movement's use of 'bruit à la masse' does demonstrate that music can be used to sway the masses through crowd psychology. The psychologist Gabriel Tarde could almost have been writing specifically about Salvation Army processions when he remarked on the *foule*'s attraction to highly expressive symbolism, asserting that they are drawn to 'ces symboles toujours les mêmes et répétés à satiété. Promener en procession des bannières et des drapeaux, [...] faire entendre des vivats ou des vociférations, des cantiques ou des chansons' ['these symbols, that are always the same and repeated until you can take no more. Walking in a procession with banners and flags and crying out vivats and vociferations, hymns or songs'] (1901, p. 42). Contrary to the assertions by journalists that the French are inherently insensible to emotive, mass musical spectacles, crowd psychology indicates no reason why this should not be as effective a means of influencing the populace in France as in Britain.

Singing for salvation 103

Indeed, according to Le Bon's theories, these processions and songs are even more likely to affect the French population because the Latin crowd demonstrates a marked volatility that is generally lacking from the Anglo-Saxon temperament: if all crowds show a tendency towards 'l'impulsivité, l'irritabilité, l'incapacité de raisonner, l'absence de jugement et d'esprit critique' ['impulsiveness, irritability, incapacity to reason, absence of judgment and critical spirit'], it is in the latinate masses that 'l'autoritisme et l'intolérance sont développés à un haut degré' ['authoritarianism and intolerance are developed to a high level'] (1895, p. 24). In the fifteen-year period following the Salvation Army's arrival in France in 1881, I have found reports of fifteen separate grievous physical assaults, including beatings, near-fatal lapidation, stabbings, and shootings, and further reports that refer to violence against the Salvationists in such a general and flippant way that they imply these acts were so commonplace that there was no need to explain the details to the reader.[12] In this era defined by anti-Semitism and the Dreyfus Affair on the one hand, and secularization and anti-clericalism on the other, it is perhaps understandable that persecution of the Salvation Army has been overlooked by scholarship and somewhat lost in historical memory, but there are two key issues to highlight here. First, this street violence was largely perpetrated by the working and lower-middle classes against Army members, and this suggests that it is not only the elites who felt troubled by issues of national and cultural identity when faced with this English invasion. Rather, in these acts of violence against the Salvation Army, the lower classes manifest their own concerns about this influx of foreign immigrants who make no attempt to adopt local customs and who openly criticize French social and religious morals – this is a story as old as humanity itself. Secondly though, and more surprisingly, we find that when newspapers *represent* this violence, they do not simply report that an assault took place and blood was spilled: instead, numerous articles from across the political spectrum lay emphasis on the presence of Salvation Army music at the same time as recording the assault – they imply more or less directly that the movement's sonic aggression both catalyses and justifies the outbursts of physical aggression that follow.

Paul Ginisty, on the occasion of some street violence against the Salvation Army in Paris, chooses to tell the readers of his column that the organization's music and theatricality are visible signs of their hidden nefarious intentions – after all, 'nous n'avons vu, à Paris, que les côtés visibles de l'Armée du Salut […] avec ses moyens de théâtre et son extraordinaire musique. Mais qui sait si on ne s'apercevra pas, dans un temps donné, que […] un plan arrêté de longue date a été opiniâtrement suivi?' ['we have only seen the visible side of the Salvation Army, with its theatricality and extraordinary music. But who knows if, after a certain amount of time, a plan will come to light that has been long-established and followed through with stubborn tenacity?'] (1890, n.p.). The Parisian aggressors, he seems to imply, were merely defending themselves and their community from this musical subterfuge. In the same paper the following year, a rather flippant report on an attack in Brussels constructs a

104 *Singing for salvation*

still-clearer connection, using a series of short, parallel sentences to tie together noise music as cause and violence as effect: 'l'Armée du Salut a fait hier une sorte de musique. Elle a été assaillie par une bande d'individus; le cortège a été mis en déroute. Quelques arrestations ont été opérées. On parle d'une salutiste grièvement blessée' ['the Salvation Army made a sort of music yesterday. They were attacked by a group of people; the procession was sent into chaos. Some arrests were made. There is some talk of a female Salvationist being seriously wounded'] ('L'Armée du Salut en déroute,' 1891, n.p.). The attack on the Salvationists here is recast as a *counterattack* on an invading army, a response to the initial aggression by the musicians, suggesting that the French are merely protecting themselves if the English insist on continuing their attempts to surreptitiously gain influence in France by way of their noxious music.

Whilst I have found no explicit accusation that the marches by the Salvation Army equate to a pseudo-militaristic invasion in France, the way in which the press chooses to present street violence as a self-defensive counterattack should be considered in the context of overt statements that, in the colonies, the arrival of the movement *does* equate to a literal invasion. As the Salvation Army made its way across the Mediterranean to France's colonial possessions, it is hardly surprising that the growing strength of a British organization bedecked in military symbolism and regalia caused some feelings of disquiet. Newspaper reports frequently allege that the organization was part of a British plot to undermine the Republic's hold over its colonies. It is perhaps to be expected that *La Croix* – a conservative, Catholic newspaper founded by the Assumptionist order – often accuses the Protestant Salvation Army of being a sinister English political apparatus. Every couple of years throughout the 1890s, they report on another case of the Salvation Army plotting actively to bring down French colonial power. For example, in an article entitled 'Agents anglais en Algérie' ['English Agents in Algeria'] in November 1893, they report that the French government's removal of Catholic priests from positions of influence in Algeria has left the field wide open to 'la propagande protestante' ['Protestant propaganda'] – and worse still, to Protestant propaganda 'faite par des agents de l'Angleterre' ['carried out by English agents']. The article is unequivocal that only one outcome can result: 'sous prétexte de distribuer des brochures salutistes aux Arabes, ces agents vont partout dans les douars fomenter l'insurrection' ['under the pretext of distributing Salvationist pamphlets to the Arabs, these agents spread insurrection throughout the douar villages'] (1893, p. 2). The story is a similar one in March 1895, in a report on the YMCA (Young Men's Christian Association), who the journalist 'Le M.' brands as 'l'arrière-garde de l'armée expéditionnaire salutiste opérant en Afrique française, [...] cette main-mise anglaise [...] à armer contre nous les populations algériennes jusqu'à présent soumises' ['the rear-guard of the expeditionary Salvation Army operating in French Africa, [...] this English stranglehold has armed the Algerian populations against us, who, until now, have been submissive'] ('L'Invasion britannique,' 1895, p. 1). In 1900, in a piece entitled 'Aoh yes!' the *La Croix* columnist 'Pierre l'Ermite'

Singing for salvation 105

states categorically, as though citing a long-established fact, that 'tout le monde sait que la [...] seule raison d'être [du protestantisme] c'est qu'il constitue un *véhicule politique*' ['everyone knows the only reason for the existence of Protestantism is as a *political vehicle*'] (1900, p. 1).

A distinct perfume of conspiracy theory is detectable here, and the clear ideological and political platform of the *La Croix* paper might initially give the impression that this is merely a storm in an ultramontane teacup. However, the same suspicions are to be found in numerous other newspapers that do not have an explicitly Catholic agenda. The Republican and anti-clerical *Rappel* warns that English members of the Salvation Army had taken the trouble to learn Arabic the better to spread both Protestantism and English propaganda in Algeria (Lefèvre, 1893, n.p.). The *Gaulois* and the *Matin* (one mondain, Boulangist, and anti-Dreyfusard, the other anti-Boulangist and moderate), both publish a speech by Georges Thiébaud that calls for government vigilance regarding protestant organizations – including the Salvation Army who are singled out by name – 'en Algérie et aux colonies [qui] font jusque dans les villages une propagande à la fois politique et religieuse' ['in Algeria and the colonies, who spread religious and political propaganda even in the smallest villages'] (Bartel, 1896, p. 3). Indeed, dedicated pamphlets were published with a view to raising awareness of and campaigning against this perceived political sabotage, such as P. Gardey's aggressive *Anglophilie gouvernementale: Manœuvres des protestants à Tahiti et à Madagascar* (1897) which details across fifty vituperative pages all the many ways in which English protestant missionaries have no interest in religion or a civilizing mission (this being considered the exclusive province of French colonialism[13]), but who seek only the extension of English political and commercial influence.

It seems dubious that these handfuls of unarmed 'soldiers' were likely to usurp any real power from the significant French military, bureaucratic, governmental, and pedagogical presence in the colonies. Importantly, however, it is when considered in the light of France's own colonial musical projects that the foundation for these suspicions does seem to follow a consistent logic. As in mainland France, Jann Pasler has observed that the French government subscribed to the theory that music and group music-making was an effective means of providing a common cultural identity and effecting that illusive *fusion des races* in the colonies (2009, p. 408). For example, an annual Orphéon competition was held in Alger in 1872, and a large part of the motivation for demanding that all the European entrants travel such a distance was to draw Algeria into French culture by way of Western choral and instrumental music. It is made quite explicit in commentaries on this event that music was believed to have actively assimilatory powers: in the *Revue et gazette musicale de Paris*, for example, Émile Mathieu de Monter writes at length over two consecutive issues about the benefits of this musical undertaking for acculturation. He asserts that

la colonisation reconnaîtra, sans doute, que l'on peut s'adresser à l'Orphéon, recourir à ses études dans les écoles franco-arabes, à ses manifestations

106   *Singing for salvation*

extérieures dans les communes, pour hâter la solution du problème ardu, je le répète, de *l'assimilation*. La communauté d'études musicales et de préoccupations artistiques est de nature à exercer sur les mœurs et sur les sympathies de deux races différentes une influence irrésistible, décisive.

(1872, p. 172)

[colonization will testify, without doubt, that you can rely upon the Orphéon movement, you can have recourse to it in Franco-Arab schools, in outdoor concerts in the provinces, in order to hasten a solution to the vexed problem, I repeat, of *assimilation*. The music-studies community and those with artistic preoccupations are of the sort to exercise an irresistible and decisive influence over the customs and sympathies of these two different races.]

Affirmations such as this testify to a clear conviction that music had the power to alter local cultural attitudes, loyalties, and identities in real terms, and it demonstrates a clear comprehension of the psychological influences that may be operated using music – as a community-building apparatus, as a means of manipulating emotions, and as a means of effacing traditional customs. In possession of this knowledge, therefore, the presence of a cluster of Salvation Army musician evangelists seems much more concerning.

Theoretically speaking, there was good reason to be concerned; though the Salvation Army's endgame was entirely different, its use of music does bear many of the same stylistic traits that would be successfully employed by twentieth-century fascist groups to galvanize crowds behind socio-political ideology a mere three decades later.[14] Peter Tregear observes in his study of fascist music that repetitive musical structures are particularly likely to become ' "stimulators" of fascistic thought, insofar as they operate by means of an unmediated submission to some kind of symbolic authority. Repetitious musical devices are, in their fascistic manifestations, cultivated to the point of idolatry' (1999, p. 46). The endlessly-repeatable refrains of the Salvation Army's sempiternal brass bands, their psalms and hymns – designed to appeal to the uneducated and disinherited – were deemed likely to have an emotive impact, even if the local populace had little education in the English language or in European musical traditions. Tregear concurs with Gustave le Bon's formulation that anyone wishing to manipulate the masses needed only three key devices: 'l'affirmation, la répétition, la contagion' ['affirmation, repetition, contagion'] (Le Bon, 1907, p. 111) – and affirmative and repetitious musical structures are plainly in evidence in the music of the Salvation Army. O'Rell claims to have heard a seemingly endless 'cantique à 99 couplets' ['99-verse hymn'] (1884b, p. 291) and de Bovet remarks upon the unceasing cycle of 'prière, hymne, psaume, hymne, psaume, prière' ['prayer, hymn, psalm, hymn, psalm, prayer'], as well as the eternal return of brass bands circulating around British towns and cities every Sunday (1898, p. 116).

Singing for salvation   107

The case of the Salvation Army appears to underwrite Jane Bennett's argument that, contrary to Adorno or Jacques Attali's ideas, the repetitive character of popular music feeds rather than starves music's capacity to inspire mass political engagement (2001, pp. 110–31). Furthermore, taking concerns about the ability of music to hypnotize and brainwash into account, even without any explicitly English political message, the concentrated essence of Englishness said by French commentators to be distilled into this accessible, infectious music could have the potential – according to this logic of musical acculturation – to turn the local populations against the French colonizers and towards the English. All the more so since, by 1894, there were over 3,300 members of the Salvation Army enlisted specifically as army musicians ('Décadence Salutiste,' 1894, p. 1). As Eyerman and Jamison have observed, 'the music of social movements transcends the bounds of the self and binds the individual to a collective consciousness' – the fear, for the French colonial powers, was that that collective consciousness to which the local populations were being bound might be an English rather than a French one (1998, p. 163). Indeed, the sound motif of the ever-recurring evangelical brass band becomes a solidification of everything that is disquieting about the British. The rum-pum-pum of the drums, fanfares of the trumpets, and tuneless singing of the choirs become akin to those most iconic of musical motifs – the -der der- of *Jaws* or -eeee! eeee!- of Hitchcock's *Psycho*; they do not merely accompany the object of fear, but they crystallize its very nature. The vague, indefinable but unavoidable feeling of psychological anxiety attached to the English is expressed in the sound motif of the Salvation Army brass section, drums, and singers.

Musical mockery

With all the issues discussed in this chapter so far – sanity, cultural identity, and political stability at home and abroad – music has been demonstrated to be a common feature and one which is placed right at the heart of how French commentators depict and engage with French concerns about the Salvation Army. It seems fitting therefore that a prominent means of deriding the Salvation Army should also be musical; given that it is in large part the *music* of the Salvation Army, as this chapter has elucidated, that is suspected of manipulating and/or undermining French power, psychological stability, or identity, then what is needed is a musical antidote – a tune still more catchy and that will persist in the mind long after the strains of the trombones have faded away. It is perhaps unsurprising, then, that music was also used in the streets as an integral element in acts of protest and even aggression against the Salvation Army. In January 1887, for example, a crowd in the town of Niort in the west of France pursued two female Salvationists through the streets, yelling, throwing stones through the windows of the café where they took refuge, and aggressively singing the Marseillaise at them (see 'Faits divers,'

108 *Singing for salvation*

29 January 1887, n.p.). The choice of the Marseillaise is clearly a significant one: the procession is not met by loud renditions of 'Ave Maria' or other religious music to inveigh against their evangelical brass bands, but rather by the national anthem with its patriotic, political message that 'ces féroces soldats' ['these ferocious soldiers'] are coming to slit the throats of your sons and wives, and that French citizens should take arms against the Salvationists.

In less openly aggressive fashion, an event so neat it could almost be an allegory rather than an anecdote is reported by Elie Frébault in the paper *L'Europe artiste* in 1889, when an unwonted battle of the bands was ongoing between a profane French theatre and the evangelical 'English' church:

> À propos d'Anglais et de musique, nous avons aussi les étranges concerts de l'*Armée du Salut* en son local, qu'un simple mur mitoyen sépare de l'Eden-Théâtre. Ce voisinage, gênant pour les deux établissements, donne lieu depuis quelque temps, aux scènes les plus désopilantes. Les hostilités sont commencées entre l'Eden et les Salutistes. C'est la lutte entre l'accordéon et la grosse caisse. Les gens de la maréchale Booth se plaignent de l'orchestre de M. Renard, et des libres propos du corps de ballet qu'on entend à travers la muraille. Ce qui empêche les épanchements religieux de produire tout leur effet sur les fidèles. À qui restera la victoire? à celui qui fera le plus de tapage, naturellement.
>
> (1889, p. 1).

[On the note of the English and their music, we also have the strange concerts of the Salvation Army in their meeting hall, separated only by a partition wall from the Eden Theatre. This proximity, a nuisance for both establishements, has recently given rise to some hilarious scenes. Hostilities are underway between the Eden and the Salvationists. It's a battle of the accordeon and the base drum. The Marechale Booth's people complain about Monsieur Renard's orchestra and the ballet company's unregulated language which can be heard through the wall. As a result, the religious outpourings aren't able to achieve their full impact on the worshippers. Who will be victorious? The side that makes the most noise, naturally.]

In this trans-mural squabble of songs we have a fitting aural metaphor for all of the cultural contentions that come to the fore in light of the Salvation Army's musical presence in France. Indeed, the tunes which accompany various popular songs, dances, and skits revolving around the Salvation Army in this period are all veritable earworms; their bright, well-pronounced rhythms, uncomplex textures and structures, recurring themes and motifs, and memorable lyrics make them ideal for counteracting any potential brainwashing, political manoeuvring, or English acculturation that the organization or its Anglo-Saxon founders might hope to achieve. The remainder of this chapter examines the treatment of the Salvation Army in popular songs; in this sphere, the foregrounded emphasis is not on the threatening or unnerving character

Singing for salvation   109

of the Salvationist as it often is in the press, but instead they are turned into a figure of fun and a butt of that characteristic Gallic wit.[15]

Given the considerable number of such works, it would require too much space to catalogue them all here, but the following gives a representative sample of the breadth of performance genres which capitalized upon the comedic potential of the Salvation Army: they include opéra-comique, with *Les Salutistes* by Bonnefond and Lajarte (performed at the Divan Japonais from May 1890), and *Miss Helyett* by Edmond Audran (which first opened at the Bouffes-Parisiens in 1890); pantomime ballet, such as *Pierrot salutiste* (in 1901 for the Automobile-Club de France); opéra-bouffe, with *Le Remplaçant* by Busnach and Duval (the headline show for the Winter season at the Palais-Royal in 1895) – a bedroom farce in which a Salvationist boarding-house keeper finds herself unwittingly providing the farcical bedroom at the centre of the plot; and Beissier and Lecocq's one-act opéra-monologue *La Salutiste* (performed at the Théâtre des Capucines in January 1905). Most widespread were the numerous comic songs that proliferated from the 1880s onwards in the cafés-concerts and music halls, often featuring amusing Salvation Army officers or magazine sellers: for example, Émile Gallé's parodic 'L'Armée du Chahut' from 1887 (see Figure 2.1); 'Les Mômes de l'Armée du Salut' by Lucien Delomel, performed in 1893 by Mlle Fougère at the Horloge; 'La Fausse Helyett,' by Byrec and Dalleroy, parodying the character from Audran's opéra-bouffe and performed in drag by Le Petit Bob at La Scala in 1893; 'Viv' l'Armée du Chahut-u-u-u-ut,' by Nalray, Deransart, Siégel, and Lémon, performed by Mlle Brissot at the Ambassadeurs in 1893 (see Figure 2.2); the part-sung skit 'Cinq Minutes à l'Armée du Salut, discours du capitaine O'Kelkuitt,' written and performed by Jules Moy at the Chat Noir cabaret in 1895, and then taken up by Plébins at La Scala and Camille Stéphani at the Cigale; 'J'ai lâché l'Armée du Salut' by Raphel Beretta and Jean Croisier from 1896; La Salutiste, by Duc, Spencer, and Barthélemy from 1896; and 'La Salutiste batignollaise!' by Émile Duhem in 1901. Even the celebrated comic singer and dancer Mistinguett, famous for her performances as a 'gommeuse épileptique' from 1897–1907,[16] appeared as a salutiste in *L'Incident est clos* at the Eldorado in 1899 (see Appendix for a list of titles and details of these songs).

Most popular of all these musical, dramatic, and comic representations was Audran's *Miss Helyett*. In this musical comedy, a female Salutiste and her family visit a French resort town from America (bear in mind that America is treated as English from a religio-cultural point of view by nineteenth-century France, the family are described as having 'English' characteristics and habits, and her official suitor James wears a tweed deerstalker cap like the stereotypical café-concert Englishman).[17] The action opens with a prudish Miss Helyett interrupting a ball with a cry of 'Shocking!' and a hymn-style song, the 'Cantique,' that criticizes the assembled French guests' moral standards, especially in terms of dress. Then, during an invigorating solitary walk in the hills, she accidentally falls from a ridge, exposing her underwear (and, it is hinted, quite a lot of her physiognomy). The man who saves her – a Parisian

110 *Singing for salvation*

Figure 2.1 Sheet music cover from 'L'Armée du Chahut' (1887).
Source: Bibliothèque nationale de France.

artist named Paul – sees her in this immodest state (and sketches her, no less), but since her skirts covered her head he is unaware of her identity, and since she has fainted she is also unaware of his. The remainder of the play involves her trying to find out who this man was so she can do her duty and marry him because he is the first man to have seen her nether regions. Conveniently, it transpires that Miss Helyett has long been in love with Paul, although he knew her as a child he has not yet learned to consider her as a grown woman. Eventually she tweaks her frumpy Salvationist dress into a feminine, attractive outfit, and after a few more twists and turns, she finally gains his interest as a desirable woman, they make a love-match, and the play draws to a rather predictable close with their engagement.

Singing for salvation 111

Figure 2.2 Sheet music cover from 'Viv' l'armée du Chahut-u-u-u-ut' (1893).
Source: Bibliothèque nationale de France.

The style of the 'Cantique' is particularly striking in its stylistic disjuncture from the familiar range of musical genres embraced in comic opera of the period. When the voice part enters, it is led not by either of the male Salvationist characters who are also on stage (the father, Smithson, and Miss Helyett's approved suitor, James) but by Miss Helyett herself, placing women literally centre stage in the zeal of the religious proselytizing. The direction to perform *bien rythmé* and with emphatic stress on every single note of the verse section echoes the stereotype of the military-esque, loud street preaching of the Salvationist *miss*; it has none of the frivolous but elegant lightness and vocal gymnastics of other female characters in the comic opera, and it stands in complete contrast to the lively 'Quadrille du Casino' which preceded it. Additionally, despite the role of Miss Helyett calling for a mezzo-soprano or

112 *Singing for salvation*

soprano, the vocal line in the 'Cantique' sits relatively low in the female vocal range (E_4 to E_5), a range which seems more suited to the contralto voice – and contraltos are rarely allotted the role of the beautiful, romantic heroine in opera or comic opera. Furthermore, Audron clearly offers up Salvationist worship practices as an object of ridicule, with a striking absence of all operatic melisma or ornamentation. Performance directions indicate that Miss Helyett should sing her simple, straight quavers 'comme un enfant qui chante à l'école,' giving a strong sense of childlike naivety to her faith and hinting that it can clearly only exist in endearing but foolish ignorance of the complexity, challenges, or nuances of real, adult existence. The exaggerated lack of ornament is perpetuated in the harmonic simplicity of Smithson and James's lines at the end of each verse: in the first verse, the male characters sing at octave intervals (James) and in unison (Smithson) with the female vocal line, and at the end of the second verse the only slight elaboration is the introduction of major thirds in Smithson's part.

The distinctness of the Salvationist 'Cantique' from familiar comic opera of the fin de siècle is all the more striking when compared with the 'Duetto espagnol' in Act I. Here, some light Spanish seasoning is provided by tambourines and a few snippets of bolero second-beat stress, but in other respects it is still heavily redolent of familiar, cosmopolitan music at this time – and even these musical hints at exoticism had been so domesticated by opera and ballet over the course of the century that they would scarcely have struck the audience as strongly Other. Indeed, the walking bass in the instrumental accompaniment to the 'Cantique' is reminiscent of the bass line in the four-part choral songs of J.S. Bach, who was strongly associated in France at this time with his composition of Lutheran church music. Decidedly, then, the audience is led to feel that the Salvationists simply do not belong in this musical world: their music is a strange, unwonted import which has no natural place in this otherwise jovial French comic opera. Its presence introduces a tension which must be resolved over the course of the play. In the end, such a resolution is provided when Miss Helyett finally becomes engaged to her Parisian artist and they close the final act with a light, trilling 'Couplet final,' which rushes, *allegro*, to a merry end with its far more typical flurries of semi-quavers and appoggiatura.

This musical comedy was one of the greatest hits of the decade: after opening in November 1890, the *XIXe Siècle* reported that it was still bringing in remarkable ticket sales for the Bouffes-Parisiens in December 1891, and in June 1892 it celebrated its one-thousandth performance (Crispin, 1891, n.p.; Perdican, 1892, n.p.). It would go on to be shown in April 1891 at the Théâtre des Variétés in Marseille, in August 1893 at the Casino in St-Malo, in July 1894 at the Menus Plaisirs in Paris; in two runs starting June 1898 and April 1904 at the Ba-ta-clan; in September 1900 at the Renaissance; in September 1902 at the Gobelins; and in June 1905 at the Variétés. Additionally, the opening tune 'Miss Helyett's Waltz' went on to be a popular number at public balls throughout the 1890s, and when the second Paris-London telegraph line was inaugurated in February 1892, of all the possible musical tributes that

Singing for salvation 113

could have been offered on this auspicious occasion, Mlle Duhamel, who first played the eponymous heroine, was asked to perform its most memorable songs in her Salvation Army costume to a select audience from London and Paris ('Échos et nouvelles,' 1892, n.p.).

When the students of Paris officially adopted the traditional Mi-Carême festival in 1893 they chose the Salvation Army as one of their six themes from all the myriad possible targets for their fun for this inaugural procession. Their carnival parade demonstrates the ubiquity of the Salvationist type in contemporaneous culture; the crowds in the street, composed of a mixed demographic in terms of class, age, gender, and even race, were expected to recognize the puns and understand the humour of the comic inversions in this new 'Armée du Chahut' – a name possibly based on the comic song 'L'Armée du Chahut' by Émile Gallé. The student Chahutistes were led through the Latin Quarter by thirty musicians making a great din with drums and brass instruments. After this orchestral racket came the standard bearers, carrying a banner with an image of a salutiste 'avec le costume classique, robe montante et chapeau Miss Helyett' ['with the classic costume, a high-collared dress and Miss Helyett bonnet'], but instead of saluting Heaven with her hands, raised in the familiar gesture of street preachers, the image instead shows a woman doing an impressive high kick to hail the carnival gods with her right heel – echoing famous contemporaneous images of chahut dancers such as La Goulue and Nini Pattes-en-l'air, as though she were dancing the cancan to the tunes of the mock-religious band that preceded her down the boulevard. The parody continues to build in its richness when considered in conjunction with the *En arrière* newspaper that their 'soldiers' handed out at the festival, and with a play on the Salvation Army uniforms, which included giving the distinctive cap of male salvationists a vastly over-sized visor and giving the modest dress of the women – rather predictably – a raunchy overhaul with the dress hitched up on one side to reveal flesh-coloured stockings (described in 'La Mi-Carême,' 1893, n.p.). So much was this spectacle in tune with the popular mood that café-concert composers Siégel, Lémon, Nalray, and Deransart immediately picked up on the idea, and their 'Viv' l'Armée du Chahut-u-u-u-ut!' was on the billing at the Ambassadeurs in the same year.

This panoply of comic songs and skits playing with the image of the Salvation Army also reveals areas in which the organization posed the most problematic questions for French society, and they probe issues through the release of laughter. There emerge a number of key, repeated themes, and it is these that indicate the ways in which French songwriters, performers, and audiences thought it most effective to deride, belittle, or simply get an easy laugh out of the idea of the Salvation Army. When seen in performance, the emotional effects of music, costume, dance, and laughter provide the audience members with a powerful experience of community togetherness and offer strong aural and visual images of what is inferior, what is culturally alien, and what is to be excluded from French national identity. Whilst the fragmented, varied nature of French society may have caused significant anxiety when

114 *Singing for salvation*

considered directly, when it is mediated via the figure of the Salvationist, this risible character that everybody could identify as 'Other' offered a means of obliquely addressing issues of individual and national identity. The English Salvationist with their honking brass bands provided France with a shared, noisy, ludicrous bogey man.

Some of these comic songs direct their mirth towards Salvationist music itself, incorporating into the comic performance snippets of music that apparently mimic Salvation Army song. In 'Cinq minutes à l'Armée du Salut,' much of the performance is spoken, but it opens, ends, and is punctuated half-way through by the instruction '[Chants sacrés ad libitum].' The tempo given for this sacred song is 'largo religioso' and, although I have found no record of precisely how this was staged, this tempo marking implies a deadpan delivery, perhaps with the performer assuming a serious 'holier-than-thou' expression. This opens the door for musical incongruity, juxtaposing the tone of the singing with the markedly secular lyrical content. The lyrics read:

> Ta-ra-ra-boum! Whiskey!
> Ta-ra-ra-boum! Brandy!
> Gin, cok-tail [sic.] and soda,
> Hip! Hip! Hourrah!
> Ah-le-lui-a!

Indeed, the first sequence of six notes is that of the popular British and American music-hall tune *Ta-ra-ra-boum-de-ay* (known in France under the title *Tha-ma-ra-boum-di-hé*, which had seen considerable success for Polaire at the Folies-Bergère in 1892). It may have taken a second for the audience to recognize the characteristic A-G#-A-D-A-A pattern at this slow *largo* tempo, but the moment of recognition would have provided a burst of merriment at the expense of the *pince-sans-rire* character of the Salutiste. What is more, Captain O'Kelkuitt announces that this psalm is number 69 – a number

Extract 2.1 'Cinq minutes à l'Armée du Salut,' by Jules Moy (1895).

Adapted from source: Bibliothèque nationale de France.

Singing for salvation   115

spoken naively by the Captain but clearly intended to raise a lewd laugh from the audience – and the lyrics are said to be available in the *En arrière* journal, recalling the parodic bawdiness of the Armée du Chahut at the Mi-Carême student cavalcade in 1893.

Though the music in 'Cinq minutes' is far from sophisticated and has only the simplest of melodies and textures, there are nonetheless multiple layers of complexity in its use of musical tropes. Notably, there are in fact three musical styles incorporated into this act – the *largo religioso* psalm, a jig (that quintessential expression of Englishness, as discussed in Chapter 1 of the present book), and a waltz. The juxtaposition between these three musical styles is important, and indeed its importance is underlined by the use of the same 'ta-ra-ra-boum-de-ay' musical motif in all three. This sequence of notes is adapted to the different time signatures and to the typical stylistic motifs of each genre; for example, for the jig, *largo* is replaced with a fast *allegro*, and for the waltz several notes are redoubled to incorporate the lilting 6/8 rhythm. From these contrasting variations the audience is invited to note several key points. First, the jig and psalm share the same 2/4 time signature and are essentially the slow minor and quick major modulations of the same tune, indicating that Englishness (metonymically in the jig) and this risible religion (in the psalm) are inextricable. It is not only a case of laughing at a small religious enclave in France, but rather laughing at the nation for which they are treated as a synecdoche – and, travelling back the other way along this joke, this evokes the immense body of popular comic song directed at the English in general (discussed in Chapter 1) to underwrite the ridiculousness of this church.

Secondly, the simple-time jig and psalm are counterposed with the compound-time waltz, a dance often seen as the epitome of French joviality and a mainstay of the *bals musettes* and of Bastille Day street parties from 1880 onwards. The audience can make no mistake here about the distinctness implied between the national characteristics of the two nations; the narrative voice assumed by the performer for the waltz section is not that of a member of the Salvation Army, but a French observer/narrator who draws the French audience into the sketch. He recounts how he was just strolling down the boulevard the other night, assuming the archetypal Parisian figure of the *flâneur*, when a young woman invited him to enter the Salvationist meeting. In he went out of curiosity, and 'ce spectacle m'a tell'ment fait rire que j'veux ici vous le r'produire' ['that spectacle made me laugh so much I want to recreate it for you here']. This frame narrative allows the audience to identify with this *curieux* – they too are all just idle Parisian flâneurs – rather than being placed in the position of members of the congregation and victims of cultural and religious brainwashing. In this, it echoes the position adopted by the narrative voice in the student cavalcade journal *En arrière*, which opens by hailing its readers as friends, and asking 'amis passants, devenus amis lecteurs, lequel de vous ne s'est vu accoster par des vierges folles, le long du boulevard?' ['passing friends, now reader friends, who among you hasn't found themselves being accosted by crazed virgins all the way down the boulevard?']

116 *Singing for salvation*

However, it becomes clear that although the organization is easy to dismiss in lyrics and texts as peculiar or eccentric, it is in fact particularly resistant to being subverted *in music*. Due to the fact that the Salvation Army's music is already a subversion of traditional religious forms of musical worship, to invert it further would logically involve a return to the typical religious hymns or plain-chant associated with Catholicism. A neutralization this might be, but as an attempt to undermine aesthetically the aesthetic practices of the Salvation Army it falls short and it risks redirecting the mockery towards French religious traditions rather than English evangelicalism. This is demonstrated further in Raphel Beretta and Jean Croisier's 'J'ai lâché l'armée du Salut' (1896). The first four lines of each verse are sung on just two notes as the female singer describes her erstwhile Salvationist appearance:

> Hier j'avais une robe plate,
> Un abominable chapeau
> Et j'allais Anglaise automate
> Évangéliser le badeau.

> [Yesterday I had a flat-fronted dress,
> A terrible hat
> And I went like an English automaton
> To evangelize the passers-by]

Combined with the moderato tempo and the *piano* dynamic, this chanted tune is clearly being used to indicate a sense of stuffy religious *recueillement*

Extract 2.2 'J'ai lâché l'armée du Salut,' by Beretta and Croisier (1896).

Adapted from source: Bibliothèque nationale de France.

Singing for salvation 117

that will then be contrasted with the cheeky chorus in which, as the title suggests, she tells us how she has dropped the Salvation Army for a lifestyle of pleasure. The tune here is akin to the sort of chanting frequently used for the call and response in sung Catholic and High Anglican services, and it would have evoked a general idea of religiosity for the audience: but in doing so, it is therefore not the Salvation Army's religio-musical identity but that of more traditional forms of Christianity that goes on to be the butt of their jokes when the same tune is used to accompany her declarations that now she is 'coquette and fantaisiste' ['coquettish and capricious'] (verse 2) and that, euphemistically, she favours 'les biens de la terre' ['earthly riches'] (verse 4). The case is a similar one in *Miss Helyett*; all songs sung by Salvation Army characters in this opéra-bouffe are presented musically as traditional psalms or chants, though the lyrics are not specifically religious, and they mostly relate to the romantic-comedy plotline. Whilst, in both cases, the audience will feel that the overall derision conveyed in the lyrics hits its Salvationist target (mocking their physical and spiritual automatism, the hypocritical pretence that the women have no sexual desires, and, in short, their dullness), this is prevented from being thoroughly driven home by the difficulty of effectively dismantling the Army's most striking feature – the appeal and the joyousness of its café-concert-style music.

Shifting signifiers

The comic treatment of female Salvation Army characters is also a striking feature of these musical acts. In many ways, this is a more straight-forward process than subverting, specifically, the musical aesthetic itself. The Salvation Army as a religious movement foregrounded an ideal of sexual purity, either in the form of abstention before marriage or of fidelity and procreation within wedlock. Uniform dress was modest, the raucousness of drunkenness was avoided through teetotalism, and all the chaos of unbridled desires and energies was redirected through corporeal and spiritual discipline into the work of the church. Consequently, it was even more than usually simple to deride the movement by suggesting that the sexual purity of its women was not all it should be (though this manoeuvre was, of course, by no means original and was also used in the same decades to belittle Jews, blue-stockings, the English in general, Orientals, the lower classes by the bourgeoisie, the bourgeoisie by the lower classes, and many more).

As one might expect in a nineteenth-century handling of both gender stereotypes in general and of female English characters, there are generally two means of negatively representing the women of the Salvation Army at this time: the unattractive prudes who would like to be sexually active but have no opportunity, and the scarcely-concealed nymphets who are extremely sexually active even though they strategically pretend not to be. The journalist Henry Fouquier foregrounds the former of these at length in his 'La Vie de Paris' column in the *XIXe Siècle*. He focuses on the interconnectedness of

118 *Singing for salvation*

unsatisfied or repressed female sexuality with Salvation Army music on the occasion of a group of missionary Salvationists passing through Paris on their way to an evangelical mission in India. Fouquier's lengthy description systematically parallels music and these women's physical attributes; both are clearly described as English, and this is taken to be explanation enough that each is as aesthetically deficient, even distasteful, as the other. Thus categorized as something of a freakshow, he uses these features to construct a logic implying that the Salvation Army can be dismissed out of hand as a religious community. Instead, the women and their music are better suited as a temporary gap-filler in the Parisian entertainments industry, a fleeting distraction, rather than something genuinely worthy of attention in its own right:

> Hier, heureusement pour les flâneurs en quête de distractions, l'Armée du Salut a comblé la lacune [d'amusements]. [...] Les femmes de l'Armée du Salut, en général, ne sont pas très jolies, ce qui fait dire aux méchants qu'une femme se met à aimer l'humanité avec cette frénésie, c'est qu'il ne lui a pas été donné de pouvoir être aimée d'un homme et l'aimer en retour. Quoi qu'il en soit, à la gaieté excitée par le spectacle d'une vingtaine de *misses* habillée en Hindous et *enturbannées* comme Mme de Staël elle-même ne le fut pas, se joignait le comique de la musique des salutistes. [...] L'Armée du Salut use et abuse du chant et des instruments. Et, comme elle est recrutée en Angleterre où le goût est resté quelque peu barbare, ses musiques sont composées de grosses caisses retentissantes, de cymbales, de clarinettes agressives pour l'oreille et de trompettes hardies ...
>
> (1888, n.p.)

> [Yesterday, happily for flâneurs in search of distraction, the Salvation Army plugged the [entertainment] gap. [...] The women of the Salvation Army are, in general, not very pretty, leading spiteful tongues to say that if a woman takes to loving humanity with such frenzy, it's because she wasn't given the means to be loved by a man and love him in return. Whatever the case may be, the merriment caused by the spectacle of twenty or so English misses, dressed up as Hindus and even more be-turbaned than Mme de Staël herself, was compounded by the comical Salvationist music. [...] The Salvation Army uses and abuses singing and instrumental music. And, as the Army draws its recruits from England where musical taste has remained somewhat barbaric, its music is made up of big rumbling drums, cymbals, clarinets that attack the ear, and brazen trumpets ...]

Fouquier is quite emphatic: there are two conjoined spectacles here, linked by the use of the verb *se joindre* [to join together] and the threading of one description into the other – the English misses who are defined by their (deficient) sexual status in society are part of one and the same entity as the comical (deficient) music of the Salvationists, and these phenomena are mutually

Singing for salvation 119

dependent. It is worthy of remark here that, although elsewhere the article mentions briefly that there are thirty members of each sex in this procession, only the female members are then described. This reveals the journalist's strategy of dismissing Salvation Army members by reducing them to their – ineffectual – feminized, sexual object status in society.

As well as the plain, prudish women, the reverse image of this is the stereotype of overtly debauched female Salvationists, disparaging the Salvation Army as a hypocritical hotbed of female desire and sexual promiscuity. Fernand de Jupilles, for example – himself a lyricist as well as a critic of British mores – exclaims that Booth 'fait hurler des psaumes en pleine rue par des bandes de fanatiques recrutées dans les prisons ou parmi [...] les femmes les plus débauchées' ['has psalms screamed out in the middle of the street by gangs of fanatics recruited in prisons or from among the most debauched women'] (1886, pp. 239–40) and Jules Vallès, with his usual vitriol, asserts that 'c'est dans des expéditions folles, toujours, que s'engagent celles [des femmes anglaises] qui osent quitter le *home*; et quand elles aiment le bruit, c'est celui du tambour, du gong, de la grosse caisse. [...] Dans ton coin, femme!' ['it is on such madcap expeditions that those English women who dare to leave the home set off; and when they like noise, it's the noise of drums, gongs, the big bass drum. [...] Get back in your corner, woman!'] (1884, p. 211).

This may also call upon contemporary stereotypes surrounding the playing of brass instruments by women, discussed fruitfully by Katharine Ellis in her study of Alphonse Sax. In this article, Ellis analyses a scheme run in the 1860s by Sax (brother of Adolphe Sax, inventor of the Saxophone) to encourage women to play brass instruments and to prove that they had the physical capacity to do so – both without injury to their fragile female bodies and indeed with positive benefits for their physical and moral welfare. She highlights the prejudices faced by the women who took part in this scheme, which cast the physical effort expended in perfecting embouchure and breathing as more an erotic display fit to be ogled by male audiences than proof of their musical abilities (1999, p. 240).[18] Although Sax's scheme ran in the 1860s, the remarks made by Sax to actively combat ideas of eroticism, grotesqueness, and indignity still chime with the sous-entendus levelled at Salvation Army bandswomen two decades later. The focus in commentaries about Sax's all-female brass sextet on their bulging eyes, flushed cheeks, and pursed lips firmly concentrate the attention on the female body and its implied sexual availability rather than on these women's talents or efforts at self-improvement.

The violent tone of male writers such as Jupilles and Vallès, then, in affirming the debauchery of Salvation Army women, echoes the criticism levelled by some at Sax's brass players, whose participation in music *was itself* seen as a deviation from their 'natural' sexual role. J.-F. Vaudin, the left-wing editor of *La France chorale*, found women's involvement in any musical societies to be in itself essentially immoral:

120   *Singing for salvation*

Quelle sera la chanson de l'enfant qui ne verra plus sa mère de la soirée? [...] Le devoir prime la musique. [...] Il y a quelque chose, selon nous, qui moralise et qui garantit un peu plus la femme, son travail et son avenir, qu'instrument à anches ou à pistons indépendants, c'est sa fidélité à la maison, c'est l'amour exclusif de ce sanctuaire.

[What will be the song sung to the child if they no longer see their mother in the evenings? [...] Duty takes precedence over music. [...] There is something which moralizes and provides greater guarantees for woman, her work, and her future than an instrument with a reed or independent pistons, and that is her fidelity to the home, her exclusive love for this sanctuary].[19]

Such distaste is only compounded when this music-making not only takes place outside the home but does so in a public place and with a view to taking a public leadership role over the spiritual actions and well-being of others.

However, when it comes to representations of Salvation Army women *in comic song*, they tend to differ in crucial ways from the depictions of women in the texts discussed so far. Whereas these writers cast aspersions about real Salvationists, most of the female 'Salvationist' characters in comic songs tell us that they are actually French girls who are merely using the Salvation Army to make an income and to fund their much more free-and-easy social life. This theme seems to have been a guarantee of audience enjoyment for comic songs on the topic, evinced by the repeated return to, and variations on, this theme in 'Les Mômes de l'Armée du Salut,' 'J'ai lâché l'Armée du Salut,' 'La Salutiste,' 'La Salutiste batignollaise,' 'L'Armée du Chahut,' and 'La Fausse Helyett.' In all of these, a French working-class woman pretends to be in the Salvation Army to sell the *En avant* journal, but really she is willing and eager to sell other more personal favours – either using the journal merely as a cover for selling her body, or using the income made as a journal seller to pay for the liberality of her social life after work. In 'Les Mômes,' the lyrics tell us that crowds of *mômes* can be seen on the streets offering passers-by the journal and singing psalms to cancan tunes. Whenever an old man asks if *En avant* is amusing, the girls immediately suggest that if he's looking for amusement, he should start by buying them a drink. The punchline in the final verse is that the singer has never sold a single copy of the newspaper in the entire year that she has been a Salvation Army *môme*, but that 'faut toujours dans sa poche / avoir un bout d'journal / Ça n'peut pas fair' de mal' ['you should always have the odd paper in your pocket, it can't do any harm']. Far from a means of evangelism, it transpires that the religious newspaper for these girls is just a savvy means of escaping anti-eliciting laws – and implies that, perhaps, this is the case for all those English Salvation *misses*, further mocking their claims to virtue.

The story is not dissimilar in 'J'ai lâchée l'Armée du Salut.' The emphasis is on the female body from the start, with a description of her Salvation

Army uniform and demeanour as she offers gentlemen in the street copies of *En avant* – and it is always gentlemen in these songs who approach the young women, although French women are more generally associated with religiousness than men in the late nineteenth century, making it clear that these approaches have nothing to do with actual religious faith. Indeed, the quaver-beat pause between 'Monsieur, voulez-vous ... *En avant?*' ['Sir, would you like ... *Forward March?*'] integrates comic timing and leaves space for the audience to silently insert their own lewd joke. In subsequent verses, she recounts that she has shed her Salutiste 'cœur de bois' ['wooden heart'], that she is now an 'artiste,' that she no longer puts up with their dullness, and that when she offers 'Monsieur, voulez-vous: En avant,' now it really *is* her body that she is offering. What is particularly striking here is that the female character has not merely left the Salvation Army behind her as a temporary blip of youthful enthusiasm, but rather she presents her time in the army as an essential *initiation* for her debut in the Armée du Chahut. The chorus lyrics explain:

> C'est mon début
> J'ai lâchée l'armée du Salut,
> Que l'on m'excuse, que l'on m'excuse,
> Et j'entre à l'armée du Chahut, oui du Chahut
> Où l'on s'amuse, où l'on s'amuse.

> [It's my debut
> I've left the Salvation Army,
> Forgive me, forgive me,
> And I'm entering the Cancan Army, yes the Cancan,
> Where you can have fun, where you can have fun.]

Rather than being antithetical, the religious organization is presented as an indispensable gateway for her progression to becoming a Chahutiste – implying that frivolous sexual mores were part of the experience and the purpose all along.

In addition to the lyrics, in both songs the combination of the melody and words gives us some indication of the dance steps and physical humour that may have gone hand-in-hand with the sung performance of this music. In 'Les Mômes,' first, there is a lively sixteen-bar musical introduction, eight bars of which are again repeated between each verse, suggesting that the performer – quite possibly with a chorus-line of dancers – would have danced energetically onto the stage, placing the physical at the forefront from the outset and framing each verse with a focus on these women's bodies. In 'J'ai lâché l'armée,' the introduction is more burlesque still, with clownesque, circus-ring style tremolo chords, followed by a dainty polka; the direction to perform this introduction 'con brio' (with vigour) hints at the performer (and possibly other dancers or acrobats) rushing frantically onto the stage, before

122   *Singing for salvation*

assuming a false air of English restraint and dancing mincingly in modest blue Salvationist dress to the delicate polka section. These contrasting musical forms demonstrate, from the very start, that this is not a restrained body or a body that can uphold the pretence of restraint for long, but a body in uproar.

The 'Salutiste batignollaise' takes a descending arpeggio, reminiscent of the military bugle call for sunset (marking the end of the regimented day), and turns it into her cry of 'En avant! en avant! en avant! en avant!' She then sings in verse 3 that it is only her uniform that restrains her by day, and that as soon as she takes it off in the evening she heads straight to the dancehall and 'je pouss' mon p'tit chahut' ['I do my little cancan'] – Salvation Army military manoeuvres being over for the day, she can signal the attack for her flirtations. Indeed, it is no doubt indicative of what audience members expected from a 'Salvation Army act' that the core criticism made by a reviewer of a performance of 'J'ai lâchée l'Armée du Salut' at the Lyon Casino by Mlle Charlotte is that 'elle ne chahute pas assez au refrain' ['she doesn't cancan uproariously enough in the chorus'] (Késanlik, 1896, p. 4). Yet amateur performances of this song were unlikely to accommodate the original visual spectacle of uproarious dance, and this raises the question, then, where the publishers thought the appeal was when they published this song as sheet music. Perhaps it is because it was not only the visual sauciness that the audience at the theatre sought, but also the message of defiance against discipline, regimentation, and traditionalism that was attached to it; the style of the music contains this signification and, even if performed without the dance, the jaunty, up-tempo melodies are so strongly associated with this theme that they are able to function alone.

It is precisely this kind of defiance of convention that becomes the crux of this comedic subgenre. The majority of the songs about the Salvation Army establish two sets of character traits. The first set encompasses poor musical taste, physical ugliness, rigidity, stuffiness, a judgmental temperament, a sense of moral responsibility, and conservative attitudes regarding sex and the value of female sexual purity for all social classes – these traits are associated with 'Englishness.' The second entails stylish musical taste, physical attractiveness, wit, freedom, a carefree spirit, and a laissez-faire approach to sex in general and working-class female sexual behaviour in particular – these are familiar as traits associated with 'Frenchness.' For example, in the lyrics to 'Viv' l'Armée du Chahut-u-u-u-ut,' the verses consist of two sets of four lines; the first four set out the unmusical (v1), frumpy and skinny (v2), flat-chested and undesirable (v3), and awkward (v4) characteristics of English Salvationist girls, and in each verse the lyrics emphatically repeat 'Ces anglais's' or 'Les English's' to underline their national identity. The subsequent four lines of each verse contrast this with the Parisian students' taste in women who are amusing (v1), have big pointy breasts (v2), are sexually available and open to having multiple partners (v3), and are not uptight (v4) – and at the same time, the melody breaks free from the clumpy confines of the straight, stomping quavers of the

Singing for salvation   123

first four 'English' bars to adopt a flowing, dancing phrase much more typical of French café-concert and bal musette music. The girls and the tune both exhibit *gauloiserie* – both in the sense of joyous, Rabelaisian bawdiness, and in the sense of being Gaulois, that is, inherently French.

In this song, the division between the English girls with English characteristics and the French girls with French (working-class) characteristics is unmistakable. However, in many comic songs the distinction struggles to remain so clear cut. It is common for the character to be a French girl who pretends to be a Salvationist by day, but really has far flightier proclivities – and she often tells us that she goes so far as to put on an English accent the better to assume the Salvationist persona. The singer of 'L'Armée du Chahut' remarks that 'il suffit et c'est très facile / d'avoir un p'tit accent anglais' ['it's enough, and it's very easy / to put on a little English accent']. On one level, this accent is deemed necessary by the character because Salvationists are seen as inherently English in contemporary culture, and thus it makes commercial sense to assume an English identity in order to advance magazine sales. Yet several of the songs also imply that this English accent does not so much advance the sale of the journal, as advance the sale of the girl herself; the accent and Englishness, then, would seem to embody an erotic fantasy for the male passer-by rather than merely embodying a risible evangelical character type. The singer in 'La Fausse Helyett' alternates between accents in the course of this song, explaining that 'she' (voiced by a male performer in drag, including Le Petit Bob at La Scala) had no success at picking up men when she street-walked as a French girl, but when men find themselves confronted with a Salvation Army uniform, prudish expression, and English accent they cannot help but eat out of her hand.

In such songs as these, Englishness, Salvationism, and Salvation music are all positioned as *performative* characteristics that may be taken up and cast off – rather than being inextricably intertwined with the English racial character as they were so emphatically depicted to be in contemporary journalism (as was discussed in the preceding sections of this chapter). As a result, the signifier 'Englishness' becomes detached from its moorings and henceforth becomes available as a derogatory signifier with a far wider scope of applicability (in the way that 'you're such a girl' or 'that's so gay' have been used as terms of abuse in the late twentieth and early twenty-first centuries even in situations when sexuality and gender are not directly relevant to the situation). Instead of Englishness being a master signifier for a series of negatively perceived inherent national traits (such as conservative attitudes to morality, to sexual and bodily behaviours especially for women, and to rigid respect for the social elites), it now becomes a *subordinate* idea under the master signifier of 'fuddy-duddy.' The Salvation Army character thus becomes not so much a metonym for Englishness as a metaphor. Its connectedness to a genuine English religious movement is loosened despite the contemporaneity of the Salvation Army's proselytization in France; it is used instead as a symbol for a traditionalist world-view that the youth culture of the fin de siècle rejects.

124 *Singing for salvation*

Of course, this conservative world-view, here termed 'English,' shares much in common with that of the French bourgeoisie; to portray the fusty Salvation Army girl as a laughable, unappealing stick-in-the-mud in comparison to her young, fun, beautiful French counterpart is also an oblique snub of the traditional bourgeois conventions by which the families of the younger generation and/or the adult bourgeois society around them encouraged them to live. In the *En arrière* journal, the anonymous student journalist mounts a protest against restrictions upon their freedom and their fun, 'une réaction et une protestation de la jeunesse qui veut rester jeune, joviale et *gauloise*, contre certaines tentatives ultra-philosophiques [...] [qui] nous conduirait tout droit au mysticisme nuageux des sectes d'Outre-Manche' ['a reaction and a protest by the youth of today who want to stay young, jovial, and *gaulois*, against certain ultra-philosophical attacks that would drive us straight to the foggy mysticism of the sects from across the Channel'] (1893, p. 1 – emphasis added). Even in the first flush of concern in the 1880s, it was highly unlikely that the Salvation Army would ever be able to gain significant enough influence over French politics to genuinely curtail the young, jovial gauloiserie of the large, educated, liberal-leaning student body or of popular culture. Consequently, we may suspect that these protestations target 'tentatives' by groups within France who *are* likely to affect their freedoms – notably from the conservative Right, anti-Malthusians, and moral reformers of all stripes.

That these songs stake their claim as 'youth culture' is clear from the racination of many of their characters in the Latin Quarter. For example, the song in the '*En Arrière*' journal places its geographical boundaries between the Place Saint Michel and the Bal Bullier (Port-Royal); the dancer in 'L'Armée du Chahut' is to be found between the Institut and the Bal Bullier; and the chahutistes of 'Viv' l'Armée du Chahut-u-u-u-ut' state explicitly that they are the girlfriends of Paris's male students. The narrative voices of these characters lay claim to a specific, carefree community of Parisian youth, with its wit, mockery, liberty, and its sexual freedoms. Like in the 1960s, this voice of a new generation rebuts any restrictions on their moral and sexual mores that the older war generation (in the case of the belle époque, the Franco-Prussian War generation) may seek to impose. By taking this position, these songs stand in contrast to many of the reactions to the Salvation Army expressed in newspapers, travel accounts, sociological texts, and so on. Whilst those texts prioritize a national agenda and use musical, sexual, and cultural behaviours to justify nationalistic feeling, these comic songs turn this dynamic on its head; they prioritize a counter-cultural, generational agenda, and use musical, sexual, and national behaviours to justify feelings of youth liberty and community.

This body of music revolving around the persona and the music of the English Salvation Army character, then, addresses keen concerns at the heart of French society in a number of ways and contexts. At times, it ridicules and belittles the organization by implying that their preaching is just superficial spiel and that a barely-controlled, unruly body is to be found just below the surface. At others, with its focus on ribaldry and merriment, it implies that nothing

Singing for salvation   125

can erase the French *joie de vivre*, and that this witty light-heartedness deemed as typically French was a solid and reliable anchoring point for national identity that no amount of brainwashing with religious or English cultural mores could change. Then, the shift away from primarily national and nationalistic concerns in the 'Salvation girl' songs has two possible effects: on the one hand, it tackles the anxieties raised in newspapers and books on the Salvation Army by femininizing the organization – reducing it to something objectifiable and pleasurable and removing it from the sphere of political anxiety; whilst on the other, the real Salvation Army is side-lined and it is used instead as an allegory for the annoyances that plague the young and curb their effervescence. Thus we can observe that in these musically simple pieces of comic song, there are complex approaches to and oblique gestures towards the network of fears, anxieties, and concerns troubling the French psyche in the face of the Salvation Army, and they create a musical mesh of different ways of facing the challenges besetting contemporary French culture and society more widely.

Notes

1 Such views are also expressed in newspaper articles following a parliamentary debate on the subject in 1896 in *Le Matin* (Paul Bartel, 1896, p. 3 and 'Contre les protestants,' 1896, p. 1).
2 On another London Sunday, Bourget writes: 'cette somnolence de la petite rue est troublée par le passage de l'Armée du Salut. Parmi les ronflements des cuivres, les fidèles de cette secte étrange défilent, et sur leur visage exalté rayonne l'ardeur des obscurs fanatismes, tandis qu'ils chantent éperdument et indéfiniment: "L'Agneau qui saigne! l'Agneau qui saigne!" Ils s'éloignent, et de nouveau la petite rue aristocratique des environs de Hyde-Park reprend sa quiétude' ['the sleepiness of the little street is disturbed by the passage of the Salvation Army. Among the rumblings of the brass, the members of this strange sect process, and their faces glow with the exalted ardour of vague fanaticisms whilst they sing frantically and indefinitely: "The blood of the lamb! The blood of the lamb!" They move away, and once more calm is restored to the aristocratic little street in the environs of Hyde Park'] (1889, p. 244).
3 A notable example of this widespread working-class and amateur instrumental movement is the Bon Marché's staff band, who played Saturday evening concerts in the square outside the store in the 1890s with a mixture of art, military, and popular music arrangements (the repertoire is discussed in more detail by Pasler, 2009, esp. pp. 291–320, 600–2).
4 This opinion is propagated when papers such as *La Croix* report the false information that the Salvation Army was invented by a woman ('une hérésie fondée par une femme [...] en notre siècle de doctoresses' ['a heresy founded by a woman in our century of doctoresses']) – that is, by William Booth's wife Catherine – and that she impelled her hen-pecked husband to support her, and indeed made him take her surname on marriage ('Gazette du jour,' 1890, p. 1). In actual fact, the organization was founded jointly by William Booth and his wife Catherine (née Mumford) as the East London Christian Mission in 1865.
5 'Dépêches télégraphiques,' 16 June 1891. *L'Univers*. n.p. This conflict is reported upon with particular frequency in *L'Intransigeant*, 'Les Déboires de l'Armée du

126 Singing for salvation

Salut,' 17 June 1891, p. 3; 'Nouvelles de minuit,' 6 September, p. 1; 'Étranger,' 28 October 1891, p. 3; and 'Les Meetings en Angleterre,' 2 February 1892, p. 2; in the *Journal des débats politiques et littéraires*, 'Étranger,' 16 June 1891 and 11 March 1892, n.p.; in *Le Matin*, 'Troubles à Eastbourne,' 19 October 1891, p. 2; 'L'Armée du Salut,' 26 October 1891, p. 2, 2 November 1891, p. 2, 4 January 1892, p. 2, 15 February 1892, p. 1, and 7 March 1892, p. 1; in the *Radical*, 'Étranger,' 22 July 1891, 28 October 1891, 25 November 1891, 6 January 1892, 16 February 1892, and 1 March 1892, n.p., and 'L'Armée du Salut,' 21 October 1891, n.p.; and in *Le Temps*, 'Bulletin de l'étranger,' 16 June 1891, 21 July 1891, and 12 March 1892, n.p.

6 These telegraphed updates about the events in Eastbourne also feature in numerous of the other papers listed above.

7 Rae Beth Gordon explains that language borrowed from the growing scientific fields of psychology and anthropology were widely adopted in the fin-de-siècle period to discuss, explain, and criticize cultural movements (2001, p. 1).

8 At the same time, this lexicon is also being used in a similarly prescriptive manner to talk, among other examples, about dance culture (discussed by Rae Beth Gordon, 2004, pp. 267–99).

9 This suspicion of the Salvation Army in regions with notable Protestant populations takes various forms, but the reports of these suspicions all tend to revolve around their music: for Daniel Courtois, writing in Strasbourg, the reformed church in France needs to create its own canon of Protestant worship music, rather than either being swung by the brash tactics of the Salvation Army or allowing sacred singing to languish still further in the French Protestant tradition (1887, esp. pp. 97–9); despite the established Salvation depot in Rouen, Octave Théoc for the *Revue normande* denies that the Salvation Army have any hope of success in Normandy and writes mocking song lyrics to popular tunes, 'Ah! Plaignez la pauvre Maréchale!' and 'Booth rimée ou Bouts rimés' (1894, pp. 3–6); and the novelist Henry Maystre set his novel *L'Adversaire* in the Basses-Cévennes, the most Protestant region in France, and dramatizes the struggle between a French Protestant preacher and the intoxicating tactics of the Salvation Army invaders (reviewed by Gaston d'Hailly, 1886, pp. 39–47).

10 In her discussion of Third Republican festivals, Jann Pasler draws attention to the prominence of the military band in Alfred Roll's *Le 14 juillet 1880: inauguration du monument à la République* (2009, p. 337), and later remarks that military bands kept the revolutionary aesthetic and pride in France's glorious military past alive long after it faded from other areas of public life (p. 613). With similar sensitivity to the affective potential of military-style music, Barbara Kelly notes that the organizers of the first Republican festivals during the Third Republic were wary of enlivening associations between Republicanism and revolutionary unrest, and that this contributed to their decision to split the first Bastille Day in 1880 into two geographically separated celebrations – the military ceremonies distanced from the populace at Longchamps, and the popular festivals in central Paris (2008, p. 2).

11 To name but a few representative examples: Fauque and Saloman's *A la santé du Boulanger!* (1888), Aron's *Boulanger vengera la France, chanson patriotique* (1888), and Guitton's *Le Général Boulanger: quadrille patriotique et militaire sur des motifs nationaux* (1890).

12 See passing reports of this violence in 'La Vérité Vraie,' *Le XIXe Siècle*, 30 June 1883, n.p.; Jean de Paris, 'Nouvelles diverses,' *Figaro*, 10 February 1886, p. 5; 'Faits divers,' *Le XIXe Siècle*, 1 May 1886, n.p.; 'Départements et étranger,' *L'Intransigeant*,

Singing for salvation 127

29 January 1887, p. 3; 'Paris: une brute,' *Le XIXe Siècle*, 9 October 1887, n.p.; Jean de Paris, 'Nouvelles diverses,' *Figaro*, 3 November 1887, p. 2; Henry Fouquier, 'La Vie de Paris,' *Le XIXe Siècle*, 19 April 1888, n.p.; 'Étranger: Bélgique,' *Le Temps*, 19 July 1891, n.p.; 'Départements: Lyon,' *Le Petit Parisien*, 9 February 1892, n.p.; 'Paris: L'Armée du Salut,' *Le Petit Parisien*, 19 November 1892, n.p.; 'Laisser faire,' *Le Temps*, 20 November 1892, n.p.; 'Paris: Chez les Salutistes,' *Le XIXs Siècle*, 2 December 1892, n.p.; 'Nouvelles diverses,' *L'Univers*, 10 November 1894, n.p.; 'Faits divers,' *Le XIXe Siècle*, 7 August 1897, n.p.

13 Robert Tombs discusses the French 'mission civilisatrice,' as a 'moral underpinning which, in the minds of French nationalists, distinguished French conquests from the selfish aggression of other colonial powers, especially Britain, the "social vampire" motivated by "mercantile egoism"' (1996, p. 202).

14 It is well recorded that the Nazi party used music to create a sense of unity and identity among its followers (see, for example, Richard J. Golsan (ed.), *Fascism, Aesthetics, and Culture* (1992); Carolyn Birdsall, *Nazi-Soundscapes* (2012); Heinz Pohle, *Der Rundfunk als Instrument der Politik* (1955); Pamela Potter, *Most German of the Arts* (1998); Frank Trommler, 'Conducting Music, Conducting War' (2004)). Vichy France negotiated with the German occupying forces for access to music broadcasting and opera companies (see Leslie A. Sprout, *The Musical Legacy of Wartime France* (2013), Chapter 1); and the Music Directorate of the British Union of Fascists enlisted music for propaganda purposes and in order to establish group homogeneity through participation in voice choirs and community singing (see Graham Macklin, "Onward Blackshirts!" (2013)).

15 Indeed, the prudish, upright Salvation Army girls are also mocked in the British music hall, though without the same connotations of *national* character: this is mentioned by Peter Bailey in the context of his study of musical comedy and the rhetoric of the 'girl' on British stages at the turn of the nineteenth century (see 1998, p. 183).

16 Polaire's 'hysterico-épileptique' style is discussed further by Rae Beth Gordon in her article 'La Parisienne dances with Darwin, 1875–1910' (2003, pp. 635–6).

17 This is seen in many aspects of the play: Miss Helyett enunciates the clichéd English expression of 'Shoking!' [sic.] on first entering the stage; her father appeals to her to maintain a stiff upper lip; the costume of her compatriot James Richter was a quintessentially English tweed suit and deer-stalker; and she is the ideal product of her father's evangelism, clearly calling to mind the English William Booth and his daughter Catherine. Indeed, in many contemporary books on England, such as Bellenger's book explicitly on London and English life, *Londres pittoresque et la vie anglaise* (1877), chapters feature in which not England but America and its religious life are the central topics, such as on the Beecher-Killon law suit (chapter 28) and on the US revivalists Moody and Sankey (chapters 37 and 39).

18 Ellis discusses in particular an image from *Le Monde illustré* (Issue 9, 30 September 1865), in which the brass instrument played by the bulging-eyed woman turns into a snake with open jaws – the caption reads, 'le *serpent* recommençant à tenter la femme' ['the *serpent* starting to tempt woman once again']. This draws an explicit parallel between the brass-playing woman and the fall of Eve, and as the serpent was an instrument typically played by men in French churches, this image is doubly freighted with criticism (1999, p. 240).

128 *Singing for salvation*

19 J.-F. Vaudin, *La France chorale*, 5 (145) (15 November 1865), n.p. – translations Ellis's from 'The Fair Sax' (1999, p. 246).

Songs cited

'L'Armée du Chahut! Chansonnette.' G. Delesalle and É. Gallé, n.d. [1887]. Paris: V. Fournier.

'Cinq minutes à l'Armée du Salut.' J. Moy, n.d. [1895]. Paris: Au Chien Noir.

'La Fausse Helyett. Chansonnette comique.' Dalleroy and L.-A. Dubost, n.d. [1893]. Paris: E. Meuriot.

'J'ai lâché l'Armée du Salut. Chansonnette.' R. Beretta and J. Croisier, n.d. [1896]. Paris: F. Brondert.

'Les Mômes de l'Armée du Salut. Chansonnette.' L. Delormel, n.d. [1893]. Paris: 7 rue d'Enghien.

'La Salutiste batignollaise! Chansonnette.' É. Duhem, n.d. [1901]. Paris: V. Lange.

'La Salutiste! Chansonnette.' Z. Duc and E. Spencer, n.d. [1896]. Paris: H. Barthélemy.

'Viv' l'Armée du Chahut-u-u-u-ut! Chansonnette.' E. Deransart, F. Lémon, P. Nalray and A. Siégel, n.d. [1893]. Paris: 7 rue d'Enghien.

Works cited

'Agents anglais en Algérie,' 1893. *La Croix*. 8 Nov., p. 2.

'L'Armée du Salut,' 1888. *Le Petit Parisien*. 18 April, n.p.

'L'Armée du Salut en déroute,' 1891. *Le XIXe Siècle*. 19 July, n.p.

'L'Armée du Salut,' 1892. *Revue encyclopédique: recueil documentaire universel et illustré*. Paris: Larousse. pp. 230–1.

Bailey, P., 1998. *Popular Culture and Performance in the Victorian City*. Cambridge: Cambridge University Press.

Baker, A., 2017. *Amateur Musical Societies and Sports Clubs in Provincial France, 1848–1914: Harmony and Hostility*. Basingstoke: Palgrave Macmillan.

Balz, A., 1893. 'Chronique,' *Le XIXe Siècle*. 2 July, n.p.

Bartel, P., 1896. 'En Province,' *Le Gaulois*. 23 Nov., p. 3.

Bellenger, H., *ca.* 1877. *Londres pittoresque et la vie anglaise*. Paris: Georges Decaux.

Bennett, J., 2001. *The Enchantment of Modern Life: Attachments, Crossings, and Ethics*. Princeton: Princeton University Press.

'Bigoterie,' 1888. *Le Petit Parisien*. 4 March, n.p.

Birdsall, C., 2012. *Nazi-Soundscapes: Sound, Technology and Urban Space in Germany, 1933–1945*. Amsterdam: Amsterdam University Press.

Blum, E., 1886. 'Zigzags dans Paris,' *Le Rappel*. 2 Sept., n.p.

Bon, G. le, 1895. *Psychologie des foules*. Reprint 1907. Paris: Félix Alcan.

Bourget, P., 1889. *Études et portraits*, 2 vols. Paris: Lemerre.

Bovet, M.-A. de, 1898. *L'Écosse: Souvenirs et impressions de voyage*. Paris: Hachette.

Brada [pseud. Henriette Consuelo Sansom Puliga], 1895. *Notes sur Londres*. Paris: Calmann-Lévy.

Brichanteau, 1886. 'Échos du jour,' *Le XIX Siècle*. 31 Aug., n.p.

Chaitin, G. D., 2009. *The Enemy Within: Culture Wars and Political Identity in Novels of the French Third Republic*. Columbus, OH: Ohio State University Press.

Champsaur, F., 1885. 'Salvation Army,' *Figaro*. 7 Sept., p. 2.

Singing for salvation 129

Chincholle, C., 1889. 'Le Mariage au drapeau,' *Figaro.* 11 Oct., p. 2.

'Choses et gens,' 1885. *Le Matin.* 13 Aug., p. 3.

'Chronique,' 1892. *L'Univers.* 2 Dec., n.p.

'Contre les protestants,' 1896. *Le Matin.* 23 Nov., p. 1.

Courtois, D., 1887. *La Musique sacrée dans l'Église réformée de France.* Strasbourg: G. Fischbacher.

Crispin, 1891. 'Les Théâtres,' *Le XIXe Siècle.* 24 Dec., n.p.

Daniel, G., 1900. 'Paris vécu: l'Armée du Salut,' *Le Matin.* 17 Dec., pp. 1–2.

'Décadence Salutiste,' 1894. *Le Matin.* 16 July, p. 1.

Dejuinne, P.-P., 1886. 'La Presse au jour le jour,' *Le XIXe Siècle.* 30 April and 6 Dec., n.p.

'Dépêches télégraphiques: Angleterre,' 1891. *L'Univers.* 6 Oct, 6 April, and 16 June, p. 3.

Desvernay, F., 1886. 'Chronique,' *Lyon-Revue.* 31 March, p. 190.

Djikic, M., 2011. 'The Effect of Music and Lyrics on Personality,' *Psychology of Aesthetics, Creativity and the Arts,* 5 (3), pp. 237–40.

Dubois, P., 1890. 'L'Armée du Chahut,' *L'Intransigeant,* 13 Sept., p. 2.

Dupain, J.-M., 1888. *Étude clinique sur le délire religieux.* Paris: Imprimeries réunies.

'Échos et nouvelles,' 1892. *Le Petit Parisien.* 29 Feb., n.p.

'Échos et nouvelles,' 1894. *Le XIXe Siècle.* 8 Aug., n.p.

Ellis, K., 1999. 'The Fair Sax: Women, Brass-Playing and the Instrument Trade in 1860s Paris,' *The Journal of the Royal Musical Association,* 124 (2), pp. 221–54.

Eyerman, R. and Jamison, A., 1998. *Music and Social Movements: Mobilizing Traditions in the Twentieth Century.* Cambridge: Cambridge University Press.

'Faits divers,' 1887. *Le Temps.* 27 Jan., n.p.

'Faits divers,' 1887. *Le Rappel.* 29 Jan., n.p.

Finot, J., 1903. *Français et Anglais.* Paris: Félix Juven.

Fouquier, H., 1883. 'Chronique,' *Le XIXe Siècle.* 20 July, n.p.

Fouquier, H., 1888. 'La Vie de Paris,' *Le XIXe Siècle.* 1 Sept., n.p.

France, H., 1883. *Les Va-nu-pieds de Londres.* Paris: Charpentier.

France, H., 1886. *Au pays des Brouillards (Mœurs britanniques).* Paris: Librairie illustrée.

France, H., 1900. *Croquis d'Outre-Manche.* Paris: Charpentier.

Frébault, E., 1889. 'Chronique,' *L'Europe artiste.* 13 Jan., p. 1.

Frollo, J., 1883. 'L'Armée du Salut,' *Le Petit Parisien.* 14 March, n.p.

Gardey, P., 1897. *Anglophilie gouvernementale: Manœuvres des protestants à Tahiti et à Madagascar.* Paris: Chamuel.

'Gazette du jour,' 1890. *La Croix.* 7 Oct., p. 1.

Général Boum-Boum, 1893. *En arrière: organe officiel de L'Armée du Chahut,* 1 (Mi-Carême).

Gérôme, 1887. 'Courrier de Paris,' *L'Univers illustré.* 26 Feb., pp. 130–1.

Ginisty, P., 1890. 'Chronique,' *Le XIXe Siècle.* 10 Dec., n.p.

Golsan, R. J., ed., 1992. *Fascism, Aesthetics, and Culture.* Hanover, NH: University Press of New England.

Gordon, R. B., 2001. *Why the French Love Jerry Lewis, from Cabaret to Early Cinema.* Stanford, CA: Stanford University Press.

Gordon, R. B., 2003. 'La Parisienne dances with Darwin, 1875–1910,' *Modernism/Modernity,* 10 (4), pp. 617–56.

Gordon, R. B., 2004. 'Fashion and the White Savage in the Parisian Music Hall,' *Fashion Theory,* 8 (3), pp. 267–99.

130 *Singing for salvation*

Gracyk, T., 2010. *Listening to Popular Music: Or, How I Learned to Stop Worrying and Love Led Zeppelin*. Ann Arbor: University of Michigan Press.

Hailly, G. d', 1886. 'Chronique,' *Revue des livres nouveaux (anciennement lettres aux châteaux)*, 11. pp. 39–47.

Johnson, B., 2002. 'Killing me Softly with his Song: an Initial Investigation into the use of Popular Music as a Tool of Oppression,' *Popular Music*, 21 (1), pp. 27–39.

Jupilles, F. de, 1885. *Jacques Bonhomme chez John Bull*. Paris: Calmann-Lévy.

Jupilles, F. de, 1886. Au Pays des Brouillards (Mœurs britanniques). Paris: Librairie illustrée.

Kelly, B., ed., 2008. *French Music, Culture, and National Identity, 1870–1939*. Rochester, NY: University of Rochester Press.

Kennaway, J., 2011. 'Musical Hypnosis: Sound and Selfhood from Mesmerism to Brainwashing,' *Social History of Medicine*, 25 (2), pp. 271–89.

Késanlik, R. de, 1896. 'En province: Lyon,' *L'Art lyrique et le music-hall*. 31 May, p. 4.

Lafond, L., 1887. *L'Écosse jadis et aujourd'hui, études et souvenirs*. Paris: Calmann-Lévy.

Lefèvre, F., 1893. 'Propagande Salutiste,' *Le Rappel*. 8 Nov., n.p.

Leger, A., 1901. 'L'Armée du Salut, *Le Correspondant: revue mensuelle*, 63, pp. 465–87.

Le M., 1895. 'L'Invasion britannique,' *La Croix*. 13 March, pp. 1–2.

Lorrain, J., 1900. *Le Vice errant*. Paris: Ollendorff.

Macklin, G., 2013. ' "Onward Blackshirts!" Music and the British Union of Fascists,' *Patterns of Prejudice*, 47 (4–5), pp. 430–57.

'La Mi-Carême,' 1893. *Le XIXe Siècle*. 10 March, n.p.

Monter, E.M. de, 1872. 'Alger: Fêtes musicales,' *Revue et gazette musicale de Paris*, 39 (22), p. 172.

Narjoux, F., 1886. *En Angleterre: Angleterre, Écosse (Les Orcades, Les Hébrides), Irlande: Le Pays, Les Habitants, La Vie intérieure*. Paris: E. Plon, Nourrit et Cie.

Nettl, B., 2000. 'An Ethnomusicologist Contemplates Universals in Music Sound and Musical Culture.' In: N.L. Wallin, B. Merker, and S. Brown, eds. *The Origins of Music*. Cambridge, MA: MIT Press.

Nordau, M., 1895. *Degeneration*. London: William Heinemann.

O'Monroy, R., 1894. 'Courrier de Paris,' *L'Univers illustré*. 8 Sept., pp. 562–63.

O'Rell, M., 1884a. *Les Filles de John Bull*. Paris: Calmann-Lévy.

O'Rell, M., 1884b. *John Bull et son île*. Paris: Calmann-Lévy.

O'Rell, M., 1887. *L'Ami MacDonald: Souvenirs anecdotiques de l'Écosse*. Paris: Calmann-Lévy.

Paris, J. de, 1886. 'Nouvelles diverses,' *Figaro*. 30 April, p. 2.

Paris, J. de, 1888. 'Nouvelles diverses,' *Figaro*. 28 Feb., p. 2.

Paris, J. de, 1891. 'La Procession des Salutistes,' *Figaro*. 9 Nov., p. 2.

'Paris: une brute,' 1887. *Le XIXe Siècle*. 9 Oct., n.p.

Pasler, J., 2009. *Composing the Citizen: Music as Public Utility in Third-Republican France*. Berkeley, CA: University of California Press.

Perdican, 1892. 'Les Théâtres,' *Le XIXe Siècle*. 10 June, n.p.

Pierre l'Ermite, 1900. 'Aoh yes!' *La Croix*. 29 July, p. 1

Pieslak, J., 2010. 'Cranking up the Volume: Music as a Tool of Torture,' *Global Dialogue Online*, 12 (1), pp. 1–11.

Pohle, H., 1955. *Der Rundfunk als Instrument der Politik: Zur Geschichte des deutschen Rundfunks von 1923/38*. Hamburg: Hans Bredow Institut.

Potter, P., 1998. *Most German of the Arts: Musicology and Society from the Weimar Republic to the End of Hitler's Reich*. New Haven: Yale University Press.

'La Presse au jour le jour,' 1887. *Le XIXe Siècle*. 13 Aug., n.p.

'Les Religions à Paris,' 1893. *Le XIXe Siècle*. 14 Nov., n.p.

Rosny aîné, J.H., 1900. *Nell Horn de l'Armée du Salut: Roman de mœurs londoniennes*. Paris: Ollendorff.

'Spectacles divers,' 1902. *Le Petit Parisien*. 22 June, p. 5.

Sprout, L.A., 2013. *The Musical Legacy of Wartime France*. Berkley, CA: University of California Press.

Taine, H., 1872. *Notes sur l'Angleterre*. Paris: Hachette.

Tarde, G., 1901. *L'Opinion et la foule*. Paris: Félix Alcan.

Théoc, O., 1894. 'Salutistes!!' *Revue comique normande: artistique, littéraire, théâtrale...*, 13. pp. 3–6.

Tinwell, A., 2015. *The Uncanny Valley in Games and Animation*. Boca Raton: CRC Press.

Tombs, R., 1996. *France 1814–1914*. London and New York: Longman.

Tregear, P., 1999. 'Sounding Fascism: T. W. Adorno and the Political Susceptibility of Music,' *Culture, Theory and Critique*, 42 (1), pp. 36–48.

Trommler, F., 2004. 'Conducting Music, Conducting War: Nazi Germany as an Acoustic Experience.' In: N. M. Alter and L. Koepnick, eds. *Sound Matters: Essays on the Acoustics of Modern German Culture*. New York and Oxford: Berghahn. pp. 65–76.

Vallès, J., 1884. *La Rue à Londres*, edited by Lucien Sheler. Reprint 1951. Paris: Editeurs Français Réunis.

Zola, É., 1894. *Lourdes*. Paris: Charpentier et Fasquelle.

3 Singing the Celts

British folk music and French identity

'Les chansons populaires d'origine celtique, conservées par la seule tradition orale, forment aujourd'hui le contingent, sinon le plus volumineux, du moins le plus caractéristique du répertoire de nos paysans.'

'Folksongs of Celtic origins, kept alive purely through oral tradition, represent, if not the most substantial, at least the most characteristic part of the repertoire of our peasants today.'

Tiersot, *Histoire de la chanson populaire en France* (1889, p. iii)

Under the impulses of Romanticism, the French gaze had frequently turned across the Channel to the wilder corners of the British Isles during the nineteenth century – to the Cumberland of the 'Lakistes' and then beyond to the nations of haunting pipes and harps in windswept landscapes, the Scotland and Ireland that held on to pockets of humble but 'authentic' culture that the Anglo-Saxon powers had failed to wipe out. However, despite the proximity of the British Isles to France, musical engagements with the cultures of these nations initially extended only to a vague, Romantic idea of a Celtic spirit or soul, particularly in the earlier part of the century. The Irish poet and song collector Thomas Moore's settings of *Irish Melodies* (1815) had been warmly received in France, especially 'The Last Rose of Summer' ('La Dernière Rose d'été') which would be arranged and rearranged by Berlioz, Gounod, and many more minor composers; this created an emotive idea of Ireland that would be reflected in dramatic adventure novels, such as Paul Féval père's hugely popular *La Quittance de Minuit* (*The Midnight Rent* – 1846). Welsh culture and songs, though not nearly as widely known, were no less the subject of study by writers such as Hersart de la Villemarqué, a scholar of Breton folk culture who is said to have been the first Frenchman to be initiated into the Welsh Gorsedd, and who published Welsh and Irish legends and folk songs alongside their Breton counterparts in his *La Légende celtique* (*Celtic Legend* – 1859). Scotland had enjoyed by far the most significant attention. Napoleon and Chateaubriand were both said to be among the throngs of enthusiastic readers of Macpherson's *Ossian*, which Le Sueur adapted into his opera *Ossian, ou les Bardes* in 1804; the tragic history of Marie Stuart captured the public imagination throughout the

DOI: 10.4324/9780367815431-4

century and was adapted into dozens of plays;[1] and, of course, the hearts and minds of a generation were enraptured by the novels of Sir Walter Scott. The literary historian Louis Maigron recalled that Scott's popularity had been so great in the first half of the century that clothing, furniture, shop décor, advertising posters, and music had all been caught up in the whirlwind. At the apogee of Scottomania (which he locates around 1827), on just one evening the Théâtre-Français was showing *Louis XI à Péronne* (an extract from *Quentin Durward*, adapted by Mély-Janin); the Odéon, *Labyrinthe de Woodstock* (an adaptation of *Woodstock*, by Duval); and the Opéra Comique, *Leicester* (adapted from *Kenilworth*, by Scribe and Auber); and then the following day Boïeldieu's *La Dame blanche* (*The White Lady*) could be seen at the Opéra Comique, inspired by a selection of Scott's works including *The Monastery*, *The Abbot*, and *Guy Mannering* (1912, p. 55). Maigron remembers that 'ce fut plus qu'un succès: ce fut un engouement. Une génération tout entière en demeura éblouie et séduite' ['it was more than a success: it was an infatuation. A whole generation was dazzled and seduced'] (1912, p. 51).

Indeed, French travellers to Scotland for several generations after Scott's own lifetime could not help but see the country through the lens of his literature and through the emotions they had felt at dramatic and musical adaptations of his plotlines. These Scottian fantasies became so entrenched that many French visitors would long be struck not by the reality beyond the fantasy nation, but inversely by fantastic qualities in the real nation. Indeed, this fantasy quality is analogized repeatedly with theatrics; the novelist and travel-writer Marie-Anne de Bovet, for example, sees the landscape just across the Scottish border as a 'joli décor d'opéra-comique' ['pretty scenery like a comic-opera set'] and near Perth she notes 'de petites gorges d'une sauvagerie d'opéra-comique' ['little gorges with a comic-opera savagery about them'] (1898, pp. 3, 108). Journalist and wit Max O'Rell quips that 'seuls ces beaux soldats *highlanders*, que les bobonnes d'Edimbourg louent à l'heure pour se promener avec elles le Dimanche, portent le costume de Dickson dans la *Dame blanche*' ['now only those handsome Highlander soldiers, who are hired by the hour by the little women of Edinburgh to walk with them on Sundays, sport Dickson's costume from the *White Lady*']. It is worthy of note that O'Rell is not making a point about the sad abandonment of the ancient dress of the clans here; rather, he is commenting that the French visitor may be surprised and disappointed at the absence from the real city of the picturesque costumes with which they were familiar from Parisian musical theatre (1887, p. 361). For all of these writers, performance, music, and fantasy constantly veil and mediate the reality of Celtic Britain, and its relevance for the French observer.

From the first half of the century, salon and art music adopted the fascination with Celtic Britain with enthusiasm. Most composers engaging musically with Celtic Britain did so in line with the vogue in Western European Romanticism to try to capture the emotional *idea* of other cultures in orchestral or operatic music, rather than to explore or recognize the inhabitants' native musical traditions or recognize them as musical and cultural subjects in their own right.

134 *Singing the Celts*

For many, 'Scottish' or 'Irish' music need only relate to folk tradition by means of a vague aural evocation of 'Scottishness' or 'Irishness,' such as the dotted reel-style rhythms present in Julien de Mallian's three-act melodrama *La Croix de feu, ou les Pieds noirs d'Irlande* (*The Burning Cross, or the Black Feet of Ireland*, 1838), in Neuland and Mme Jourdain's wistful romance *Écosse est ma patrie,* (*Scotland is my Homeland,* 1845), or Coquelin and Frouart's equally wistful *Écosse ma patrie* (*Scotland, my Homeland,* 1847), but without a felt need to replicate any identifiable connection to any specific Irish or Scottish song. Other composers, perhaps inspired by Beethoven's *Twenty-Five Irish Songs* (WoO 152) and *Twenty-Five Scottish Songs* (Opus 108), integrated short musical quotations from collections of real folksongs into their orchestral or operatic compositions; Boïeldieu, for example, integrated a motif from 'Wi' a Hundred Pipers' into his *Dame blanche*, though for the listener this is in no way differentiated from musical sections by Boïeldieu which pastiche Scottish music, or from sections which are fully detached from Scottish tradition and entrenched in the middle- and high-brow operatic fashions of 1820s France.

In many ways, this approach continues to be espoused with gusto during the Third Republic. In the art-music world, Saint-Saëns still included snippets of Scottish and Irish themes in the 'Idylle écossaise' and 'Entrée des clans' for his opera *Henry VIII* (1883), and manifold variations on the folk songs 'The Last Rose of Summer' and 'My Heart's in the Highlands' found their way into drawing-room singing books and piano-tuition primers for French young ladies. Where the fin de siècle differs, however, is the growing interest in 'authentic' folk music as an important signifier of inherent character traits in the context of evolutionary theory and the growing body of contemporaneous race 'science.' A conviction had existed for some time that national spirit and folk-music traditions were intertwined in some deeply organic way: in 1835, for example, G. Fulgence articulates this in the preface to his *Cent Chants populaires des diverses nations du monde* [*One Hundred Folksongs from Around the World*]:

> les chants populaires sont le miroir le plus fidèle des mœurs et de l'esprit d'un peuple, ses goûts, ses coutumes, ses traditions s'y peignent avec une merveilleuse exactitude. Toutes les circonstances extérieures qui créent le caractère d'une nation, influent également sur ses chants.
>
> (*ca.* 1835, p. 1)

> [folksongs are the most faithful mirror of cultural mores and of the spirit of a people; their tastes, customs, and traditions are painted there with marvellous precision. All the external circumstances that create the character of a nation also influence folksong].

Building on these ideas, with the increasing colonial movement and its cultural appropriations, and with the racializing evolutionary science of the Darwinian era (as discussed in the introduction to the present book), the final decades of

Singing the Celts 135

the nineteenth century saw a spike in interest in traditional music as a manifestation of national and racial identity and character in a more specific and more direct manner than ever before (discussed by Pasler, 2007, p. 160). Such ideas were not the province of a small intellectual elite or restricted to highbrow discussions among music theorists; rather, the considerable crowds who gathered to hear the international musical performers at the World Fairs of 1878, 1889, and 1900 are testament to a wider public interest in the folk music of the ordinary populations of other countries as a key signifier of identity, race, and each people's place in the natural order. As Annegret Fauser observes,

> by 1889, the rhetoric of folk music as the authentic, uncorrupted voice of the people had been firmly established in European thought. [...] While art music was a universal language spoken by individuals, folk music was specific to a linguistic community and region but, at the same time, a shared, collective expression of the "génie du peuple"
>
> (2005, p. 253)

Jann Pasler goes on to note that there was a decisive drive after 1870 by many from across the political spectrum to forge an idea of France as a nation with unified traits in spite of its multiple languages and dialects, ethnic origins, religious customs, and cultural differences; moreover, to do so not just in general cultural terms, but more specifically in terms of inherent birth traits, variously termed racial, ethnic, of the blood, or national according to the chosen terminology of each writer or theorist. She remarks that the same racial theories, used and abused by both Republicans and conservative nationalists in the colonial sphere, were implemented to explicate regional identities, to analyse French folk music, and to connect the two together (see 2007, pp. 147–67). Of course, the appeal of such a unifying perspective is understandable in the wake of a century of civil conflict, defeat in the Franco-Prussian War, colonial struggles, and the increasing social and racial tensions within France that would crystalize during the Dreyfus Affair. These were no doubt crucial motivational factors behind the foundation of associations for the study of folk traditions, such as the Société des traditions populaires in 1877, and in Romain Rolland's advocation of folk singing within primary school syllabi with the hope of fostering a sense of national sentiment in the young through music (1908, p. 264). Indeed, there was considerable disagreement over the definition of the inherent French character that should be arrived at through its music: Pasler writes perceptively that

> when the term race appeared in reference to the French as a homogenous entity, it was in some ways a term of desire as well as self-delusion [...]. Both republicans and monarchists seized on the notion of music as a sign and symbol of race because, to them both, it idealized a certain identity associated with their ancestors.
>
> (2006, p. 489)

136 *Singing the Celts*

This chapter explores the role and reception of Scottish, Irish, and, occasionally, Welsh traditional music in this historical and cultural context during the Third Republic, focusing on music destined for the large market of amateurs, non-art music performances, and related commentaries. The terms 'traditional' and 'folk' song are, of course, fluid and rather ambiguous signifiers: this is all the more so in French, where the descriptor 'chanson populaire' could merely indicate that the song be well known, that it be widespread in its popularity, and that it originate outside the art-music sphere. Nonetheless, musicians and writers from this time imply that, to be worthy of study, 'folk' music should have emerged in some way organically from the people, be that from the peasantry lost in the mists of time, from more recent poets seen as figureheads for that historic people's folk culture (in the case of Scotland, Walter Scott and Robert Burns, and for Ireland, Thomas Moore), or with songs of protest associated with historic popular movements in which one whole population is being oppressed by another – often along lines understood to be analogous with ethnic identity. In general, the populace in question should not be urban, the songs should not originate from organized entertainment venues such as music hall or vaudeville, and they should appear to convey something much more profound about identity and ethnic essence than their melodic and harmonic simplicity would initially seem to imply.[2] This non-specific approach to defining and selecting what counts as 'folk' or 'authentic' in music is addressed in places as this chapter progresses, but more often than not these questions are significant to French approaches to British folk culture in as much as they are *not* asked by writers. French commentators often extrapolate about ethnicity and national culture from Celtic-British music as though this process were unproblematic – even though they rarely accept such an unproblematic version of identity on their own side of the Channel.

Though it is not strictly accurate from either an historical or an ethnic point of view, I use the rough term 'Celtic' (and 'Celtic British') in this chapter to refer to the traditions of Scotland, Ireland, and Wales, employing the term in much the same loose way as it was used in nineteenth-century France. Despite the common interchangeability of the terms 'Angleterre' and 'Grande-Bretagne,' 'anglais' and 'britannique' in almost all contexts in the nineteenth century, such was generally not the case when engaging in subjects touching the world of folk culture. Here, almost all French writers were emphatic that the Anglo-Saxons (i.e. the English) were devoid of folk culture – especially folk music – whereas their Celtic neighbours had a wealth of it, in spite of – or thanks to – the oppression and cultural erasure inflicted upon them through history by their Anglo-Saxon overlords, tinted rose with nostalgia for the Franco-Scottish Auld Alliance and the brotherhood of Catholic tradition with Ireland. The writer Louis Lafond, for example, having reached the far-distant shores of the Outer Hebrides, is enchanted by the native musicality of Barra fisherman, singing as they go out to sea with 'chants pleins d'une étrange et gracieuse mélodie comme tous ceux que conserve ce peuple si

Singing the Celts 137

bien doué pour la musique' ['songs full of a strange and graceful melody, like all those songs preserved by this musically-gifted people'] (1887, p. 175). The music critic and historian Albert Soubies, asserted that 'l'élément saxon [...] a [...] fait preuve, en musique de dons moins brillants que ceux des Celtes [...]. Pour ce qui concerne les Celtes, leur goût et leur aptitude pour la musique ont été en quelque sorte reconnus de toute antiquité' ['the Saxon element of society has demonstrated less dazzling musical talent than the Celtic part. As for the Celts, their taste in and aptitude for music has been recognized to some extent throughout history'] (1904, p. 2). Indeed, in an almost unique instance of Scottish culture being used as a generic catch-all for English culture rather than the reverse, in Paul Lacôme's *Le Tour du monde en dix chansons nationales et caractéristiques* [*Around the World in Ten National and Characteristic Songs*], 'Angleterre' is represented by 'La Plainte du barde: ballade écossaise' ['The Bard's Lament: a Scottish ballad'] (1875, pp. 24–5).

The present chapter discusses the fascination and heightened significance of Celtic-British traditional music within the debates around French national identity, racial origins, and the significance of folk song – a fascination that was, paradoxically, both cast in the light of the increasing 'sciencification' of ideas around race, but that was also in many ways the product of the French imaginary. Where Celtic Britain is concerned, the newly evolutionary, racialist turn in contemporaneous thinking resulted in a tension between the desire for romantic, emotional affect and the desire to use folk music to discover something incisive about Celtic ethnic characteristics. Much like more distant and/ or colonized nations, these countries are treated as an object of both ethnological interest and exoticist fantasy; indeed, numerous collections of music arranged for piano, voice, or violin published for amateurs at this time place Celtic-British folksongs side-by-side with music from the cultures of Hungary, China, and the Maghreb.[3] Britain's proximity to France, their shared history, and their longstanding legacy of cultural exchanges did not exempt Scottish, Irish, and Welsh folk music from such treatment, either in terms of how it was represented in textual discourse, or in terms of how it was transcribed, translated, arranged, and edited for performance by musicians in France. Similar paradigms are used by the French in their musical representations of both the Orient and Celtic Britain, substantially problematizing the usefulness of published versions of their folksongs as source material for better understanding these nations through the music of their people.

It might seem incongruous to raise concepts and language drawn from colonialism and post-colonialism here, given that there was no military or political colonization – and no expectation of colonization – of any part of Britain by France. General sentiment in France was sympathetic towards the plights of Scotland and Ireland, and crucially (and ironically) this sentiment was largely due to the fact that these countries were seen as being subjected to pseudo-colonial rule by the English to the detriment of their own distinct cultures and freedoms. Nonetheless, the hallmarks of orientalism, exoticization, and cultural appropriation are demonstrably present in arrangements of Celtic-British

138 *Singing the Celts*

folksongs and in writing about those traditions – and the absence of real-life political or military power hierarchies between France and these nations makes it all the more striking to ascertain their presence here. Matthew Head asserts in his discussion on Mozart's Turkish music that musical orientalism is characterized by 'the tropology of the unchanging Orient, of the Middle East as intrinsically and eternally ancient, it denies "the East" its own access to the imaginary timeline' (2000, p. 17). This was complexified, suggests Head, by the Romantic movement, which focused on the 'Ideal' – 'the inner universal substance, which is abstract and indeterminate' (2000, p. 143) We can see direct parallels between all these aspects of musical orientalism and the treatment of Celtic-British music which will be discussed in this chapter; reading French adaptations and translations of folksong with a critical eye informed by postcolonialism can, then, be revelatory.

This chapter looks, first, at the discursive frameworks and the selective vision of Celtic-British folk music privileged by Third Republican writers and musicians, before exploring this further in the context of French myth-making about their own Celtic heritage. Detailed readings of a selection of arrangements and translations of Scottish and Irish folksongs reveal ways in which, by turning the gaze upon the Celtic world of Britain rather than that of France, French writers and commentators are able to gain salutary distance from the complex contemporaneous world of French socio-political conflicts, providing a space in which to work through questions, anxieties, and contradictions about the French Self and what having a common 'racial' identity might mean for the Third Republican French population.

Imagining the Celtic-British margins

In French perceptions of British folk tradition, Scottish, Irish, and Welsh songs are privileged to the near exclusion of English music. This imbalance is particularly notable because it differs markedly from the approach that had been taken during the boom for folksong albums in Britain during the seventeenth and eighteenth centuries. These were almost as likely to collect together songs from the various regions of England as they were songs from Scotland, Ireland, or Wales, and a rich selection of English folksongs was widely available from British publishing houses.[4] Yet collections of typical, traditional, or folk music from Britain for the amateur musician in France, including the substantial *Échos d'Angleterre* by Gallet and Weckerlin (*Echoes of England, ca.* 1877), generally present songs from England differently to those from the other constituent nations of Britain. The songs of Scotland, Ireland, and Wales in this particular collection are presented as traditional songs, which may have been mediated by song arrangers such as Thomas Moore, Walter Scott, and Robert Burns but are nonetheless represented as preserving intact their authentic folk roots. In contrast, of the twenty-one English songs, only a handful are flagged as traditional and drawn from the mists of time (such as 'The Three Ravens,' translated as 'Les Trois Corbeaux');

Singing the Celts 139

instead, most are given specific points of origin and noted as coming from courtly entertainments, urban theatre, or popular music hall – for example, the *Échos* contains Henry Bishop and John Howard Payne's 'Home Sweet Home' ('Le Foyer' in French – from an 1823 operetta), and Thomas Haynes Bayley's ballads 'I'd be a Butterfly' ('Si j'étais papillon,' *ca.* 1840) and 'Oh, no, we never mention her' ('Souvenir,' *ca.* 1840). Unsurprisingly, the songs most frequently included in such books as exemplifying English tradition are 'God Save the Queen' and 'Rule Britannia!' woven through as they are with imperial and jingoistic associations; in terms of age, these songs predate both Robert Burns and Thomas Moore, but they lack the aura of traditional, rural, pre- or extra-imperial culture and they are presented as the stuff of what O'Rell dubs, in the title of his popular book, the colonial 'Maison John Bull et Co.' Such nationalistic songs feature in lieu of the large body of traditional music strongly connected to specific English regions, such as 'The Lincolnshire Poacher,' 'Go no more a'rushing,' or 'Matty Groves.'

Publication decisions such as these and the interpretations they invite both reveal and foster a French interest in British *musique populaire* firmly fixed upon the Celtic fringes. Though the reasons for this focus are never discussed explicitly by contemporaneous writers and musicians, its explanation may in part be due to, first, the French tendency to overlook the local and regional quality of culture within England itself. That there were songs and distinctive local identities in Tyneside, the West country, or the Wash fenland only made sense if one recognized that 'Englishness' was not itself a uniform cultural or ethnic entity but a collection of diverse regional populations with sometimes radically different concepts of lifestyle, identity, and, in some cases, dialect – a premise that runs contrary to the homogenous clichés of John Bull (for the lower and middle classes) and Mylord (for the aristocracy) promulgated by café-concert song, journalism, sociological texts, caricature, and literature alike. Secondly, contributing to this attitude may have been the fact that the English already appeared as political and military rivals in *French* traditional songs going back several centuries: for example, the song 'La Princesse mariée à un Anglais' ['The Princess married to an Englishman'] from the Nord region, dating back to at least 1700, in which the king's daughter begs her father not to marry her off to an Englishman, and when she is forced to go through with the wedding to the 'maudit Anglais' ['cursed Englishman'], the whole of Paris weeps for her. In the early-modern 'Le Ronde du roi d'Angleterre' ['The Dance of the King of England'], a French shepherdess on the Pont Neuf heckles the 'maudit roi d'Angleterre' ['cursed King of England'] and hits him with her distaff – after which he dies, to everybody's great satisfaction, and the crowd celebrate that 'le maudit roi est mort, nous n'aurons plus de guerre' ['the cursed king is dead, we'll have no more war'].[5] England, even centuries previously, was ever seen in French culture as a pressing political reality, not a folkish seat of bucolic shepherds and timeless, soil-rooted peasant life.

Thirdly, the French disregard for English folksong may be caused by the restricted compass of travel within England itself attempted by most French

140 *Singing the Celts*

travellers and therefore featuring in most travel writing. Although those who ventured across the Channel very often pursued their exploration along the East or West coast mainlines from London all the way to Edinburgh or Glasgow and thence to the Highlands, the large expanse of England that fell between King's Cross station and the Scottish borders was experienced as a mere streak of green fields or rain-drenched coastline. To the best of my knowledge, no major travel account from the Third Republic makes any significant mention of a French visitor exploring the rural parts of counties such as Lincolnshire, Norfolk, Shropshire, and Suffolk – areas that might well have afforded them encounters with continued traditions of non-urban English song. Only London, Oxford, a few aristocratic estates in the Home Counties, a handful of industrial rail interchanges such as Birmingham and Manchester and, occasionally, the touristy heart of the Lake District are graced by the bulk of French Third Republican travellers – and it is these atypical locations that are used to extrapolate information about the English as a whole. Additionally, for those French tourists and travel writers who express their pre-existing interest in folk culture, his or her preconception that this was an exclusively Celtic gift becomes a self-fulfilling prophecy; it led them to construct a travel itinerary around this assumption, and their belief that folk culture was to be found at the margins of Britain dictated that they travel straight through the England of the café-concert Englishman who we met in Chapter 1 of the present book, straight to those Celtic margins. On finding folksong in these places, they may well also deduce that they were quite right that it was not to be found anywhere else. In this respect Wales, too, often misses out; its traditional musical culture was often cast by French writers as entering its decline during the persecution of the bards by Edward I in the thirteenth century, and thus is placed so far back in history as to leave only an impoverished trace of its former character – attracting, in consequence, very little touristic attention.

At the same time, a tendency to overlook the local and regional qualities of culture within Scotland, Ireland, and Wales was similarly essential; the impossibly complicated web of local or regional warfare and vengeful clan feuds that so many traditional songs narrate would require some substantial history lessons (for example, the Scottish 'The Battle of Harlaw,' about warfare between Donald of the Isles and the Earl of Mar in 1411). The Barra fishermen mentioned above, for example, are not seen by Lafond through the local lens by which they likely understood their own musical identity, but as a product of pure, intense, and unadulterated Scottishness. Instead, the narratives in these folksongs offer more both conceptually and emotionally to a French audience – particularly a French audience after the Franco-Prussian War – if taken reductively as a fight of an oppressed, proud *nation*, united by their Celtic bloodline, resisting a militarily and economically strong one. Equally essential was the tendency to discount the multiple meanings that folksongs had for their singers and audiences in their countries of origin, which evolved over the course of the nineteenth and early twentieth centuries

Singing the Celts 141

with the waves of national feeling, political protest, emigration, industrial and economic development, and so on. Such evolution is overlooked in French discussions and adaptations of these songs, and they are treated as a crystallization of a glorious and fixed former time – as giving voice to the blood that was seen as still remaining constant in these countries *beneath* all the transient contingencies of modern life.

It is not only through simplification that the Celtic margins of Britain are reimagined and conceptualized in France – rather, racializing and exoticizing vocabulary abounds. Prevalent vocabulary of savagery and wildness in travel writing and sociological texts about the Irish, Scottish, and Welsh indicate that their milieus and their native populations are considered subjects worthy of *ethnological* study – more akin to African tribes than Western civilized societies. Marie-Anne de Bovet describes the landscape that provided the setting for Walter Scott's novels and poetry as an 'âpre et sauvage chaos' ['bitter and savage chaos'] (1898, p. 2). On observing the fishwives in Newhaven near Edinburgh going about their work, she does not just describe what she sees them do and wear, but treats this as evidence that their population has preserved 'son caractère typique et ses usages fort primitifs' ['its typical character and extremely primitive customs'] as a 'race hardie et forte' ['strong and hardy race'] (1898, p. 54). For the Parisian teacher and essayist Firmin Roz, the Scottish peasant crofters of the Highlands offer 'une image de vie simple, noble, indépendante et fière toute pénétrée de douceur sauvage que la solitude insinue dans les âmes comme pour conserver leur pureté' ['an image of a simple, noble, independent, and proud life, penetrated by a savage sweetness that solitude has planted in their souls to preserve their purity'] (1905, p. 227). Further still, despite their shared Catholic heritage, Ireland is deemed so wild and savage that writers drift towards superlative and hyperbole: de Bovet asserts first that Donegal is 'le comté le plus sauvage et le plus pauvre de la pauvre et sauvage Erin' ['the most savage and the poorest county in poor, savage Erin'] (1908, p. 282); the celebrated novelist and critic Paul Bourget calls Connemara 'de toute la sauvage Irlande le plus sauvage endroit' ['of all savage Ireland the most savage place'] (1889, II, p. 60); and Paul Joanne's guidebook series informs the reader that County Mayo and Achill Island are wild Ireland's 'district sauvage et pittoresque' ['wild and picturesque district'] (1908, p. 174). Unlike the efforts to denigrate the English as barbaric which are shot through with nationalistic rivalry (as discussed in Chapter 1), the context is different when the British Celts are in question; the tone is more neutral, less belligerent or acerbic, and more tinted with anthropological curiosity, exoticist fantasy, and culturally-appropriative desire than political competitiveness.

As the products of these wild milieus, writers tend to assert that the aesthetic qualities of Celtic-British music are also characteristically primitive and savage. O'Rell describes 'la mélodie primitive et sauvage des chansons écossaises' ['the primitive and savage melody of Scottish songs'] (1887, p. 260). In the appendix to his translation of Thomas Moore's *Mélodies*,

142 *Singing the Celts*

Henri Jousselin observes with more poetry than precision that, in Irish folk songs, 'la mesure, la coupe du vers, le rythme et l'harmonie donnent une saveur étrange et comme un parfum sauvage' ['the timing, the shape of the verse, the rhythm and harmony have a strange flavour, something like a wild perfume'] (1871, p. 30). Welsh music, too, is treated in these terms by the musicologist Carl Engel in his study of primitive world music from 1866, being compared to the ancient music imported by rampaging Viking invaders (1866, p. 355). Indeed, in this context Robert Burns is valued above Thomas Moore because the former fits into French stereotypes of the 'natural' and the 'authentic': Jousselin expresses a typical assessment by reflecting that:

> aux accents de ces vieux airs qui chantaient dans son souvenir, y excitant des images de douleur et de liberté, son imagination s'est éveillée plus vive et plus tendre. Non pas qu'il ne se soit jamais monté à ce ton de sensibilité profonde et passionnée, qui étonne et ravit dans les poésies de Robert Burns, un patriote d'une autre trempe. Mais ce Robert Burns était une âme forte, un peu rude; mais que de naturel et de vigueur!
>
> (1871, p. 13)

> [with the traces of old airs singing in his memory, enlivening images of suffering and liberty, his imagination awoke all the livelier and more tender. Not that he never rose to the pitch of profound and passionate sensitivity that is so striking and delightful in the poetry of Robert Burns, a patriot of a different metal. But Robert Burns was a strong soul, a little tough, but so natural and vigorous!]

For all its literary brilliance, Jousselin considers it an undesirable betrayal of nature that Moore demonstrates poetic and musical sophistication, his 'imagination prodigue d'ornements,' his 'goût exquis et brillant des détails,' and his 'parfum d'antiquité classique' ['prodigiously ornamented imagination,' his 'exquisite and glittering taste for detail,' and his 'scent of classical antiquity'] (1871, p. 13). Burns, in contrast, is lauded by his translator Richard de la Madelaine by dint of being a 'poète ignorant [qui] ne voyait pas la nature à travers les lunettes des livres' ['an ignorant poet who didn't observe nature through a bookish lens'] (1874, p. xxxix), and by his biographer Angellier as a bard for a musical genre 'sortie du sol' ['emerged from the earth'] (1893, II, p. 3). In a circular gesture, as well as the savage primitiveness of the land and people resulting in savage, primitive music, so too such primitive and savage music is presented as evidence of the savage primitiveness of the people.

Similarly, Scottish and Irish folk culture are explicitly analogized with the Oriental Other as well as a generic primitiveness despite their white European ethnicity. De la Madelaine, for example, records in the preface to his translation of Burns that a rendition of 'Scots wha hae wi' Wallace bled' which he heard performed by a piper and singer whilst descending the Caledonian Canal sounded 'plaintif comme les psalmodies des muezzins des mosquées'

Singing the Celts 143

['plaintive like the mu'addhin from a mosque'] (1874, p. xii). In a curious combination of the northern and eastern exotic, Louis Ganne – known for his patriotic songs such as the café-concert hits *La Père la Victoire* (1888) and *La Marche Lorraine* (1892) – composed *La Gipsy: mazurka ecossaise* (1899), a mash-up avant la lettre for piano which takes characteristic Scottish-style musical tropes,[6] and bends them to fit the 3/4 time signature and second or third-beat stress of the mazurka form. The cherry is placed upon the cake of this bizarre exotic melange by the cover image for the sheet music, which offers a dark-haired gypsy character, complete with tambourine and saucy over-the-shoulder smile, but whose clothing comprises a glengarry bonnet, a wide tartan band around her dress, and fastenings reminiscent of those found on highland-dress sporrans and broaches. A primitive violence, too, often associated with more exotic lands, is also evoked in association with Celtic-British musical tradition. Angellier states that the cultural mores and bloody battles depicted in Scottish ballads 'ne sont pas supérieures à celles de nos sauvages de l'Amérique du Sud' ['are not superior to those of our South American savages'] (1893, II, p. 306), and although there is a recognition that violence and warrior culture is a thing of the past in Scotland, the fact that there is still a taste for its representation *in music* in the nineteenth century is treated by many French writers as evidence that the same character traits have nonetheless been passed down in the blood of the people ever since.

Such lexicon of savagery, exoticism, and primitive violence is compounded by an insistent return to terms evoking ancientness in late nineteenth-century texts on Celtic-British folk music. There is a determined emphasis on an idealized golden age that has come and gone, diminishing the worth and the cultural importance of these once-musical nations in the present day. The past dominates every text on Celtic Britain. Firmin Roz could not be clearer in his displacement of Ireland's cultural richness into the past, stating that 'l'Irlande est la terre du passé [où] tout y rappelle les temps qui ne sont plus' ['Ireland is the land of the past, where everything recalls days that are gone'] (1905, p. 107). Scotland, too, in a selective forgetting of the modern cities of Edinburgh and Glasgow that Roz has himself visited, gives 'cette impression que le pays *a été*. Les jours semblent ne survivre à l'Histoire que pour en refléter le prestige' ['the impression that this is a country that *has been*. Days seem to live on beyond the Past only to serve as a reminder of its former prestige'] (1905, p. 214). On visiting Wales, Roz recounts that in Llandudno he thinks 'avec mélancolie aux pittoresques cités de jadis' ['with sadness of the picturesque medieval towns of old'], and faced with the absence of Romantic ruins in North Wales he simply loses interest: 'rien n'attire, rien ne retient. Nul édifice ne raconte l'histoire' ['there is nothing to attract you, nothing to hold you there. Not a single building speaks of history'] (1905, p. 242).

Music, balladry, and legend are treated as the key remnants of these past golden days; the ancient music still bears witness to authentic traces of these glory years but in doing so it underlines that there is no realistic prospect of further glory in the future. In Ireland, Marie-Anne de Bovet remarks in

144 *Singing the Celts*

the imperfect tense, 'la musique était en grand honneur dans l'antique Erin, et le collège des sages comprenait une section consacrée à l'enseignement de l'harmonie universelle' ['music used to be greatly honoured in ancient Erin, and the school of the sages included a section consecrated to teaching universal harmony'] (1908, p. 332). The novelist and architect Félix Narjoux implies that Scottish skill and natural inclination towards singing is a lingering historical trait from the days when 'les puissants lairds autrefois entretenaient autour d'eux des bardes qui célébraient leurs exploits et racontaient les hauts faits de leur famille; mais ces chants parlés et non écrits ont disparu' ['in the past powerful lairds maintained bards in their retinue who would sing of their exploits and tell of the great deeds their family had accomplished; but these songs, being performed orally rather than being written down, have disappeared'] (1886, p. 252). On a similar note, Lafond describes the role of erstwhile 'harpers' (minstrels) who would have sung the legends of Ossian and were once the heart and soul of the musical tradition of the Highlands – but who sing no longer (1887, pp. 118–9). Even the capacity to appreciate music, Lafond implies, has degraded over time, and he laments the reduction of St Cecilia's Hall in Edinburgh from the musical concert venue par excellence to a beer merchant and second-hand clothing shop (1887, p. 33).

When combined, this joint emphasis on savagery, exoticism, and pastness clearly paints the music of Celtic Britain both as more primitive than that of France, and of interest *only* in as much as it is primitive. On the one hand, this feeds into the general Romantic fascination with the noble savage – a vague, imagined figure of an Edenic past that modern man has had to sacrifice for the benefits of civilization and that he likes to contemplate wistfully over fine wine in cut-crystal glasses and to use as a means of contemplating the state of modern institutions and mores. On the other hand, by the Third Republic this goes deeper due to both the 'scientific' turn in Western scrutiny of the cultures and races of the world in general, and due to more localized interest in defining a 'French' identity in the wake of the Franco-Prussian War and revolutionary upheaval. As Jane Goodall explains in her study of performance culture in the age of evolutionary theory, ideas from the realm of science were embraced with enthusiasm in all realms of culture, inspiring 'fertile associative games that played with ideas which captured the imagination of the general public,' but which also often took 'a cavalier attitude to comprehension' (2002, pp. 5–6).

It is not surprising, then, with these competing motives and inconsistent approaches, that the recurrent lexical fields of primitivism, exoticism, and pastness are also threaded through with internal contradictions and inconsistencies, and these linger under the surface to pose oblique, awkward questions. Such uncertainty can be sensed bubbling beneath the surface of some of the more hostile responses to Celtic-British music, such as the essayist Félix Rémo's comments on Welsh music in his series of articles about the 'Mouvement musical en Angleterre' in *L'Europe artiste* from September to December 1896. As is so often the case, 'Angleterre' in the title here refers to Britain, and includes instalments on Scotland (20 September), Ireland (27 September), and Wales (4 October). The section on Wales sets out the ancientness of Welsh music according to their national legends, their pride in their musical heritage, their strong belief in musical aptitude as a cornerstone of Cymric identity, their tradition of harp music and sung ballads, the attack on the Welsh bards by Edward I, and, finally, their modern but less mystic forms of contemporary bardic culture centring around the Eisteddfod. One might assume – given that Rémo is unusual in choosing to write about Welsh music at all and given that the Welsh were hardly political or economic challengers to French supremacy – that the tone of this article would be one of general historical and musicological interest. However, this is by no means the case, and instead the predominant tone is mocking and belittling. For example, Rémo opens with the exclamation: 'Allez donc vous aventurer à toucher à leurs croyances! Écoutez-les évoquer leurs souvenirs, leurs convictions, leurs traditions' ['Go ahead and try touching their beliefs! Listen to them evoking their memories, their convictions, their traditions'] (4 October 1896, n.p.). The exclamation mark and use of the imperative seek to impress upon the reader a sense that the Welsh pride in their music is mere silliness and that they are living in an infantile fantasy-land rather than their being in possession of a rich national culture worthy of genuine interest or respect.

We might well wonder why Rémo writes in this sarcastic, rather vehement manner. The desire to take England down a peg or two would by no means be a surprise, as we have seen in Chapter 1 of the present book, but it is quite unlikely that many of his general readership yearned for an opportunity to belittle the Welsh.[7] Yet belittle them Rémo certainly does, adding salt to the typical descriptions of primitiveness and savagery by scoffing that the Welsh are puerile and deluded in their national obsession with their musical heritage. This surprising stance might have two possible motives. First, there may be an underlying political motivation regarding Brittany and its currents of political separatism. Heather Williams has discussed the enthusiastic contact between Breton musicians and learned societies with Welsh harpers and bards during the latter half of the century (including a notable Breton visit to the Eisteddfod in 1899 – see Williams, 2013, pp. 27–35); in a Republican France confronting the difficulties of forging a sense national identity and unity, directly or indirectly evoking the oppositional stance of Brittany was undoubtedly undesirable. Moreover, Rémo's sarcasm may also be explained by his observation that the Welsh claim their national musicality is older, greater, and richer than other musical traditions in Europe (including, by implication, in France). The examples chosen by Rémo evince that he feels, consciously or subconsciously, that these Welsh claims threaten French pride and the validity of traits seen as central to French identity. This is particularly so because Welsh bardic tradition lays claim to the use of harmony and counterpoint by harp players as early as the twelfth century, well before they were in use in France; Rémo dismisses the evidence (that is, Welsh medieval manuscripts which include written musical notation with harmonies) and asserts that any

146 *Singing the Celts*

musical sophistication achieved by the medieval Welsh was merely down to chance when a harp player happened to let their fingers fall upon several strings at once, creating a 'harmonie aussi naïve que primitive' ['a harmony as naïve as it was primitive'], rather than being a sign of intellectual and artistic sophistication, and a step beyond the musical impulses of raw human nature.

A sense of underlying uncertainty at the implications of Celtic-British music for the French subject is also apparent in the often rather anxious accounts by French travellers of first-hand experiences of music when in Ireland and Scotland. They may have been eagerly enchanted – and psychologically pre-prepared – to hear bagpipes in the hills and harps in the valleys, but when aural encounters are involuntary, uncomfortably up-close, imbedded in the realities of poverty, or generally run counter to their expectations, singing and music spark more unease than interest. Marie-Anne de Bovet is unsettled by the uncontrolled, unromantic singing that emanates from a group of priests in the Irish spa town of Lisdoonvarna, 'buvant du punch au whiskey et chantant à tour de rôle des chansons comiques bêtes à pleurer, et des romances sentimentales en façon de complainte d'aveugle' ['drinking whiskey punch and taking turns to sing woefully silly comic songs, and sentimental romances like a blindman's lament'] (1908, p. 205). In Scotland, Narjoux casts the noise of spontaneous music and singing at public festivals as decidedly negative rather than charmingly Celtic or rustic: on coming across some drunken singers at a 'fête champêtre' near Perth, he bemoans that 'le bruit de la fête contrastait avec le calme et le silence de la campagne. Ces gens surexcités [...] poussent maintenant des hurrahs frénétiques, des cris assourdissants; la bête est lâchée et son contact n'a rien d'agréable' ['the noise of the festival contrasted with the calm and silence of the countryside. Now, these overexcited people are crying out frenetic hurrahs, deafening shouts; the beast is unleashed, and there is nothing agreeable in having any contact with it'] (1886, p. 122). Linked in a subordinate clause by the semi-colon, there is no possible doubt that this string of sound images and the animality they encapsulate are to be judged as emphatically disagreeable. Perhaps, as Edward Hughes says of French encounters with Polynesians, these uncontrolled aural encounters in Scotland and Ireland fill the French listener with the anxiety that 'the centre might slide into barbarism [...]. Thus the ethnographic fantasy [...] readmits European fears about the brittle foundations of its own civilization' (2001, p. 27) – an anxiety all the more alive given the shared bloodlines between the French and these Celtic savages which did not feature in the typical Eastern encounter.

A Celtic France?

The language of orientalism and exoticism, the reductionism of Celtic-British folk music traditions, and the evidence of disquiet and uncertainty when faced with reality rather than the imagined Celtic margins – all these aspects gravitate around and are informed by the wider, often conflicting

Singing the Celts   147

ideas and debates on music and concepts of race and national character from the mid-nineteenth century onwards. During the Third Republic, as ethnomusicologist Bruno Nettl has remarked in his study of folk traditions, 'it is assumed by some that each people or culture has only one kind of music, one musical style, which really fits its personality and an authentic song would have to be a song with this character' (1965, p. 9). The authentic song with its authentic character, once located, could be read alongside theories of musical and ethnological progress as indicative of the evolutionary sophistication of any one people and their relative level of civilization and ethnic value. This interpretive impulse is not only turned outwards, but the ethno-musicologists emerging in the Third Republic also seek to divine what this means for music from within France – to the point that the idea of an 'authentic' version of each song is enforced by composers and scholars without any great regard for logic: for example, even on hearing a wide range of styles and versions of the same song in situ in the Basse-Breton region, Bourgault-Ducoudray actively ignores the clearly fluid character of the tradition and comments that 'on est quelquefois obligé de recueillir vingt versions du même air avant de trouver la bonne' ['sometimes one has to collect twenty versions of the same tune before coming across the right one'] – though how he is able to identify the 'right' from the 'wrong' version is never explained (1885, p. 6).

There is a general agreement that France as a nation is inherently musical from the grassroots upwards: Julien Tiersot, for example, asserted that 'la France est une grande province sur les diverses parties de laquelle sont répandues les mêmes poésies naïves et frustes, les mêmes mélodies tour à tour vives, gracieuses ou mélancoliques' ['France is a vast province across which are spread the same naïve and rough poetry, the same melodies, whether they be lively, graceful, or melancholic'] (1890, III, p. 3). The folklorist Gabriel Vicaire goes so far as to affirm with emphatic use of the singular that 'la poésie populaire française, c'est la France elle-même' ['French folk lyric is France itself'] (1886, p. 255). Yet statements of unity such as this are not unproblematic. What becomes apparent from both discussions of folk music in general and of Celtic-British folk music in particular, is not so much the unified character of the national folk-musical traditions of France, but the intensity of the *need* to locate (or construct) an ideal, shared, racial and national identity for France, and the persisting magnetism of folk music as the raw material for that process. As folksong collectors delved into the rockiest and remotest corners of the country to catalogue the nation's native musical essence from the Second Empire onwards, their discoveries evinced the variety of traditions, languages, and musical styles within the politically-defined entity of the French nation;[8] folksong seemed to demonstrate the diversity of cultures, languages, bloodlines, and identities rather than its shared origins and identity. After all, until this point traditional music had often been seen as an expression of *regional* character, both by the Parisian elites as a means of marking out the Otherness of provincial populations and by those dwelling in the regions as a marker of their unique identity and community togetherness;

148   *Singing the Celts*

for example, the compendious series of pen portraits from around France, *Les Français peints par eux-mêmes* (*The French Painted by Themselves*, 1840–42), had used snippets of folk music as explicit evidence of characteristics deemed inherent to different regional types – among other instances, both musical notation and lyrics are printed to describe to the reader the songs sung by Norman peasants to ask for alms at Christmas time, to celebrate the Fêtes de la Saint-Jean, and to make merry with cider drinking during the Saint Vivien festivities. The author Émile de la Bédollièrre deduces from this music that the Norman people have unique, rather savage character traits, and he conveys through his descriptions of this music how fundamentally different Normans are from Parisians or any other regional community (1840–42, pp. 146–7, 150–1).

One means of seeking unity in the face of this diversity was to search further back in time to a moment that the land known in the nineteenth century as France was thought to have been occupied largely by one ethnically cohesive group: and the time most often seized upon is pre-Roman, Celtic Gaul. Habitation of France's landmass by the Celtic race predated the dilution of bloodlines brought about by successive invasions by Romans, Vikings, and Franks and thus this Celtic era and heritage indicated the possibility of common French racial origins, albeit (conveniently) shrouded in the mists of time. This fascination with a Celtic origin took several forms and built upon the work of a number of influential theorists of both music and race from earlier in the century whose legacies would colour the French reception and conceptualization of Celtic-British folk music during the Third Republic considerably. Augustin Thierry had revived the idea of a connection between ethnicity and class for the readers of post-Revolutionary France, positing that the aristocracy had descended from the Franks whilst the rest of the French people could find the origins of their bloodline among the Celtic Gauls (1840, Chapter 2). In Arthur de Gobineau's widely read *Essai sur l'inégalité des races humaines* (*Essay on the Inequality of the Human Races*, 1855), a key element of his argument is that Celts are a 'masculine' race, introducing strong character traits into the French bloodline which would be diluted in the south by intermixing with 'feminine' Mediterranean races but which would remain dominant in the north (1855, I, p. 87). The highly-influential music theorist François-Joseph Fétis sees musical talent and the capacity for progress towards musical sophistication as the unique province of the Aryan race (1869, I, p. III), and he explores the music of the Celts – as direct descendants of the Aryans – in terms of archaeological artefacts of the French (and to some extent European) musical past which could be usefully investigated in Wales, Ireland, and Scotland (see 1874, IV, book 11). These ideas left a powerful legacy for the next generation of musicians and music theorists, who in turn took an eager interest in Celtic folk music and the secrets it could reveal about *French* ethnic identity.

Revivifying the dormant Celtic blood running through the veins of the French population becomes a motivational impulse behind numerous artistic,

Singing the Celts 149

educational, and political movements around the turn of the twentieth century. The *école romane* movement of the 1890s, for example, sought to 'renoue[r] la chaîne gallique rompue par le romantisme et sa décadence' ['re-tie the gallic chain that was broken by Romanticism and its decadence'] (Moréas, 1891, p. 1), and books were published on all manner of aspects of Celtic heritage, including Celtic roots to the French language (Pierre Malvezin's *Dictionnaire des racines celtiques* [*Dictionary of Celtic Root Words*], 1903), on Celtic arch-aeological sites (Henri Martin's *Études d'archéologie celtique* [*Studies in Celtic Archeology*], 1872), and on the Celtic origins of French legends (Part 4 of Édouard Schuré's *Les Grandes Légendes de la France* [*The Great Legends of France*], 1892). Tiersot remarks explicitly upon the importance of studying Celtic history – including folksong – because, in France:

> l'influence celtique n'a pas complètement disparu. [...] Les légendes, les contes et les chansons populaires d'origine celtique, conservés par la seule tradition orale, forment aujourd'hui le contingent, sinon le plus volumineux, du moins le plus caractéristique du répertoire de nos paysans.
> (1889, p. iii)

> [the Celtic influence has not completely disappeared. The legends, stories, and folksongs of Celtic origin, preserved solely through oral tradition, form today if not the most numerous then at least the most characteristic part of the repertoire of our peasants.]

Yet the spectre of impending cultural loss hovers over France's own Celtic past; Weckerlin expresses his sorrow, asking, 'grâce à la facilité des communications, où sont-ils ces pays sauvages et primitifs, qui ont gardé leur ancien langage et la tradition des mœurs de leurs pères? [...] Les anciens airs auront complètement disparu avant la fin de l'année' ['thanks to the ease of modern communications, where are those savage and primitive lands that have kept their ancient language and the traditional customs of their forefathers? The old ballads will have completely disappeared before the end of the year'] (1886, p. xxxi). It is to address these problematic identifications, desires, and anxieties that Celtic-British folk music is brought to bear as at once a thinking space, archaeological artefact, and idealization – it provides a conceptual detour which makes it possible to consider issues of Celtic-French racial identity and folk traditions via those of Celtic Scotland, Ireland, and Wales.

Indeed, that a shared heritage exists, passed down in the blood of both Celtic Britain and France, is evoked repeatedly by French writers. Burns's jocular poetry is taken by de la Madelaine as evidence of 'un fond de joyeuseté celtique, peut-être l'influence française' ['a background of Celtic joyousness, perhaps a French influence'] (1874, pp. 305–06). It leads Angellier to ponder that 'il semblerait bien plutôt fait pour prendre sa place dans la littérature française [...], l'idée qu'on se fait ordinairement de notre race' ['he would seem more suited to take a place in the French literary canon, with the idea

150   *Singing the Celts*

of race normally associated with ourselves'] (1893, II, p. 399). The essayist and historian Firmin Roz suggests that the Scottish soul 'était quelque peu sœur de la nôtre' ['is somewhat the sister of our own'], with the proud 'petit peuple' of Scotland giving glimpses of 'l'idéalisme, la grâce et la courtoisie du pays de France' ['the idealism, the grace, and the courtesy of France'] (1905, p. 234). Author, orientalist, and antiquarian James Darmesteter suggests that the study of old Irish heritage should become 'presque une branche des études d'antiquités françaises: seule, l'Irlande sait encore une partie de ce que nous avons été' ['almost a branch of the study of French antiquity: Ireland alone recalls a part of what we have been'] (1896, p. 236). Taine places Thomas Moore as 'le plus gai et le plus français de tous' ['the most cheerful and French of them all'] (1863, p. 255). Gaelic and Cymric cultures in Celtic Britain were represented as the keys to the Celtic world,

> [qui] subsistent en Irlande, dans les Highlands d'Écosse et dans le pays de Galles, c'est-à-dire dans les contrées de la langue gaélique et galloise où les éléments celtiques et kymriques sont restés le plus purs. Ces contrées sont peuplées des descendants des malheureuses populations du sud de l'Angleterre qui se sont réfugiées, lors des invasions romaines [...] et qui, soustraites par leur manière de vivre, de leur langue, à l'influence subie par les autres compatriotes, sont demeurées les dépositaires fidèles des purs vieilles traditions nationales.
>
> (Brueyre, 1875, p. x.)

> [which persist in Ireland, in the Scottish Highlands, and in Wales – that is, in the regions where Gaelic and Gallic languages are spoken and where Celtic and Cymric elements have remained the purest. These regions are populated with the descendants of those unfortunate communities from the south of England who sought refuge from the Roman invasions and who were shielded by their lifestyle and language from the influences undergone by their compatriots. They have therefore remained the loyal custodians of the pure old national traditions.]

For all these writers, France and Celtic Britain are overtly linked by the parallel manifestations in modern times of their ancient shared bloodline – and the study of Celtic Britain and its folk music, which maintain Celtic traits in a more primitive but stronger concentration, are presented to the reader as worthy of interest precisely for the insights they offers into *French* heritage.

Moreover, to read the culture of nineteenth-century Celtic Britain as the enduring product of 'pure' Celtic and Cymric blood is so compelling an idea that writers seem to find it hard to avoid. After all, the lands of Scott, Byron, Burns, Moore, and the Gorsedd were known to be rich in folk music – what could be more Scottish than the bagpipes or more Irish or Welsh than the harp? Although Auguste Angellier declares specifically in his preface that, unlike Taine, he will *not* be trying to define 'quelle part [de la génie de Burns]

Singing the Celts 151

revient à la race, au climat, aux habitudes de la vie' ['which part of Burns's genius is the result of race, climate, and the customs of daily life'], he none-theless seems to be unable to resist mentioning the Celtic blood in Burns's maternal line and its undoubted impact upon the poet's musical and cultural life: 'c'est à l'influence maternelle que revient la partie lyrique, ses adorables chansons si légères, hymnes joyeuses aux couleurs clairs qui laissent deviner le sang vif des Gaulois' ['the lyrical qualities come from his maternal side; his loveable, light songs are joyous, brightly-coloured hymns that allow us to glimpse his rich Gaelic blood'] (1893, II, p. iii). Being ascribed to his Gaelic blood, rather than merely to his individual family or to nurture by a musical mother, the reader is given to understand that it is Burns's Celtic characteristics that endow him with 'le goût, bien celte aussi, de la grâce dans le movement et des sons harmonieux' ['the taste – a very Celtic taste too – for grace in movement and harmonious sounds'] (1893, II, pp. 5, 18). Similarly, when Robert de Bonnière, in his novel *Lord Hyland* (1895), seeks to explain the characteristics of his melancholic protagonist, folk music and ethnic heritage are placed hand in hand: Hyland describes the musical gifts of his Irish mother, asserting that 'je ne doutais pas [...] qu'au pays où elle était née, les chansons sacrées, autrefois chantées sous les chênes, n'eussent gardé assez de vertu pour agir en elle' ['I had no doubt that in the land of her birth, the sacred songs, once sung beneath oak trees, still carried enough virtue to act from deep within her'] (1895, pp. 69–70). Despite the fact that the druids themselves are characterized as a relic of the past by de Bonnière, their musical and spiritual essence is presumed to persist, being passed down the generations in the blood and being able to manifest themselves actively still through the nineteenth-century individual.

Ralphe Locke has remarked that 'internal Others' (such as, in his example, the Puerto Ricans in West Side Story) are often exoticized by a society's dominant culture (2009, p. 7); we can see in the case of Celtic-British folk music that this exoticism is taken a step further. The margins of Britain pro-vide a means of exoticizing an *external* Celtic Other despite the fact that an *internal* Celtic Other also exists (both evidently in Brittany, and throughout the population if these claims for French Celtic ethnic heritage be correct), but without the detrimental effects of directly exoticizing internal Otherness; Scotland, Ireland, and Wales serve then as a sort of 'external-internal' Other. As the French observer was likely to have minimal direct contact with British cultures of music-making, the conceptual detour via Celtic Britain made it easier to draw compelling conclusions about the relationship between Celtic music and Celtic-French racial identity that could be acceptable and access-ible to a far greater number of people. This is not unlike the use of the Orient as mirror discussed by Edward Said (1978, Introduction), although in the case of Celtic Britain the Otherness is largely a chronological one (it reflects an ancient bloodline) rather than a geographical or religious Otherness (reflecting Eastern, non-white, and non-Christian peoples). Celtic Britain offers the sup-posedly authentic remnants of a people who had withstood Germanic (in

152 *Singing the Celts*

this case, Anglo-Saxon) invasion, and onto which the French could project their concerns about identity in the modern era and after military defeat by Germany. Celtic Britain offers a less politically sensitive way of connecting outside of France with the idea of an ancient, pre-Germanic past inside of France – and it offers, too, concrete examples of Celtic music and lyrics to stir the Celtic blood still said to be coursing through French veins without any French regional associations.

Arranging and translating Celtic-British folksong

One might expect, in the context of both the 'scientific' discourses around race and music, and the desire to explore French ethnic heritage through her Celtic neighbours, that a light-touch approach would be taken to arranging and translating Celtic-British folk music for consumption by the broad French audience of amateur musicians and music consumers. However, more often than not, appropriation appears to dominate strongly over desires for appreciation or education. This partakes in the longstanding trend, as discussed by Matthew Riley and Anthony Smith, of arranging 'folk' music in a way that is palatable for the desired consumer (2016, p. 37); the key nuance, however, for the fin-de-siècle generation, is that this is blurred beneath glosses which claim the ability of their palatable arrangements to nonetheless convey insights into national identity, character, and psychological makeup. Typical in this respect is W.R. Binfield's *Bluette* (subtitled 'Transcription de chants nationaux écossais,' 1877 – see Figure 3.1).[9] This piece comprises four Scottish folksongs with variations, arranged for piano. Each song is introduced in more-or-less recognizable form, though the arrangements present the tunes with a considerably thicker texture and ornate style than any traditional song would usually have: in the first sixteen bars, for example, 'Scots wha hae wi' Wallace bled' is to be performed *maestoso pesante* (majestic and weighty), with a generous scattering of arpeggi, and a dramatic crescendo to the peak of the third phrase, which is held with a pause before falling away in a fading decrescendo. This is followed by an extremely elaborate variation of busy, Italianate stylistics, show-casing any talented French amateur pianist who had purchased this sheet music to their friends, family, and acquaintances. The weighty crochets of the theme splinter into a maelstrom of hemi-demi-semi-quavers racing up and down the keyboard, with tremuli, septuplets, and long appoggiaturas marked *veloce* (swift).

Clearly, the primary concern here is not to acquaint the amateur musician or the audience with 'national Scottish songs' through an objective transcription as the subtitle suggests, but rather a thoroughgoing adaptation to provide material for virtuosic display, French musical pleasure, and as a signifier of talent to other members of the player's French social circle.

To some extent, composers such as Binfield simply exhibit the very natural desire to seek inspiration and to extend the range of aesthetic forms available to them by drawing upon other cultures. Jonathan Bellman argues

Singing the Celts 153

Figure 3.1 The first page of W.R. Binfield's *Bluette*, with variations on the theme of 'Scots wha hae wi' Wallace bled.'
Source: Bibliothèque nationale de France.

persuasively that the 'transcultural' in music need not always be pernicious or domineering – indeed, without it, local musical styles would descend into stagnation and exhausting repetitiveness (2011, p. 433). Bellman agrees with Edward Said's interpretation of orientalism in music (in the latter's *Culture and Imperialism*, 1993), which allows room for transformation, learning, sharing,

154 *Singing the Celts*

and exchanging, as well as for the hegemonic strictures of Western colonial conquest and appropriation (summarized by Bellman in 2011, pp. 417–22). However, especially in instrumental music, it is hard to define with any precision where the line stands between neutral inspiration and exoticist appropriation, particularly in light of the minimizing, rather belittling use of linguistic tropes of savagery and orientalism which, as we have seen, are so often used to frame the folk music of Celtic Britain by French writers, musicians, and arrangers, and the minimal allowance made for learning or sharing through mutual discussion. In view of the wider context of Othering Celtic Britain through language, there are then clearly elements which Matthew Head criticizes in musical orientalism. In his discussion of Mozart's Turkish music, Head argues that in such musical exoticism 'signs of difference are "relegated" to the status of details within a pre-existing European framework: Turkish music is represented not only though decoration but *as* decoration,' (2000, p. 27) and the Orient appears in music as 'estranged essence: divine, remote, imaginately glimpsed, ancestral' (2000, p. 143). Though Celtic-British nations are neither Oriental nor French colonies, these elements of decorativeness, fantasy, and ancestral essence are all clearly present in arrangements and variations such as that by Binfield. However, this position too should be nuanced with the fact that the substantial cultural appropriation of Scottish folk tradition in Binfield's variations is not generic enough to be likely to be written or heard as entirely neutral, there is also no direct power relation over Scotland in the wider socio-political reality that would invite us to fully espouse the condemnation meted out by Head on musical orientalism more widely.

The complexity and ambivalence of this relationship is still more evident in arrangements which combine the translation of lyrics with the adaptations and elaborations wrought upon the melodies of folk music. Naturally, to some extent every transcription of a folksong requires cultural infidelity. Folksongs, by their very nature, have no one definitive form or performance context, and their very fluidity and space for improvisation, inspiration, and crowd participation is a crucial part of such musical culture. Indeed, the very idea of writing down and fixing folk music within western stave notation and within all the codified regularity of Western art-music tradition is anathema to its nature. On gathering Celtic-British folk music into musical collections in the nineteenth century, French translators and arrangers had to select and impose a fixed form upon these songs – and they did so in response to their own musical training, anticipated audience, and their preconceptions about Celtic character that they perceived these songs should express. In doing so, they were, of course, generally preceded by British song collectors who had already transcribed and reformulated popular folk music from around Great Britain to make it accessible and appealing to the drawing-room amateur musician and salon or concert performer. Many British song collectors were, as David Harker reminds us, 'prepared to go to considerable lengths not only to expropriate workers' culture, but to alter what they found so as to fit their

Singing the Celts 155

own class-based preconceptions, prejudices, and needs' (1985, p. 77) – Harker points to Scott as a notable example of such a collector, and Jules Janin wrote with positive overtones in the introduction to Jousselin's translation of the *Mélodies irlandaises* that Thomas Moore took traditional Irish airs, 'les dépouillant avec art de ces paroles vides et de ces refrains sonores, qui sont la base et le fond des chansons primitives, et il introduisait sous l'air rustique une poésie élégante' ['skillfully stripped them of the empty words and loud choruses that are the building blocks for primitive songs, and introduced an elegant poetry underneath their rustic tunes'] (1871, p. xxii).

Such changes include the switch from traditional instruments such as harp, pipe, fiddle, or drum to drawing-room or orchestral alternatives, effacing original timbres and sounds from the songs and resulting in a voice that has lost much of its identity. Similarly, transcribing this music into the twelve-semi-tone scale results in a change in the harmonics of much Celtic folk music. In its traditional form, a pentatonic scale and simple texture often provided the basis for many traditional Scottish and Irish melodies, creating iconic acoustic signatures.[10] This style invited singers and instrumentalists to improvise with melismatic ornamentation in the spaces between those five core pitches, in a manner more flexible than Western art-music traditions typically invite (this is recognized by Tiersot, 1905, p. 49). The imposition of a diatonic scale removes these spaces and the characteristic freedoms they offer. Distinctive traits are lost as the popular music is tamed within the socially-structured rigour of music lessons, salon entertainments, and concert rooms, made 'melodious' for the classically-attuned ear, and made learnable and perfectible to satisfy bourgeois cultural ideals in less dynamic performance contexts.

However, it is significant that French arrangements of such songs also differ substantially from their British bourgeois predecessors, and that significant adaptations, changes, and variations are introduced by even those nationalistic composers and arrangers who explicitly voice the inherent connectedness between folk music and national identity – and who are therefore most aware of the false impressions that they convey to their audience of non-expert, amateur musicians and listeners. Notably, many further changes are affected to the musical arrangements that are entirely unnecessary from a practical point of view, given that the work of rendering these songs into standard Western notation had already taken place, and given that they have already been adapted to the instruments and tastes of drawing-room musicians and audiences on both sides of the Channel. The decisions made in Gallet and Weckerlin's *Échos d'Angleterre* are a case in point. Although Weckerlin attributes several of these songs explicitly to Thomas Moore (who himself had adapted them from various Irish folk sources), Weckerlin's piano accompaniments deviate considerably from Moore's *Irish Melodies*. Nearly all of the Irish songs in Weckerlin's *Échos* have one generalized pattern of accompaniment, with sets of rapid triplets rolling up the arpeggio from the left to the right hand.

156 *Singing the Celts*

Extract 3.1 Weckerlin's arrangement of 'Minstrel Boy' (translated as 'Le Jeune Ménéstrel'), from *Échos d'Angleterre* (*ca.*1877, p. 112).

Extract 3.2 The equivalent passage from the original publication of Moore's verse arranged by John Andrew Stevenson, from *A Selection of Irish Melodies*, vol. 5 (1813, p. 31).

Extract 3.3 Weckerlin's arrangement of 'Has Sorrow thy Young Days Shaded' (translated as 'Une larme'), from *Échos d'Angleterre* (*ca.*1877, p. 107).

Extract 3.4 The equivalent passage from the original publication of Moore's verse arranged by John Andrew Stevenson, from *A Selection of Irish Melodies*, vol. 6 (1815, p. 57).

Yet such musical patterns are almost entirely absent from Moore's musical transcriptions of the *Irish Melodies*. This may suggest that Weckerlin was familiar with the compound metre of the traditional jig; however, a number of these airs are not and never were jigs, and thus Weckerlin enforces a narrow, stereotypical musical trope onto a rich, diverse musical tradition. In doing so, he significantly reduces the amateur French musician's exposure to and awareness of that richness, giving the impression that the Irish have a narrow stylistic palette and limiting the French public's exposure to the variety of their artistic imagination. Such a decision is all the more striking when one takes into account that Weckerlin was, himself, an influential and prominent figure in the study and collection of French folksongs, and that he wrote at length

158 *Singing the Celts*

in his *La Chanson populaire* [*Folksong*] on the inextricable links between folk music and racial origins (1886 – see, for example, pp. 188–9). The substantial audience for his arrangements, too, demonstrates the scope of how widely misleading these adaptations could be; for example, songs from this *Échos d'Angleterre* album were selected and played at the 'auditions de musiques pittoresques' at the 1889 World Fair, being framed in an explicitly educational, factual context (mentioned by Tiersot, in his 'Promenades musicales à l'exposition' for *Le Ménéstrel*, 4 August 1889, p. 244).

Additionally, French versions of Celtic-British folksong rarely incorporated the grace notes or the drone common in bagpipe music from both Scotland and Ireland, even though these traits were often included in transcriptions of songs for piano, violin, or voice circulating in Britain. Still more strikingly, the 'Scotch catch' (a semi-quaver followed by a dotted quaver) is nowhere to be seen, despite the fact that it does appear in French Romantic music *inspired* by Scotland and Ireland, and despite the fact that British song collectors had a tendency to rather *over*-exaggerate the use of this stylistic ornament (Engel, 1866, p. 98). This reflects, as Locke has argued, that 'musical exoticism is not "contained in" specific devices. Rather it arises through an interaction between a work, in *all* its aspects, and the listener': the erasure of traits such as drones and Scotch catches from French arrangements therefore may be seen as an active aesthetic decision, carrying a specifically French meaning, and attuned to the anticipated French listener (2009, p. 3).

Similarly, nearly all fast-moving Irish and Scottish dance tunes are designated as 'gigues' by French music books and writers, yet very often the melody to which they refer is, in fact, a hornpipe or strathspey. A typical jig in Scottish and Irish folk music and dance is set in a compound metre (often 9/8 or 12/8), and the stress falls on the first note in each group of three quavers. A hornpipe, or the slower strathspey, by contrast, is usually set in simple time (2/4 or 4/4), and typically comprises uneven dotted rhythms, usually a dotted semi-quaver paired with a demi-semi-quaver (or the same in reverse order). Although there are certainly aural similarities between these styles of music, the jig, hornpipe, or strathspey all tended to be played on different sets of instruments, were danced with different figures of steps, were danced primarily in different communities and settings, by different genders (the hornpipe being largely danced by sailors by the nineteenth century) and using different modes of bodily comportment. This conflation of genres was widespread, and was likely due in no small part to the pseudo 'jigs' familiar from (but misidentified in) the café-concert, as discussed in Chapter 1 – but the implications of this misidentification are more significant in light of the presentation of the music by many song arrangers as a source of *ethnological* information. This series of interpretations and obfuscations, both musical and sociological, dilutes the distinctiveness of acoustic identities, histories, subjective voices, acts of resistance, communities, and performing bodies. The implication in titles and subtitles that these are transcriptions of authentic, traditional folksongs (not merely songs about or inspired by Celtic Britain) in spite of the unnecessary imposition of aesthetic alterations, enacts a silencing and a process of cultural erasure even where no power relationship exists in political reality. Far from endeavouring to explore the 'genuine' or 'natural' character through folk music, instead such composers enact a process of appropriation all the while claiming authenticity for the arrangements of the songs that they have substantially altered and using them as inaccurate evidence for racialist assumptions.

That considerable changes are made to the music of Celtic-British folksong is all the more notable because, when French travellers to Scotland and Ireland hear folk music in picturesque settings whilst visiting these countries, they assert that the music has an ability to express something profound about these countries and the traits of their native inhabitants. During Marie-Anne de Bovet's Scottish travels, for example, she religiously documents every occasion on which she hears the bagpipes. Although their 'son aigu et nasillard' ['shrill and nasal sound'], the 'grand fracas de pibrochs glapissants' ['great din of squealing pipers'] does not always seem to her taste from an aesthetic point of view, she expresses repeatedly the revealing and eloquent nature of this music, insisting that it embodies 'le caractère à la fois pastoral et martial de la population des highlands' ['the character of the highlanders, at once pastoral and martial'] (1898, pp. 24, 153, 121) (see Figure 3.2). Similarly, Henri Jousselin, in his translation of Thomas Moore, remarks that had

Figure 3.2 One of several plates with images of bagpipe players from Marie-Anne de Bovet's *L'Écosse: Souvenirs et impressions de voyage* (1898).

160   *Singing the Celts*

Hippolyte Taine actually *heard* Moore's melodies in Ireland as well as having read the lyrics before writing his *Histoire de la littérature anglaise* [*History of English Literature*] then he would have found more substantial meaning therein than mere sentiment: 'dans ces mélodies chantées par une belle voix irlandaise et à des Irlandais. [...] il y eût vu autre chose que des *mélodies sentimentales*' ['in these melodies sung by a beautiful Irish voice to Irish people he would have seen something more than *sentimental melodies*'] (1871, p. 74 – emphasis in original text).

It is particularly interesting to observe that the Scottish, Irish, and Welsh folk musicians behind these traditions are even at times silenced where their Oriental counterparts are afforded some – limited – ability to have a voice and contribute to the conversations about their musical traditions. Given the ethnological interest taken in their shared Celtic heritage by arrangers and writers, one might imagine that interviews might be conducted with folk musicians the better to understand the traits, origins, and living cultural practice surrounding this music – particularly since Tiersot does conduct precisely such conversations with, and tries the instruments of, musicians from countries as unfamiliar as Senegal and Java during the 1889 World Fair.[11] Yet there is little evidence of any such steps being taken when it comes to Celtic Britain.

Moreover, not only do French arrangers and writers not travel to conduct interviews or research in Britain, but they also perpetuate the process of silencing and deculturation in their translations of the lyrics of Celtic-British folksongs – be they from songs in standard English, in regional varieties of English, or in Gaelic and Cymric languages. Given the contemporaneous belief among race theorists and anthropologists in the intrinsic link between folksong and national character, the translation strategy adopted to convert these unintelligible tongues into French carries considerable weight for the idea of Celtic Britishness that they convey. Translating Celtic-British folksong does, admittedly, present a number of considerable difficulties: those which face any translator (for example, the need to find equivalences for idiomatic expression and cultural references); those that face any translator of poetry (such as rhyme, phonetic patterning, musicality, and so forth); and those particularly apparent in folksong and legend – conveying the *génie* not only of the individual poet and the language, but of the whole national character for which folksong was thought to be the truly authentic expression. This is complicated further because, although singing in Italian and German would have been a commonplace experience to even amateur musicians in France, songs in English were rare,[12] and English language skills were generally limited throughout the Third Republic (as has been discussed in Chapter 1 of the present book). This alone would make singing and understanding the folksongs difficult, and it is exacerbated further by the fact that Celtic-British songs are often not in standard English but in regional varieties such as Scots English (generally referred to as 'Doric') or Hiberno-English (generally referred to as 'brogue irlandaise'), or in the distinct languages of Welsh, Scots Gaelic, or Irish; indeed, many native English speakers in Great Britain would have

Singing the Celts 161

struggled to understand these regional varieties of English, and would have been entirely at sea with the meaning and pronunciation of Celtic languages. I am not aware of any French translators working directly from Welsh, Scots Gaelic, or Irish in their song transcriptions, but many translators do record in their prefaces the difficulties of working with regional varieties of English. In his book on Burns, Buisson du Berger notes that Burns's lyric is relatively unknown in France because his Scots Doric is 'une sorte de patois qui en rend la traduction presque impracticable et dont nous ne prétendons donner que la saveur affaiblie' ['a kind of patois that makes translation almost unworkable and of which the present text claims to give only a diluted flavour'] (1889, p. 289). Indeed, so complex is this process that Buisson du Berger adds a footnote to remind the reader of the obstacles he faces each time he comes across a phrase that poses some especially knotty challenge: for example, in the translation of 'A Man's a Man for a' that' ('Pour tout ça et tout ça'), he begs the reader's indulgence, reminding them that 'il faut quelque bonne volonté chez le lecteur de toute traduction, surtout quand il s'agit d'un poète aussi difficile que Burns' ['the reader needs to approach any translation with some good will, especially when it is a translation of a poet as complex as Burns'] (1889, p. 297).

If folksong is to provide an insight into the Celtic race in Britain (and France), a foreignizing approach to translation would seem the most logical – that is, a method that retains elements of the original language and/or style – instead of a domesticating strategy which, as Lawrence Venuti explains, effaces 'the linguistic and cultural difference of the foreign text in favour of the transparent discourse dominating the target-language culture' (1992, p. 5). A very small number of translators do embrace this foreignizing approach, particularly in publications that anticipate a specialist-interest audience who would primarily be *readers* of the lyrics as silent poems rather than songs. This is the case at times, for example, in the *Revue des traditions populaires*; for its self-selecting group of folk-culture lovers and scholars, contributors to this journal sometimes offer translations such as that of an Irish ballad entitled 'Lámhóigín,' in which a number of words are retained from the Irish and are accompanied by a pronunciation guide and definitions in the footnotes (September 1890, pp. 605–11). Very occasionally, musical publications provide songs with parallel texts so that the amateur French musician can be exposed to the original language – for instance, the unusual choice by Gallet and Weckerlin to publish the Welsh lyrics to the 'March of the Men of Harleck' [sic] alongside the French (as 'Marche des Hommes de Harlech'), even though their French translation appears to have been achieved by way of an interim translation into English as it only maps loosely onto the Welsh (1877, n.p.).

More frequently, however, a domesticating translation methodology is firmly in evidence. Of course, it would be unjust to judge these French translators too harshly for many of the necessary compromises they must make. Translating some of these extremely complex specificities faithfully into French is an impossibility; indeed, there are few ways of translating 'wee, sleekit, cowran,

162 *Singing the Celts*

tim'rous beastie' into standard English that would be an adequate rendering of the original, let alone into French (de la Madelaine simply writes 'petite bête, timide et craintive'; accurate, but unevocative – 1874, p. 15). Furthermore, for those translators whose priority is to make these songs singable for the French public, a principally domesticating translation strategy is often an understandable solution, as authenticity must compromise with the exigencies of the musical form and of French rules of versification.

However, it is particularly salient to note some occasions on which translation loss – often considerable translation loss – was easily avoidable but was nonetheless enacted by French song translators, and to consider the motivation behind these active choices. Sometimes whole lines or sections are simply missed out, presumably because their translators were unable to comprehend the original texts. For example, in de la Madelaine's version of Burns's 'Lament of Mary Queen of Scots,' the French text simply skips the lines 'The mavis wild wi'mony a note / Sings drowsy day to rest,' and in 'Scotch drink' he decides not to attempt the visual description of the 'guid auld Scotch drink / whether thro' wimpling worms thou jink / Or, rickly brown, ream owne the brink' (1874, pp. 5, 69). More frequently, translation is attempted but there is a marked dilution of cultural specificity. This is especially significant in the context of the racialized readings of folk traditions in the late nineteenth century; the dilution of musical, cultural, and linguistic specificity gives a false impression of precisely those aspects that translators and commentators on Celtic-British folksong uphold as evidence of particular national and racial characteristics. For example, de la Madelaine's translation of 'Auld Lang Syne' ('Le Bon Vieux Temps') presents us with a drinking song about wine without any of the fundamental nostalgia for old friendships and times gone by; it replaces the cup of kindness with a stereotype of raucous alcohol consumption (quite aside from the fact that it places wine glasses in hands much more likely to raise a beer or whiskey) (1874, pp. 67–8). This deviation leads one to suspect the translator of being imbued with so strong a preconception of what a Scottish song *should* represent that ultimately it is what they *make* it represent in French: cliché had instilled, after all, the received wisdom that the Scots were inveterate drinkers.[13] Similarly, Gallet's translation of Lady Anne Lindsay's 'Auld Robin Gray' ('Le Vieux Robin Gray,' 1877), deprives the song of most of its core characteristics. Where the original reads:

> When the sheep are in the fauld and the kye at hame,
> And a' the weary world tae rest are gane,
> The waes of my heart fa' in showers frae my e'e,
> When my gudeman lies sound by me.

it is translated as:

> Tandis que sommeille mon vieux mari Robin Gray,
> Seule je veille: mon cœur est navré…

Et dans l'ombre un rêve sombre me surprend…
En vain mon cœur s'en défend!

The crofter setting and the farm animals have been removed, despite a number of contemporary texts and novels insisting on the centrality of this unique rural lifestyle to Scottish culture and identity;[14] what is left is melancholia and troubled dreams, the stuff of Romanticism's Scotland, but in truth there is little of the identity of the source text left here.

Historical specificity often disappears in what appears to be an effort to avoid the complications of pronouncing Gaelic place names. In the Gallet translation of Walter Scott's 'Pibroch of Donuil Dhu' (rendered as 'Cri de guerre écossais,' 1877), most of the culturally-specific detail is decontextualized into a generic war song. The only reference to anything specifically Scottish are the terms 'clan' and 'claymore,' although these are not in fact in Scott's version of the song:

Voici la guerre! La plaine s'éclaire,
Venez tous! A nos cris le clan se lève!
Armez-vous de la claymore ou du glaive!
Que vos coups frappent sans pitié, sans trêve!

[Pibroch of Donuil Dhu, Pibroch of Donuil,
Wake they wild voice anew, Summon Clan Conuil!
Come away, Come away, Hark to the summons!
Come in your war array, gentles and commons.]

Yet the text itself does not force the translator to sacrifice and domesticate so much of the source-text's character here: rather than changing the rhyming patterns, the rhyme words could easily have been maintained and with it more of the original flavour, with a translation along the lines of 'Pibroch de Donuil Dhu, Pibroch de Donuil / De voix sauvage éveillez le Clan Conuil.' There seems to be an assumption here that the French singer and audience would rather have smooth and familiar sounds than exposure to authentic phonetics and specific references to episodes from Scottish history. Further still, the substantive content of these traditions is often whitewashed by the selection process of which songs to translate and which to exclude; for example, Robert Burns's many bawdy, earthy lyrics are side-lined in favour of his deep expressions of love, patriotism, and bucolic nature. I have not found any translations or adaptations of 'Tha was Twa Wives,' in which Burns merrily describes Maggie who, after hitting the brandy, farts repeatedly until 'beans and peas cam down her thighs / And cackit a' her stockins.' This is not, it would be fair to say, an image of Burns that would appeal to French sensibilities about the profundity of the Celtic spirit, or provide an idea of the Celtic character that they – especially the bourgeoisie – would be eager to incorporate into their own sense of national identity.

164 *Singing the Celts*

This level of domestication even appears in that prototypical song of Scottish national feeling, 'My Heart's in the Highlands' ('Mon cœur est en Écosse'). Not only does the translation of the title imply that the Highlands, more isolated as they were from Anglo-Saxon and other outside influence, are the only 'real' Scotland, but in its prototypicality Gallet's French translation goes on to proffer a non-specific song of patriotism which evokes nothing of the rugged Highlands with their deer, snow-covered mountains, and raging streams:

> Mon âme est partie sur l'aile des vents,
> Vers toi ma patrie, vers tes cieux riants!
> Si loin que m'enchaîne le destin jaloux,
> J'oublierai ma peine en pensant à vous.

> [My heart's in the Highlands, my heart is not here;
> My heart's in the Highlands a-chasing the deer.
> A chasing the wild deer and foll'wing the roe,
> My heart's in the Highlands wher'ever I go.]

As in 'Pibroch of Donuil Dhu,' the domesticating translation robs this song of its specificity as a song of clan loyalty or Scottish patriotism, of the Scottish landscape (the 'cieux riants' are certainly not the weather most habitually associated with the Highlands), and as a locus of specifically Highland identity and historical memory. Both song translations produce a generic song of nationalist feeling and patriotic nostalgia that could apply to any country.

Ironically, this potential for reductionism from the specific to the generic may be central to the appeal of such songs for French song arrangers and their audiences: regardless of their prefatory statements concerning the insights into innate Celtic racial character that may be gained through folk song, Gallet and Weckerlin and Richard de la Madelaine focus in their adaptations on the potential scope for a *French* audience to identify with the overarching themes and general aesthetics, far more than they attempt to convey any more profound sense of Celtic-British history or identity. In the wake of the Franco-Prussian War and with the rising tide of nationalism in France, songs that are manifestations of the Scottish (specifically, Highland) voice rejecting Anglo-Saxon oppression by the English appear to be co-opted to give voice to the Celtic blood supposed to be found running through French veins; they become songs obliquely about French national patriotism in the face of oppression by their own Germanic neighbour. The first-person voice (either singular or plural), its message of strength and determination, and its expression of subjectivity are the only aspects of these folksongs that are systematically translated with any accuracy or consistency.

There is an irony here: French translators of and writers on Irish and Scottish folk music frequently claim that it will reveal some deep, Celtic

Singing the Celts   165

essence useful to an exploration of their own national identity; yet at the same time they strip these folk songs of their performance contexts, their acoustic signatures, their linguistic power of expression, and their cultural and historical specificity – that is, of all the factors that might reveal any notable imprint of 'ethnic' identity. It appears, then, that Scottish or Irish music and their lyrical voices are culturally colonized and sidelined here by the French claims to Celtic identity; the French voice declares ownership of the positive characteristics expressed in these songs and appropriate their 'Celtic characteristics' for France. As the French versions of Celtic-British folk songs efface native musical and linguistic hallmarks and historical references, they create songs that not only suffer some translation loss but are also appropriated as a product of French culture. The tension that this provokes opens up an awareness, perhaps only subconsciously, of the space between the two languages in the process of translation. Language and music become spheres of ambivalence. In this respect they share points of correspondence with the exotic novel in the colonial era; as Yee observes, in such texts 'language itself is problematic and fragmented.' Language and music may not be actively portrayed as 'plural and opaque' in translations of folk song, but the near-complete absence of any cultural specificity in the target-language text no less reveals similar disturbances to those identified by Yee as prefiguring postcolonial literatures in the nineteenth century (2008, p. 14). In seeking to make the songs appealing to the target-language audience, these French translators and composers encode the source texts with incongruous target-language values, and provide the audience with 'the narcissistic experience of recognizing his or her own culture in a cultural order, enacting an imperialism that extends the dominion of transparency with other ideological discourses over a different culture' (Venuti, 1992, p. 5).

A shared Celtic esprit

Throughout the discussion so far, the representational choices – in accounts of hearing Celtic-British music in situ, of depicting it in text, of arranging the music, and of translating the lyrics – are all riven with problematic logic. In large part these logical issues arise from the contemporaneous desire to analyse cultural phenomena as part of the growing body of 'race science'; to see music culture as an inborn and essential behaviour produced by unconscious impulses of the blood rather than the conscious mind; and from the fascination with how the cultures of other 'races' reflect upon concepts of race and nation in France itself.

One such logical non-sequitur is the inconsistent mixing of vocabulary associated with racial categorizations. As we have seen, at times the Scots and the Irish seem Oriental or savage, at times French, and yet the Orient and France are generally considered as binary opposites: how then could it be that one country, and a Western European one at that, could be akin to both at the same time? The metaphoric nature of these terms becomes apparent

166 *Singing the Celts*

here, undermining their use as useful objective descriptors of Celtic-British song culture – or indeed as racial categories or signifiers. Furthermore, if the widespread belief that culture is an adaptation by a human subspecies to their milieu be correct, how could it be that musical traditions that are the natural product of the rugged septentrional landscape, climate, and milieu could engender identical acoustic tropes to the sun-baked lands of Hindu and Arabian traditions, such as the pentatonic scale?[15] Tiersot tries to rationalize this by using common musical tropes across different locations as proof of the ability of folk music itself to adapt to new habitats:

> Parfois une mélodie, sans subir pour cela des modifications fondamentales, peut, en passant d'un pays dans un autre, prendre un caractère tout nouveau, qui est le caractère propre à la région où elle a élu son nouveau domicile. Il y a là un phénomène d'acclimatation musicale très digne d'être noté. Le peuple est, d'instinct, un grand symphoniste.
>
> (1894, p. 27)

> [Sometimes a melody, without undergoing fundamental changes, can, on passing from one country to another, take on an entirely new character – the individual character of the region where it has taken up residence. We see in this a very noteworthy phenomenon of musical acclimatization. The populace is instinctively a great composer.]

However, this deft justification is destabilized by the numerous logical leaps elsewhere in Tiersot's writings on musical cultures: for example, while music from the East is considered as the product of race – Arabian music, Asian music, and so on – he deems music from France as inherently *French* rather than Aryan, Celtic, European, Frankish, or other similar supranational ethnic grouping (Tiersot presents this standpoint throughout his *Notes*, 1905). Also, although his *Notes d'ethnographie musicale* [*Notes on Musical Ethnography*] have a remarkably detailed methodology – studying genres and subgenres of folk stories, tonal and technical aspects of folk songs and their evolutions over time, and the role of folksong in the development of modern music – the whole argument is constructed upon the premise that Celtic traditions are more authentically French despite being rarer in France; a premise for which he provides no further explanation or evidence.

The poet Gabriel Vicaire does have an astute explanation to defuse this apparent deadlock. He explains that 'l'esprit gaulois ne meurent pas. Il est immortel. [...] Mais il s'écarta de plus en plus de la forme populaire. À la spontanéité ingénue, à la barbarie, si l'on veut, des premiers âges, se substitua insensiblement je ne sais quoi de parfaitement noble et de superbement orné' ['the gallic spirit does not die. It is immortal. But it has become more and more distant from its traditional folk form. The naïve spontaneity, the barbarousness if you like, of early epochs, has gradually been substituted for something somehow noble and superbly ornamented'] (1886, p. 262). Vicaire implies that the disappearance of Celtic folk music as the summa of local culture in France (outside of Brittany) in fact reveals the *strength* of the Gallic bloodline, which has naturally and beautifully evolved into France's nineteenth-century art world: in an adroit intellectual leap, far from traditional song being the victim of the decadent process of decay that many associated with modernity, Vicaire claims that its dwindling presence is due to France's *upward* progression along the path of evolution. The same racial impulses that once led the Celts to sing their ballads (and which still do express themselves in the less developed corners of France) now find their ideal means of expression in more sophisticated forms of art music. This is a neat and wonderfully appealing rationalization.

However, still more problems arise from the ambivalent layering of power relations in many Celtic-British songs for the French context. On the one hand, the bards are model nationalist heroes, and their folk songs are ideal patriotic anthems for a nation oppressed under the Germanic Anglo-Saxon yolk, perfect for adaptation to the Celtic Gaul being oppressed under the German yolk after 1871. On the other hand, however, the nationalist Celtic bard is also a rebellious colonial subject creating a subversive counterculture that challenges the legitimacy and the superiority of the centralized, legitimate government. Thus, the degree to which the bardic spirit is desirable depends entirely on which borders the French observer focuses upon hearing these songs. If looking towards the German border, the Celtic-British bard provides a rich model of cultural identity in the face of tragic oppression – an allegory worthy of emulation for post-1871 France, for militarily *revanchistes* and those in favour of peacefully fostering cultural superiority alike. However, if looking south and eastwards towards the French colonies, this rich model of native, ethnic cultural identity and resistance is an explicit threat to the identity of *la plus grande France* whose colonial mission sought to efface local, 'savage' culture in favour of the gifts of French civilization. If the former, the French musician and audience can identify with the Celtic bard as a noble-spirited and afflicted hero; but, if the latter, they are identified with England as an oppressive and tyrannical power with no artistic soul. Indeed, this also problematizes the very contention of a civilizing mission at all, at a time when the colonial movement and the civilizing mythology attached to it were becoming increasingly important for France. If the Scots and Irish are still driven by the primitive impulses that they are often said to be in the discourses surrounding their folk music, in spite of all the railways and schools and industrial infrastructure within their borders, then the idea of a 'civilizing' mission is shown – even within Europe and within the white races – to be an impossible quest.

Of course, in practice no nation has ever consistently applied their principles and philosophies, and this problematization does not claim an exceptional inconsistency for this failure of logic. Nonetheless, it is interesting to note that logical conflicts such as these arise in particular due to the focalization on music as the product of racial, essential impulses – and, moreover, the

168   *Singing the Celts*

desire to find in the traditions of Scotland, Ireland, and Wales not merely cultural parallels but musico-archaeological evidence of *French* ethnic heritage. One occasion where such discussions are more fruitful and less undermined by their own internal logic is when the tendency to decontextualize – which dominates as we have seen in the appropriative arrangements and translations of these songs – is curtailed. This is the case in the frequent association drawn by French writers between folk, popular, and traditional music and the specific context of the Irish Home Rule movement. French accounts in journalism and travel writing of public protests surrounding this political cry for freedom systematically feature song, and the impulse to sing in the face of political adversity is seen as emerging directly from the heart of the Irish people. Moreover, it is often described and foregrounded in lieu of any explanation of the bill's political demands or the more concrete socio-historical situation. For example, Narjoux, on depicting a political meeting in Galway, chooses to focus on 'des bandes de piétons [qui] défilent dans toutes les rues, musique en tête. [...] Les chants, les cris retentissent par toute la ville' ['groups of people on foot walking down every street with music in their heads. [...] Songs and shouts ring out across the city'] (1886, p. 349). On the way to a 'meeting monstre,' De Bovet frames her account of a mass political meeting with music, preceding it with a description of the fanfares of the National League's bands and the singing from groups from across the local Irish population (including female workers' cooperatives, mutual aid societies, temperance societies, football clubs, land league members, and parish priests) and concluding with a depiction of a public banquet punctuated by spontaneous eruptions of Irish ballads (1889, pp. 8, 12). Indeed, she later lifts this episode from her travel writing and elaborates it for her novel *Terre d'Émeraude* (1908, pp. 186–99), ensuring that a still wider French readership would be familiar with the idea that an intimate connection existed between the Irish freedom movement and typically Irish music.

Even telegraphed newspaper communications, which were restricted to very short character limits, still saw fit to dedicate space to conveying the powerful, affective presence of traditional Irish protest music in such situations. A representative example can be found in the insistent reporting about Irish protestors, rebels, or townsfolk singing *God Save Ireland*, a rebel song from 1867 which celebrates the three Fenians known as the Manchester Martyrs, but which quickly entered the annals of music seen as wrought of intrinsically Irish spirit. For example, during a visit of the Prince and Princess of Wales to Cork in April 1885, the *Gaulois*, *Temps*, and the *Intransigeant* newspapers all report on how the crowd's sullen silence erupted into noisy conflict when a group of Orangemen cheered the Royal cortege and the locals replied 'par des protestations tumultueuses, en chantant l'hymne *God save Ireland*' ['with tumultuous protestations whilst singing the anthem *God save Ireland*'] (respectively, 16 April 1885, p. 1; 17 April 1885, p. 1; 18 April 1885, p. 1). A few weeks later, this song again reverberates at the centre of a clash at the Londonderry opera house, reported by the *Temps* and the *Petite*

Singing the Celts 169

Presse; the pantomime show included a tableau representing the royal family, at which loyalist members of the audience stood and sang *God Save the Queen*, provoking numerous people seated in the stalls and upper circles to holler back *God Save Ireland*. This conflict of songs soon turned into physical conflict, eventually pouring out into the streets and resulting in several serious injuries (respectively, 30 April 1885, p. 2; 1 May 1885, p. 1). When word spread of a revolt in a women's workhouse in New Ross, the *Temps* and *Intransigeant* report that a substantial crowd of Irish people gathered outside the walls, '[qui] poussait des cris et se mit à chanter le *God save Ireland* et jeta des pierres à la police' ['[who] yelled and started singing *God save Ireland* and threw stones at the police'] (21 February 1887, p. 2; 22 February 1887, p. 2). In September 1893 when the Second Home Rule Bill was passed by the House of Commons – only to later be defeated in the Lords – the *Matin, Temps*, and *Petit Journal* all depict the anxious crowds waiting outside parliament, who greeted the announcement of the vote with cries of 'Long live Gladstone! Down with Balfour!' before joyously singing *God Save Ireland* (2 September 1893, p. 2; 3 September 1893, p. 1; 3 September 1893, p. 2).

This is by no means an exhaustive list and in all such reports typically Irish song is contextualized, linked to the present rather than conveyed as a manifestation of the ancient past alone, and it is represented by the French journalists as a politically-powerful stone thrown in the face of the authorities. It becomes a musical shorthand for the suffering and the struggle of the Irish nation, and becomes a symbol so eloquent as to be meaningful to French readers from across the political and class spectrums as well as to Irish nationalists. It is particularly interesting to observe that the minimizing or belittling nature of the ethnological interpretations that had so habitually been attributed to Irish music in non-political contexts evaporates in these numerous and frequent accounts of the music of political protest. This is not because these protest songs are unique in having a political subject matter; much of the music typically treated as Irish folk music by the French – including those arranged by Thomas Moore and inspired by the Irish Rebellion of 1798 – also has political protest at its origin (such as 'The Minstrel Boy' and 'The Harp That Once Through Tara's Halls'). Nor it is to say that they cease to be interpreted as linked to innate Irish nature; on the contrary, this music is seen as expressing an inherent Irish love of freedom, justice, brotherhood, and courage. Rather, the contextual setting of contemporary political revolt makes it possible to read these songs and the Irish ethnic character that produces them in a newly modern light, and as sharing parallel positive traits to French Republicans in the here and now. These shared traits are still rooted in a sense of a common Celtic heritage; the image of the Gallic warrior was commonly depicted as possessing these characteristics in plays, sculptures, children's schoolbooks, musical compositions and more during the Third Republic to, as Pasler has explained, 'inspire patriotism and nourish French confidence in their military might. With powerful images of bravery, their images of idealized heroes, like Vercingetorix, represented French strength and resilience as a people,

170   *Singing the Celts*

emblems of the Gallic spirit unchanged over time' (2006, p. 481). The idea that the shared positive traits of the present are somehow 'Celtic' would have been familiar from the popular images of these Celtic heroes of the past and would invite the reader to see common inherited traits between the modern French and, unlike in other examples seen in this chapter, the *modern* Irish. Indeed, at a dinner held by the Congrès International des Traditions Populaires for important international guests at the 1889 World Fair, the French organizing committee chose Gallet and Weckerlin's arrangement of Thomas Moore's Irish patriot song 'The Minstrel Boy' alongside folksongs from various regions of France, without clearly separating this out as a foreign borrowing not originating in France (see A. Certaux, 1889, p. 499).

Such a sense of a shared Franco-Irish character is revealed in Hector France's account in *Gil-Blas* of a march in favour of Home Rule in London in 1887 ('Chez John Bull,' 1887, p. 2). On following this march, the French author is particularly struck by the constant accompaniment of music, and he recounts that it is through this music that the gathered crowd responds to everything along their path as they march. *God Save Ireland* strikes up with lively tones as they pass the Reform Club and on entering Hyde Park. In contrast, a funeral march is played as a message to the more conservative clubs such as the Carlton, and a jig is danced by some 'horribles mégères ivres' ['horrible drunken shrews'], embodying for Hector France the scorn-worthy English populace. But then, on traversing Trafalgar Square and on Park Lane, the crowd bursts out into the Marseillaise – and Hector France declares that 'j'eus un moment de légitime orgueil' ['I had a moment of legitimate pride'] (p. 2). Although much of his description in this account focuses its rhetoric upon expressing contempt for the English masses who tag along with the march, here there is a clear moment of fraternal connection between the French patriot and the Irish cause through the medium of revolutionary music.

In this sudden identification that Hector France experiences with the protestors, on both a personal and national level, we find an instance of one of the more convincing comparisons between French and Irish character types – not in the nebulous realm of abstract generalities based on ancient heritage and problematic racial theory, but in terms of the contemporary use of music during periods of political upheaval. Both French and Irish populations make frequent and seemingly instinctive use of music for polit-ical, even revolutionary, self-expression – indeed, the two populations some-times use the *same* songs for that revolutionary self-expression, as France's account of the Marseillaise here suggests. Certainly, the century of revolutionary tumult in France had been marked throughout with a long tradition of grassroots political protest music. For example, during the Revolutionary period, Laura Mason observes that Paris

> was a city that encompassed a cacophony of voices as revolutionaries and royalists filled streets, theatres, and cafés, organizing festivals, giving

Singing the Celts 171

speeches, rioting and, throughout all, singing. Common citizens rhymed political opinions, which some sang privately even as others trumpeted them forth before legislative and sectional assemblies. [...] Songs [...] become one of the most commonly used means of communication of the French Revolution.

(1996, p. 2)

As Mason indicates, this dynamic musicality in the face of political change was not just the province of the common people but was espoused by all sectors of society and all political opinions, and it would be remembered as a characteristic trait of French popular and political culture for many decades to come. So well-known was the emotional attraction to music that successive governments and ruling elites in France sought to channel this emotional responsiveness, either through the active top-down organization of musical events, or through censorship of popular, bottom-up modes of musical expression.[16]

Despite, then, the frequent tendency when focusing on the traditional songs of Ireland to treat them and their singers as primitive, ancient, and only related to France by distant, historical ancestry, when the focus is on the musical impulses of the people as modern political subjects, a kind of shared Celtic *esprit* is evoked by French writers which places the French and Irish as equals and brothers rather than distant and unequal cousins. Scotland and Wales, having succumbed to British rule longer ago, having succumbed to Protestantism, and having no immediate revolutionary or independence movements against their monarchical overlords, are not included by the French in this verve – even where their songs still express a passionate and defiant sense of self-determinism. A clear example of the sense of shared Franco-Irish esprit can be found in the salon music about Irish freedom composed by Augusta Holmès, and it is with a brief glance at her song the *Chanson des gas d'Irlande* (1891) – a salon re-imagining of popular Irish protest music – which I will end this chapter.

The various paradoxes and approaches to Celtic-British folk music discussed in this chapter so far can be found threaded together in the work of this composer – a particularly interesting case, as she was born to an Irish father and British mother but was naturalized as French in her early twenties and has tended to be considered as a French composer. She is best known for her emphatically patriotic, epic compositions lauding French nationhood, notably *La Montagne noire* (1895) and the *Ode triomphale* (1889), the latter of which she composed for the centrepiece concert of the 1889 World Fair. Alongside these, she wrote a number of exoticist works evoking familiar fantasies of the Middle East, Spain, and gypsies such as *Danses d'almées* (1861), *Astarté* (1870), *Carmen nuptiale* (1870), and *Rêverie tzigane* (1888). Contemporaneously, she also composed a handful of works about Ireland, including the symphonic poem *Irlande* (1882), and the songs *La Chanson des gas d'Irlande* (1891) and *Noël d'Irlande* (1897). In many ways, then, we might expect to find a similarly exoticist approach in both her Irish and

172   *Singing the Celts*

Oriental works, echoing the standpoint taken to Celtic Britain by many other composers and writers among her generation. However, her Irish heritage and her life experiences of Ireland and Irish music lead us to question whether a more complex process may be at work – and they demonstrate the need for nuance in the musicological analysis of cultural appropriation in this context.

The *Chanson des gas* comprises a rather thick-textured piano line, composed in the unusual key choice of G-sharp minor, and with soaring high G sharps in the soprano vocal line; it is immediately clear that this is not a composition aimed at the skill set of the simple village folk musician, nor the average Parisian café-concert singer, but for a singer and pianist trained and competent in art-music techniques.[17] In the introduction and the verse section, there is little that calls upon the French listener's preconceptions of Irish folk music; there are no dotted rhythms, grace notes, or simple and repetitive motifs. What is particularly notable about this song is its split personality between minor and major keys: the verse has a solemn, measured melody in the minor key, performed *moderato* and *piano* for the first three phrases, before suddenly jumping up to the high G sharp, sung *fortissimo* on the exclamation 'Hurrah!' in a cry of patriotic fervour. But then, rather than return from this climax to the solemnity of the opening, it modulates into A-flat major for the chorus, and the performers are instructed to go quickly and very gaily (*allegro – très gaiement*). The dynamics alternate playfully between *piano* and *forte*, and the rather weighty crochets of the piano accompaniment in the verse section are replaced with light, almost laughing sequences of quavers. The lyrics, most strikingly, abandon their woeful and angry message that

> Nous souffrons tous les affronts
> Et notre misère est très grande
> Mais nous souffrons en criant: Hurrah!
> Nous souffrons pour l'Irlande.

> [We suffer every insult
> And our misery is very great
> But we suffer whilst crying: Hurrah!
> We suffer for Ireland.]

for the lively

> Tra la la la la la la la la
> Buvons, oublions nos misères,
> Chantons, oublions nos haillons,
> En dansant vidons nos verres!
> Au son du cors et des harpes d'or
> Ainsi buviez nos pères;
> Au nom des aïeux et des jours glorieux

Singing the Celts 173

Vidons nos verres
Tra la la, vidons nos verres!

[Tra la la la la la la la la la
Let's drink, let's forget our miseries,
Let's sing, let's forget our rags
By dancing and emptying our glasses!
It was to the sound of the trumpets and the golden harps
That our fathers used to drink;
In the name of our ancestors and their glorious days
Let's empty our glasses
Tra la la, let's empty our glasses!]

At first, we appear to be firmly situated in the realm of stereotype and demeaning triviality: the drunken, tra-la-la-ing Irishman harping on about the past golden age but unable to improve his lot because he always has his nose in a whiskey glass. However, the contrast between these two musical sections, poised on the boundaries between drinking song and vengeful war song, challenges this recourse to cliché. Although as we have seen the theme of war was by no means a novelty in the songs about Ireland – and Scotland – already familiar to the French audience, this degree of bloodthirstiness is out of the ordinary. In the final verse, the lyrics incite –

Et c'est du sang qu'en bondissant
Nous boirons sur la verte lande!
Oui c'est *leur* sang qu'en criant: Hurrah!
Nous boirons à l'Irlande!

[And it is blood that, leaping,
We will drink on the green land!
Yes, it's *their* blood that, whilst crying: Hurrah!
We will drink to Ireland!]

This message, set to uplifting, merry musical strains, is significantly more redolent of the Marsaillaise with its 'qu'un sang impure abreuve nos sillons' ['let impure blood flow in our furrows'] than it is of the ubiquitous and softly nostalgic 'Last Rose of Summer' or even the rousing 'God Save Ireland.' Given such parallels between the *Chanson des gas* and the Revolutionary anthem of the French, it is worth observing that the target audience of this song is clearly French, despite the apparent dramatization of an Irish 'nous' in whose Irish breasts an upsurgeance of nationalistic pride seems to be invited. To some extent, the lyrics and general mood of Holmès's composition again echo Matthew Head's critique of musical orientalism: Holmès subordinates the Irish voice; she co-opts their plight for the emotional excitement of a

174 *Singing the Celts*

French audience; and we might well see an appropriation and reduction of their struggle here as a generic allegory for nationalistic rage, encouraging resistance against another Germanic, Protestant oppressor – all the while maintaining *gaieté* and *joie de vivre*.

However, the lyrical references specifically *to music* within the song indicate additional layers of meaning here. The -or- rhyme between 'cors,' 'or,' and 'glorieux' places riches and glory after the musical sounds of the trumpets, to which they are subordinate. This link is emphasized further for the listener by each of these words being sung on a C in the vocal line, with an A flat in the left hand of the piano, and an A flat-C chord in the right. This recurrent return to the tonic draws the ear to the repeated phonetic sound, and it places music at the heart of a coming golden age for Ireland.

Perhaps, then, in addition to a generic musical allegory for political fury against Germanic oppression in all its forms, Holmès is also both offering up a cry of political anguish and solidarity specifically between Ireland and France, and a means of engaging with the wider discourses surrounding Celtic ethnic identity – all at the same time. When she invites the musician and audience to identify with a Celtic heritage it is a heritage awakened explicitly and directly *by music*. The Celtic Ireland she offers them is one that fosters robust nationalistic song – and one that responds to that song with robust nationalistic spirit. She invites the French listener to be inspired by her music to identify with a kind of Celtic identity and togetherness, which will invigorate them to pull together as a nation and to fight back. Thus, Holmès offers a means of engaging with a shared sense of Celtic spirit through music, that goes further than most of her contemporaries by maintaining the focus on music – not as an aesthetic attribute of each nation that *passively* shows something profound about inherent character (placing racial character as cause and music as effect) but as something that can *actively* elicit similar patriotic responses in both the Irish and the French (placing music as cause and racial character-response as effect). Whilst many of the translators and arrangers of Celtic-British folksong encourage the French musician and audience to take a conceptual detour to think about French racial and national identity obliquely through the music of the Celtic-British Other, Holmès suggests instead that it is through their shared musical spirit that the boundaries between Self and Other fall, and that both Ireland and France's mutual Celtic selfhood past, present, and future can be located.

Notes

1 Works dramatizing the life of Marie Stuart across the century include, for example, the musical drama by Eugène de Planard, Jean-François Roger, and François-Joseph Fétis, *Marie Stuart en Écosse, ou le Château de Douglas* (1823); the Romantic opera by Théodore Anne and Louis Niedermeyer, *Marie Stuart* (1844); the sentimental history by J.-A. Petit, *Histoire de Marie Stuart* (1875); the Catholic pseudo-martyrologies by V. Canet, *Marie Stuart, la Reine martyr* (1888)

Singing the Celts   175

and by Abbé Joubert, *Marie Stuart: Tragédie en 5 actes* (1897). So widespread is this fascination with the Scottish queen that Flaubert entered her name into his dictionary of received ideas from the Second Empire and Third Republic: 'Stuart (Marie): s'apitoyer sur son sort' (1910, p. 443).

2 These general characteristics are summarized by Weckerlin in his *La Chanson populaire* (1886), and draw upon influential predecessors, including Adrien de la Fage (*Miscellanées musicales*, 1844), Joseph d'Ortigue (*La Musique à l'église*, 1861), and François-Joseph Fétis (notably his *Résumé philosophique de l'histoire de la musique*, 1835, and *Histoire générale de la musique*, 1869). The ambiguity of defining 'authenticity' in folk music is discussed in cogent detail and at length in the context of British folksong throughout Dave Harker's *Fakesong* (1985).

3 For example, in the eighteen instalments of A. Rabuteau and R. de Vilbac, *Airs populaires: Chants nationaux et motifs célèbres de tous les pays, arrangés pour piano et violon* (1869–1886), an 'Air écossais' ('The Blue Bells of Scotland') and 'Air irlandais' ('Robin Adair') can be found alongside songs from Hungary, Spain, Italy, Germany, Bohemia, Turkey, North Africa, America, and more. The cover of this edition includes two Scottish figures in kilts, whilst the 'Petit Pianiste' series advertised on the inner leaf mentions pieces inspired by North Africa, Germany, Italy, Spain, and China.

4 There was a verve among English ballad collectors for music from the various regions of England, such as Joseph Ritson's *The Northumberland Garland* (1793), G. Dursart's *Old English Songs, as Now Sung by the Peasantry of the Weald of Surrey and Sussex* (1843), James Halliwell's *The Yorkshire Anthology* (1851), and John Harland's *Ballads and Songs of Lancashire* (1865), to name but a few.

5 These songs are arranged for voice and piano by Tiersot in his compendious survey of typical French regional folk music (1921, IV, p. 44, p. 66).

6 Notably, as this piece is in a minor key, varying between the use of the major and minor 6th – associated with Scottish bagpipe music by Fétis (1874, IV, p. 403).

7 Indeed, Rémo is either neutral or, at times, remarkably positive about English musical promise in his book-length study *Musique au pays des brouillards* (1885) – unlike the majority of his contemporaries, as shall be discussed at length in Chapter 4 of the present book. Though no Anglophile from a political point of view, Rémo praises musical evenings held by the English aristocracy and upper classes for their display of taste in music and performers (pp. 36–41); he promotes England's interest in amateur orchestras as a valuable pastime (p. 67); and he excuses the lack of English operatic composition as the result of an inadequate support structure rather than a question of inherent talent (p. 199). Overall, he considers that England is not musically incapable per se, but that the milieu is an ill-tilled field of which more could be made with the right support structures and encouragement (p. v).

8 Such collections became particularly popular after Louis-Napoleon commissioned the French Minister of Public Education, Hippolyte Fortoul, to catalogue French folksong and poetry on a wide scale in 1852. To give a small representative sample: songs from the Alpes françaises collected by Julien Tiersot (*Chansons populaires recueillies dans les Alpes françaises*, 1903); from the Vivarais and Vercors regions, collected by the composer Vincent d'Indy (*Chansons populaires recueillies dans le Vivarais et le Vercors*, 1892); from Alsace, after its secession to Germany, collected by J.B. Weckerlin (*Chansons populaires de l'Alsace*, 1883); and from Poitou, Saintonge, Aunis, and Angoumois, collected by Jérome Bujeaud (*Chants et chansons populaires des provinces de l'ouest*, 1895).

176 *Singing the Celts*

9 Although little is known about W.R. Binfield, despite his anglosaxon-sounding name he appears to have been a French-born composer.

10 Fétis works through the typical scales used in traditional Irish and Scottish music at length in Vol. IV of his *Histoire générale de la musique* (1874, Book 11).

11 Tiersot contributes a series of articles on exotic music at the World Fair to the *Ménéstrel* journal under the titles of 'Promenades musicale à l'exposition': for Senegal, see 6 October 1889, p. 316; and for Java, see 28 July, p. 235 and 18 August 1889, p. 259.

12 In 1833, Fétis had remarked that 'la langue anglaise est si peu favorable à la musique, et si peu connue des étrangers, que jamais on ne publie la partition d'un opéra anglais. Quelques airs, devenus populaires, sont seuls achetés par les marchands de musique qui, moyennant une somme peu considérable, profitent de la vogue qu'ils obtiennent' ['the English language is markedly unfavourable to music, and it is so little known by foreigners, that nobody ever publishes the scores to English operas. Only a handful of airs that have become popular are sold by music merchants who, for a meagre sum, profit from their temporary popularity' – 'Essai sur la musique en Angleterre' (1833, p. 163). A survey of the sheet-music collection of the Bibliothèque nationale de France suggests that the state of affairs was much the same in the final decades of the nineteenth century, and even when music-hall hits became popular exports from England to the French stage, these were very often translated or rewritten for their Francophone audience.

13 O'Rell offers this pseudo-nostalgic witticism on Scottish drinking: 'On boit encore dru en Écosse; mais où est le vieux temps où l'hôte écossais cassait le pied des verres, afin que ses invités eussent à les vider d'un trait [...]? On boit encore dru en Écosse; mais où est le bon vieux temps où l'on croyait manquer d'égards envers son hôte en montant à la chambre à coucher sans l'aide de deux domestiques? [...] On boit encore dru en Écosse; mais où est le temps où, sur les onze heures du soir, les femmes de la maison se sauvaient et allaient s'enfermer sous clef dans les chambres à coucher pour échapper aux fureurs des hommes?' ['They still drink heavily in Scotland; but where have the olden days gone, when Scottish hosts would smash the feet of their glasses so that the guests had to empty them in one go? They still drink heavily in Scotland; but where have the good old days gone when it seemed a slight to the host to make your way to bed without the help of two servants? They still drink heavily in Scotland; but where have the olden times gone when, at eleven in the evening, the women of the house ran to lock themselves in their rooms to save themselves from the mad lust of the men?'] *L'Ami MacDonald* (1887, pp. 98–100).

14 This is the message sustained by Charles Guernier in his *Les Crofters écossais* (1897) in his discussion of the Crofters' Holdings Act (1886), and by Auguste Angellier in his biography of Burns, where he emphasizes the poet's upbringing in a crofter's cottage, rooted to the land (1893, I, especially Chapter 1).

15 Tiersot notes the prevalence of pentatonic scales in both East Asian and Celtic folk music (1905, p. 49).

16 Pasler discusses the Third Republic's efforts to rehabilitate and co-opt the legacy of Revolutionary music in the interests of shaping national identity (2007, Chapter 2); Jane Fulcher scrutinizes Third Republican initiatives by the state and individual composers and musicians including Vincent d'Indy and Gustave Charpentier to disseminate ideology through music, music making, and group singing (1999, Chapter 2); and the decades of censorship and limitations placed

Singing the Celts 177

on the goguettes, cafés chantants, and cafés-concerts testify to a keen awareness across the social and political spectrum of dynamism, affect, and capacity for influence in France and, in particular, in Paris (see Sallée, 1985, p. 13; Loosely, 2003, pp. 27–39).

17 A full digitized copy of the *Chanson desgas d'Irlande* can be found online within the *Mélodies pour piano et chant* collection, at https://imslp.org/wiki/ M%C3%A9lodies_pour_piano_et_chant_(Holm%C3%A8s%2C_Augusta_ Mary_Anne)

Works cited

Angellier, A., 1893. *Robert Burns*, 2 vols. Paris: Hachette.

Anne, T. and Niedermeyer, L., 1844. *Marie Stuart: opéra en 5 actes*. Paris: s.n.

Bédollièrre, E. de la, 1840-42. 'Le Normand.' In: *Les Français peints par eux-mêmes: encyclopédie morale du dix-neuvième siècle*, 10 vols. Paris: Curmer. VII, pp. 121–84.

Bellman, J., 2011. 'Musical Voyages and their Baggage: Orientalism in Music and Critical Musicology,' *The Music Quarterly*, 94. pp. 417–38.

Bohlman, P.V. and Radano R. (eds), 2000. *Music and the Racial Imagination*. Chicago: University of Chicago Press. pp. 1–53.

Bonnière, R. de, 1895. *Lord Hyland: histoire véritable*. Paris: Olendorff.

Bourgault-Ducoudray, L.-A., 1885. *Trente mélodies populaires de Basse-Bretagne*. Paris: Lemoine et fils.

Bovet, M.-A. de, 1898. *L'Écosse: Souvenirs et impressions de voyage*. Paris: Hachette.

Bovet, M.-A. de, 1908. *Trois mois en Irlande*. Paris: Hachette.

Brueyre, L., 1875. *Contes populaires de la Grande-Bretagne*. Paris: Hachette.

Buisson du Berger, A., 1889. *Poètes anglais contemporains: Robert Burns – John Keats – Elisabeth Browning – Bailey Robert Browning*. Paris: Henri Gautier.

Bujeaud J., 1895. *Chants et chansons populaires des provinces de l'ouest: Poitou, Saintonge, Aunis et Angoumois, avec les airs originaux*, 2 vols. Niort: L. Clouzot.

'Bulletin de l'étranger,' 30 April 1885, 21 February 1887, and 3 September 1893. *Le Temps*. p. 2.

'Bulletin du jour,' 1885. *Le Temps*. 17 April, p. 1.

Canet, V., 1888. Marie Stuart, la Reine martyr. Lille: Desclée.

Certaux, A., 1889. 'Le Congrès international des traditions populaires,' *Revue des traditions populaires*, 4 (8–9). p. 499.

Darmesteter, J., 1896. *Nouvelles études anglaises*. Paris: Calmann-Lévy.

'Émeute à Cork,' 1885. *Le Gaulois*. 16 April, p. 1.

Engel, C., 1866. *An Introduction to the Study of National Music Comprising Researches into Popular Songs, Traditions and Customs*. London: Longmans.

'Étranger,' 1885. *La Petite Presse*. 1 May, p. 1.

Fauser, A., 2005. *Musical Encounters at the 1889 Paris World's Fair*. Rochester, NY: University of Rochester Press.

Fétis, J.-F., 1869–1874. *Histoire générale de la musique depuis les temps les plus anciens jusqu'à nos jours*, 5 vols. Paris: Firmin Didot.

Fétis, J.-F., 1883. 'Essai sur la musique en Angleterre,' *Revue des Deux Mondes*, 3. pp. 129–70.

Flaubert, G., 1910. 'Dictionnaire des idées reçues.' In: *Œuvres complètes de Gustave Flaubert*, edited by L. Conard. Paris: Louis Conard. pp. 415–44.

178 *Singing the Celts*

France, H., 1887. 'Chez John Bull,' *Gil-Blas*, 16 April, p. 2.

Fulcher, J., 1999. *French Cultural Politics and Music: from the Dreyfus Affair to the First World War*. Oxford: Oxford University Press.

Fulgence, G., *ca.* 1835. *Cent Chants populaires des diverses nations du monde avec les airs, les textes originaux, des notices, la traduction française* [musical score]. Paris: Ph. Petit.

Gallet L., and Weckerlin, J.B., *ca.*1877. *Échos d'Angleterre: Mélodies populaires de l'Angleterre, de l'Écosse, de l'Irlande, et du Pays de Galles* [musical score]. Paris: Durand, Schoenewerk et Cie.

Ganne, L., 1899. *La Gipsy: mazurka écossaise* [musical score]. Paris: Costallat et Cie.

Gobineau, A. de, 1855. *Essai sur l'inégalité des races humaines*. 1884 reprint. Paris: Firmin Didot.

Goodall, J.R., 2002. *Performance and Evolution in the Age of Darwin: Out of the Natural Order*. London and New York: Routledge.

Guernier, C., 1897. *Les Crofters écossais*. Paris: Arthur Rousseau.

Harker, D., 1985. *Fakesong: the Manufacture of British 'folksong', 1700 to the Present Day*. Milton Keynes, Open University Press.

Head, M., 2000. *Orientalism, Masquerade and Mozart's Turkish Music*. London: Royal Musical Association.

Holmès, A., 1891. 'La Chanson des gas d'Irlande' [musical score]. Paris: Léon Grus.

'Le Home Rule voté,' 1893. *Le Matin*. 2 Sept., p. 2.

Hughes, E.J., 2001. *Writing Marginality in Modern French Literature from Loti to Genet*. Cambridge: Cambridge University Press.

Indy, V. d', 1892. *Chansons populaires recueillies dans le Vivarais et le Vercors*. Paris: Librairie Fischbacher.

Joanne, P., 1908. *Angleterre – Écosse – Irlande*. Paris: Hachette.

Joubert, Abbé, 1897. Marie Stuart: Tragédie en 5 actes et en vers. Paris: Librairie catholique de l'œuvre Saint Paul.

Jousselin, H., 1871. *Appendice aux mélodies irlandaises de Thomas Moore traduites en vers français par Henri Jousselin*. Paris: E. Maillet.

Lâcome, P., 1875. Le Tour du monde en dix chansons nationales et caractéristiques. Paris: Choudens.

Lafond, Le Comte L., 1887. *L'Écosse jadis et aujourd'hui, études et souvenirs*. Paris: Calmann-Lévy.

'Lámhóigín – Conte irlandais de la Saint-Martin (Cork),' 1890. *Revue des traditions populaires*, 5 (9). pp. 605–11.

Locke, R., 2009. *Musical Exoticism: Images and Reflections*. Cambridge: Cambridge University Press.

Loosely, D., 2003. 'In from the Margins: *Chanson*, popular and cultural legitimacy.' In: *Popular Music in France from Chanson to Techno: Culture, Identity, and Society*, edited by Hugh Dauncey and Steve Cannon. Aldershot: Ashgate. pp. 27–39.

Madelaine, R. de la, 1874. *Burns: traduit de l'écossais*. Rouen: s.n.

Maigron, L., 1912. *Le Roman historique à l'époque romantique: essai sur l'influence de Walter Scott*. Paris: Honoré Champion.

Mason, L., 1996. *Singing the French Revolution: Popular Culture and Politics, 1787–1799*. Ithaca and London: Cornell University Press.

Moréas, J., 1891. 'Sur l'école romane,' *Figaro*, 14 Sept., p. 1.

Narjoux, F., 1886. *En Angleterre: Angleterre, Écosse (Les Orcades, Les Hébrides), Irlande: Le Pays, Les Habitants, La Vie intérieure*. Paris: E. Plon, Nourrit et Cie.

Nettl, B., 1965. *Folk and Traditional Music of the Western Continents*. Englewood Cliffs, NJ: Prentice-Hall.

O'Rell, M. [pseud. Léon Paul Blouet], 1887. *L'Ami Macdonald: Souvenirs anecdotiques de l'Écosse*. Paris: Calmann-Lévy.

O'Rell, M., 1894. *La Maison John Bull et Cie*. Paris: Calmann-Lévy.

Pasler, J., 2006. 'Theorizing Race in Nineteenth-Century France: Music as Emblem of Identity,' *The Music Quarterly*, 89 (4). pp. 459–504.

Pasler, J., 2007. 'Race and Nation: Musical Acclimatization and the *chansons populaires* in Third Republican France.' In: *Western Music and Race*, edited by Julie Brown. Cambridge: Cambridge University Press. pp. 147–67.

Petit, J.-A., 1875. *Histoire de Marie Stuart, Reine de France et d'Écosse*. Paris: Bloud et Barral.

Planard, E. de, Roger, J.-F., and Fétis, F.-J., 1823. *Marie Stuart en Écosse, ou le Château de Douglas*. Paris: Lelièvre.

'Politique à l'étranger,' 1893. *Le Petit Journal*, 3 Sept., p. 2.

'Le Prince de Galles en Irlande,' 1885. *L'Intransigeant*, 18 April, p. 1.

Rabuteau, A. and Vilbac, R. de, 1869–1886. *Airs populaires: Chants nationaux et motifs célèbres de tous les pays, arrangés pour piano et violon* [musical score], 18 vols. Paris: H. Lemoine.

Rémo, F., 1885. *La Musique au pays des brouillards, suivi de quelques biographies inédites d'artistes contemporains. Étude humoristique et anecdotique de l'état actuel de la musique en Angleterre*. Paris: s.n.

Rémo, F., 1896. 'Le Mouvement musical en Angleterre,' *L'Europe artiste*, 4 Oct., n.p.

Renan, E., 1882. *Qu'est-ce qu'une nation? Conférence faite en Sorbonne, le 11 mars 1882*. Paris: Calmann-Lévy.

'Révolte dans une prison de femmes,' 1887. *L'Intransigeant*, 22 Feb., p. 2.

Riley, M. and Smith, A., *Nation and Classical Music: from Handel to Copland*. Suffolk: Boydell and Brewer.

Rolland, R., 1908. *Musiciens d'aujourd'hui*. Paris: Hachette.

Roz, F., 1905. *Sous la couronne d'Angleterre: l'Irlande et son destin: Impressions d'Écosse: au pays de Galles*. Paris: Plon.

Said, E., 1978. *Orientalism*. London and New York: Routledge and Kegan Paul.

Said, E., 1993. *Culture and Imperialism*. New York: Knopf.

Sallée, A. and Chauveau, P. (eds), 1985. *Music-hall et café-concert*. Paris: Bordas.

Soubies, A., 1904. *Histoire de la musique: Îles britanniques*. Paris: Librairie des bibliophiles.

Stevenson, J.A. and Moore, T., 1808–34. *A Selection of Irish Melodies with Symphonies and Accompaniments by Sir John Stevenson and Characteristic Words by Thomas Moore*. 10 vols. London: J. Power.

Taine, H., 1863. *Histoire de la littérature anglaise*. 1878 reprint. Paris: Laloux fils et Guillot.

Thierry, A., 1840. *Récit des temps mérovingiens, précédés de Considérations sur l'histoire de France*. Paris: Just Tessier.

Tiersot, J., 1889. *Histoire de la chanson populaire en France*. Paris: E. Plon et Nourrit.

Tiersot, J., July – October 1889. 'Promenades musicales à l'exposition,' *Le Ménéstrel*. n.p.

Tiersot, J., 1890. *Mélodies populaires des Provinces de France: recueillies et harmonisées*, 10 vols. Paris: Au Ménéstrel.

Tiersot, J., 1894. *Les Types mélodiques dans la chanson populaire française*. Paris: Sagot.

180   *Singing the Celts*

Tiersot, J., 1903. *Chansons populaires recueillies dans les Alpes françaises.* Grenoble: Librairie Dauphinoise.

Tiersot, J., 1905. *Notes d'ethnologie musicale.* Paris: Fischbacher.

Tiersot, J., *ca.*1921. *Mélodies populaires des provinces de France: recueillies et harmonisées*, 10 vols. Paris: Au Ménéstrel.

Venuti, L. (ed.), 1992. *Rethinking Translation: Discourse, Subjectivity, Ideology.* London and New York: Routledge.

Vicaire, G., 1886. 'La Poésie populaire et les poètes français,' *Revue des traditions populaires*, 1 (9–10). pp. 253–65.

Weckerlin, J.-B., 1883. *Chansons populaires de l'Alsace.* Paris: Maisonneuve & Cie.

Weckerlin, J.-B., 1886. *La Chanson populaire.* Paris: Firmin Didot.

Williams, H., 2013. 'Cultural Changes and Exchanges: Brittany and Wales.' In: *Regards croisés sur la Bretagne et le pays de Galles /Cross-Cultural Essays on Wales and Brittany*, edited by Anne Hellegouarc'h and Heather Williams. Brest: CRBC. pp. 27–35.

Yee, J., 2008. *Exotic Subversions in Nineteenth-Century French Fiction.* Oxford: Legenda.

4 Singing in London

Dubious music in French travel writing

'Un homme qui a beaucoup voyagé peut mentir impunément.'

'The well-travelled man may lie with impunity.'

A French proverb, quoted as a Scottish proverb by
Max O'Rell (1887, p. 275)

In 1877, the exiled Communard journalist Henri Bellenger asked his French readers: 'Avez-vous parfois rencontré à Londres un Français venu là pour se distraire? Jamais, et ils ont bien raison' ['Have you ever met a Frenchman who has come to London for his own amusement? Never, and they have good reason not to'] (1877, p. 117). The ready availability of guidebooks for French leisure travel to Britain suggests there may be some hyperbole at work here, but it no less echoes a common perception that Britain, and especially London, is a serious place where amusement simply is not the order of the day – the French seek it out as a land of necessary political exile or of business, not as a land for frivolity and vacation.[1] Yet if they do not visit for amusement, we may well ask how French travel writers find the time around their unspecified but practical, unamusing engagements in Britain to take notes, to walk in parks, to attend theatres, to visit slums, and to dine at private houses, restaurants, and pubs, all the while collecting ample material for lengthy travel narratives. Travel diaries published by French visitors, though varied in style and context, all convey that their writers have been on a voyage of exploration and discovery, with a tone of astonishment not unlike that of their contemporaries who ventured to more exotic and distant lands.

In David Scott's analysis of travel and semiology, he comments that 'travel writing is a paradox in that it is a rite of passage both to the *real* – that is, to an epistemic system different from that of the writer and which thus provokes a profound re-assessment of experience and values – and to the *ideal* – that is, to a world of renewed and heightened meaning' (2004, p. 5). In this respect, texts on Britain are not unlike travel narratives about the Orient, though more rain-drench and less sensual; the United Kingdom becomes a land of discovery, where many stereotypes colour the French traveller's vision of what they see, but where some reality is confronted in this different epistemic system, and

DOI: 10.4324/9780367815431-5

182 *Singing in London*

where many of the lessons learned by French travellers (and their readers) are about the real and the ideal versions of themselves and of their own home country contemplated vis-à-vis this ethnic Other. This state of affairs is encapsulated in the best-selling Guide Joanne travel guides. The guidebook to London and its surrounding regions affirms that, in London:

> Le caractère de la race anglaise se trouve là reflété sous tous ses aspects, car Londres résume l'énergie créatrice de la Grande-Bretagne, et met en relief l'esprit, le commerce et les arts libéraux. Le génie à la fois intellectuel et pratique, dont le développement a eu pour effet de fonder un empire pour ainsi dire universel, se révèle à l'observateur par le spectacle imposant que lui offre la grandiose cité assise sur la Tamise. C'est là que se trouve le cœur et la tête de la grande puissance, c'est là qu'elle apparaît dans toute sa vitalité.
>
> (1898–1899, pp. 143–4)

> [Every aspect of English racial character can be seen there, for London encapsulates the creative energy of Great Britain, and it casts light upon the nation's mind, its commerce, and its liberal arts. The distinctive nature of its spirit, at once intellectual and pragmatic – whose development has founded an empire one might call universal – is visible in the imposing spectacle of this grandiose city astride the Thames. That is where the heart and the head of this great power can be found, that is where it can be seen in all its vitality.]

The guidebook manifests several preconceptions here – notably, that London is representative of Britain more widely (which is to some extent a stereotype received in advance by French travellers from their predecessors, and to some extent also an attitude of urban dwellers in general that will have irked anyone who has lived outside the principal cities of any country). However, a consciousness that Britain entails a distinct epistemic system is also glimpsed here, conveyed in the impression of the imposing grandiosity and power of London. Additionally, it is noticeable that the areas that attract the attention of the writer and that are of supposed interest for the French reader are areas in which something might be gleaned from Britain for France; pragmatism, a can-do mindset that is the product of their education system, imperial successes, and global power gained through savvy commercialism. London is a clue that the traveller seeks to decipher, a riddle to be solved, and its meaning signifies something for France.

Yet by the end of the nineteenth century, it had become a convention of travel notes or social studies of British culture to open with an assertion of how difficult Britain was to comprehend; no mere holiday or business trip would suffice to open the French mind to the true nature of British peculiarities, for which only an extended stay would suffice. This was the argument expressed in particular by the regular stream of exiles who found their

Singing in London   183

way to London after the *coup d'état* in 1851 and again after the repression of the Commune in 1871. According to Alfred Hamonet, exiled during the Second Empire and still residing in London through the Third Republic, as many as twenty-eight years might be needed to gain a reasonable level of acquaintance with British habits (1880, p. 51). This is in part because of how deeply French preconceptions about Britain were intrenched, necessitating lengthy exposure to the real thing to subdue reflex responses and allow the French observer to see their surroundings objectively; and in part because the British, for all their shared history with France and their geographical proximity, were considered to be so entirely different. This is often expressed with the same exoticist analogies that were present in writing on British folk music, as discussed in Chapter 3 of the present book; Hamonet remarks, for example, that the everyday French traveller to Britain 'emporte généralement une fausse idée de ce grand pays. De retour au foyer, il parle avec dédain, avec horreur quelquefois, de cette "*perfide albion*," qu'il connaît moins bien que la Chine ou le Japon' ['generally takes away an erroneous idea of this great country. On returning home he speaks with disdain, sometimes with horror, of that "perfidious Albion," though he knows it less intimately than he knows China or Japan'] (1880, p. 51).

Certainly, Britain is a strange enough land that it resists casual French interpretation and penetration. The travel account worth its salt, therefore, must proclaim that the author has been there and witnessed everything. Augustin Fillon asserts with confidence in the preface to his short stories set in England that 'j'ai observé la vie anglaise d'aussi près et aussi profondément qu'il était possible à un étranger de le faire' ['I have observed English life as closely and as deeply as it is possible for a foreigner to do'] (1888, p. v), while Henri Bellenger advises from his exile in London that 'il ne suffit pas d'être sur les lieux, il faut *savoir voir*' ['it is not enough to be physically present, one must *know how to see*'] (1877, p. 93). However, on assessing the content of such travel texts in the Third Republic, it is not only *voir* that is important, but also *entendre* [to hear] and *écouter* [to listen]; travel writers return again and again to the aural experiences of being in Britain and being surrounded by the British, in their descriptions of each new street, pub, park, and event. The French travellers' sensitivity to sound in Britain – and especially in London – is striking in such texts and it forms a key element of the physical and moral shock that was experienced. Perennially popular novels set in London by Dickens, Jack London, and Paul Féval prepared the eye for what they might see but did little to prepare the ear for what it might hear. Explicatory prefaces may seldom draw attention to sound and music as ineluctable aspects of a visit to Britain, but the body of travel writing nonetheless overflows with references to theatricals, music, noise, and even deafening silences. These texts reveal that the music and sounds of Britain are equally expressive of Otherness for the French adventurer across the Channel as they are in encounters with the non-European Other.[2] Britain sounds different, perhaps unsettling, thus Britain *is* different and unsettling.

184 *Singing in London*

On travelling to Britain, on wandering around its major cities and its Scottish and Irish hills, the French visitor is confronted repeatedly with sound and music; religious music, street music, music-hall song, workers singing, seaside bands playing. These music-making practices become part of the foreignness of the British experience – indeed, they serve to actively foreignize Britain. The author and dramatist Gabriel Mouray is so struck by street performers on each occasion he passes them that he notes them individually, including two women in brightly coloured gowns doing a high-kick dance to a jaunty band, and a colossal man in a kilt playing the bagpipes (1895, pp. 44–5). Bourget's visit to the Isle of Wight rings with musical sounds; on the promenade at Ryde people stroll 'au son d'une musique militaire [...] [et les musiciens] après une valse de Waldteufel, entonnent comme il convient le "God save the Queen!"' ['to the sound of a military band which, after a Waldteufel waltz, struck up "God Save the Queen!" as is right and proper'] and in the summer idyll of Oxford, the tranquil air quivers with 'un orchestre caché sous les arbres du jardin de *Christ Church* [qui] joue des airs à la mode, avec force ronflement de cuivre' ['an orchestra hidden among the trees of the Christchurch gardens playing fashionable tunes, with great rumblings from the brass section'] (1889, II, pp. 9, 230). On a boat from Llandudno to Liverpool, one of the rare leisure tourists writing about Wales, Albert Huet, finds himself on deck with 'une troupe de musiciens [...], et bientôt les violons et les harpes alternent avec des voix un peu éraillées, mais qui répètent assez mélancoliquement des chansons anglaises' ['a troupe of musicians, and soon the violins and harps alternate with voices that are slightly gravelly, but which all rehearse English songs with melancholic intonations'] (1877, p. 38). In Scotland, Burns scholar Auguste Angellier declares that it is impossible to visit the country without taking away 'une vive impression musicale' ['a powerful musical impression'], such as that of a summer evening on Carlton Hill when he heard 'deux cornemuses [qui] jouaient de vieux airs en marchant vite de long en large; [...] quelques heures solitaires [...] tandis que le Pibroch montait d'en bas, perçant tous les bruits confus de la cité' ['two bagpipers who played old songs as they marched briskly up and down; a few solitary hours spent as the sounds of the Pibroch rose from below, piercing through the muffled noises of the city'] (1893, II, p. 26). These street performances seem to strike the French ear as so fundamentally different from the public music-making common to French cities – such as bands playing adaptations of opera tunes in public parks, or even the humdrum accordion or organ grinder – that the foreignizing effect of music even occurs when the music did in fact originate in France; Paul Bourget notes in his diary entry from Shanklin that, during a cricket match, 'un orchestre de musiciens, en costume bourgeois, attaque de temps à autre un air d'opérette *française*, [...] tableau bien *anglais* par les plus menus de ses détails' ['an orchestra of musicians, dressed in suits, attack a *French* operatic aria from time to time, a very *English* picture in all its smallest details'] (1889, II, p. 31 – emphasis added). Far from music being the art form par excellence that elevates the mind, that goes beyond language, and that

Singing in London   185

transcends boundaries in geography and lifestyle, music-making in Britain, for the French, is always inherently British; on each occasion, hearing music is an experience that lingers long with the French writer.

Tim Youngs reminds us that travel writing is never an objective exercise, but that 'it is influenced, if not determined, by its author's gender, class, age, nationality, cultural background and education' (2006, pp. 2–3). Therefore, the preoccupation with music, noise, sound, and silence is also an eloquent reflection on the French subject who writes about them. Indeed, descriptions of sound are among the key differentiating factors between the more objective textual form of the guidebook and the various forms of personal account by writers as diverse as the middle-class international journalist Max O'Rell, the exiled left-wing radical Jules Vallès, the female, upper-class novelists Marie-Anne de Bovet and Brada, and the chauvinistic architect Félix Narjoux. This implies that music and sound are particularly affective at the subjective level, and that they express something different to the visual input which is revelatory both about the British people being observed and the French person doing the observing. Youngs goes on to note that travel writing is ideological (2006, p. 2), and travel texts on Britain from this period project not only meaning but also values onto what they hear whilst across the Channel. As will be discussed presently, this is no rigid, prescribed value system – not least because their aural experiences in Britain strike them as so different to their everyday exposure to sound in France that they have scarce terms of reference by which to judge them. Rather, music and sound become fundamental terms in a negotiation over the meaning that may be ascribed to Britain, and to the French Self in relation to it.

This chapter aims to show the extent to which hearing music and sound become fundamental axes in the French mental conception of British character and culture. Unlike the ubiquitous presence of the comic Englishman songs at the café-concert, discussed in Chapter 1 of the present book, these disconcerting experiences are undergone by a necessarily narrow portion of the French population: leisure travel to England was reserved largely for those with wealth and free time; those with such freedoms were often drawn south to the Mediterranean rather than north; and poor workers or exiles who did reach England were relatively unlikely to have the time, literacy, or connections to write and publish about their experiences. Nonetheless, within this narrower segment of French society, it is with striking insistence and consistency that French writers place music at the forefront of their eye (or ear) witness accounts of 'real,' 'natural' British characteristics, whether they be in comfortable or impoverished streets, middle-class salons or spit-and-sawdust bars. First, this is explored through the alien impression of the music, noise, and sound in the streets of Britain made upon travel writers and their representations of these disconcerting experiences. Next, it steps into the drawing room to experience a musical soirée alongside French visitors, before accompanying Jules Vallès for an evening at the music hall, and finally following Hector France to the sleazy nude theatres and strip joints of East London.

186 *Singing in London*

Sound values

Before delving into specific musical anecdotes from these travel texts, it will first be useful to explore the impression made upon French writers by the British soundscape in a general sense, which struck them as a continuum from general, irritant noise into noisy music. Throughout the lengthy descriptions of British music – and particularly English music – French travel writers frequently employ a lexical field more generally associated with noise and the clamorous urban landscape than with harmoniousness. Writers are quite clear that what they hear are musical instruments and singing voices, but they ascribe so little aesthetic value to them that they blur into the wider soundscape, which itself often overwhelms the French writer. Despite all of these writers living in Paris for a substantial portion of their lives and thus being used to the noises and decibel levels of a modern urban environment (albeit in many cases the noises of relatively comfortable Parisian neighbourhoods), the sonic world of the cities of Britain presents them with what Habermas has termed a 'dialectic of shock and revelation,' in which things are dislodged from familiar frames of reference and re-presented as new (1981, p. 48).

That sound is of central concern to these writers is apparent in the fact that many of them open their texts with descriptions of the sound world of London rather than its visual landscape. The first lines of Félix Narjoux's *En Angleterre* depict the dawning of a London day in a middle-class residential neighbourhood as the city goes from sleepy silence to a chorus of characteristic sounds:

> La ville s'éveille, la journée commence. Le premier bruit qui se fasse entendre est le cri du boy annonçant les 'papers' (journaux) du matin. Puis viennent les marchands de viande à chat: 'Meat, meat!', les chiffonniers, ou plutôt les enleveurs d'ordures ménagères, les 'dustmen': 'Dust, oh!', 'Dust, dust, oh!'.
>
> (1886, p. 1)

> [The city awakes, the day begins. The first noise that makes itself heard is the boy announcing the morning papers. Then come the cat food sellers: 'Meat, meat!' the *chiffonniers*, or rather the household waste collectors, the 'dustmen': 'Dust, oh!' 'Dust, dust, oh!']

Here, the beginning of the day is commensurate not with first light, but with first noise. Narjoux builds an impression of the city for the reader by opening with an aural rather than a visual description, layering sound onto silent foundations (the contemporary reader might well at this point be hard pressed not to imagine the famous strains of Lionel Bart's 'Who will buy?' from the 1968 musical comedy *Oliver!* as the street sellers ply their trade around matinal Bloomsbury). A similar approach is taken by Vallès in the opening page of the first instalment of his *La Rue à Londres* (1884), where he evokes a first

Singing in London   187

impression of London on Oxford Street – and in so doing, beginning as he means to go on, he evokes the inhuman national character of the British.

Il y a du tapage, des rires, des rayons et des éclairs; il y a des pétillements d'ironie, une odeur de plaisir, des souvenirs de poudre. La rue de Londres est ou énorme et vide, – muette alors comme un alignement de tombeaux – ou bourrée de viande humaine, encombrée de chariots, pleine à faire reculer les murs, bruyante comme la levée d'un camp et le torrent d'une déroute. Mais ce sont des bruits sourds, un grondement d'usine, le tumulte animal – point une explosion de vie et de passion. On entend grincer les roues, hennir les chevaux; mais on n'entend pas *parler* les hommes: ni parler, ni rire!... Ils vont, ils viennent comme les *pistons* de machines.
(1884, p. 19 – emphasis in original text)

[There is noise, laughter, beams and flashes of light; there are fizzes of irony, a scent of pleasure, lingering hints of gunpowder. The London street is either enormous and empty – and thus silent, like a row of tombstones – or packed full of human flesh, obstructed by carts, so full as to make the walls shift back, noisy like an army striking camp and the rush of a retreat. But they are dull noises, the rumble of a factory, an animal uproar – not an explosion of life and passion. You hear wheels grate, horses whinny; but you never hear men *speak*: neither speak, nor laugh!... They come and go like the *pistons* of a machine.]

There is a clear desire to create an effect on the reader that fits in with his idea of Britain rather than one seeking to create an objective record; it would be miraculous if Britain functioned without anybody speaking to each other at all in the streets, and we are never sure where those 'rires' in the first line come from if one never hears anybody 'ni parler, ni rire!' by the end of the paragraph. However, regardless of its relationship with reality, this characteristically Vallèsian use of hyperbole underlines the fact that hearing Britain can, at all times, be felt as a strange and alienating sensory experience for the French visitor; in the London street, 'étonné des grognements, ahuri par la rumeur [...] le Français perd la tête' ['astonished by the groans, stunned by the rumblings, the Frenchman loses his head'] (1884, pp. 23–4).

Aberrant sound here forms a continuum of incomprehension and strangeness between the aural experience of musical sounds in the theatres and streets, and the aural experience of the everyday for Vallès and his reader. To some extent, the descriptions of the British city pre-empt Russolo's ideals for Futurist sound; like the Futurists, French travellers cross the large modern capital with their ears more sensitive than their eyes, they are alert to the mechanical noises of the city, and as they traverse its streets, we can often imagine Russolo's *Noise Music: Awakening of a City* for howlers, boomers, cracklers, scrapers, exploders, buzzers, gurglers, and whistles (see Cox and Warner, 2004 [1913], p. 12). However, the ecstasy attached to this world of noise by the

188   *Singing in London*

Futurists is almost entirely absent from accounts of British noise by French writers at the fin de siècle. Such noise is cast as negative: indeed, noise is, by definition, sound so intense or irritating that it causes us physical or psychological pain, a sound, according to the Oxford English Dictionary 'that is loud or unpleasant or that causes disturbance.' This is no Futurist experience of ecstasy in noise or the 'noise music' associated with an industrial, urban world that creates cathartic pleasure through the intensive pain it causes.

When travel writers seek to condemn the morals and mores of the British, it is often achieved by taking this adverse experience of noise and taking the behaviour of a specific group or on a specific occasion as metonymic for the English as a whole. Narjoux describes the vulgar 'instincts naturels' ['natural instincts'] of the 'grossier et brutal' ['coarse and brutal'] Englishman, and qualifies this by describing not only his drinking, eating, and smoking, but also his tendency to sing – and that he sings badly is so obvious that it does not even need to be said (1886, p. 126). When the noisy lower-middle classes let their hair down on holiday, they are 'bruyants, tapageurs' ['noisy, raucous'], they 'parlent haut' ['speak loudly'], and, worst of all, 'chante[nt] à tue-tête' ['sing at the top of their lungs'] (1886, p. 201). At the Derby, the textual presence of the middle and lower classes for Hector France is composed almost entirely of noise, with their 'tohu-bohu, ripailles, ivrogneries, paris, miaulements, sermons, chants, bousculades, disputes, baisers' ['commotion, feasting, drunkenness, betting, meowling, sermons, singing, jostling, fights, kisses'] until the starting pistol fires and ten-thousand voices all cry together '*The y* [sic] *are off*' (1900, p. 226). Indeed, the impression is so deafening that it produces noisy text, the better for the reader to share the aural overload:

> C'est la saturnale sportique [...]: cris de camelots, ronflements des bugles, beuglements des bookmakers, hurlements des saltimbanques, glapissements des marchands de programmes, chansons des minstrels, chants des salutistes avec accompagnement de banjo, de castagnettes, de tambours de basques, de grimaces et de gigue.
>
> (1900, p. 226)

> [It's a sporting Saturnalia: the cries of peddlers, rumblings of bugles, bellowing of bookmakers, shouts of acrobats, squeals of program sellers, songs of minstrels, hymns of Salvationists accompanied by banjos, castanets, tambourines, grimaces, and jigs.]

Here, France fills his description with alliteration and rhyme, with phonetic threads of /s/, /k/, /b/, /m/, and /g/, and the heavy repetition of the article 'de' or 'des.' In case we misread this poeticism as a positive advocation of carnvalesque joyousness, à la Rabelais or Bruegel, France makes it clear that sound is a corollary of vulgarity here: the multitude are 'indécente et bruyante' ['indecent and noisy'] (1900, p. 225). In the unreadable social surroundings of Whitechapel, the East End, or any heavily-populated area, the braying,

Singing in London   189

shrieking noises of the lower classes are like the shadowy, monstrous figures in a child's nightmare.

It would seem that the more disconcerted and fearful the French visitor feels, the less able they are to comprehend and control their surroundings in language, and the more they record hearing noise, discordant music, and inhuman sounds. Indeed, under the French pen, the working classes, beggars, the homeless, and prostitutes are seldom portrayed as a purely visual entity; the familiar *physionomie* image is nearly always accompanied by a soundtrack of noise. This is all the more striking because French writers mention frequently that these people sing but they never discuss that singing in terms of music; they are reduced to a level of humanity and civilization below even that ascribed to the Hottentots by Darwin in *The Descent of Man* (1875, pp. 567–73). Crowds of street urchins sing and scream mocking gibes at drunken prostitutes who have been thrown out of the pub (Bellenger, 1877, p. 26); gin-fuelled banshees 'sortaient en trébuchant des *public-houses*, la chanson et le rire aux lèvres' ['left the pubs, stumbling, song and laughter on their lips'] (France, 1883, p. 99); and beggars and pickpockets 'parcouraient les rues en chantant' ['roamed the streets whilst singing'] (Poisson, 1895, p. 38). This prevalence of singing is not experienced with the passing curiosity of the tourist enjoying local colour; it is, on the contrary, felt as a threat upon the civilized selfhood of the French bourgeois visitor (as it may well have been perceived, of course, by wealthier British people too) – and unlike any tolerable music, which no doubt was to be found in Britain as elsewhere, it is deemed typical of the national propensity for music as a whole.

Many of these sounds, from noise through to noisy music-making, are, in principle, little different from those familiar to the Parisian city dweller. However, where this repeated return to the noises and semi-musical sounds of London's streets differs critically is in the extrapolations that are drawn from these sonic experiences. As the above texts show, comfortable residential streets, the wealthy pavements of Oxford Street, the petty bourgeoisie on high-days and holidays, and the working-class slums (and indeed many more locations that there is not space to discuss here) are all equally the focus of this aural attention and they all create a striking impression on the French ear. This is not, as in Paris, generally a means of discussing the character or morality of just the lower classes for a middle-class reader; Gustave Charpentier's working-class opera *Louise* (1900), for example, incorporated the street cries of market hawkers into the music, and though Émile Zola is not generally inclined to place musical scenes in his novels, the one volume in which he does so is his working-class *L'Assommoir* (1876), in which no fewer than seventeen popular songs are sung and referred to by name.[3] Rather, street noises and noxious music from Britain is treated as a cross-class, cross-community phenomenon so ubiquitous and so unique that the French visitor feels justified in using it as evidence of the essence of Britishness.

The reader of these texts is left with an ambiguous picture both as to the true sonic surroundings in Britain, and of the connotations that they should

190   *Singing in London*

attach to British sounds. There is little doubt that some kind of value *is* to be attached to it – it is used too often as an emotive, affective indicator for it to be otherwise. Yet faced with the difficulty of ascribing any clear semantic sense to the sounds they hear, they instead ascribe value to sound's very presence. The spectrum of music, sound, and noise in Britain fascinates the French ear and the feelings it induces result in affective assessments of not only the sound itself, but also the nation that makes it and lives with it. It may be extrapolated from the fluctuating, inherently contradictory value system attached to British sound that aural irritation from sounds in what are deemed the 'wrong' places is actually a symptom revealing as much if not more about the French visitor's psychological experience than about anything they might dispassionately witness.

Music in the drawing room

Value judgments are not only applied to sounds, music, and noise heard – perhaps unwillingly – in the street but are also the dominant feature in representations of middle-class, drawing-room music. Max O'Rell describes that, on one musical evening,

> J'ai entendu jusqu'à vingt-cinq romances en moins de deux heures, et quand je me prenais à songer au nombre incalculable de petits ronds noirs qui avaient voltigé dans le salon sans qu'aucun des amateurs ait réussi à en attraper un de juste, je me disais: 'C'est vraiment jouer de malheur; jamais je n'ai vu de déveine pareille. C'est insensé, c'est prodigieux, quand on songe à la théorie des chances, au calcul des probabilités.' 'Concert, dit Littré, action d'agir ensemble.' Pas en Angleterre aux soirées d'amateurs: action de courir l'un après l'autre sans jamais parvenir à s'attraper. Ces excellents gens m'ont toujours fait l'effet, dans leur duos, de se crier à tue-tête: 'Tu ne m'attraperas pas, Nicolas!'.
>
> (1884a, pp. 145–6)

> [I have heard as many as twenty-five romances in less than two hours, and when I considered the incalculable number of little black dots that had flown around the drawing room without any of the amateurs managing to catch one, I said to myself: 'It's incredible, when you think of the theory of chance, when you calculate the probability.' 'Concert,' says the Littré dictionary, 'the act of acting together.' Not in England at an amateur musical evening: the act of running after one another without ever managing to catch each other up. These excellent people have always given me the impression, during their duets, of yelling at each other at the tops of their voices: 'You can't catch me, Nicolas!']

Of course, it is entirely likely that numbers of English amateur musicians were of a standard not calculated to dazzle; it is after all not only French authors

Singing in London 191

who get comedic or critical mileage from such scenes, and Jane Austen's Mary Bennet in *Pride and Prejudice* and Charles Dicken's Mr Jinkins in *Martin Chuzzlewit* demonstrate that the general public in England were only too well acquainted with individuals of both sexes whose desire to perform far outstripped their natural capacities. These draw entertainment value from highlighting the absence of musical talent, especially when those who lack it show a remarkable absence of self-awareness in their deficiencies – none, however, approach individual musical talent as evidence of national character as a whole, as these French travel texts do.

In travel texts such as O'Rell's *Les Filles de John Bull* and *John Bull et son île* and Fernand de Jupilles's *Jacques Bonhomme chez John Bull*, readers are invited from their very titles onwards to take the anecdotal narratives as representative of not just social types (Austen's plain, overly-serious gentleman's daughter, or Dickens's man 'of a fashionable turn') but to stand synecdochically for an entire nation. Although the context of the drawing room is class specific, the fact that the drawing rooms are treated as characteristic of John Bull in all three cases asserts their national typicality. In these anecdotes, both O'Rell and Jupilles extrapolate from instances of learned cultural behaviours or of individual lack of skill to make assertions about the inherent nature of every 'insulaire.' Jupilles, for example, states that a meagre, skinny vocal timbre without ringing or mellow qualities constitutes 'the' English singing voice and is 'l'expression de cette nature sèche et prosaïque. Quel son un pareil instrument pourrait-il rendre?' ['the very expression of that dry and prosaic nature. What sound could such an instrument be expected to produce?'] (1885, p. 179). Yet the example he gives to justify this conclusion never even describes the singer's tonal qualities; all we learn of the performance by an anonymous young *miss* is that she makes unfortunate mistakes in her French pronunciation, replacing the romantic line 'portez-lui mes soupirs' ['take him my sighs'] with 'portez-lui mes soupières' ['take him my tureens'] (1885, p. 179). Indeed, immediately after his somewhat ambitious extrapolation about inherent national character demonstrated through vocal tone, Jupilles returns again not to musicality itself, but to pronunciation, complaining of English ladies who want to practice their French with him but have poor accents. The only comment he actually makes about their musical behaviours is that it is popular in England to sing in German, Italian, and French, that English men and women alike are crazy for music, and that they appreciate French musical traditions. Yet taste and cultural appreciation alone are not in themselves deemed sufficient signifiers of value here – genuine Frenchness alone qualifies an individual for praise, and as no English manifestation of French artistic tastes can redeem them, he conveys that this is a question of racial heritage rather than cultural values. The English are cast in a dynamic akin to that explicated by Homi Bhabha in his 'Of Mimicry and Man'; they exhibit many of the same traits and tastes as the French, but they are no less treated as inferior because they are not actually French, however much they seek to emulate them (see 1984, pp. 125–33).

192 *Singing in London*

This is, of course, questionable logic on a number of levels from Jupilles, as well as bearing the trace of somewhat chauvinistic exaggeration. First, most strikingly, because of the argument's circularity – Frenchness is superior because of its greater artistic spirit, but if the English share that spirit, they are still not equal because they are not French. However, it goes deeper than this. Unlike literary poetry or prose, which is inscribed in linguistic systems of signification, music's expressiveness is generally deemed to have extra-linguistic properties, particularly as instrumental music typically has no linguistic content. Consequently, to excel in musical communication, especially in the art-music traditions of nineteenth-century Western Europe, expression must be transmitted in the *mode* of performance with relatively minimal emphasis being placed upon the purely linguistic communication of the lyrics. Indeed, operatic stylistics often render the words only partly comprehensible due to vibrato and the privileging of open vocal passageways regardless of everyday pronunciation (this is reflected in the late twentieth and twenty-first century trend for sur-titling by companies such as the English National Opera, Canadian Opera Company, and New York City Opera, whether the opera be sung in the original language or in an English translation). To repeatedly justify a hierarchy of values, then, using primarily lyric-centric criticisms is a curious choice and one that seems to undermine its own assessment.

The situation is taken a step further in O'Rell's account of a middle-class musical evening. Unlike Jupilles, he does give specific details of the lack of expressiveness in English music-making, using anecdotes to support his statements that 'pour plaire à un auditoire de salon, il faut ici jouer ou chanter comme une mécanique' ['to please a salon audience here, you have to play or sing like a machine'] (1884a, p. 148) and that 'on y rencontre quelquefois de jolies voix, mais elles ne vous disent rien, c'est du bruit' ['you sometimes hear a pretty voice here, but it doesn't say anything to you, it's just noise'] (1884b, p. 189). However, precisely how such statements should be interpreted is immediately cast into doubt because subsequent details reveal that it is not that the English are unable to empathize with feelings through and in music, but that cultural habits tell them to *repress* such expression: after all, 'l'Anglais qui montre ses sentiments perd son *self-control* et se voit renié de ses compatriotes' ['the Englishman who shows his feelings loses his *self-control* and is shunned by his compatriots'] (1884a, p. 148). O'Rell (supposedly) has it from a French composer and music teacher, Monsieur B, that the headmistress of a girls' school at which he was employed responded to his complaints over his pupils' lack of emotion that 'je ne vous ai pas engagé pour enseigner le sentiment à mes jeunes demoiselles' ['I did not employ you to teach emotion to my young ladies'] (1884b, p. 189). This seems to imply that it is not a case of ingrained character – that the English are constitutionally unable to be expressive – but rather of changeable cultural norms – the English are capable of being expressive, but choose not to be.

Of course, their choice to conceal their feelings, even in the arch-expressive form of music, could itself be read as an ingrained characteristic of

Singing in London 193

Englishness, itself a sign of their inferiority to the French – and there is scope for O'Rell to make this a convincing argument here in the context of contemporaneous ideas on racial characteristics and the frequently-repeated trope of English moral and emotional hypocrisy. However, O'Rell undermines this argument in his own desire to be witty. He intertwines his interactions with the English guests and musicians with asides made in inner-monologue, which demonstrate that he is socially adept and charming but also entirely alive to the aesthetic inferiority and the ridiculousness of the music he hears. He approaches one singer who, he says, has just massacred Tito Mattei's *Non è ver*, even though there was no need to talk to him and even though O'Rell has just explained to the reader that the best trick is to stay glued to one's seat throughout the evening. He then offers the singer false flattery about his performance. This little dialogue, it would seem, is intended to highlight the fatuousness and complete lack of musical sense of the singer, but it also demonstrates that O'Rell is an adept hypocrite who hides his feelings the better to succeed in society. Again, when the hostess on one occasion sighs that English pianos 'sont un peu sourds' ['are a little muted' – but literally in French, a little deaf], he quips to himself 'ils ont de la chance' ['they are lucky'], but never gives his honest opinion to the mistress of the house (1884a, p. 146). This hypocritical concealment of feeling differs little in its essentials from precisely that criticism of emotional dishonesty for which he belittles the English; the only key difference is that he dissembles here when speaking whereas they dissemble when performing music. Indeed, O'Rell's hypocrisy is perhaps the greater since he uses conventionally-accepted linguistic signification to mislead and express the opposite to what he thinks, whereas the English musicians simply void their performances of emotion and mislead nobody. If Britain is the home of hypocrisy, O'Rell inadvertently challenges boundaries of national identity here and shows himself to have more than a little bit of Britishness.

There is a sense in the lengthy, over-emphatic nature of Jupilles and O'Rell's lambasting of English drawing-room music that they feel some particular, profound need to discredit it. This is conveyed further by the recurrent lexicon of pain and torture used by both writers. For Jupilles, his after-dinner musical experience is 'un nouveau supplice' ['a new form of torture'] that exists 'pour vous mettre à la torture' ['to subject you to torture']. O'Rell goes further, repeatedly emphasizing the agony of hearing such music. He begins by quipping that 'c'est une affaire de quelques égratignures aux oreilles. On en revient' ['it's a matter of a few scratches to the ears. You recover from it'], but the physical suffering soon worsens:

> J'étais au supplice depuis deux mortelles heures. [...] Un jeune homme à la voix cuivrée venait de massacrer *Non è ver*, la jolie romance de Tito Mattei. [...] On chante plus ou moins fort, plus ou moins faux. Quand la maîtresse de la maison vient vous dire: 'vous allez entendre ce monsieur, il a une voix magnifique,' cela signifie qu'il a une voix de stentor.

194 *Singing in London*

Si j'avais à donner une idée à peu près exacte de ce que l'on ressent aux soirées musicales de mistress John Bull, je dirais que ce sont des douleurs intolérables que je ne pourrais mieux comparer qu'au mal de dents dans les intestins. Figurez-vous qu'on vous arrache une molaire au fond de l'estomac.

(1884a, pp. 146–9)

[I had been suffering torture for two deadly hours. [...] A young man with a brassy voice had just massacred *Non è ver*, the attractive romance by Tito Mattei. [...] They sing more or less loudly, more or less out of tune. When the hostess comes over to tell you 'you're going hear this gentleman sing, he has a magnificent voice,' that means that he has a stentorian voice. To give you a more-or-less precise idea of what one feels during a musical soirée at Mistress John Bull's house, I would say it is a kind of intolerable pain that can best be compared to a toothache in the intestines. Imagine that someone is extracting a molar from the pit of your stomach.]

This language of torture draws upon the fin-de-siècle figure of the cruel English character. The figures of Swinburne's poetic persona and Jack the Ripper had created a caricature of English sadism that would form the crux of novels and short stories such as Maupassant's 'L'Anglais d'Étretat' ('The Englishman of Etretat,' 1882), Villiers de l'Isle-Adam's 'Le Sadisme anglais' in *Histoire insolite* ('English Sadism' in *A Bizarre Story*, 1888), Octave Mirbeau's *Le Jardin des supplices* (*The Torture Garden*, 1899), and Jean Lorrain's *Monsieur de Phocas* (1901). That both Jupilles and O'Rell refer to the experience as torture implies that they are unwilling victims to the sonic cruelty of their English hosts and fellow guests – and music certainly can be an effective instrument of persecution, as scholars such as Jonathan Pieslak and Bruce Johnson have studied in relation to modern acts of sonic discomfort and torture.[4] Yet, there is no imperative for O'Rell or Jupilles to attend such evenings; and if this was an experience that they had been subjected to on numerous occasions (thus justifying their claims for its typicality), we might well wonder why they keep accepting such invitations. O'Rell even offers us an inventive way of getting out of invitations by blaming one's wife for supposedly having made a prior engagement.

So why do they deliver themselves up into the hands of their torturers, if indeed the music is so utterly terrible? Perhaps what they express here is not so much a tale of sadistic torture, as masochistic immolation. In the masochistic scenario, Suzanne Stewart explains, there is an aesthetic tendency and pleasure is to be found 'in the staging or make-believe of torture, enslavement, and humiliation' (1998, p. 3). As a result of this fictional quality, Gilles Deleuze notes, 'the body of the victim remains in a strange state of indeterminacy except where it receives the blows' (1989, p. 26). Although these musical events entail no literal violence, the perceived aggression to the ear does result in a narrative where the Frenchman is, primarily, a hearer; he refuses to adopt the role of performer or listener, and instead his body becomes little more than an agonized ear. This echoes a wider tendency in late nineteenth-century literature that has been explored by Stewart, especially in decadent texts, for male authors to cast themselves as masochistic victims, expressing 'both a crisis of male subjectivity and the positive valorization of that crisis whereby crisis itself became a constitutional feature of that same masculinity' (1998, p. 13). Jupilles and O'Rell express their anguish and seem to imply a powerlessness in the presence of this hideous noise that causes them physical pain, but at the same time as they undergo this apparent crisis of powerlessness over their own bodies and the situation around them, they also affirm their subjectivity with a clear, assertive narrative voice that in its critical tone and its claims for aesthetic superiority assumes a position of power that would be impossible without this experience of suffering.

Yet it should be remembered that Decadence and this idea of masochistic selfhood was a symptom of cultural crisis in France. The need for this artificial construct in order to establish power relations implies that the French individual is being confronted by a significant and serious challenge to their selfhood during their travels in Britain to make this necessary. Surrounded by strangers, communicating outside of their mother tongue, operating in a social situation where the status or connections they enjoyed in France are rendered somewhat irrelevant and where they are identified as French first and an individual subject later, it is perhaps not surprising that O'Rell and Jupilles need to fabricate a narrative of constructed powerlessness here as they undergo a loss of selfhood – as a remedy for their real powerlessness. They must accept these social invitations, in spite of their apparent dislike for the music, in order to be an integral part of society and to ward off loneliness; however, this dependence on the whims of Mistress John Bull places them in an uncomfortable position of powerlessness, and they compensate by attacking the characteristics of their host nation (which, in O'Rell's case, is also the nationality of his wife).

By denigrating British music, they operate the bipartite procedure: first, of demonstrating their intellectual and artistic superiority as Frenchmen, traits that they portray as ingrained in their very racial makeup, and which are therefore incontestable; and secondly, of making it possible to pretend to have a level of control over the situation, in which it is the masochist who chooses his torture and only *plays* the part of a desubjectified victim. Indeed, if they were genuinely in pain, Elaine Scarry has explained that there would be little room for this cool, controlled, pithy narrative voice. Even after the fact, 'physical pain does not simply resist language but actively destroys it,' and its experience is characterized by 'its unsharability' (1985, p. 4). Instead, it is clear that this is primarily a psychological manoeuvre for the French visitor's own benefit. For both of these reassuring claims, it is vital that English music be deemed aesthetically bereft, to ensure the writer dominance as both a Frenchman and an individual – especially when attending musical evenings with members of their own social class rather than their social inferiors, over whom a position

196 *Singing in London*

of power is more easily established. The fact that O'Rell – despite the title of his book, the *daughters* of John Bull – primarily focuses on male musicians in this scene underlines this process; by degrading men rather than 'just' women, he is able to reduce his torturer to the objectified position of a musical Wanda, stripping the subjectivity from the bourgeois Englishman with all his confident pretensions to imperial, masculine, and class power.

Such emphatically negative assessments of middle-class, drawing-room music are particularly interesting when viewed in contrast to the occasional mentions of social music-making in more rural areas of England. In *Les Filles de John Bull*, O'Rell remarks warmly upon the musical gatherings in country towns and villages, where throughout the year a relatively humble but self-improving population gather of an evening to share songs and literary readings. It is quite possible that the average musical proficiency in these smaller communities was considerably lower than in the city, yet there are no comments here upon the refinement of the pieces chosen, the skill of the musicians, their accents, the number of items on the programme, the rapidity of tempo, and so on as there were in London. Indeed, O'Rell feels so favourable about these events that he excuses himself to his French reader, reassuring them that his 'étude critique' ['critical study'] is not about to take 'la tournure d'un panégyrique' ['the direction of a panegyric'] – and it is with the above section on drawing-room music and the molars being extracted from his stomach that he then exculpates himself from any such accusation (1884a, p. 139). This reflects in several key ways upon O'Rell's motives and upon his anticipated audience. Whilst his books sold widely to an international, cross-class, and both a rural and urban audience, this rose-tinted, sympathetic view of country life implies that he anticipates either an urban reader (who might nurture a pleasant fantasy of rural life), or a higher-class rural reader who might share in wider concerns for the education and improvement of rural populations in France. This book, published shortly after the introduction of universal, free primary education in France, offers an image of a self-improving, culture-seeking, peaceful rural population, far from the numerous negative portrayals of French rural life at a similar time.[5] At no point does O'Rell seek to use the details of this musical event as a means of critiquing or analysing this English countryside community in any significant detail; rather, he provides his audience with a message that does not attack their own behaviours, but that reflects upon their social subordinates, that implies an area of concern alive in the contemporary mindset, and that possibly suggests areas in which they might take an interest as employers, masters, patrons, or legislators.

However, this fleeting, positive glimpse of music in rural England is problematic and contradictory in light of O'Rell's general appurtenance to the widely-held belief that the musical Self is expressive of profoundly ingrained national characteristics. He often associates music with ideas of 'racial' traits that are at the heart of how a national community think, feel, and act – indeed, that prescribe the bounds within which they are *able* to think, feel, and act.

Singing in London   197

The considerable body of contemporaneous writing on folk music at this time indicates that rural populations present a more 'authentic' vision of racial character and inherent national traits than their urban counterparts who are adversely influenced by the homogenizing effects of modernity, urban life, and the melting-pot of cosmopolitanism (as has been discussed in Chapter 3 of the present book). Yet if this be the case, then the humble, sociable, culturally-interested populations of rural England should in fact be privileged as an expression of 'genuine Englishness.' The vague and cursory nature of this description, and its immediate juxtaposition with the emphatic critique and mockery of middle-class musicking, to recall Christopher Small's term (the premise of his 2011 work), suggests a need to glaze over the challenges this raises for the clear-cut distinctions between France and England.

Music hall!

London, as it was discussed in the introduction to this book, was positively overflowing with music for the three-to-four-month duration of the Season every year; according to the *Ménéstrel* journal, theatres, concert halls, meeting rooms, and every conceivable space were adapted to serve the musical insatiability of English audiences (Moreno, 1872, p. 253). This level of demand cannot possibly have been generated solely by the relatively small number of wealthy, landed gentry who made their way to London from their country estates; rather, it reflects the equal yearning for musical entertainment from the lower-classed servants who travelled with them, the influx of seasonal workers in the tertiary sector who descended upon the city to cater to their every need, and ordinary Londoners. This Season is quite an event, one might think, and one well-worthy of remark by the French explorer seeking out the unusual in London; nonetheless, in the majority of contemporaneous travel narratives, diaries, and notes the musical delights of the Season in London are hardly mentioned at all. Yet English language-learning books available in France provide set phrases for use at the theatre and concert hall, implying that it was anticipated that the French visitor would habitually frequent – and presumably enjoy – such entertainment whilst on their travels.[6] O'Rell does remark upon the glamour of the compulsory black-tie dress code at the more sophisticated theatres, though he still makes scant remark upon the musical performances themselves (1884a, pp. 66–7), and even here, the paucity of lines consecrated to such glittering audiences in comparison to the lengthy description of other more popular musical genres and performances is telling. Perhaps this kind of music – artistic, operatic, orchestral – is too familiar to the French listener to be remarkable: it is, after all, a cosmopolitan genre and a theatre like the Covent Garden Opera House thrived on 'la confusion des langues musicales' ['an intermingling of musical languages'] (Bertrand, 1872, p. 3). It is a common paradox of explorations of Britain that anything witnessed that contradicts the assumptions that Britain is always and at all times inherently British is often pushed to one side as an irrelevant

198   *Singing in London*

anomaly, rather than taken as evidence that Britain may be more like France than anticipated.

This dismissal of high-culture music in favour of the low whilst in London is revelatory of the key position that music holds in the French psychological appraisal of Britain; it is the familiarity of the *aural* experience that renders the striking *visual* spectacle of this annual musical mania almost entirely uninteresting for writers beyond the musical press. In terms of Britain's own theatrical and musical repertoire, the average show in this land of Shakespeare is dismissed as a – very – poor derivative of theatre in France: the rife second-rate adaptations of French plays and comic operas are described derogatively by Jules Vallès as 'des serpents dont on a terni la peau et dont les anneaux se déroulent dans la poussière' ['snakes whose skin has been tarnished and whose coils unfurl in the dust'] (1884, p. 52). Original British writers of comic opera go unnoticed: Gilbert and Sullivan, whose fourteen collaborative comic operas saw tremendous success from 1871 to 1896, and whose works were staged over five thousand times by their original theatrical companies alone, are to my knowledge not mentioned in books of travel writing, although their names were likely to be familiar to many French readers from newspaper reports on their shows in major titles such as the *Figaro*.[7] Rather, the musical spectacles that are sought out are from significantly lower down the artistic spectrum: generic music-hall acts (with no mention of the national – and indeed international – celebrity of singers such as the Queen of the Music Hall Marie Lloyd in the 1880s and 1890s), variety shows, and striptease shows.

On these performance genres, nearly every visitor has something to say (including, with the exception of the strip shows, female visitors). A common theme is the French bemusement at English behaviour in these rowdy theatres. Brada is surprised to find that 'ce qui les divertit au suprême degré, c'est le côté grotesque et naturellement plus ou moins inconvenant [...] [du] travestissement; [...] on *hurle* de joie aux bons endroits' ['the thing that amuses them the most is the grotesque and more or less indecorous side of cross-dressing; they *scream* with joy at the best bits'] (1895, p. 236), and even the largely neutral Guide Joanne suggests that 'les chansons comiques, les farces théâtrales grotesques, la foule qui fourmille dans ces lieux de divertissement, sont là pour témoigner de l'absurdité de nos idées [par rapport aux Anglais] à cet égard' ['comic songs, grotesque theatrical farces, and the crowd that swarms into these places of entertainment, are all evidence of the absurdity of our ideas about the English in this respect'] (1898, p. 135). French writers testify to their great surprise that the English, on home soil, do not demonstrate the prudery that stereotypes had led them to expect and that they welcome not just naughtiness but genuinely grotesque corporeality well beyond *le shocking*.

However, this degree of surprise is in part because the French visitors pay minimal regard to the implications of class difference in the cultural milieu of the music hall, especially the music hall outside the heart of the West End – and this in spite of the markedly obvious distinctions between these venues and the bourgeois drawing-room settings discussed in the previous section.

Unlike in the halls and variety theatres of the West End, it is rarely the ruling elites who they meet in these neighbourhood London theatres, nor for the most part the aspirational middle and upper-middle classes who seek to penetrate those upper social echelons; rather, the principal part of the audience would have been composed of the lower-middle and working classes, especially in the earlier decades of this period. Now, this is not to say that French writers are incapable of identifying the class to which the people around them belong when they choose to slum it for an evening: on the contrary, Vallès is aware that the clerk or shop-keeper John Bull, his family, miners, and factory workers are the target audience at the music hall (1884, p. 54), and O'Rell recognizes *le cockney* (his shorthand for all working-class Londoners) during his evening at the music hall (1887, p. 11). Rather, what they do not identify is the fact that it is deeply problematic to take this section of society as representative of 'Britishness' (or even 'Englishness') as a whole; they overlook the specificity of lifestyle, community structures, exposure to outside cultures, and even diverse ethnic heritages entailed in the popular audiences of this modern, industrial city. Its attendees are frequently referred to as John Bull just like the hosts of musical evenings in the middle-class drawing room despite the majority of them having markedly different socio-cultural and economic existences. It is unlikely that any of these travel writers would have made the same oversight about the population of Paris; an author declaring that the Parisian workers were representative of all Parisians, or that they were representative of Gascony or Brittany as much as Paris would either have caused a scandal or have been laughed out of the bookshops.

Nonetheless, almost no consideration is given to the implications that such class-specific differences might have on the performance styles and the signification of the content at the music hall. It is particularly surprising to find issues of class disregarded by Vallès given his collaboration with the workers in the Commune of 1871 and his record of outspoken criticism against the capitalist culture of the Second Empire. His depiction of music hall in England is among the most extensive in any French account at the time, notably in the instalment entitled 'Le Soir' from a series of articles published by *L'Événement* in 1876–1877 during his exile, and then later in book form as *La Rue à Londres* in 1884. 'Le Soir' details the various entertainments available in London, briskly touching on theatre and art music, striking glancing blows at the poor quality of the directing, the lack of talent on stage, the absence of elegance or grace, and the indifferent theatrical journalism, before arriving at the proliferation of music-hall theatres and their immense size (quantity at the expense, he implies, of quality). Here, Vallès lingers, and his use of highly affective, derogatory descriptors from the outset of the instalment demonstrates that there is no intention here of simply providing a detached depiction of a curious cultural phenomenon.

Instead, what Vallès hears and sees (and, it is reasonable to assume from the hyperbolic tone, paints with a degree of artistic licence) is employed to reinforce pre-existing negative stereotypes of the English and reaffirm his

200   *Singing in London*

own and France's superiority rather than to seek out new insights. The first key stereotype, in the opening lines of the section on the music hall, revolves around the Chairman: Vallès asserts that he is not a mere host or announcer, but he is like an auctioneer proposing the acts as objects for sale. This is to be expected, as the French are familiar with the cliché of the English as a nation of shopkeepers and merchants without human feeling – in a circular gesture Vallès uses the stereotype to explain the behaviour of the Chairman, and uses the Chairman to prove the veracity of the stereotype. In case the reader has failed to recognize that the Chairman is not depicted here as an anomaly but as the manifestation of the flaws of the whole nation, Vallès clarifies explicitly that:

> ce *chairman* [...] c'est bien l'Angleterre, – l'Angleterre de la *respectability* et du *business*, qui, frac au dos, marteau au poing, – appelle les artistes comme les recrues, et ne permet pas que les belles filles restent sur la scène pour rien. [...] Chanté! Dansé! Adjugé! – À un autre! Comme je te reconnais d'un coup, ô brutale Angleterre!
>
> (1884, pp. 36–7)

> [this *chairman* is England itself – the England of *respectability* and *business*, who, with a suit on his back and a gavel in his hand, calls up the artists like army recruits and doesn't just let pretty girls stay on the stage for no good reason. Sung! Danced! Sold! – Next! Oh, how I recognize you at a glance, brutal England!]

Following the Chairman, each character in turn is rooted in a familiar stereotype with a similar degree of insistence; there is the audience (who are fuelled by the capitalized 'Orgueil anglais' – 'English Pride'), the jig dancer ('cette marionnette'), and the female performer ('[qui] a l'air d'un garçon en fille' – 'who looks like a boy dressed as a girl') (1884, pp, 38, 37, 43). Of course, some allowance must be made here for Vallès's unenviable position as an exile in London and for the destitution he suffered during this time; his struggle to make an adequate living and London society's indifferent treatment of him as just another faceless *immigré* would naturally have added humiliation to his intense solitude, have caused bitterness, and have given him reason to want to take a position of linguistic agency to counteract his social powerlessness. However, the target of his anger here seems radically misdirected: first, even when the capitalists of London had treated him brusquely, they are not the class of most of the people he encounters in the music-hall audience – indeed, it is quite probable that many other music-hall goers would have suffered similar or even worse treatment at the same hands; and secondly, the *degree* of violence and hatred expressed in depictions of the disadvantaged and destitute of England is positively vindictive. In the first instalment of *La Rue*, Vallès had already described with overwhelming disgust the filth of impoverished, brutalized women eking out a living as flower-sellers and of the half-starved children of slum housing, in a tone of scorn rather than pity. He goes on to complain callously that London's 'viande à plaisir' ['pleasure flesh'] offend him because they wear rags and because they have the unattractive habit of complaining that they are hungry (1884, pp. 4, 54, 62). His own unstable and uncomfortable situation seems, paradoxically, to translate a nostalgic sympathy for the French *peuple* into a hostility against the English populace, shifting the focus of his ideology from one of class to one of nationalism. This experience of hardship that he shares to some extent with the lower classes of England, rather than deepening his sense of class brotherhood, instead leads him to vituperate against England as a whole.

There are two acts at the music hall that Vallès describes in detail and that are particularly striking. First is his scathing critique of the black-face minstrel act.[8] The music he describes is represented as merely the sum of a number of disagreeable sounds: 'l'orchestre grince [...] qu'on est dans un pays de spleen et de cauchemar, plein de gens qui sont saouls de religion ou de gin' ['the orchestra squawks that you are in a land of spleen and nightmares, filled with people drunk on religion or gin'], and the music is 'criard comme un public-house' ['shrill as a public house']; the banjo tune played by *Kaffir à l'œil blanc* (White-Eyed Kaffir – the stage name of G. H. Chirgwin) is a 'musique monotone et nue' ['monotonous and bare music']; the typical female singer has a voice 'trempée de vinaigre, accordée sur un miaulement' ['dipped in vinegar, tuned to a mewling note'] or otherwise '[elle] vomit des notes graves, aussi grosses que celles lâchées par les boulangers' ['she belches out low notes, as substantial as those hollered by bakers']; and Vallès draws from all this a conclusion about the whole nation, that 'avant d'être un peuple d'artistes, ils sont une nation de boxeurs' ['rather than a nation of artists, they are above all a nation of boxers'] (1884, pp. 41, 44, 45). Vallès dismisses the music as mere noxious sound, foregrounding a lexical field associated with noise, industry, and aggression; the orchestra plays 'comme les coups de sifflet [qui] accompagnent le départ d'un train' ['like the whistles of a departing train'], and the expression vibrating along the strings is 'l'électricité de la mélancolie comme sur le fil des télégraphes' ['the electricity of melancholy as if on telegraph wires'] (1884, p. 41). This draws a direct parallel between this particular musical experience and his sweeping assessment of the population who mill constantly along London streets and who move like 'des *pistons* de machine, ils passent comme des courroies se mêlent, comme les trains se croisent. [...] Allez, le piston!' ['machine *pistons*, crossing like drive belts, like passing trains. Work on, piston!'] (1884, pp. 1–2 – italics in original text). Indeed, the very nature of the English mind itself is compared to a discordant box of instruments; instead of having heart strings to pull, English reverie is hung 'comme un gong, aux parois de cerveaux anglais' ['like a gong on the walls of the English brain'], and eccentricity is a 'fifre qui a son clou, près du gong, sous le crâne de John Bull' ['fife on a hook next to the gong inside the skull of

202 *Singing in London*

John Bull']. Music – or rather, noise music – is deemed by Vallès to be the best possible way of conveying the nature of the English mind.

If we take Vallès at his word, by all the standards of 'good' musical taste, this music is demonstrably 'bad.' Yet the audience's incongruously positive reaction to these terrible, nightmarish noises hints that there is something here which Vallès fails to understand – particularly given the apparent sobriety of the audience (this is one of the few occasions Vallès does not insist on the inebriation of the English). Without being aware of it, Vallès has recorded here the aural aesthetics that would soon be championed by modernism on both sides of the Channel. Music comes to reflect the sounds of the city, the mechanical and repetitive aspects of industry to which the workers are subjected in their daily occupations, and it speaks of the struggles of their existence.[9] Through the veil of Vallès's aesthetic distaste, we catch a glimpse within music hall of an art form for the modern proletariat, encapsulated within what Narjoux rejected as 'un spectacle commun, qui n'est pas fait pour plaire à des esprits raffinés et délicats' ['a common spectacle, not made to please refined or delicate minds'] (1886, p. 69). Narjoux is, though not for the reasons he imagines, correct; these performances are *not* made for the pleasure of the refined elites, but are moulded by and for the labouring population of the fin de siècle's industrialized, alienating urban environment – and as such music hall is that population's entertainment of choice.

The lower strata of society were not without affordable opportunities to hear more 'refined' music if they so wished, albeit not necessarily performed by the most successful or highly-trained musicians: even in deepest rural Ireland, Marie-Anne de Bovet remarks that touring companies passed through country towns with selections from Gounod's *Faust* and Bizet's *Carmen* (1908, p. 91). Rather, the lower classes actively choose the musical modes of entertainment and expression associated with the music hall. This discordant, shrill music seems to speak eloquently to this audience – and in reaction to different pieces of music which sound to Vallès to be of equally poor quality, they manifest diverse, active, physical responses. They do not, as Berthold Brecht would later say of art music, allow the sounds and their aesthetic values to wash over them, being 'transported into a peculiar state of intoxication, wholly passive, self-absorbed, and according to all appearances, doped' (1964, p. 89), but rather they are galvanized into enthusiasm by jigs and are nearly brought to tears by White-Eyed Kaffir's banjo music. Indeed, the very shape of the banjo seems to be a parody of classical tropes, being neither violin, nor cello, nor classical guitar, yet its form, the physics of its acoustics, and its player's postures and gestures all call to mind and parody its high-culture counterparts. Instead of the feminine curves of the violin or cello (that would later be played upon by Man Ray in 'Ingrès's Violin'), it presents the rounded potbelly of the clown. No matter how forcefully Vallès argues that the entire audience and thus nation lack the *esprit* for either aesthetic judgement, proper human emotion, or distinction of character, the intense pleasures expressed by this class-specific audience imply that such music

Singing in London 203

should not in fact be interpreted according to questions of national character, but rather of engaged, deliberate lower-class counterculture.

Vallès ascribes the popularity of black-face minstrels to an inherent English thirst for asserting power. The English audience member:

> se prend, pendant un quart d'heure, pour un planteur ou un commandeur de par-delà l'Océan, qui a le droit de faire sauter et gémir les esclaves. [...] C'est comme s'il régnait pour un moment sur une des possessions au-dessus desquelles flotte l'*Union Jack* et où des milliers de gens de couleur s'inclinent devant les favoris roux d'une centaine de marins anglais.
>
> (1884, pp. 38–9)

> [thinks of himself, for quarter of an hour, as a plantation owner or colonial commander overseas, who has the right to make slaves jump and howl. It's as though he reigned for a moment over one of those possessions where the Union Jack flies and where thousands of coloured people bow down before the ginger sideburns of a hundred English sailors.]

British (and French) colonialism certainly did entail numerous episodes of inexcusable cruelty, but for the vast majority of the John Bulls and the 'gens de mines et d'usines' in this music-hall audience, the oppression of colonized subjects is something of which they likely had limited concrete understanding and with which they were complicit only at several removes; for example, as shopkeepers selling exotic goods or dockworkers eking a precarious poverty-line existence from unloading cargo ships. Most of the lower and working-class men in the theatre had only just been granted the vote (in the 1867 Reform Act), the women would have to wait several decades longer, and they may well all have had only a general sense of what colonialism meant in practice – especially if they were illiterate, since compulsory primary education was only introduced in 1880. Michael Pickering has remarked that

> minstrelsy was just as much about English social relations as it was about a scantily known Afro-American populace. What was being symbolically worked out in minstrelsy, at a metalevel of commentary, were questions about the status of white Victorian society.
>
> (1986, p. 84)

Though originally imported from the United States of America, by the late nineteenth century it had been adapted and become naturalized to appeal and speak to its British audiences. So, in this context, where is the slave in the room? Far from identifying with the masters, whip in hand, much of the audience at these neighbourhood music halls would themselves have been wage slaves to Capitalism: enslavement was in fact a long-standing metaphor in nineteenth-century literature for the suffering of the working classes,[10] and as Engels explained,

204   *Singing in London*

the slave is sold once and for all; the proletarian must sell himself daily and hourly. [...] The individual proletarian [is] property as it were of the entire bourgeois class which buys his labour only when someone has need of it.

(1952, pp. 7–8)

Thus, when Vallès represents the audience being moved nearly to tears by the 'slave' music played by White-Eyed Kaffir, it suggests that far from identifying with the slave driver, they actually identify with the figure of the slave; they find in his music a means of vicariously expressing their own oppressed lot in society. The socially disadvantaged see a photographic negative of themselves being brought to life, they hear in his aesthetically-marginal music the sound of their own social marginality, and they find therein a distraction from and coping strategy for their precarious social existence.

Vallès seems insensitive to this. He will, however, represent one act in over-whelmingly positive terms. A singer, decked as a London beggar, emerges from behind the audience, Vallès tells us, dragging his foot, decked in rags, and smeared with dirt, who proceeds to sing 'd'une voix d'écrasé [...] des mots qui sont une plainte d'abord, mais qui, peu à peu, deviennent une raillerie féroce et douloureuse' ['with the voice of a crushed man, words that start as a groan but, little by little, become a ferocious and painful jeer'] (1884, p. 39). As the song goes on, this beggar character lambasts the socio-political system in a satirical tirade that attacks the glory of Britain, the supposed generosity of the rich, the virtue of the queen, the integrity of Gladstone and Disraeli, and the persistence of poverty and hunger with an 'ironie sanglante' ['bloody irony'] and a 'menace voilée!' ['veiled threat!'] (1884, p. 39) – the likes of which would be impossible in France until 1906 due to the enduring 'censure pre-ventative [qui] condamne le café-concert à des rengaines qui vous feraient pleurer' ['restrictive censorship that condemns the café-concert to staging woeful ditties'] (1884, p. 41).

On this occasion, faced with such evident socio-political protest, Vallès does recognize a truly proletarian voice and is overjoyed at finding that such liberty of expression is possible. At first, he seems taken aback, exclaiming that: 'ce n'est plus le chauvinisme britannique, c'est la liberté anglaise! Écartez-vous, censeurs du pauvre pays de France [...]! Ce cabot en haillons vient de tirer avec le pistolet de la blague sur la souveraine et sur les ministres' ['this is no longer British chauvinism, it's English freedom! Step aside, censors of poor old France! This ham actor in rags has just shot the Queen and the govern-ment ministers with the pistol of his jokes'] (1884, pp. 56–7). Vallès even goes so far as to suggest that 'c'est le souvenir de ces hardiesses d'outre-Manche qui fait que celui qui a connu l'Angleterre bâille aux refrains banals de l'Alcazar ou de l'Eldorado, et peut avoir pour une heure la nostalgie des soirées d'exil' ['it's memories of this audacity on the other side of the Channel that makes anyone who has been to England yawn at the banal refrains at the Alcazar or the Eldorado, and can make you nostalgic for a while for those evenings spent

Singing in London   205

in exile'] (1884, p. 57). The forces of order allow it (no policemen arrest the singer); the audience seems neither astonished to witness such an act, implying its familiar and habitual inclusion on hall billings, nor do they protest that their sacred cows are being denigrated (indeed, they seem to be in consensus with his critical views); and all of this despite the fact that the English authorities, like the French, were actively aware of the political utility of music as a propaganda tool.[11] Like the figure of the slave, the song of the beggar-man seems to accord with the audience's social disenfranchisement and to provide them with both a sense of class identity and a means of expressing their disadvantaged lot. Yet even though there is such a clear correlation between the deliberately jarring style of the singing and the jarring political message, between the musical dynamics (that is, sound volume) and the strained social dynamics indicated in the lyrics, still Vallès does not consider looking for similar analogies in the other acts at the music hall – or indeed, he does not consider extrapolating from this one act to inform his understanding of Englishness more widely. So ingrained is his belief in 'Orgueil anglais,' and so firmly does he consider the English lower classes to be cowardly and fawning, that rather than being able to make objective observations, he is blind – or more accurately, deaf – to the signification of what he hears.[12]

This selective hearing inevitably introduces contradictions into his text and Vallès's preconceptions are confronted repeatedly by the complexities of reality. Such a confrontation often poses problems for travel writers (this has been widely discussed in scholarship on Oriental travels),[13] but rare is the degree of absolute self-contradiction that follows here. Quite contrary to his preceding remarks upon the Chairman as the embodiment of Englishness, Vallès now claims that the beggar character represents the 'génie de l'Angleterre' ['English spirit/genius'] (1884, p. 41) – even though the two characters, one oppressive, conservative, and inhuman, one liberated, politically engaged, and intensely human, manifest sets of mutually exclusive traits. He does not address this flagrant contradiction, but simply leaves the reader to confront the tension themselves. This may be read alongside one unique moment of clarity in the previous instalment of *La Rue* when Vallès cries, seemingly in despair, 'quelle ville!... toute pleine de contradictions énormes, amas de confusion! [...] Des silences de cimetières, des mines de chemin où l'on tue – et, à deux pas, des grognements d'inondation et des déchirements de tempête!' ['what a city!... filled to the brim with enormous contradictions, a heap of confusion! [...] Cemetery-like silences, cut-throat-alley faces – and, just two steps away, the roaring of a flood and rending of a storm!'] (1884, p. 14). Uniquely here, rather than choosing to overlook or reduce the urban confusion into neat stereotypes as he did during the black-face minstrel act, he instead acknowledges the impossibility of such an endeavour – and indeed, in this moment, Vallès conveys the complexity of *all* modern, urban existence, built on irresolvable contradictions and compromises. The text indicates then, obliquely, that France, like England, is too complex, class-divided, inconsistent, and diverse to possibly have one, unified national character.

206 *Singing in London*

Jigs and strippers

At the bottom of the spectrum of musical encounters in London's theatres is the debauched world of the strip show, where music and dance unite not for primarily artistic purposes, but to fuel male sexual fantasies. Typically, in novels by French authors that are set in Britain – even in Rachilde's atypical *L'Homme roux* (*The Red-haired Man*, 1889) – there is rarely more than the occasional glimpse of nakedness, and there are none of the lengthy passages revelling in descriptions of breasts, hips, and thighs so familiar from novels set in France such as *Nana, Manette Salomon*, or decadent novels such as *Là-Bas* (*Over There*) and the *Marquise de Sade*. One stereotype of the British – confirmed and strengthened by translations of the Romantic poets and Charles Dickens – is that British women are modest (or prudish, depending on your perspective) by nature. However, in descriptions of London theatricals, there are as many if not more descriptions of female strippers than of British actresses or singers of more 'respectable' credentials; what is more, they always appear in conjunction with music particularly inflected with associations of 'Britishness' for the French reader, such as a jig or a military march. As we have seen in Chapter 1, French café-concert song had already disseminated the idea that these genres were inseparable from not just British music culture, but from the very nature of the British individual, their inner character, and their body. Jigs and marches are the soundtrack to the generic British being and thus the presence of this music has a powerful reality effect for the French reader. To write repeatedly about the presence of such musical genres in immoral strip shows subtly persuades the reader that vice has just as intrinsic a relationship with British character as these tunes do.

Hector France pays this aspect of British mores particular attention in his *Les Va-nu-pieds de Londres* (1883). In this text, France describes a nude Tableaux Vivants show in a gentlemen-only theatre, where, as the curtains opened 'au son d'une gigue légère jouée sur un piano invisible, les *tableaux vivants* se déroulaient' ['to the sound of a light jig played on an unseen piano, the tableaux vivants began'], and the audience behold '[des] exhibitions malsaines de femmes avachies, de crapuleux voyous et de filles à peine pubères' ['unwholesome exhibitions of sagging women, debauched delinquents, and barely-pubescent girls'] (1883, pp. 287–9). Of course, the highly affective adjectives here seek to demonstrate disgust at such immorality; yet this condemnation is contestable since Hector France attends more than one night of such entertainments, and his notes reveal concentrated attention on the sexualized bodies of the girl and women performers. On another occasion, he visits a private theatre in Whitechapel, where he and his companion buy gin for the child-singers and dancers before the latter hurry backstage to get ready for their acts on the spit-and-sawdust stage. First 'cinq ou six jeunes drôlesses chantèrent [des] chansons graveleuses, firent les mêmes gestes immondes, suivis des mêmes gigues' ['five or six young hussies sang bawdy songs, made

Singing in London 207

the same filthy gestures, followed by the same jig steps'] (1883, p. 298). Then the dance act – the main attraction – takes to the stage, which I will quote here at some length:

Triangle, piston et tambour entamèrent une marche militaire, et voici que défilèrent les demoiselles du corps de ballet. [...] *Ran plan plan! Ran plan plan!* Au pas, comme des soldats, elles traversèrent la scène, lentement, l'une derrière l'autre par rang de taille et sur un seul rang afin d'être bien vues, faisant bruyamment et en cadence retentir leurs talons sur les planches. Elles avaient la tête couverte d'un schall à la façon des madones ou des Irlandaises des jours de pluie. La pointe tombait jusqu'au-dessous de la croupe et, retenu devant par leurs mains croisées, le schall ne dépassait pas les hanches. Les jambes sans maillot montraient leurs blanches nudités. [...] Alors, retenant le schall de leurs deux mains comme si elles craignaient de laisser voir leur poitrine, elles commencèrent la gigue. Cette grotesque danse, caricature de l'art chorégraphique, sans laquelle il n'est pas de fête populaire, semble l'exacte expression du caractère national, raide, disgracieux, d'une lascivité hypocritement voilée.

Frénétiquement, avec des éclats de derviche en délire, l'orchestre accompagnait, et rien de plus étrange que ces filles la tête et le buste couverts, agitant par des mouvements épileptiques leurs jambes amaigries par la croissance, les nuits sans sommeil, la débauche hâtive, car la plus âgée comptait quinze ans à peine, et sur les vingt de la bande la moitié n'avait que douze ans. Mais le ballet eût paru monotone s'il eût duré longtemps ainsi; bientôt les schalls glissèrent à terre, et je compris le nom donné à cette érotique chorée, *drawers' ballet*, ballet des caleçons. Entièrement nues jusqu'à la chaussure, elles ne portaient, pour cacher leur puberté naissante, qu'un caleçon de coton de baigneur, et dans le cynisme enfantin de leur vice, elles s'étaient ingéniées à lui faire tenir le moins de place possible, afin que le public ne perdît rien de leur nudité. Et toutes ces petites ribaudes, prises de rage, enfiévrées sous les regards ardents des mâles, continuèrent pendant quelques minutes, avec des gestes et un piétinement de convulsionnaires, cette danse digne du sabbat. Et empourprées, l'écume aux lèvres, l'œil perdu, ruisselantes de sueur, elles s'arrêtèrent haletantes, reprirent leurs schalls, s'en enveloppèrent et, s'élançant de la scène, se répandirent dans la salle, tandis que l'orchestre continuait ses airs de gigue endiablée.

(1883, pp. 300–01)

[The triangle, brass, and drum struck up a military march and the girls of the ballet corps came onto the stage. [...] *Rum-pa-pa-pum! Rum-pa-pa-pum!* Marching like soldiers, they crossed the stage slowly, one behind the other in order of size in a single row so that they were all completely visible, and they drummed their heels loudly on the boards in time with the music. They had their heads covered in shawls like Madonnas or like

208   *Singing in London*

Irish women in the rain. The points at the back of the shawls fell below their hindquarters and, at the front, they were held together with crossed hands, going down only as far as their thighs so that their bare legs were on show in all their white nudity. [...] Then, holding the shawl with their two hands as though they feared letting the audience glimpse their chests, they began to jig. This grotesque dance, a caricature of the art of choreography, a fundamental part of any popular festival, is the exact expression of British national character – inflexible, disgraceful, and with a lasciviousness concealed by hypocrisy.

Frenetically, with outbursts like whirling dervishes, the orchestra accompanied them, and there is no stranger sight than those girls with their heads and torsos covered, moving their legs with epileptic agitation. Their legs were thin from adolescent growth, sleepless nights, and premature debauchery – the oldest was hardly fifteen, and of the troupe of twenty, half of them couldn't have been more than twelve years old. But the ballet would have seemed monotonous if it had long continued in that way. Soon, the shawls slipped to the floor and I then understood the name given to this erotic dance, *the drawers' ballet*. Entirely naked from head to foot, they wore nothing but a pair of cotton bathers to cover their budding puberty, and, in the childish cynicism of their vice, they had worked wonders to make them cover as little flesh as possible so that the audience would miss nothing of their nudity. And all these debauched little girls, crazed and feverish under the ardent male gaze, continued this infernal dance for several minutes with their convulsive hand gestures and footwork. Then, crimson, foaming at the lips, with a distant gaze, dripping with sweat, they stopped, panting for breath, and grabbed their shawls, which they threw around their shoulders and ran from the stage into the audience whilst the orchestra continued its diabolical jig.]

Throughout this description, France emphasizes the jig's inherently British nature, both as a genre in general and in terms of this performance in particular. We are told that no popular festival is possible without it (although France attends no popular festivals in the course of this book), and that it is the *exact* expression of national character. So inherent is the jig to Britishness that the frenetic music even seems to trigger an instinctive response in the girls' bodies. France orders his description carefully with a series of causes and effects in order to convey this idea: first, this delirious music begins playing, and shortly afterwards the girls begin to dance like 'épileptiques' and 'convulsionnaires,' as though the madness of the music almost unwittingly triggers the madness of their physical movement. Then, at the end of the piece, the diabolical music does not stop, and thus nor do the girls: instead of retreating backstage as we might expect, the 'airs de gigue endiablée' continue and the music seems to force the girls to keep dancing as they skip off into the audience to find transient sexual customers.

Singing in London 209

Understand the jig, Hector France contends, and you understand the nation. Whilst this dance might have once been the stuff of innocent peasants, France presents an image of a degraded nineteenth-century jig that, like Britain as a whole, he implies, has fallen from its pastoral origins and entered a period of decline and decadence. Indeed, it is clear that Hector France ascribes a considerable significatory power to music as he composes a text that endeavours to make an aural as well as a visual impact upon the reader. We are informed of the precise instruments in the small ensemble so we can imagine the tonality; we are not only told that the drums were playing, but are given a rendering of their *ran-plan-plan*; we not only see the girls march but are given to hear their heels pounding loudly on the boards; and the jig music accompanies the girls' every move, punctuating the narrative, so that the two are rendered inextricable. Both march and jig were familiar musical genres to the fin-de-siècle French audience and they would have been able to imagine how the transition would sound between the straight rhythms of the march as the girls entered the stage (often based on strings of quavers in a 2/4 time signature) and the tertiary rhythms of the jig (typically triple sets of quavers in a compound time signature). By placing the music that accompanies this dance in both the first line of text and the last, France implies that this national musical genre is also a musical metaphor for all the other manifestations of vice that he indicates therein; the strangeness of the aural experience that he depicts in the text impresses upon the reader how remote all of this is from French culture.

Within this framework, France makes this image of immorality as shocking as possible: the long, detailed description makes uncomfortable reading with its clear sexual exploitation of children and its projection of vice away from the adult viewer and onto the child performers; it is the 'hussies' who are debauched, he says, who want to show off as much as possible of their nudity, and who desire to enflame the ardent eyes of their male audience rather than performing simply out of economic necessity. The *Va-nu-pieds de Londres* claims at the start to be a text written in sympathy for the poor, so the reader initially approaches this description expecting to be presented with an object of pity; yet in the presence of the 'gigue endiablée,' a cognitive dissonance makes itself felt. First, there is dissonance because the promise of pity appears instead under Hector France's pen as scorn; it transpires that the critique is not primarily to promote reform, but simply to denigrate Britain – an appealing idea for many readers, no doubt, at a time of fear about degenerating national morality, of low birth rates, and of rampant syphilis in France. As Britain grew in wealth and in political strength in the colonial scramble, to explain such lewdness not merely as immorality but as inherent to British nature and culture, rooted even in their most authentic music and dance, suggests that they might not be victorious in the Darwinian survival of the fittest in the long run after all. Secondly – and more strikingly – dissonance emerges because the reader's ability to assimilate Hector France's deeply negative image of British character is undermined by the laughter response that is triggered by the presence of the jig throughout these erotic revelries.

210 *Singing in London*

Whilst the jig certainly does connote Britishness for the French reader, it also brings to mind the funny accents, hilarious dancing, frumpy tweed, and outrageous stick-on mutton chops of the cafés-concerts that were discussed in Chapter 1 of the present book. The reader may struggle, therefore, to take the seriousness that Hector France seems to espouse entirely seriously.

The lowest echelon of Hector France's voyage of discovery through the strip joints of East London takes him to a tawdry tavern in Whitechapel. Here, although without the same implications of child sexual exploitation, France treats the reader to another long, detailed rendition of the music he hears, the dance he watches and nicknames 'Eve's Jig,' and the sight of the gradual removal of the dancer's clothes:

> Tout à coup, faisant signe au violoneux, elle monta sur la table du milieu en s'aidant de l'épaule d'un jeune drôle à mine de furet, et le violon ayant entamé l'air *Speed the Plough*, le gigue commença. Les mouvements furent lents d'abord, puis se se [sic] précipitèrent; la fille s'anima, frappant du talon à crever la table, et le musicien ayant accéléré la mesure, elle sembla bientôt prise d'une folie hystérique. Alors se passa une scène étrange: le vieux jeu du *clown*, dans les cirques forains, lorsque vêtu en campagnard il se hisse sur un cheval, et, se dépouillant peu à peu de toutes ses hardes, paraît, aux yeux émerveillés, dans son maillot éclatant de paillettes. […]
>   --- here there is a detailed account of each piece of
>   clothing as it falls ---
>
> La danseuse en chemise, ou plutôt en peignoir, continua une gigue folle au milieu des applaudissements des spectateurs. Et, souriante, le front calme, confiante, son chapeau de velours transformé en aumônière, elle fit lentement le tour de la société. […] Elle remonta sur la table. Alors, avec une pudeur que je n'attendais guère, elle baissa, sourde aux protestations de l'assemblée, l'unique flamme de gaz, et quand il ne resta plus qu'une petite lumière tremblotante, son peignoir glissa. […] Les fureurs des mâles en rut éclataient dans les profondeurs intimes de ces gueux.
>   (1883, pp. 79–80)

> [All of a sudden, she gestured to the fiddle player and climbed up onto the table in the middle of the room, leaning on the shoulder of a weasel-faced young rake. The fiddle began playing *Speed the Plough* and the Eve's Jig began. The steps were slow at first, then became faster; the girl became increasingly lively, striking the table with her heel so hard it seemed it would break, and as the musician picked up the tempo, she soon seemed in the grip of an hysterical madness. Then a strange scene took place: it was that old trick of the clown in a travelling circus who is dressed in rustic clothes and, as he vaults up onto a horse, takes off one piece of clothing after another until, under the astonished gaze of the audience, he appears in a shimmering, spangled costume. […]

Singing in London   211

The dancer in her petticoat, or rather in a dressing gown, continued her crazed jig to the applause of the audience. And, smiling, with a calm expression, confidently, she made a circuit of the room with her velvet hat in the guise of a money bowl. [...] She climbed back up onto the table. Then, with a modesty that I hadn't expected, she lowered the one gas lamp, deaf to grumbles of protest from the audience, and when there was no light left but a small flicking flame, her robe slipped down. [...] The raging passion of rutting men burst out from the inner depths of these paupers.]

Although his attention is, of course, substantially occupied by the visual stimulus on show, France nonetheless also places significance on the aural in this scene; he elaborates upon the type of instrument, the name of the tune, the progressive accelerando of the fiddle-player's rhythm, and the dancer's heel stomping on the table. However, again, his desire to emphasize the strange, unseductive, almost uncanny nature of the dance and the associated desires evokes instead figures of fun from the French comic song repertoire. The clowning reference recalls the Hanlon-Lees and numerous acrobatic troupes at French circuses (clowning being considered so inherently British that the French language adopted the word *clown* directly from English) – thus, at the same time as they read about the grimiest of Whitechapel taverns, the sound-scape and the mental image are layered with memories of the light-hearted milieu of Parisian entertainment.

The problematization of this episode goes further here due to errors in the identification of the music. First, the folk tune *Speed the Plough* is not a jig at all but a reel, which has a 4/4 time signature and thus does not easily accommodate the compound rhythms of the jig; the dance steps that result from this are thus likely to be very different. Clearly, the primary focus for this performer and her audience is not the faithful replication of folkdance genres; but this misidentification is significant because France is emphatic is his assertions that the jig is the lifeblood of British culture and the mirror of its national spirit, and he confidently extrapolates 'facts' about Britishness from his experiences of watching and hearing dance and music. Yet he is clearly not sufficiently familiar with its features to distinguish it from other musical or dance forms. Logically, therefore, he may also not be able to distinguish between features that are 'typically British' and those pertaining to other social or national groups.

Further, his censure of this episode as a quintessentially British moral iniquity is called into question by his particular choices of extremely negative lexicon to condemn this spectacle. More often than not, his rhetoric implies that his disgust is primarily an *aesthetic* one: those 'femmes avachies,' the surroundings in the theatre where the wallpaper peels like a leper's skin, the fact that he is forced to confront the 'détails ignobles, les côtés écœurants et immondes' ['ignoble details, the sickening and filthy side'] (1883, p. 295), the diabolical music, and the crazed 'mouvements épileptiques' that are far from

212 *Singing in London*

a smooth, seductive burlesque dance. France's text implies that his main irritation is that the sex industry he finds in London feels ugly and dirty from an aesthetic point-of-view, rather than because he dislikes the sexual objectification or exploitation of vulnerable women and children per se – yet, as Stallybrass and White have argued in their discussion of lowbrow culture, 'disgust always bears the imprint of desire. These low domains, apparently expelled as "Other," return as the object of [...] longing and fascination' (1986, p. 191). Thus, whilst lambasting the British for their moral hypocrisy on the one hand, at the same time he demonstrates the very same hypocrisy himself: he does, after all, pay the entrance fee and facilitate the industry; he attends strip joints on at least three separate occasions; he turns his fascinated attention onto the sexualized bodies of the girls on stage; he increases the vicarious audience to these performances by sharing every detail with his readers; and he never actively condemns the theatrical managers who hire child performers, who sexually exploit impoverished women, or who provide venues for lewd acts.[14] Thus, at the same time as he tries to convince the audience of the ingrained association between British national character and moral hypocrisy by way of these erotic jigs, so too he exhibits those supposedly British characteristics himself; he demonstrates that national character is fluid at the very moment that he seeks to demonstrate its exclusiveness.

The last problematic aspect of the anecdote of 'Eve's Jig' that I shall discuss here can be found in the emphasis placed on the arousal experienced by the audience. Though it can be assumed that the audience of the Tableaux Vivants and the Drawers' Ballet were aroused by the performances too, this is not described in the text – but in the tavern the French reader can witness these East-Enders as they are enflamed by the visual fantasies of striptease and by the aural effect of the fevered music. Roland Barthes remarks in his writing on striptease that the gradual exhibition of flesh conceals rather than reveals the true locus of desire and thus leaves a lingering dissatisfaction that serves to keep desire circulating: 'le nu qui suit reste lui-même irréel, lisse et fermé comme un bel objet glissant, retiré par son extravagance même de l'usage humain' ['the nude body that appears remains unreal, smooth, and closed like a slippery, beautiful object, excluded by its very extravagance from human use'] (1957, p. 139). Furthermore, Barthes contends that the dance aspect of striptease, 'faite de gestes rituels, vus mille fois [...] cache la nudité, enfouit le spectacle sous un glacis de gestes inutiles' ['composed of ritualized gestures, seen a thousand times before, conceal the dancer's nakedness, bury the spectacle beneath a glaze of useless gestures'] (1957, p. 140). Hector France's tavern stripteaser performs ritualized gestures in the form of the jig, and as a result the spectacle of her nakedness is hidden to some extent behind these gestures, resisting the French reader's desiring gaze. Indeed, the jigging stripper or the drawers' ballet girls are still more resistant than the French burlesque dancer, using as they do gestures that have not only been ritualized within the world of dance, but also ritualized by French comic singers and by decades of French travel writing about the English. Corinne Perrin has

Singing in London 213

rightly remarked that the idea of 'the English' was recognizable not through its relatedness to a referential reality, but 'par référence à d'autres Anglais de papier, [...] des représentations collectives' ['with reference to other paper English people, other collective representations'] (2003, p. 10); whilst Hector France has these girls remove their clothes, the presence of the heavily-stereotyped music and dance of the jig veils them under layers of older songs and texts, and rather than being contained in the categorical judgements he proclaims, the mystery of Britishness evades Hector France.

Furthermore, in the British context, those ritualized gestures are not ones of reassuring feather boas or ostrich-feather fans, but rather they are gestures that are perturbing, composed of repulsive physicality and maddening music. Barthes argues that striptease could be seen as 'un spectacle de la peur, ou plutôt du "fais-moi peur," comme si l'érotisme restait ici une sorte de terreur délicieuse' ['a spectacle of fear, or rather of the "go-on-and-scare-me," as though eroticism stood here for a sort of delicious terror'] (1957, p. 138). Barthes intends this in a primarily Freudian sense – a fear of seeing the reality of the female sexual organs and of the castration they are thought to imply – but in the jigging female body the scope for fear reaches further than a purely primal horror. Watching the British girls and women jig, strip, and then jig naked entails an aesthetic horror, but is also horrifying as a challenge to French masculinity; the hyper-energetic jig is so unerotic by their ideals of sensuality as to imply that the women have no desire to seduce them. The music and the dance steps actively refuse to emphasize a rounded female form and to caress the eye and the ear; instead, Hector France is distressed by the sharp, pointed, rigid shapes and melodic phrases that are performed before him and that are antithetical to his French ideas of sensuality and eroticism. Even more than Barthes's practiced Parisian stripteaser, 'les quelques atomes d'érotisme, désignés par la situation même du spectacle, sont en fait absorbés dans un rituel' ['the few atoms of eroticism, indicated by the very setting of the spectacle, are in fact absorbed into a ritual'] (1957, pp. 138–9). Thus, the French male observer may be disconcerted in two principal ways: first, on an individual psychological level, as his subjectivity is not reaffirmed through the acknowledgement of his desires by the female sexual object; and secondly, perhaps still more disconcertingly, because these unsensual jigs and the unromantic music accompanying them *do* seem to gratify the desires of the British men around him – they do seem to give these Londoners a sense of power and assurance. This suggests that there is an entirely different epistemic system at work here, to recall Tim Youngs's phrase, and one that utterly excludes the French male subject. Hector France's reaction to these scenes suggests that he feels himself powerless and de-subjectified on an individual level by these performances by women, in a nation that already threatens the power of his country on a geo-political one.

Thus it appears from these travel narratives that the musical and quasi-musical soundscapes of Britain present the French ear with a particularly resistant sound habitus, to play on the term coined by Pierre Bourdieu (see

214   *Singing in London*

Questions de sociologie, 1984). The social mores of the British are peculiar, but long exposure and good will make it possible for the French individual to adapt to these – Alfred Hamonet's lengthy exile and excellent command of the language, for example, allow him to gain an understanding and sometimes an admiration for his country of adoption, asserting justifiably that 'il a donc pu se former une idée juste des Anglais, et secouer quelques-uns de ces préjugés absurdes que le Français traîne partout avec lui quand il voyage à l'étranger' ['he has thus been able to form a fair idea of the English, and to shake off some of those absurd prejudices that the Frenchman drags around with him everywhere when he travels abroad'] (1880, p. 51). Yet the way that British individuals make, perceive, and react to their music and their sonic surroundings remains mystifying, and they constitute a set of embodied dispositions that the French individual cannot acquire or begin to comprehend. Often, French writers project interpretations over this music – claiming it is a sign of racial banality, delinquency, or a society on the point of collapse – but like the caricatures of the British on the French café-concert stage, these projections build more on French stereotypes of Britain than on an objective and an up-to-date reality.

There is a strong sense that the French visitor experiences the British soundscape – from music hall, to jigs, to drunken prostitutes singing – as a Verfremdungseffekt. Rather than being able to codify and conceptualize Britain by the eye, as Realism and Naturalism had helped a generation of writers codify Paris, noise and silence, music, un-musical singing, and instrument playing turn fairly ordinary and accessible objects into something peculiar and unsettling. Culturally and visually, Hyde Park is not so different from the Bois de Boulogne, but instead of the gay restaurant orchestras it has its vociferating preachers on speakers' corner. Oxford Street is not so alien to someone who has seen the Rue de Rivoli after Haussmannization, but in London bagpipers and black-face minstrels busk on the corners. The London music hall is not so different from Parisian cafés-concerts, but its acts are punctuated with jolting jigs instead of lyrical waltzes, and beggar tirades replace innocuous love songs. This Verfremdungseffekt makes it impossible for the French observer to identify with their surroundings and the people that populate them, in spite of the many cultural similarities between fin-de-siècle France and Britain in comparison to, say, the alterity of North Africa or Indo-China. And yet the French visitor to Britain writes in such a way, often with such vehemence or confusion, that this near neighbour seems to strike them as stranger – or rather, less assimilable to a familiar and pleasant French fantasy – than the Orient. Rather than sound revealing an 'authenticity effect' that, according to James Buzzard's analysis of contemporaneous travel writing, provides 'the epiphanic moment in which the unified essence of the place shines forth' (1993, p. 188), instead the only epiphany is one that reveals their own alienation.

Notes

1 Census data from 1870 to the turn of the century indicate a resident French population in London of 10,179 (1871), 8,251 (1881, after the amnesty in France), 12,834 (1891), and 11,300 (1901) – with nearly as many again living in the rest of Britain.

2 Philip V. Bohlman and Ronald Radano discuss European descriptions of music around the world in the introduction to *Music and the Racial Imagination* (2000, p. 17).

3 Music in this novel is discussed in more detail by Robert Lethbridge (1991 – with a focus on the potential political subversion in popular music) and in my own forthcoming essay, 'Songs in the Laundry: Musical Meaning in Zola's *L'Assommoir*.'

4 See: Pieslak, 'Cranking up the Volume' (2010); Johnson, 'Killing me Softly with his Song' (2002).

5 For example, the rural lower-middle classes in many of Maupassant's short stories, including the banal Bovary-esque wife in 'Une aventure parisienne' (1881) and the sexually-abusive master's son in 'Histoire d'une fille de ferme' (1881); Maupassant's selfish, brutal peasants such as in 'Coco' (1884) and 'La Mère aux monstres' (1883); the conniving, greedy peasants in Huysmans's *En rade* (1887); and the drinking, flatulent peasants who Zola would portray so derogatorily in *La Terre* (1887).

6 See, for example, J.P. Grace-Smith and F. Thémoin, *Cours d'Anglais d'après la Méthode Gouin* (1905), pp. 104–8.

7 This is all the more striking since newspapers have little positive comment to offer on Gilbert and Sullivan and they would therefore seem ideally suited to be mentioned in a critique on British musical culture in travel writing. For example, on the occasion of Arthur Sullivan's knighthood in 1883, a reporter for the *Figaro* newspaper sneers that 'il est comme compositeur très inférieur à J. Offenbach ou à Lecocq à l'ennoblissement desquels on n'aurait jamais songé en France' ['as a composer, he is very inferior to J. Offenbach or Lecocq, and in France we would never so much as consider their elevation to the nobility'] (Johnson, 16 May 1883, p. 3); a reporter in anticipation of a production of *The Yeomen of the Guard* at the 1889 World Fair wills the show to fail: 'la chute qui attend cette opérette prouvera que MM. Guilbert et Sullivan sont bien loin, bien loin de MM. Meilhac et Halévy et du regretté Offenbach' ['the failure of this operetta will prove that Misters Guilbert and Sullivan are far, far less talented than Misters Meilhac and Halévy and the much-lamented Offenbach'] (Johnson, 27 March 1889, p. 3); and an article damns Sullivan's *The Golden Legend* with faint praise, by scoffing that 'je ne dirai rien de la *Légende dorée*, c'est de la musique anglaise qui n'est évidemment pas faite pour des oreilles continentales, car j'avoue ne pas comprendre l'enthousiasme des 20000 Anglais des deux sexes qui ont *cheered* ce soir Empereur, musique, et musiciens!' ['I won't say anything about the *Golden Legend*; it's English music that obviously isn't made for continental ears, and I confess that I cannot understand the enthusiasm of the 20,000 English men and women who cheered the Emperor, the music, and the musicians this evening!'] (Jacques St-Cère, 1891, p. 2).

8 The fact that the minstrelsy tradition of mimicking and mocking dark-skinned people is inherently racist was not recognized by the nineteenth-century European mind, and consequently for the purposes of the present study I will leave this aspect aside and direct the reader to the fruitful discussions

216 *Singing in London*

elsewhere – including: Annemarie Bean and James V. Hatch (eds), *Inside the Minstrel Mask* (1996); Dale Cockrell, *Demons of Disorder* (1997); and, on the late Victorian tradition specifically, Michael Pickering, 'John Bull in Blackface' (1997).

9 A growing body of scholarship has begun exploring this link between urban noise and modernity, including with reference to Paris in Aimée Boutin, *City of Noise* (2015); to the London of Virginia Woolf, for example in Kate Flint, 'Sounds of the City' (2003) and Angela Frattarola, 'Developing an Ear for the Modernist Novel' (2009); and to the Futurists' vision of noise music, for example in Robert P. Morgan, 'A New Musical Reality' (1994).

10 For example, A. Templar's poem 'Infant Slavery, or the Children of the Mines and Factories' (1840); in Elizabeth Gaskell's *Mary Barton*, where Barton cries that 'we're their slaves as long as we can work; we pile up their fortunes with the sweat of our brows' (1848, p. 8); and this was still common currency when Robert Tressell published his controversial *Ragged Trousered Philanthropists* in 1914 and his socialist character Owen explains that 'instead of enjoying the advantages of civilization we are really worse off than slaves, for if we were slaves our owners, in their own interest, would see to it that we always had food' (1914, p. 51).

11 This is discussed in compelling detail in Fulcher, *French Cultural Politics and Music* (1999) and Pasler, *Composing the Citizen* (2009). It also became a significant and powerful part of fascist political movements in the twentieth century, see: Peter Tregear, 'Sounding Fascism' (1999); Ron Eyerman and Andrew Jamison, *Music and Social Movements* (1998); and Carolyn Birdsall, *Nazi-Soundscapes* (2012).

12 Vallès decries the working-class Englishman as someone who 'se pressera alors, au nom de la servilité nationale, court lécher le pied des hiérarchies' ['will hurry along, in the name of national servility, to lick the feet of people of rank' – p. 10], without taking into account the frequent and often bloody working-class uprisings, protests, and strikes throughout the nineteenth century, such as Peterloo (1819), the Cato Street Conspiracy (1820), the Reform Riots (1831), the Preston Strike (1842), the Sunday Trading Riots (1855), and the Reform League Hyde Park Demonstration (1866).

13 This underlying complexity is discussed by Edward Said in *Orientalism* (1978); Tim Youngs, *Travel Writing* (2006); David Scott, *Semiologies of Travel* (2004); and Benedict Anderson, *Imagined Communities* (1991).

14 Similar ambivalence to the sexual exploitation of young girls is to be found on a far wider scale at the Paris Opéra, where the ballet chorus girls, the *petits rats*, were generally expected to be 'patronized' by a wealthy male abonné of the theatre, who had special access rights to the backstage areas, dancers' dressings rooms, and, in many cases, the dancers' bodies (see Lorraine Coons's 2014 article, and the dramatization of this sexualized commerce in countless contemporaneous novels, short-stories, and magazine articles, including Ludovic Halévy's novel of a family of ballet dancers, *La Famille Cardinal* (1883)).

Works cited

Anderson, B., 1991. *Imagined Communities: Reflections on the Origins and Spread of Nationalism*. London and New York: Verso.

Angellier, A., 1893. *Robert Burns*, 2 vols. Paris: Hachette.

Barthes, R., 1957. *Mythologies*. Paris: Seuil.

Singing in London 217

Bean, A. and Hatch, J.V., eds, 1996. *Inside the Minstrel Mask: Readings in Nineteenth-Century Blackface Minstrelsy.* Hanover, NH: Wesleyan University Press.

Bellenger, H., *ca.* 1877. *Londres pittoresque et la vie anglaise.* Paris: Georges Decaux.

Bertrand, G., 1872. *Les Nationalités musicales, étudiées dans le drame lyrique.* Paris: Didier.

Bhabha, H., 1984. 'Of Mimicry and Man: The Ambivalence of Colonial Discourse,' *October*, 28, pp. 125–33.

Birdsall, C., 2012. *Nazi-Soundscapes: Sound, Technology and Urban Space in Germany, 1933-1945.* Amsterdam: Amsterdam University Press.

Bohlman, P.V. and Radano, R., 2000. *Music and the Racial Imagination.* Chicago: University of Chicago Press.

Bourdieu, P., 1984. *Questions de sociologie.* Paris: Éditions de Minuit.

Bourget, P., 1889. *Études et portraits*, 2 vols. Paris: Lemerre.

Boutin, A., 2015. *City of Noise: Sound in Nineteenth-Century Paris.* Urbana: University of Illinois Press.

Bovet, M.-A. de, 1898. *L'Écosse: Souvenirs et impressions de voyage.* Paris: Hachette.

Bovet, M.-A. de, 1908. *Trois mois en Irlande.* Paris: Hachette.

Brada, [Henriette Consuelo Sansom Puliga], 1895. *Notes sur Londres.* Paris: Calmann-Lévy.

Brecht, B., 1964. *Brecht on Theatre*, translated and edited by J. Willett. London: Methuen.

Buzzard, J., 1993. *The Beaten Track: European Tourism, Literature, and the Ways to 'Culture,' 1800–1918.* Oxford: Clarendon Press.

Cockrell, D., 1997. *Demons of Disorder: Early Blackface Minstrels and their World.* Cambridge: Cambridge University Press.

Coon, L., 2014. 'Artiste or coquette? Les *petits rats* of the Paris Opera ballet,' *French Cultural Studies*, 25 (2), pp. 140–64.

Darwin, C., 1875. *The Descent of Man*, 2nd edn. New York: Appleton.

Deleuze, G., 1989. *Masochism: Coldness and Cruelty*, translated by J. McNeil and A. Willm. New York: Zone Books.

Engels, F., 1952. *Principles of Communism*, translated by P. M. Sweezy. New York: Monthly Review.

Eyerman, R. and Jamison, A., 1998. *Music and Social Movements: Mobilizing Traditions in the Twentieth Century.* Cambridge: Cambridge University Press.

Filon, A., 1888. *Amours anglais: nouvelles.* Paris: Hachette.

Flint, K., 2003. 'Sounds of the City: Virginia Woolf and Modern Noise.' In: H. Small and T. Tate, eds, *Literature, Science, Psychoanalysis, 1830–1970.* Oxford: Oxford University Press. pp. 181–94.

France, H., 1883. *Les Va-nu-pieds de Londres.* Paris: Charpentier.

France, H., 1900. *Croquis d'Outre-Manche.* Paris: Charpentier.

Frattarola, A., 2009. 'Developing an Ear for the Modernist Novel: Virginia Woolf, Dorothy Richardson and James Joyce,' *Journal of Modern Literature*, 33 (1), pp. 132–53.

Fulcher, J., 1999. *French Cultural Politics and Music: from the Dreyfus Affair to the First World War.* New York: Oxford University Press.

Gaskell, E., 1848. *Mary Barton.* Reprint 1994. London: Penguin Books.

Grace-Smith, J.P. and Thémoin F., 1905. *Cours d'Anglais d'après la Méthode Gouin*, 2 vols. Paris: Hachette.

218 *Singing in London*

Habermas, J., 1981. 'Modernity: an Unfinished Project.' In: M. D'Entrèves and S. Beahabib, eds, 1996. *Habermas and the Unfinished Project of Modernity.* Cambridge: Polity Press. pp. 38–55.

Halévy, L., 1883. *La Famille Cardinal.* Paris: Calmann-Lévy.

Hamonet, A., 1880. *Annuaire commercial et industriel ou Guide général à l'usage des Français en Angleterre.* Paris: Hachette.

Huet, A., 1877. *Un Tour au pays de Galles.* Paris: Imprimerie centrale des chemins de fer.

Joanne, P., 1898–9. *Guide-Joanne: Londres et ses environs.* Paris: Hachette.

Johnson, B., 2002. 'Killing me Softly with his Song: an Initial Investigation into the use of Popular Music as a Tool of Oppression,' *Popular Music*, 21 (1), pp. 27–39.

Johnson, T., 16 May 1883 and 27 March 1889. 'Correspondance anglaise,' *Figaro.* p. 3.

Jupilles, F. de, 1885. *Jacques Bonhomme chez John Bull.* Paris: Calmann-Lévy.

Lethbridge, R., 1991. 'Reading the Songs of *L'Assommoir,*' *French Studies*, 45 (4), pp. 435–47.

Moreno, H., 1872. 'Saison de Londres,' *Le Ménéstrel.* 30 June, p. 253.

Morgan, R.P., 1994. 'A New Musical Reality: Futurism, Modernism, and "The Art of Noises",' *Modernism/Modernity*, 1 (3), pp. 129–51.

Mouray, G., 1895. *Passé le détroit.* Paris: Ollendorff.

Narjoux, F., 1886. *En Angleterre: Angleterre, Écosse (Les Orcades, Les Hébrides), Irlande: Le Pays, Les Habitants, La Vie intérieure.* Paris: E. Plon, Nourrit et Cie.

O'Rell, M., 1884a. *Les Filles de John Bull.* Paris: Calmann-Lévy.

O'Rell, M., 1884b. *John Bull et son île.* Paris: Calmann-Lévy.

O'Rell, M., 1887. *L'Ami MacDonald: Souvenirs anecdotiques de l'Écosse.* Paris: Calmann-Lévy.

Pasler, J., 2009. *Composing the Citizen: Music as Public Utility in Third Republic France.* Berkeley, CA: University of California Press.

Perrin, C., 2003. 'Anglais en papier: le cliché et le miroir.' In: A. Court and P. Charreton, eds, *Regards populaires sur l'Anglo-Saxon: Drôles de types.* Saint-Étienne: Publications de l'Université de Saint-Étienne. pp. 9–29.

Pickering, M., 1986. 'White Skin, Black Masks: "Nigger" Minstrelsy in Victorian England.' In: J. S. Bratton, ed., *Music Hall: Performance and Style.* Milton Keynes and Philadelphia: Open University Press. pp. 70–91.

Pickering, M., 1997. 'John Bull in Blackface,' *Popular Music*, 16 (2), pp. 181–202.

Pieslak, J., 2010. 'Cranking up the Volume: Music as a Tool of Torture,' *Global Dialogue*, 12 (1), pp. 1–11.

Poisson, L'Abbé, 1895. *Angleterre – Écosse – Irlande: Souvenirs et impressions de voyage.* Orleans: H. Herluison.

Russolo, L., 1913. 'The Art of Noises: Futurist Manifesto.' In: Christopher Cox and Daniel Warner, eds, 2004. *Audio Culture: Readings in Modern Music.* New York and London: Continuum. pp. 10–14.

Said, E., 1978. *Orientalism.* New York: Pantheon Books.

Scarry, E., 1985. *The Body in Pain: the Making and Unmaking of the World.* Oxford and New York: Oxford University Press.

Scott, D., 2004. *Semiologies of Travel: from Gautier to Baudrillard.* Cambridge: Cambridge University Press.

Small, C., 2011. *Musicking: the Meanings of Performing and Listening.* Middletown, CT: Wesleyan University Press.

Stallybrass, P. and White, A., 1986. *The Politics and Poetics of Transgression*. London: Methuen.

St-Cère, J., 1891. 'À Londres', *Figaro*. 11 July, pp. 1–2.

Stewart, S., 1998. *Sublime Surrender: Male Masochism at the Fin de Siècle*. Ithaca and London: Cornell University Press.

Tregear, P., 1999. 'Sounding Fascism: T. W. Adorno and the Political Susceptibility of Music,' *Culture, Theory and Critique*, 42 (1), pp. 36–48.

Tressell, R., 1914. *The Ragged Trousered Philanthropists*. Reprint 2012. London: Wordsworth Editions.

Vallès, J., 1884. *La Rue à Londres*, edited by Lucien Scheler. Reprint 1951. Paris: Éditeurs Français Réunis.

Youngs, T., ed., 2006. *Travel Writing in the Nineteenth Century*. London and New York: Anthem Press.

Epilogue

'Les chants de haine sonnent aujourd'hui d'une façon étrange à nos oreilles.'
'Today songs of hatred ring strangely in our ears.'

Jean Finot (1903, p. 292)

As Europe took its first steps into the twentieth century and towards the gathering clouds of World War I, the political and cultural landscapes in and surrounding France had changed character considerably since the dawn of the Third Republic. Universal primary education had begun to loosen class boundaries for the lower classes; the progression of women's liberation movements, especially in the UK and USA, began to destabilize long-held certainties about gender roles and capabilities; and secularization movements weakened the Catholic church's influence over social structures, cultural norms, and hierarchies. On the international stage, France's sense of the primary causes for concern shifted, as the presumed superiority of the 'white race' was shaken by the so-called 'Péril jaune' ('Yellow Peril') as Japan saw victories in the Russo-Japanese Wars (1904–05); as America progressively raised its head as a global superpower;[1] and as Germany began to flex its imperial muscles in earnest to carve out its own colonial footholds in Africa. Indeed, Christine Geoffroy has argued that 'ce fut avant tout la menace représentée par l'Allemagne qui fut l'élément déterminant de l'alignement politique [entre la France et le Royaume-Uni]' ['it was above all the threat posed by Germany which proved the decisive factor in the political alliance between France and the United Kingdom'] (2004, pp. 284–5).

The Entente Cordiale was signed between France and Britain on 8 April 1904 and comprised a suite of compromises and agreements on trade and, especially, on which of the two colonial powers should have unopposed control of which corners of the world. Geoffrey notes that, even at the proverbial eleventh hour, both the political elites and public opinion were often lukewarm at best and raised numerous obstacles for the diplomatic talents of its four chief proponents, Théophile Delcassé, Paul Cambon, Lord Landsdowne, and Edward VII. The pragmatic political expediency of the Entente came

Epilogue   221

to converge with the belief that France and Britain could accede to greater promise and prosperity through mutual cooperation instead of persistent hostility and competitiveness. Though this was not an entirely novel idea and had been aired periodically throughout the nineteenth century, now the political situation was ripe for it to come to fruition. The philosopher Jean Finot, for example, highlights to his readers the mutually beneficial trade arrangements that had arisen since the turn of the twentieth century and offers them up as markers of their shared fraternity (in 1901, Britain had purchased thirty per cent of French goods on the global market), followed by a lengthy explanation of the moments of amity in their long parallel histories and cultural developments (1903, pp. 32–6).[2] This is all posited as evidence of the fact that the racialist and ethnological theories habitually reeled out about the British were gravely misleading:

> notre terminologie scientifique est remplie de préjugés comme l'âme d'une dévote. […] Les haines entre peuples, basées sur la prétendue contradiction de leurs origines ou la fausse analyse de leur sang, ne cessent de se manifester d'une façon inquiétante. C'est ainsi que les Français considérés comme un peuple 'latin' sont censés haïr les Anglais, envisagés comme un peuple germanique.
>
> (1903, p. 159)

> [our scientific terminology is as full as prejudice as a devout soul. […] Hatred between different peoples, based on their supposedly opposite origins or on the false analysis of their blood, has not ceased to manifest itself to a worrying degree. It is this attitude that posits that the French as a 'latin' people should hate the English, seen as 'germanic.']

He concludes that 'les vociférations des énergumènes des deux côtés de la Manche manquent de fonds réel' ['the vociferations of maniacs on both sides of the Channel lack any real foundation'], in a powerful vindication of the mutual benefits of closer relations between the two nations (1903, p. 240).

However, old preconceptions, rivalries, and lingering scorn held firm even against the profound sense of fraternity arising from the shared suffering of World War I. In 1919, in a book unironically entitled *Notre nouvelle amie l'Angleterre* [*Our New Friend England*], the French writer John Charpentier opens by advocating for the 'importance essentielle' of continued close relations between France and England (that is, Britain) (1919, p. 1), yet then scatters his text with the familiar old generalizations and casually deprecating remarks. Among others, in Chapter 3 he airs clichés about the stocky, muscular, lean English physique, their business mind, their emotionless drive, their rather small-minded love of the home, self-sufficiency, belligerence, conservatism, sense of duty, and cynical use of religion for political and financial advantage. Chapter 6 is equally reminiscent of nineteenth-century travel writing as it describes the 'English Home,' with snide remarks on

222 *Epilogue*

English women's lack of financial management, stolid but passionless fidelity, Christmas celebrations, and so on – indeed, the majority of the reference points for 'facts' on English women are fictional works from at least some seventy years prior, such as *Clarissa*, *Jane Eyre*, and Balzac's chauvinistic representation of Lady Dudley in *Le Lys dans la vallée* (*The Lily of the Valley*, 1836, pp. 164, 173–5), and he makes not the slightest mention of women's war work or the recent Representation of the People Act which had seen a proportion of the female population gain the right to suffrage.

The ambivalence of this situation is reflected aptly, as the reader of this book might by now anticipate, in the sphere of the song and music. Kelly and Thumpston have remarked in their review of art music and musicological relations between France and Britain that although musical connections became increasingly strong over the course of the twentieth century, British interest in French art music was not generally matched by French interest in British music (2017, p. 638). However, the same does not apply for popular music, in which the influence of British (and American) music hall was ever increasing and consistently interwoven with the wider purview of contemporary social and political events. The Entente Cordiale was no exception. In 1906, the English writer and wit Raymond Needham hypothesized swapping national anthems to temper the revolutionary verve of the French, quipping that

> the first bar [of the Marseillaise] will put a Frenchman beside himself. [...] It would, indeed, be a prudent thing for the French to give us the 'Marseillaise' in exchange for our 'God Save the King.' The necessary adaptations and adjustments could easily be made and this simple act of barter would do more to promote the peace of nations than a thousand conferences at the Hague. The French are a volatile people and need something dirge-like by way of antidote: 'God save the Republic' would be just the thing for them.
>
> (1906, pp. 214, 217)

The extensive body of witty songs about the English discussed in this book also did due homage to the Entente; for example, songwriters Mérall and Ryp created 'L'Entente cordiale: ou la visite des délégués anglais,' published as a song sheet in *Les Refrains de la Butte: Derniers succès Montmartrois* (*Songs from the Mound: latest hits from Montmartre*) in 1904. Since this was set to the catchy, well-known tune of 'Cadet Rousselle' rather than an original melody, it was clearly intended to invite audience participation, and indeed to be sung outside as well as inside the café-concert performance context. This song opens by placing the Entente in the context of 'ces temps de gros armements' ['these times of mass armaments'], and then sets the scene with the French députés wanting to treat their British colleagues to a proper Parisian night out. The singer asserts that, after all, 'on voit, dans un bon r'pas / Si l'entente est cordiale, ou pas' ['you can see at a good meal / If the entente is cordial, or

Epilogue 223

not']. Thence it pursues themes familiar to the café-concert audience, who for more than thirty years had witnessed the exploits of comic English characters letting their hair down in Paris on the café-concert stage. The French député characters within the song seem to have missed this comic tradition, however, and they express their profound astonishment at the English 'gaité débordante' ['overflowing jollity'], wondering whether ' "Ces Anglais sont trop gais: / Pas possibl!" C'est des Portugais!' ['These Englishmen are too cheerful: / It isn't possible, they must be Portuguese!']

It is intriguing that the monuments which the entente députés invite the English to take in on their tour of Paris – described as 'nos plus superbes monuments' ['our most superb monuments'] – are not the Arc de Triomphe, Louvre, or Notre-Dame, but instead are signifiers of recent, Republican origin and speak to a more popular model of identity: the song signals a visit to the districts of Montmartre and Montsouris, both on the peripheries of Paris to the north and south in 1904, with passing admiration for the Lion de Belfort at Montrouge (which celebrates the heroic resistance of Parisians during the Prussian siege), as well as the Château-Rouge and the Moulin-Rouge (lively night-spots in the working-class 18th arrondissement). The only reference to the more central, more wealthy arrondissements comes in verse five when the French and English representatives go on a group trip to a brothel on the Place de Louvois (now, in a happy coincidence, home to the BNF's music archives). In this, we see the traditional hierarchies of power and their inscription on the topography of Paris being laughingly reversed and so we are alerted to a mixed message at work. On the one hand, the choice of such an upbeat tune and the playful naughtiness of the lyrics imply an atmosphere of celebration of the newly-established amity, revolving around Edward VII whose Francophilia and youthful playboy behaviour as Prince of Wales had earned him popularity with the French. On the other hand, there is also a clear tone of scoffing disrespect for the social and political elites and their hierarchies. It seems an entirely apt recognition of the seriousness of the Entente to celebrate it, this song quips, by going on a Franco-British lads' night out at a brothel, where the female staff are exhorted euphemistically by the respectable French députés to 'recevez savamment / Tous ces membres du Parlement' ['skillfully receive / All these members of parliament']. Such a farcical reception of their diplomatic achievement is not, perhaps, everything the French and English negotiators could have desired.

A similarly mirthful ambivalence is to be found in songs about the project for a Channel Tunnel or bridge. The idea to establish a civil-engineering solution to crossing the short stretch of sea separating the two countries was no new initiative by the first decade of the twentieth century: Napoleon had engaged in conversations to this end with the English government, which stalled as the Napoleonic Wars progressed; the French engineer Thomé de Gamond had begun thoughtful study of the possibilities in 1838 and presented his plans for a tunnel at the 1867 World Fair in Paris, gaining serious interest from both sides until the events of 1870 halted its development; negotiations

224   *Epilogue*

had recommenced in 1873, but public fears in Britain about an increased threat of invasion from Europe once more blocked substantial headway from being made; and in 1876, excavation had advanced under the seabed to the extent of 3 kilometres of tunnel on the English and 1.8 kilometre on the French side before once more drawing to a halt ('Le Pont sur la Manche,' 1890, pp. 951–2; D'Avout, 1895, p. 18). These faltering beginnings, though periodically reported upon in passing in the press, do not to the best of my knowledge inspire any musical repartee in the nineteenth century, but the Entente Cordiale also saw discussions reopen on the subject of the Tunnel and it found its way back into the public eye – especially when the House of Commons and Sir Henry Campbell-Bannerman's government subsequently decided that, once again, the public interest in Britain was best served in not pursuing the scheme for the present moment (Campbell-Bannerman, 1907, *cc.* 1203–04). This time, the idea inspired a Théâtre Marigny review show staging a series of explicitly fantasy tableaux – among which was Tup Tup and Octave Rudde's music-hall tribute, 'Le Tunnel sous la Manche' (1907 – reviewed by Nicolet, 1907, p. 3), and shortly after in June 1907 Georges Méliès made a silent film entitled *Le Tunnel sous la Manche, ou le cauchemar Franco-Anglais* (*The Tunnel under the Channel, or the Franco-English Nightmare*).[3] In Tup Tup and Rudde's song, the singer, with pronunciation very lightly inflected with popular Parisian twang (notably in dropping vowels and in the elision of syllables), recounts that newspapers have recently reported the imminent commencement of work on the tunnel – lucky for the Montmartre ladies, he suggests, who will no longer have to wait patiently for wealthy Englishmen to arrive by boat. The old stereotypes rise to the surface as he recounts that, in the past,

> Lorsqu'il fut question des sondages,
> Tous les mangeurs de plum-pudding
> Se voilèr'nt aussitôt l'visage
> En s'écriant "Aoh! shocking!"

> [When it came to running opinion polls,
> All the plum-pudding eaters
> Immediately covered their faces
> And cried out, "Oh! Shocking!"]

but that now the House of Commons had a more virile member (euphemistic pun intended) to provide the leadership needed to see the project through. Thanks to him, work would soon commence – and this would definitively seal 'l'entent' cordiale et féconde' ['the fertile and cordial entente']. This song is broadly positive about the idea of a tunnel: the two countries' mutual accord would be cemented, travel would be easier, gaiety would be the order of the day all around. The lyrics are set to a melody with few of the jaunty jig-style rhythms typically associated with the buffoonish Englishmen of the café-concert tradition, creating instead a statelier air that reduces the tone of

Epilogue   225

biting satire so often present in such songs. Yet the contextual setting casts this broadly positive approach in an explicitly satirical mode. There is, as before, the euphemistic punning on the 'members' of parliament, reducing matters of state to so many men competing over their virility. Moreover, after Britain's recent renewal of its opposition to the scheme – and their emphatic denial that it had anything to do with military matters[4] – the idea that a Tunnel might one day exist is placed alongside a series of other comical and often fantastical scenarios. In this review show, the Tunnel in scene four sits among burlesque scenes about 'Le Flirt franco-anglais' ('The Franco-English flirtation' – scene 5), a historical fantasy about 'Les Champions de jadis' ('Heroes of Yesteryear' – scene 6), a jovial science-fiction vision of 'La Ville aérienne' ('The Aerial City' – scene 9), and an unlikely version of the world in which women are in charge as 'Nos belles directrices' ('Our Beautiful Lady Directors' – scene 10).

Songs engendered both by the Entente Cordiale and the Channel Tunnel echo the mischievous relationship between the popular stage and the world of ideas and politics highlighted by Jane Goodall in her discussion of evolutionary theory and the world of popular performance. She remarks that

> entertainments established their own forms of ironic distance from the views generated by the opinion-making classes (who were, of course, also among their audiences), and from the long-term cultural and economic investments with which these views were underpinned. [...] There was a sense in which performers literally tried ideas on, testing them out through enactment.
>
> (2002, p. 6)

This ironic distance allows the popular entertainers and their audiences to play with the ideas held and disseminated by the elites, without any obligation 'to take the issues seriously, or to get the ideas right, or to be consistent in their approach' (2002, p. 7). We see in 'Le Tunnel sous la Manche,' as in all the lowbrow music discussed in this book, a shifting, ambivalent, exploratory means of engaging with the wider social and political world, of seeking to better understand the relative place of France and Britain in the modern world – and, above all, the implications of this for the French individual, for French identity, and for the French nation.

This book has sought to shed light upon lowbrow music's role as a soundtrack to the elaborate swirl of identity politics at this turning point in Republican history – whilst racialist 'science,' anthropology, and colonialism trickled down to affect thinking in every sphere of life; whilst different segments of society vacillated between yearning for togetherness and for self-distinction; and whilst class, generation, gender, region, religion, philosophy, political affiliation, and more all jostled to carve out their relevance for the twentieth-century French Self. The same songs, traditions, and performances are experienced as variously frivolous, as literal evidence of inherent national

226 *Epilogue*

character, and as a key to unlocking the mysteries of France's relative position in the hierarchies of evolution and of civilizations. Furthermore, the music and the musicking evoked in these pages are no mere passive or static reflections upon a society in a moment in time. Rather, lowbrow music, in all the forms evoked here, was an active and fluid participant in a social conversation that allowed its audiences to confront issues of their national past, present, and future, and provided a means of contemplating the place of the individual in the context of wider Parisian and French society's ideals, interdictions, politics, and prejudices.

The various forms of relationship that France might want with Britain are played upon and acted out within the musical kaleidoscope explored here – from repetitive comic stereotypes of the Anglais in café-concert chansonnette, to romanticized and culturally-appropriated Celtic folk song, to disquieting sounds of the Salvation Army in France and its colonies, and to the auditory experience of hearing noisy lowbrow music in London. Should French citizens happily accept, as Bellenger remarked, that 'l'Anglais et le Français possèdent précisément les qualités et les défauts contraires et se complètent merveilleusement l'un par l'autre, en leur supposant un but identique' ['the Englishman and the Frenchman have precisely the opposite qualities and failings and they would complement each other marvellously, were they to have a common purpose']? (1877, p. 3). Or, should they side with the sceptical Georges Viernot, and maintain that 'l'Angleterre, notre ami d'aujourd'hui, est fatalement notre ennemie de demain ou d'après-demain' ['England, our friend today, will inevitably be our enemy tomorrow or the day after']? (1908, p. 150). Or perhaps strike a grudging middle ground with Charpentier, casting the Entente Cordiale as a *mariage de raison*, 'surtout de notre côté, – et pourquoi ne pas en convenir? Nous plaisons plus aux Anglais qu'il ne nous plaisent. Nous tenons moins à leur estime qu'ils ne tiennent à la nôtre... .' ['especially on our side – and why not say so? We please the English more than they please us. We care less for their respect than they do for ours... .'] (1919, pp. 54–55). Popular song culture does not exist to provide clear answers or sure sets of instructions for navigating these complexities – after all, the café-concert laughs outrageously at everything, while French writers on British religious music and music in London have a marked tendency to take everything awfully seriously. Often, song faces the contemporary world by repressing uncertainties with denial, erasure, projection, evasion, and simply by turning its back on them and laughing. However, common ground can be found across the spectrum of lowbrow music in the shared resonance, *sotto voce*, of an underlying fear that a failure to draw the French community together behind at least one facet of shared national identity, after a century of internecine conflict, could undermine France's future as a global power once and for all.

♌

For over a hundred years, and as the 120th anniversary of the Entente Cordiale approaches, France and Britain have found themselves consistently

Epilogue 227

on the same side in all the major military conflicts of the twentieth and twenty-first centuries and have gradually distanced themselves from the rancour of colonial rivalry. Yet the vast majority of the stereotypes and snide jokes that characterized their more cantankerous nineteenth-century relations still persist. Comedy has remained a familiar part of the Franco-British relationship; for those of us who grew up in the Anglophone world alone, jokes about the French feature prominently, in Monty Python's *Holy Grail* (1975), *Allô, Allô* (1982–1992), *Blackadder* (for example, the 'Nob and Nobility' episode, set during the French Revolution, 1987), and in sketches and stand-up from the likes of Catherine Tate ('Lauren's French Exam,' 2006), Dylan Moran ('French Skit,' 2007), and Alexis Dubus (as his alter-ego Marcel Lucont since 2009). There is little systematic equivalent to this for either France or England in relation to any other European nation.

Nor has the importance of music and its active role in both directing and commenting upon how the French and British understand each other waned – and its persistence shows clearly that this is by no means a niche, fleeting phenomenon of the nineteenth century. Today, in the era of Brexit and the uncertainty it brings for Britain's relationship with its European neighbours, 2016 and 2017 alone saw dozens of songs on both sides of the Channel (and indeed the Atlantic) trying to influence, mock, critique, and, occasionally, praise the outcome of the June 2016 referendum. Comic song writers, unsurprisingly, have been the first to set their thoughts to music at each stage of the painful process: Fascinating Aida, at the Edinburgh Festival, sang an apology to Scotland who, taken separately as a country, had voted to Remain ('So Sorry Scotland' – August 2016); on the radio station France Inter, Frédéric Fromet sent Britain on its way with a catalogue of old-school stereotypes in 'Rosbif, mon Rosbif' (24 June 2016); and the BBC radio comedy *Now Show*'s Mitch Benn has written 'Article 50 Day' (March 2017), 'Just Keep Believing in Brexit' (October 2017), and 'A Brexit Wish' (November 2017). Internationally-famous singers, too, have contributed their musical pennyworth to the debate; Paloma Faith explores post-Brexit guilt in 'Guilty' (October 2016); Mick Jagger released songs inspired by the referendum outcome ('England Lost' and 'Gotta Get a Grip,' July 2017); and French rock singer Bertrand Cantat critiqued the insular attitude of Brexit in his 'L'Angleterre' (October 2017). Of course, in the modern world of self-publication on the internet, it is not only performers with access to a stage and live audience who seek to make their voices heard through music: indeed, it is through the medium of YouTube that most of the pro-Brexit songs have found their platform, such as UKIP candidate Mandy Boylett's pastiche on Baddiel, Skinner, and the Lightening Seeds' football anthem 'Three Lions' entitled 'Britain's Coming Home' (February 2016) and a Union-flag-bedecked Peter Parson's confident pro-Brexit 'Brexit Song: We'll be Strong' (September 2017). Meanwhile, Les Moineaux de Paris's 'Le Brexzut!' (August 2017) and Une Chanson comme ça's 'Le Brexit ou pas?' (April 2019) sing back about the lack of clarity in the British government's approach to the process. As in the

228 *Epilogue*

nineteenth century, these are not songs sung in isolation: they have generated media attention and comment from fans, internet trolls, the wider public, and politicians, demonstrating the potential for music to engage with and influence opinions and decision-making in wider society, politics, and culture.[5] Lowbrow music today, just as in the belle époque, is of central importance and remains a site of instinctive recourse for people seeking to express and to explore their opinions and feelings about the events and the uncertainties of contemporary life and the ties that reach across the Channel between France and Britain. Popular music remains active in our social dialogue and in the connections between our personal and communal sense of identity with a vibrancy which we cannot afford to overlook.

Notes

1 Finot includes a chapter on 'Le Danger américain' in his 1903 book on the benefits of a Franco-British rapprochement (1903, Chapter 2: Section 3).

2 Finot follows this with a lengthy discussion of their shared history from pp. 36–190.

3 This short film opens with a scene representing two bedrooms belonging to Edward VII and the president of France, Armand Fallières. Both men settle down to sleep and begin dreaming parallel dreams. We see them looking at each other from either side of the Channel through telescopes, waving, and then stretching out monstrous arms to shake hands mid-way across the stretch of sea. In the next scene, we go beneath the waves to see tunnel digging in progress until workers from both sides meet in the middle, and the first train passes through to great celebration. But the celebrations are short-lived, as two trains crash into each other in the tunnel – and then both king and president awaken from this nightmare with a start. They run into each other's rooms and share their harrowing dream – only for a man with the plans for the projected tunnel to enter the room and be chased out vigorously by both national leaders.

4 The underlying military and national defence concerns behind these repeated refusals are discussed at length by Georges Viernot in 1908; he details, through a series of strategic approaches, how an invasion of England by way of the tunnel could be defeated, and therefore mediated against. Curiously, in his conclusion, having spent some 150 pages of the book seeking to deflate the perception of military threats to the UK, he then demonstrates how the threat to France might actually be the greater: 'L'Angleterre, notre ami aujourd'hui, est fatalement notre ennemie de demain ou d'après-demain, et le jour où elle sera notre ennemie, elle cherchera et trouvera sur le continent, conformément à sa tradition et ses besoins, les alliés qui lui furent nécessaires pour frapper la puissance continentale que nous sommes' ['England, today our friend, will inevitably be our enemy tomorrow or the day after; and the day that she becomes our enemy, she will seek and find on the continent, in accordance with her traditions and needs, the allies she requires to strike us as a continental power'] (1908, p. 150).

5 For example, Mandy Boylett's song was upbraided by the *Guardian* and commended by the *Daily Mail* (24 February 2016), and Paloma Faith received considerable backlash after the release of her song, notably from members of the public on Twitter.

Works cited

Avout, Bon A. d', 1895. 'Notes de voyage en Angleterre et en Écosse.' In: *Mémoires de la Société bourguignonne de géographie et d'histoire*. Dijon: Darantière.

Balzac, H. de, 1836. *Le Lys dans la vallée*. Reprint 1919. Paris: Charpentier.

Bellenger, H., *ca.* 1877. *Londres pittoresque et la vie anglaise*. Paris: Georges Decaux.

Campbell-Bannerman, Sir H., 1907. 'Adjournment: *House of Commons Debate,' Hansards, 171. 21 March, cc. 1203–04*.

Charpentier, J., 1919. *Notre nouvelle amie l'Angleterre*. Paris: Hachette.

Finot, J., *ca.* 1903. *Français et Anglais*. Paris: Félix Juven.

Geoffroy, C., 2004. *Les Coulisses de l'Entente cordiale*. Paris: Grasset.

Goodall, J., 2002. *Performance and Evolution in the Age of Darwin: Out of the Natural Order*. London and New York: Routledge.

Kelly, B. and Thumpston, R., 2017. 'Maintaining the Entente Cordiale: Musicological Collaborations between the United Kingdom and France,' *Revue de musicologie*, 103 (2), pp. 615–40.

Mérall, M. and Ryp, 1904. 'L'Entente cordiale ou la visite des délégués anglais' [musical score]. Paris: Plessis.

Needham, R., 1906. *L'Entente Cordiale (more or less) – a little mild abuse*. London: Everett & Co.

Nicolet, 1907. 'Spectacles divers,' *Gaulois*. 3 May, p. 3.

'Le Pont sur la Manche,' 1890. *Les Merveilles de l'Exposition de 1889: histoire, construction, inauguration, description détaillée des palais*. Paris: Librairie illustrée. pp. 951–9.

Rodde, O. and Tup-tup, n.d. [1907]. 'Le Tunnel sous la Manche. Chansonnette,' [musical score]. Paris: A. Rougier.

Le Tunnel sous la Manche ou Le Cauchemar franco-anglais, 1907. [film]. Directed by G. Méliès. France: s.n.

Viernot, G., *ca.* 1908. *Un grand problème international et militaire – Le Tunnel sous la Manche*. Paris: Henri Charles-Lavauzelle.

Appendix

Café-concert comic songs about the English

Song title	Year composed	Composer	Lyricist	Key performers and performance venues
L'Anglais au dictionnaire: scène comique [The Englishman with the Dictionary: comic scene]	1875	H.C. de Ploosen	Langat	Jably at the Ambassadeurs
L'Anglais aujourd'hui [The Englishman Today]	1876	Lhuillier	Lhuillier	Armand des Roseaux
L'Anglaise en voyage: scène comique avec parlé [The English Lady on her Travels: comic scene with monologue]	1876	Pourny	Joly	
Gig-Gigue: gigottement à jet continu [Jig-Jig: Endless Burst of Jiggery]	1876	Linas	Bataille	Desir at the XIXe Siècle; Pichat at the Concert Européen; Hervy at the Ambassadeurs; Jably at the Pépinière; Suiram at the Gaité-Rochechouart; Laforgue at the Alcazar d'été; Darville at the Concert du Cadran; Barjon at the Scala

Song title	Year composed	Composer	Lyricist	Key performers and performance venues
Aoh! Je étais très content: Chansonette anglaise mêlée de danse [Oh! I was very happy: comic English song mixed with dance]	1877	Baumaine and Blondelet	Duhem	Dufour at the Ambassadeurs
Miss Kokett: Scène-type [Miss Kokett: Character Act]	1877	Berthelier	Bousquet	
Les Leçons d'Anglais [The English Lessons]	1877	Boisselot	Chassaigne	Céline Chaumont
Oh! le Angleterre: Chansonnette [Oh! England: comic song]	1878	Petit	Lambetti	Jably at the Grand Concert Parisien
Mylord Gig-Gig! Excentricité anglaise [Mylord Jig-Jig! English eccentricity]	1879	Tac-Coen	L. Gabillaud and J. Rocca	
L'Anglais rageur: Chansonnette comique [The Angry Englishman: comic song]	1879	Deransart	Laroche and Hurbain	Bousquet at the Scala; Stainville at the Alcazar; Pisarello at the Ba-ta-clan; Titre at the XIXe Siècle; Jably at the Concert Parisien
Le Jeune Homme de London et la demoiselle de Breda Street [The Young Man from London and the Girl from Breda Street]	1880	Duhem	Delormel	Reval and Nancy at the Alcazar d'été; Duhem and Volay at the Horloge
L'Anglais à Paris [The Englishman in Paris]	1881	Frieda	Fourcaud and Suirain	

(*continued*)

Song title	Year composed	Composer	Lyricist	Key performers and performance venues
L'Anglaise en voyage [The English Lady on her Travels]	1882	Villemer	Delormel	
L'Anglais timide [The Timid Englishman]	1883	Desormes	Durafour	Paul Chevalier at the Alcazar d'été; Jably at the Grand Concert Parisien
Very good! Very well!	1883	Bourges	Kuhn	Bourges at the Scala; Limat at the Eden-Concert; Plébins at the Folies-Rambuteau; Henriot at the Alcazar d'Hiver; Jably at the Concert Parisien
Miss Gig: Chansonnette avec danse [Miss Jig: comic song with dance]	1885	Duhem	Delormel	
Anglaises Misses: Chansonnette [The English Misses: Comic Song]	1885	Duhem	Durozel	Dufour at the Horloge; Dassy at the Alcazar d'été
La Bouteille de l'Anglaise: Chansonnette comique [The English Woman's Bottle: comic song]	1885	Traiffort and Valer	Villemer and Delormel	Reval at the Alcazar d'été
Je pôvais pas! Chansonnette anglaise avec gigue [I just couldn't! English comic song with jig]	1885	Paulet and Hurbain	Strauss	
L'Anglaise malade [The Sick English Woman]	1887	Pourny	Lebreton	
Miss Rage! Chanson-monologue [Miss Rage! song and monologue]	1887	Petit	Marcel	

Song title	Year composed	Composer	Lyricist	Key performers and performance venues
Yes! No! Tribulations anglaises [Yes! No! English Tribulations]	1887	Chaudoir	Belhiatus	Vaunel at the Eldorado
L'Anglais embarrassé: chansonnette comique [The Annoyed Englishman: comic song]	1887	Courtois	Delormel and Garnier	Paulus at the Théâtre des Menus Plaisirs; Hymack at the Empire [1914]
L'Anglais rieur! Éclat de rire [The Laughing Englishman: Burst of Laughter]	1887	Ouvrard	Pizoir	
Milady Plumpudding! Chansonnette anglaise, avec danse et parlé [Milady Plumpudding! Comic song with dance and monologue]	1887	Tac-Coen	Jambon and Stainville	
Anglais et Français: Chanson monologue [The Englishman and the Frenchman: Song and monologue]	1888	Laroche	Ouvrard	Ouvrard at the Scala
L'Anglais formaliste: Chanson-monologue [The Formal Englishman: song and monologue]	1888	Delormel	Garnier	Vaunel at the Alcazar d'été; Libert at the Horloge
L'Anglais au théâtre: Scène comique britannique [The Englishman at the Theatre: comic British act]	1888	Duhem	Laroche	

(continued)

234 *Appendix*

Song title	Year composed	Composer	Lyricist	Key performers and performance venues
L'Anglais mal reçu: chansonnette [The Ill-Received Englishman: comic song]	1888	Chaudoir	Belhiatus	Vaunel at the Eldorado
Mister Barbe bleue: Chansonnette [Mister Blue Beard: comic song]	1888	Chaudoir	Delormel and Garnier	Paulus
L'Anglais malcontent: Chansonnette comique [The Discontented Englishman: comic song]	1888	Duhem	Laroche	Vaunel at the Eldorado; Limat at the Eden-Concert; Rivoire at the Horloge; Charlus at the Concert Parisien
L'Anglais aux courses [The Englishman at the Races]	1888	Duhem	Bonin and Charbonnet	
Le Joyeux Anglais: Scène comique avec parlé [The Joyous Englishman: comic act with monologue]	1889	Letellier	Letellier	
Mister et mistress John Bull [Mr and Mrs John Bull]	1889	Stretti	Delormel and Stretti	Paulus
Milord Balabrelock! Chanson-gigue [Milord Balabrelock! Song and jig]	1889	Baneux	Wachs	
Miss Valérie	1890	Byrec	Houssot	Mme Duparc at the Eldorado
Mister Malbrough: rengaine Anglo comique [Mister Malbrough: Corny old comic song]	1890	Gangloff	Delormel and Garnier	Paulus

Song title	Year composed	Composer	Lyricist	Key performers and performance venues
Le Plum Pudding	1891	Poret	Delormel	Mme Duparc at the Alcazar d'été
Les Anglais chez nous: chansonnette [The English in our Country: comic song]	1891	Duhem	Jouy	Dufay at the Eldorado
Les Anglais au poste [The Englishmen in a Prison Cell]	1892	Ferry	Ferry	[?] at the Chat Noir
L'Anglais triste: chanson-monologue [The Sad Englishman: song and monologue]	1892	Leonvic	Gerny	Vaunel at the Eldorado
La Leçon d'Anglais [The English Lesson]	1892	Petit	Delormel	Mlle Irène Henry at the Ambassadeurs
A Practical Medecine: Fantaisie Anglo-Louffoquiste [A Practical Medicine: silly English fantasy]	1893	De Croze	De Croze	
Ratatapoum purée! Type réaliste d'anglais [Ratatapoum Heck! Realist English character]	1893	Paigne	Dufor	Dufor
Ell's danse pas le d'gigue [They don't dance the jig]	1893	Chassaigne	Aupto	Louise Roland
Schocking! Cri anglais [Shocking! English Cry]	1893	Gruber	Dupré de la Roussière	Yvette Guilbert

(continued)

Song title	Year composed	Composer	Lyricist	Key performers and performance venues
Les Anglais: Polka-Marche	1893	Courtois	Jouy	Kam-Hill at the Horloge
Miss Plumpudding	1894	Waiss	Lemercier	Marguerite Duclerc at the Ambassadeurs
Les Petites Miss! Chanson [The Little Misses! Song]	1894	Teramond	Weiller	Mme Edmée Lescot
Mylord Poukc'fort: Chansonnette [Mylord Poukc'fort: comic song]	1894	Fragson	Duhem and Bonin	Lucienne Muguet at the Jardin de Paris
Schoking! Chansonnette [Shocking! Comic song]	1894	Chaudoir	Damien and Flic-Flac	Polaire at the Ambassadeurs
La Revanche de John Bull: Scène comique [The Revenge of John Bull: comic act]	1894	Letellier	Letellier	
L'Apéritif d'un Anglais: Chansonnette comique [The Englishman's Aperitif: comic song]	1894	Ducreux	Disle	Delmarre at the Eden-Concert; Charlus at the Moulin Rouge
English Obsession	1894	Sinclair	Dreynier	Paulus at the Ba-ta-clan
Yes! Nâo! Chansonnette [Yes! No! Comic song]	1894	Sinclair	Delormel and Garnier	Paulus at the Ba-ta-clan
Le Chic anglais! Chansonnette [English Chic! Comic song]	1894	Spencer	Belloche	Mlle B. Duchamp at the Parisien; Bourguit at the Ba-ta-clan; D'Harvier at the Parisiana

Song title	Year composed	Composer	Lyricist	Key performers and performance venues
L'Amour anglais! Chansonnette comique [English Love: comic song]	1895	Holzer	Rosario	
Miss Oh! Yes! Chansonnette	1895	Perpignan	Delormel	
L'Anglais parisien: chansonnette [The Parisian Englishman: comic song]	1895	Fragson	Briollet and Mortreuil	Fragson at the Parisiana; Maurel at the Scala
Miss Rodin: Chansonnette	1895	Carle	Delormel and Briollet	Fougère at the Ba-ta-clan
Consolation anglaise! Chanson-gigue [English Consolation! Song and jig]	1896	Percier	Mario	
Les Policemen	1896	Del and Poncin	Delormel and Briollet	
L'Anglais entêté: chansonnette comique [The Stubborn Englishman: comic song]	1897	Laurain	Garnier and Phillips	Vaunel at the Ba-ta-clan
Paris-London: chanson monologue [Paris-London: song and monologue]	1897	Del and Fragson	Garnier and Héros	Paulus at the Parisiana; Amelet at the Cigale
Les Mots Anglais: Chansonnette [English Words: comic song]	1897	Delormel	Briollet and Gerny	Max-Morel at the Cigale; Ransard at the Gaité-Rochechouart

(continued)

Song title	Year composed	Composer	Lyricist	Key performers and performance venues
Miss La Pudeur [Miss Prudery]	1897	Byrec	Desmarets	
L'Anglais et le Bourgeois: duo comique [The Englishman and the Bourgeois: comic duet]	1897	Queyriaux	Gerny	Chavat and Girier
L'Anglais et l'Allemand, ou la leçon d'amour, scène comique [The Englishman and the German, or the Lesson of Love: comic act]	1897	Martin	Dales	
L'Anglais poivrot! [The Drunken Englishman!]	1897	Graves	Cologne	
Le Flègme [Flegmatism]	1898	Del and Fragson	Gerny	Fragson and Maurel at the Parisiana
Polka des English's	1898	Mortreuil and Allier	Christine	Mayol at the Concert Parisien; Portal at the Scala
L'Anglais gelé, ou John c'est épatant, Chansonnette comique [The Frozen Englishman, or John it's Astonishing: comic song]	1898	Grimaldi	Christine	
L'Anglais faubourien: chansonnette [The Englishman from the Parisian Suburbs: comic song]	1899	Fragson and Del	Briollet and Poupay	Fragson at the Scala

Song title	Year composed	Composer	Lyricist	Key performers and performance venues
L'Anglais éduqué: Chansonnette [The Educated Englishman: comic song]	1899	Derouville and Del	Dearly and Mortreuil	Dearly at the Scala
Ce sont les Anglais! Chansonnette comique [Those People are English! Comic song]	1899	Valabrègue	Valabrègue	
L'English curieux: chansonnette [The Curious Englishman: comic song]	ca. 1900	Derouville	Arnould	
Les Fils d'Albion [The Sons of Albion]	1900	Pizoir	Altery and Marty	
Vertus d'Outre-Manche: Chansonnette à refrain [Cross-Channel Virtues: song and refrain]	1900	Deschaux	Chicot and Jost	
Le Chic anglais [English Style]	1900	Garnier and Jeunil	Lasaïgues and Bans	
Gigue-obsession! [Jig Obsession!]	1900	Lemercier	Poncin	
Le Spleen: Chansonnette anglaise [Spleen: English comic song]	1901	Fragson	Briollet	Fragson at the Alcazar d'été
L'Anglais sobre [The Sober Englishman]	1901	Christine	Briollet and Lelièvre	

(*continued*)

Song title	Year composed	Composer	Lyricist	Key performers and performance venues
Pourvu qu' j'ai l' Chic anglais! [As Long as I have English Style!]	1901	Garnier and Jeunil	Lasaïgues and Bans	
L'Anglaise à Paris [The Englishwoman in Paris]	1903	Favart	Cambon	
Miss Orchestre! Chansonnette - duo franco-anglais [Miss Orchestra! Comic song, Franco-English duet]	1903	Taillefer	Sibre	Brésina, Sœurs Lajallières, and Sœurs Harlett
Article anglais! [The English Object]	1903	Charton	Briollet	
Charley! Chansonnette d'Outre-Manche [Charley! Cross-Channel comic song]	1903	Trewey	Scale	Miss Ixa at the Théâtre des Folies Dramatiques; Miss Claudine Briais at the Scala; Mlle Alice de Tender in London
Oh! Miss…Miss…: Chansonnette	1904	Fragson	Forgettes	Fragson at the Alcazar d'été; Victor Lejal at the Ambassadeurs
L'Entente cordiale	1904 (to the tune of Cadet Rousselle)	—		

Café-concert comic songs about the Salvation Army

Song title	Year composed	Composer	Lyricist	Key performers and performance venues
L'Armée du Chahut [The Cancan Army]	1887	Gallé	Delesalle	Mme Gabrielle Lange at the Eldorado; Mlle Juliette Perrin at the Alcazar d'Hiver
Les Mômes de l'Armée du Salut [The Salvation Army Chicks]	1893	Delormel	Delormel	Mlle Fougère at the Horloge
La Fausse Helyett: chansonnette comique [The Fake Helyett: comic song]	1893	Byrec	Dalleroy	Le Petit Bob at the Scala
Viv' l'Armée du Chahut-u-u-u-ut [Long Live the Can-an-an-an-can Army]	1893	Nalray and Deransart	Siegel and Lemon	Mlle Brissot at the Ambassadeurs
Cinq Minutes à l'Armée du Salut (discours du capitaine O'Kelkuitt) [Five Minutes with the Salvation Army (the Speech of Captain O'Kelkuitt)]	1895	Jules Moy	Jules Moy	Jules Moy at the Chat Noir; Plébins at the Scala; Camille Stéphani at the Cigale
J'ai lâché l'Armée du Salut [I've Left the Salvation Army]	1896	Beretta	Croisier	
La Salutiste: chansonnette [The Salvation Army Girl: comic song]	1896	Spencer	Duc	
La Salutiste batignollaise! [The Salvation Army Girl from Batignolles]	1901	Duhem	Duhem	

Index

Adorno, T. 8–9
'L'Anglais au dictionnaire' 44–5
'Les Anglais chez nous' 36
'L'Anglais en voyage' 44
'L'Anglais et le bourgeois' 49
'L'Anglais formaliste' 34
'L'Anglais malcontent' 36
'L'Anglais parisien' 53
'L'Anglais rieur' 64–6
'L'Anglais triste' 61–2
Anglomania 53–55
'L'Armée du Chahut' 123–4
art music, 29–30
audiences: café-concert 11–12, 63–4,
    70–2; London music hall 201–05;
    London strip shows 212–3

blackface minstrels 201–4
Bourget, Paul 85–6, 125n2, 141, 184
Bovet, Marie-Anne de 83–4, 93, 106,
    133, 141, 143–4, 146, 159, 168, 202
Brada 81–82, 198
Brexit songs 227–8
Burns, Robert 142, 149–52, 161–3

café-concert: comic 'German' songs
    48; criticism 11–12, 28–9, 70–2; as
    mirror of society 30, 73–4; song
    genres 30–1
cake walk 63
Celtic Britain: as ethnological evidence
    137, 141–2, 166, 168; exoticization
    137–8, 141–3, 151–2; as golden age
    143–4; as mirror for France 151–2,
    164–5, 167, 169–74; musical talent 137
censorship 11, 28, 204
census 16–17, 23n15
Channel Tunnel 223–5
'Le Chic anglais' 54

'Cinq minutes à l'Armée du Salut'
    114–15
colonial rivalry 18, 48
comic 'English' songs: character types
    33–4, 35–6; costume 38–43; style 31,
    33, 56–8; see also language; see also
    Salvation army
cultural appropriation 154–65
cultural influence 62–3

Darwin, Charles 5
Dreyfus Affair 10

'Ell's danse pas le d'gigue' 56–7
'Englishing up' 51
entente cordiale 19, 220–5
'L'Entente cordiale: ou la visite des
    délégués anglais' 222–3

'La Fausse Helyett' 123
Fétis, François-Joseph 2, 6, 148
folksong: English 139; French 147–8;
    French adaptations 155–65; as
    product of national character 134–5,
    147–8; as Romantic idea 132, 134;
    see also Burns, Robert; see also
    Moore, Thomas; see also Scott,
    Walter; see also Wales
France, Hector 40, 84, 87, 90, 102, 188,
    206–14
Franco-British relations 12–7

'Gigue-obsession' 52–3
Guide Joanne, 182, 198
Guilbert and Sullivan 198, 215n7
Guilbert, Yvette 58, 65–6, 73

Handel, G.F. 2
Holmès, Augusta 171–4

Index   243

Home Rule 168–71
hypocrisy, moral 67–71, 81, 87–9

'J'ai lâché l'armée du Salut' 116–17, 120–2
'Je pôvais pas' 44, 49
jig 34–5, 55–64, 156–9, 206–14
'Le Joyeux Anglais' 34, 66
Jupilles, Fernand de 4–5, 67, 81, 119,
  191–2

language: anglicisms 52–5; English as
  patois 50; skills of the British 33,
  44–50; skills of the French 46–9
laughter: as national trait 64; psychology
  of 46, 52–4
Literature, British characters in 17–18,
  35, 44
London: drawing room music 190–5;
  music hall 197–205; noise 186–90; the
  Season 3–4, 197; street music 188–9;
  strip shows 206–14
Lourdes 98

'Miss Gig' 59
Miss Helyett 109–13
'Miss! Oh yes!' 46–7
'Miss Plumpudding' 68
'Les Mômes de l'Armée du Salut' 120–1
Moore, Thomas 132, 141–2, 150, 155,
  157, 159–60
'Les Mots anglais'
'Mylord Gig-Gig' 56

Narjoux, Félix 4, 90, 144, 146, 168, 186,
  188, 202
national difference 43, 70, 72–3, 221–3

O'Rell, Max 67, 80, 84–5, 87–9, 106, 133,
  141, 190–9
orphéons 105–06

'Paris-London' 72–3
political song 36–7
Protestantism 82

racial characteristics, British 7, 14, 50–2,
  58–62, 221–2
religious delirium 97–9

'La Salutiste batignollaise' 122
Salvation Army: brainwashing 93–9; in
  Britain 84–91; as colonial threat
  104–06; in comic song 107–17,
  120–5; as cultural invasion 99–102;
  establishment in France 91–3;
  persecution 103–4; as political threat
  102–4; Salvation Army women
  117–25; in theatre 109
'Schoking!' 69–70
Scott, Walter 133, 163–4
sheet music 31

Taine, Hippolyte 5, 35, 66, 67, 82,
  150
Tiersot, Julien 6, 147, 149, 160,
  166
translation 160–5
travel 16
travel writing 15, 83–91, 133, 140,
  141–3, 146, 159–60, 168, 170–1,
  181–214
'Le Tunnel sous la Manche' 224–5

Vallès, Jules 119, 186–7, 199–205
'Viv' l'Armée du Chahut-u-u-u-ut!'
  122–4

Wales 140, 142–6
Weckerlin, Jean-Baptiste 6, 28–9, 149,
  155–7, 161
World Fairs 41–3, 61, 135, 158

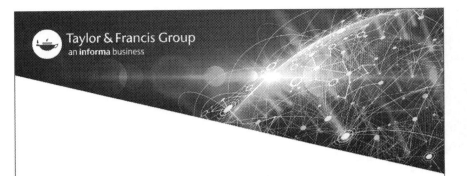

Printed in the United States
by Baker & Taylor Publisher Services